Environmental Taxation in the Pandemic Era

CRITICAL ISSUES IN ENVIRONMENTAL TAXATION

Series Editors: Mikael Skou Andersen, *Aarhus University, Denmark*, Hope Ashiabor, *Climate Policy Consultant, Australia* and Janet E. Milne, *Vermont Law School, USA*

The *Critical Issues in Environmental Taxation* series provides insights and analysis on environmental taxation issues on an international basis and explores detailed theories for achieving environmental goals through fiscal policy. Each book in the series contains pioneering and thought-provoking contributions by the world's leading environmental tax scholars who respond to the diverse challenges posed by environmental sustainability.

Previous volumes in the series:

Original book published by CCH Incorporated
    Volumes I–IV published by Richmond Law and Tax
    Volumes V–VIII published by Oxford University Press
    Volume IX onwards published by Edward Elgar Publishing

Recent titles in the series include:

Volume XVII	Green Fiscal Reform for a Sustainable Future Reform, Innovation and Renewable Energy *Edited by Natalie P. Stoianoff, Larry Kreiser, Bill Butcher, Janet E. Milne and Hope Ashiabor*
Volume XVIII	Market Instruments and the Protection of Natural Resources *Edited by Natalie P. Stoianoff, Larry Kreiser, Bill Butcher, Janet E. Milne and Hope Ashiabor*
Volume XIX	The Green Market Transition Carbon Taxes, Energy Subsidies and Smart Instrument Mixes *Edited by Stefan E. Weishaar, Larry Kreiser, Janet E. Milne, Hope Ashiabor and Michael Mehling*
Volume XX	Innovation Addressing Climate Change Challenges Market-based Perspectives *Edited by Mona Hymel, Larry Kreiser, Janet E. Milne and Hope Ashiabor*
Volume XXI	Environmental Fiscal Challenges for Cities and Transport *Edited by Marta Villar Ezcurra, Janet E. Milne, Hope Ashiabor and Mikael Skou Andersen*
Volume XXII	Economic instruments for a Low-carbon Future *Edited by Theodoros Zachariadis, Janet E. Milne, Mikael Skou Andersen and Hope Ashiabor*
Volume XXIII	Environmental Taxation in the Pandemic Era Opportunities and Challenges *Edited by Hope Ashiabor, Janet E. Milne and Mikael Skou Andersen*

Environmental Taxation in the Pandemic Era

Opportunities and Challenges

Edited by

Hope Ashiabor

Climate Policy Consultant, Australia

Janet E. Milne

Professor of Law and Director of the Environmental Tax Policy Institute, Vermont Law School, USA

Mikael Skou Andersen

Professor of Environmental Policy Analysis, Aarhus University, Denmark

CRITICAL ISSUES IN ENVIRONMENTAL TAXATION, VOLUME XXIII

Cheltenham, UK • Northampton, MA, USA

© The Editors and Contributors severally 2021

All rights reserved. No part of this publication may be reproduced, stored in a retrieval system or transmitted in any form or by any means, electronic, mechanical or photocopying, recording, or otherwise without the prior permission of the publisher.

Published by
Edward Elgar Publishing Limited
The Lypiatts
15 Lansdown Road
Cheltenham
Glos GL50 2JA
UK

Edward Elgar Publishing, Inc.
William Pratt House
9 Dewey Court
Northampton
Massachusetts 01060
USA

A catalogue record for this book
is available from the British Library

Library of Congress Control Number: 2021939242

This book is available electronically in the **Elgar**online
Law subject collection
http://dx.doi.org/10.4337/9781800888517

ISBN 978 1 80088 850 0 (cased)
ISBN 978 1 80088 851 7 (eBook)

Printed and bound in Great Britain by TJ Books Limited, Padstow, Cornwall

Contents

Editorial review board	viii
List of contributors	ix
Foreword: fake twins by Christian de Perthuis	x

PART I CARBON TAX THEORY IN THE PANDEMIC ERA

1 A post-crisis assessment of carbon taxation for members of the Coalition of Finance Ministers for Climate Action 3
   Simon Black and Ian Parry

2 Setting a price for carbon to achieve carbon neutrality in the European Union 20
   Alberto Majocchi

3 The Green New Dividend: a cost neutral market-based alternative to the Green New Deal 34
   Russell Mendell

PART II COVID-19 AND EU-WIDE TAX POLICIES

4 100 years of externalities 49
   Astrid Ladefoged and Mirka Janda

5 Promoting a green economic recovery from the Corona crisis 66
   Holger Bär, Matthias Runkel and Kai Schlegelmilch

6 Reconciling EU tax and environmental policies: VAT as a vehicle to boost green consumerism under the EU Green Deal 81
   Francesco Cannas and Matteo Fermeglia

PART III CARBON PRICING IN LATIN AMERICA IN THE PANDEMIC ERA

7 Carbon pricing in Perú: a matter of climate justice in the Covid-19 context 96
   Carlos Trinidad Alvarado and Daniela Soberón Garreta

8 The Carbon Tax in Argentina is sick with COVID-19 111
   Rodolfo Salassa Boix

9 Public finance, taxation, and environment post-Covid-19: perspectives for Brazil 126
   Daniel Giotti de Paula and Lígia Barroso Fabri

10 Tax incentives for electric vehicles and biofuels: a Brazilian case study 140
    Rafaela Cristina Oliari, Carlos Araújo Leonetti and Elena Aydos

PART IV EUROPEAN NATIONAL CASE STUDIES

11 Environmental taxation in an age of COVID-19: an Italian approach 155
    Alberto Comelli

12 COVID-19 and urban mobility: has the time come for a paradigmatic shift? The potential of environmental tax policies in the pandemic age 169
    Marina Bisogno

PART V ENVIRONMENTAL SUPPORT SCHEMES IN THE MIDST OF THE PANDEMIC

13 A taxonomy of environmentally sustainable activities to orient Covid-19 tax measures to environmental objectives 184
    Sébastien Wolff

14 Assessing public aid for true green digital recovery: a matter of good tax governance in the European Union 198
    Marta Villar Ezcurra and María Amparo Grau Ruiz

15 The purposefulness and serviceability of renewable energy support schemes in view of the COVID-19 crisis 214
    Theodoros G. Iliopoulos

PART VI LESSONS FOR ALLOWANCE TRADING

16 Covid-19 and EU climate change linking 229
    Stefan E. Weishaar

17 Enforcing sustainable auction-based ETS in
    a post-COVID-19 world: evidence from and lessons for
    Northeast Asia 242
    Joseph Dellatte and Sven Rudolph

Index 255

Editorial review board

The chapters in this book have been brought to publication with the help of an editorial review board dedicated to peer review. The members of the board are committed to the field of environmental taxation and are active participants in environmental taxation events around the world.

Chair
    Ashiabor, Hope, Climate Policy Consultant, Australia

Members
    Andersen, Mikael Skou, Aarhus University, Denmark
    Belletti, Elena, Columbia University, USA
    Cottrell, Jacqueline, Green Budget Germany, Germany
    Duff, David, University of British Columbia, Canada
    Grau Ruiz, María Amparo, Complutense University of Madrid, Spain
    Jarvie, Deborah, University of Lethbridge, Canada
    Majocchi, Alberto, University of Pavia, Italy
    Mann, Roberta, University of Oregon, USA
    Meyer, Ina, Austrian Institute of Economic Research (WIFO), Austria
    Milne, Janet E., Vermont Law School, USA
    Mortimore, Anna, Griffith University, Australia
    Pirlot, Alice, University of Oxford, United Kingdom
    Roberts, Tracey, Samford University, USA
    Rudolph, Sven, Kyoto University, Japan
    Speck, Stefan, European Environment Agency, Denmark
    Stoianoff, Natalie, University of Technology, Australia
    Teusch, Jonas, Organisation for Economic Co-operation and Development, (OECD), France
    Villar Ezcurra, Marta, Universidad San Pablo-CEU, CEU Universities, Spain
    Weishaar, Stefan E., University of Groningen, The Netherlands
    Zachariadis, Theodoros, Cyprus University of Technology and The Cyprus Institute

Contributors

Aydos, Elena, University of Newcastle, Australia
Bär, Holger, Green Budget Germany, Germany
Bisogno, Marina, University of Naples Federico II, Italy
Black, Simon, International Monetary Fund, Fiscal Affairs Department, USA
Cannas, Francesco, Hasselt University, Belgium
Comelli, Alberto, University of Parma, Italy
De Paula, Daniel Giotti, Institute of Tax and Financial Studies of Juiz de Fora, Brazil
De Perthuis, Christian, Université Paris Dauphine – PSL, France
Dellatte, Joseph, Kyoto University, Japan
Fabri, Ligia Barroso, Lawyer at HLL Advogados, Brazil
Fermeglia, Matteo, Hasselt University, Belgium
Grau Ruiz, María Amparo, Complutense University of Madrid, Spain
Iliopoulos, Theodoros G., Hasselt University, Belgium
Janda, Mirka, European Commission, Belgium
Ladefoged, Astrid, European Commission, Belgium
Leonetti, Carlos Araújo, Federal University of Santa Catarina, Brazil
Majocchi, Alberto, University of Pavia, Italy
Mendell, Russell, RMI, USA
Oliari, Rafaela Cristina, Federal University of Santa Catarina, Brazil
Parry, Ian, International Monetary Fund, Fiscal Affairs Department, USA
Rudolph, Sven, Kyoto University, Japan
Runkel, Matthias, Green Budget Germany, Germany
Salassa Boix, Rodolfo, Pompeu Fabra University of Barcelona, Spain
Schlegelmilch, Kai, Green Budget Germany, Germany
Soberón Garreta, Daniela, Climate Policy Institute, Peru
Trinidad Alvarado, Carlos, Climate Policy Institute, Peru
Villar Ezcurra, Marta, CEU San Pablo University, Spain
Weishaar, Stefan E., University of Groningen, The Netherlands
Wolff, Sébastien, Catholic University of Louvain, Belgium

Foreword: fake twins

Christian de Perthuis

Covid-19 and CO_2 are similar in many ways. It is the scientists who warn society of the risks to which these expose us. Politicians who refuse to listen to Intergovernmental Panel on Climate Change (IPCC) climate warnings are also those who deny the seriousness of the epidemic threat.

Covid-19 and CO_2 have another similarity. They both threaten a global public good: public health and the climate stability. This is why it is necessary to align the behaviors of each one by tracking down the free riders to fight them effectively.

These twinning traits between Covid-19 and CO_2 have clearly appeared in short-term action in the face of the pandemic. By shutting down economies, politicians have cleared the sky and reduced CO_2 emissions like no other policy before. Action against health risk and action against climate change have been mutually reinforcing.

Can we draw more lasting lessons from action against the pandemic to strengthen action against global warming? I see two main ones that we will be able to implement if we take into account the differences between the action of CO_2 and that of the virus, in fact two fake twins.

Firstly, the temporality of the threat is not the same. Between the time the lockdown is decided and the first results appear on the speed of the virus circulation, it takes two to three weeks. In terms of climate change, it takes two to three decades because it is the stock of greenhouse gases that warms the planet and not the annual flow of our emissions.

There would be no sense in wanting to prolong the rationing mechanisms that have reduced CO_2 emissions over several decades. But the economist has, in his toolbox, an instrument to achieve the results of rationing while maintaining the flexibility required for the economy to run efficiently: Emissions Trading Schemes (ETS). This is why all avenues for strengthening these mechanisms must be explored, particularly in Europe where ETS has suffered numerous dysfunctions in the past and in China where it will begin to be implemented at the national level from 2021.

Secondly, the virus is not a human production. It has been transmitted from the animal world, following a path still unidentified, but certainly favored by our lifestyles and the way we treat nature. To combat this circulation, science is enabling the development of vaccines that will become essential weapons in action.

When it comes to warming, there will be no vaccine. For a basic reason: the pathogen is none other than ourselves since the excess CO_2 in the atmosphere is of human origin. In reality, we will need to be vaccinated against ourselves, by radically modifying our ways of producing and consuming. Here again, carbon taxation seems the best instrument to trigger these increasingly urgent changes in view of the climate emergency.

This is why the pricing of carbon, via taxes or ETS, is an even more important issue in the era of the pandemic. I therefore have great pleasure in introducing this book which sheds multiple lights on these questions and shows us that the health crisis has in no way altered the dynamism and creativity of the network of researchers, policymakers, and international organizations that has formed over the years to work on environmental taxation.

Christian de Perthuis
Professor at Université Paris Dauphine – PSL
Founder of the Climate Economics Chair
Paris, France

PART I

Carbon tax theory in the pandemic era

1. A post-crisis assessment of carbon taxation for members of the Coalition of Finance Ministers for Climate Action

Simon Black and Ian Parry[1]

1. INTRODUCTION

The health and economic crisis precipitated by the novel coronavirus (COVID19) is unprecedented but the urgent need to reduce carbon emissions to address climate change remains. The Intergovernmental Panel on Climate Change (IPCC) put the 'budget' for containing expected warming to 1.5°C at the equivalent of 10 years of current annual greenhouse gas (GHG) emissions, underscoring the need for an immediate and drastic scaling back of global emissions.[2] Though the crisis substantially dented global emissions in 2020, emissions are rebounding in 2021.[3] Given this, there remains an urgent need for transitioning to zero-carbon energy systems by midcentury.

The landmark 2015 Paris Agreement laid the foundations for meaningful action to stabilize the global climate system. The centerpiece of the Agreement is commitments made by 192 parties to reduce GHGs, as specified in their Nationally Determined Contributions (NDCs). The first-round commitments were consistent with containing projected warming to approximately 3°C,[4] though countries are required to submit revised pledges, preferably with greater ambition, every 5 years starting with COP 26 in November 2021. Current NDCs have intermediate emissions targets, mostly for 2030, though pledges differ considerably in their nominal stringency. Additionally, over 100 countries and almost 400 cities have pledged to achieve 'net zero' emissions by midcentury,[5] as required by the 1.5–2°C goal of the Agreement.

It is widely accepted that carbon pricing—charges on the carbon content of fossil fuels or their emissions—could play a central role in implementing mitigation pledges. As carbon charges are reflected in higher prices for fossil fuel-based energy, this provides across-the-board incentives to reduce energy use and shift firms and households towards cleaner energy sources. Carbon pricing also provides the critical price signal for redirecting investment towards low-carbon technologies.[6] As economies stabilize, shutdowns ease, and recoveries commence, fiscal policymakers should seek to promote a 'green' recovery. Carbon taxes or similar measures can play a critical role in getting energy prices right, thereby helping ensure new investment is efficiently allocated to low-carbon technologies.

Finance Ministers—such as the 52 members of the Coalition of Finance Ministers (referred to here as the 'Coalition')[7]—and their ministries have a central role in climate mitigation, notably through carbon taxation. While environment ministries typically have responsibility for emissions inventories and regulatory/trading programs, finance ministers hold many of the key fiscal levers that can help countries achieve their mitigation commitments. Existing pledges among Coalition members are to cut emissions by around 15–35 percent by 2030, relative to historical or business as usual (BAU) emissions projections (i.e., emissions in the absence of mitigating measures). Overall, Coalition countries represented 16 percent of global carbon dioxide (CO_2) emissions in 2017, and 30 percent of global gross domestic product (GDP), and had about half the global average emissions intensity of GDP.[8]

This chapter seeks to provide a transparent and comprehensive assessment for Coalition countries of carbon taxes and their environmental, fiscal, and energy price implications. The analysis is based on an International Monetary Fund (IMF) and World Bank spreadsheet model, updated for the most recent (post-COVID) GDP and energy price forecasts and focusing on CO_2 emissions from fossil fuel combustion.[9] This analysis is intended to provide quantitative guidance to inform policymakers about the effective stringency of pledges and the policy actions needed, though it should not be used to rank countries. Appropriate mitigation effort will vary across countries depending, for example, on the willingness of electorates to accept higher energy prices, the ease of switching to cleaner energy sources, per capita income, and historical contributions to atmospheric GHGs.

2. CARBON TAXES AS A CLIMATE MITIGATION TOOL

Carbon pricing can, in general, take one of two forms. Carbon taxes are taxes on fuel supply—with rates scaled to the carbon content of the fuels—and are straightforward from an administrative perspective as an extension of fuel excise collection by finance ministries.[10] Emissions trading systems (ETSs) require regulated entities to acquire allowances for their emissions—they are usually implemented by environment ministries who fix the supply of allowances and monitor emissions while trading in allowance markets establishes emissions prices.

In principle, each instrument can be designed to mimic features of the other. In practice the coverage of ETSs has typically been limited to power generators and industrial firms (with large smokestacks) though they could be extended to cover suppliers of fuels for transportation and buildings. ETSs could also (for the same emissions coverage and price) raise the same amount of general revenue as carbon taxes through allowance auctions. However, this has not generally been the practice to date, as allowances are often given away via free allocation. Additionally, auctioned revenues are often earmarked—for example for environmental spending—and hence may offer less fiscal flexibility. Revenues from carbon taxes are sometimes earmarked, though more commonly they are used for broader fiscal reforms or go to the general budget.[11] Pure ETSs provide more certainty over annual emissions from covered sectors but the trade-off is uncertainty over emissions prices, which might deter private investment in low-emission technologies. ETSs can, however, be augmented through price floors (e.g., implemented, for example, through a minimum auction price) to make them behave more like taxes, while carbon tax rates can be periodically adjusted to keep emissions in line with future targets. Given the focus on finance ministries, this chapter focuses on carbon taxes.

About 60 carbon pricing schemes have been implemented to date at regional, national, and sub-national levels (Table 1.1). Prices in 2020 were around $5 to $25 per ton[12] in most schemes, but in a few cases (e.g., Scandinavian countries) carbon taxes are much higher. Some countries make use of both carbon taxes and ETSs—for example, Denmark, France, Ireland, Sweden, and Portugal apply carbon taxes to emissions outside of the EU ETS. From a global perspective, however, carbon pricing schemes are barely scratching the surface of what is needed. Existing and prospective pricing schemes cover only a fifth of global GHGs and the explicit carbon price, averaged across global emissions, is only around $2 per ton of CO_2.[13]

Carbon taxes need to be part of a broader policy package and the appropriate timing depends on national circumstances. Where there are limits on the political acceptability of higher energy prices other (albeit less efficient) mitigation instruments can have a reinforcing role, by promoting some of the key behavioral responses of carbon taxes while avoiding a significant impact on energy prices. These may take the form of regulatory standards for emission rates and energy efficiency, though a more flexible and cost-effective approach is feebates.[14] More generally, mitigation instruments will need to be supported by public investment (e.g., in smart grids, electric vehicle charging stations) and incentives for technology development and deployment. The appropriate time for introducing carbon taxes will depend on prevailing factors such as the urgency of fiscal consolidation and likely opposition from the public.

Table 1.1   *Selected carbon pricing schemes, 2020*

Country/Region	Year Introduced	Price 2019, $/ton CO$_2$	Coverage of GHGs 2018 Million Tons	Percent
Carbon taxes				
Chile	2017	5	47	39
Columbia	2017	5	42	40
Denmark	1992	26	22	40
Finland	1990	65	25	38
France	2014	50	176	37
Ireland	2010	22	31	48
Japan	2012	3	999	68
Mexico	2014	1–3	307	47
Norway	1991	59	40	63
Portugal	2015	14	21	29
South Africa	2019	10	360	10
Sweden	1991	127	26	40
Switzerland	2008	96	18	35
Emissions Trading Systems (ETSs)				
California	2012	16	378	85
China	2020	n/a	3232	
European Union	2005	25	2132	45
Korea	2015	22	453	68
New Zealand	2008	17	40	52
Regional GHG Initial	2009	5	94	21
Carbon price floors				
Canada	2016	15	n/a	70
United Kingdom	2013	24	136	24

Note: Regional GHG Initiative is a cooperative effort among Connecticut, Delaware, Maine, Maryland, Massachusetts, New Hampshire, New Jersey, New York, Rhode Island and Vermont.
Source: WBG (2019a), IMF (2019a).

3. QUANTITATIVE ASSESSMENT

This part discusses, for Coalition member countries, the following issues: fossil fuel CO$_2$ emissions projections under current policies; emission reductions needed for intermediate emissions targets; carbon prices implied by emissions targets; revenues from carbon taxes; energy price implications; comparisons of pricing with other mitigation instruments; and broader energy price reform.[15]

The analysis is based on an IMF and World Bank spreadsheet tool.[16] This tool projects uses of fossil and other fuels by the major energy sectors in a BAU scenario with no new or tightening of existing mitigation policies (e.g., current fuel taxes and EU ETS emissions prices are taken as given). The impacts of carbon taxes on fuel use and emissions depend on assumptions about the price responsiveness of fuel use which are based on empirical and modelling literature, though significant uncertainty surrounds these parameters. Data availability permits analysis for 44 Coalition countries.

Future BAU emissions growth depends on GDP growth, changes in the energy intensity of GDP, and changes in the carbon intensity of energy. Figure 1.1 shows projected changes in the BAU between 2017 and 2030 (2017 is the last year for which cross-country fuel use data is comprehensively available). GDP is expected to rise across Coalition countries by a simple average of 37 percent to 2030, though growth is faster in populous developing countries like Philippines (80 percent), Kenya (90 percent), and Bangladesh (122 percent). Increases in GDP raises emissions, as does the increasing CO_2 emissions intensity of energy as countries like Indonesia (16 percent) and Ethiopia (66 percent) scale up their energy systems.[17] However, the energy intensity of GDP is expected to fall by an average of 13 percent over this period, reflecting improving energy efficiency and the demand for energy rising less than in proportion to GDP. Overall, CO_2 emissions are expected to increase across the Coalition by an average of 22 percent over this period, but the increase exceeds 30 percent in 12 cases. Seven countries (Finland, Greece, Ireland, Italy, Poland, Portugal, and Spain) are expected to reduce emissions in the baseline. The effective stringency of mitigation pledges is significant but varies across Coalition countries (Figure 1.2). Reductions below BAU levels in 2030 needed to achieve (first-round) mitigation pledges range from reductions greater than 40 percent in 12 cases to less than 10 percent in 8 cases.[18] In part, these differences may reflect countries' varying preferences for being leaders on climate change. Separately, some advanced countries have, or are planning to introduce, stricter domestic climate plans.[19]

The emissions reductions needed to meet mitigation pledges have not changed significantly (Figure 1.2). In level terms, IMF GDP projections for Coalition countries have been revised downwards by a GDP-weighted average of 3 percentage points by 2024 over previous forecasts.[20] The overall impact on emissions is fully counteracted, however, by an increase in emissions due to lower oil, natural gas, and to a lesser extent coal price forecasts for 2030.[21] On a simple average basis, emissions reductions required to meet current NDCs are 29 percent below BAU levels in 2030, about 1 percentage point below their pre-COVID forecasts.

Carbon prices implicit in mitigation pledges vary from over $75 per ton in 2030 in 14 cases, between $25 and $75 in 13 cases, and below $25 in 17 countries. Figure 1.3 compares emissions reductions under different carbon taxes in 2030 to reductions required for mitigation pledges. The cross-country differences in prices needed to meet mitigation pledges reflect differences in the stringency of commitments as just discussed, but also in the price responsiveness of emissions. For example, emissions reductions below BAU levels from a $50 carbon price exceed 25 percent for countries consuming a lot of coal (e.g., Indonesia and Poland) and are less than 10 percent in some countries where coal use is minimal or zero (e.g., Costa Rica, Ethiopia, Panama).

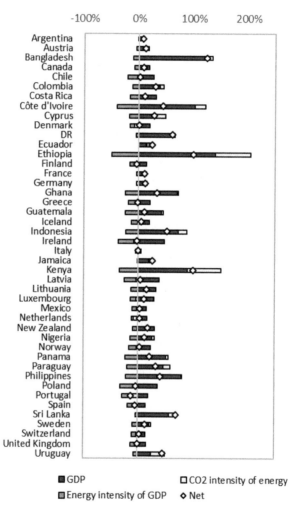

Figure 1.1   Percent change in CO_2 emissions 2018–30

The need for other mitigation instruments to reinforce carbon pricing will be especially important in cases where emissions reductions under carbon pricing alone fall short of target reductions, even under high carbon prices. Cross-country dispersion in needed carbon prices also underscores the case for international coordination mechanisms like carbon price floors.[22]

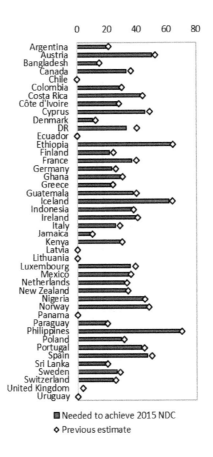

Figure 1.2   Emissons reductions versus BAU 2030 (%)

Comprehensive carbon taxation can mobilize a valuable revenue stream. In 2021, a $25 per ton carbon tax in 2021 would raise revenues of around 0.2–0.7 percent of GDP for most Coalition countries. In 2030, a $50 tax would raise revenues (Figure 1.4) of around 0.6–1.3 percent of GDP. Cross-country differences reflect (most importantly) differences in BAU emissions intensity in 2030 but also differences in the price responsiveness of emissions. Revenues are about 65–80 percent higher under the $50 per ton carbon tax in 2030 compared with the $25 tax (they are less than double, due to tax base erosion).[23] Ultimately, carbon pricing revenues would need to be replaced by other revenue sources as economies are de-carbonized, but this is an issue for the longer term.

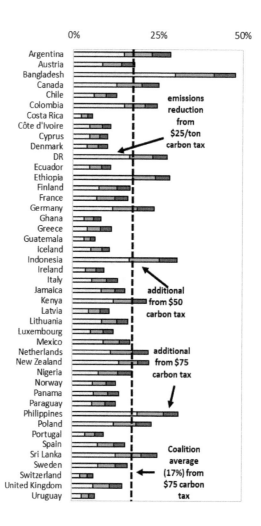

Figure 1.3   Percent change in CO_2 emissions in 2030 against baseline

A post-crisis assessment of carbon taxation

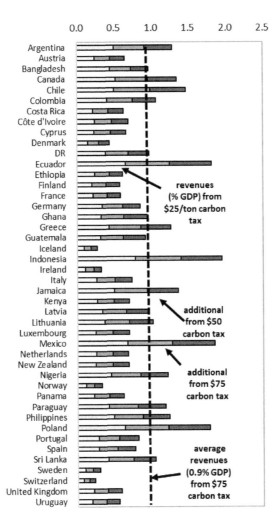

Figure 1.4   Revenues collected in 2030 (% GDP)

Carbon pricing has substantial impacts on coal and natural gas prices, but more moderate impacts on electricity and gasoline prices (Black and Parry 2020). On average, coal prices increase 144 percent above BAU prices for a $50 CO_2 price in 2030 while natural gas prices increase 46 percent. In contrast, retail electricity and gasoline prices increase on average about 10 percent. There are significant differences across countries, however, due to differences in

BAU prices (e.g., BAU prices for coal and natural gas are relatively high for European countries) and, in the case of electricity, differences in the carbon intensity of production (e.g., price increases exceed 30 percent in countries with large shares of coal or natural gas generation like Chile, Indonesia, Mexico, Philippines, Poland).

The mitigation potential of carbon pricing differs across sectors (Figure 1.5). Under a uniform carbon price applied to all Coalition members, on a simple average basis industrial sectors would account for about 54 percent of total emissions reductions, followed by power (21 percent), transport (13 percent), and residential (12 percent) sectors. Accordingly, countries with large abatement potential (Figure 1.3) tend to be those whose composition of CO_2 emissions comprises a significant amount of coal (Figure 1.6). However, achieving the Paris Agreement's long-term temperature goals requires full decarbonization of all sectors, including those that are harder to abate like transport and housing. By providing the long-term price signals needed to spur investment in low-carbon technologies, including in these sectors, carbon pricing can support decarbonization efforts beyond 2030.

Other mitigation instruments are less effective at reducing CO_2 than comprehensive carbon pricing (Black and Parry 2020). Policies are compared for the same CO_2 price increase ($50 per ton in 2030) they impose on emissions covered by the policy. ETSs are typically around 40–60 percent as effective as broad carbon pricing, not because of the instrument itself but rather its assumed coverage (based on general practice to date) of power generators and large industry. Road fuel taxes have effectiveness of mostly around 5–20 percent of carbon taxes as these fuels typically account for a minor proportion of emissions and carbon charging has a relatively modest impact on retail prices. In some coal-intensive countries (e.g., Philippines, Poland), taxing coal alone can be nearly as effective as a broad carbon tax. A combination of measures (feebates, regulations) that promote fuel switching in power generation and major opportunities for energy efficiency improvements has around 60–75 percent of the effectiveness of broad carbon pricing.

Other instruments also raise far less revenue (Black and Parry 2020). For example, coal taxes raise less than one-third of the revenue raised by comprehensive carbon taxes in most Coalition countries. Even if allowances are fully auctioned, the revenue potential of ETSs limited to the power and industrial sectors is generally below half of that for the carbon tax. And although feebates and regulations have smaller impacts on energy prices, a trade-off is that they forgo revenue opportunities.

A post-crisis assessment of carbon taxation 13

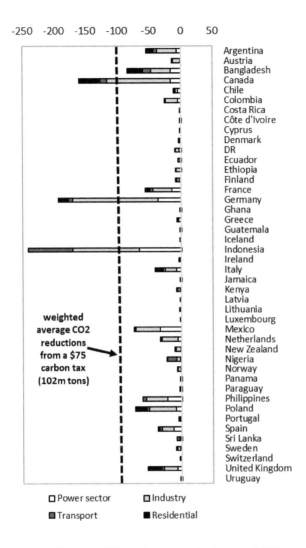

Figure 1.5   *Million tons CO$_2$ emissions reductions in 2030*

Broader fossil fuel price reform would be needed for fossil fuel prices to reflect supply costs and the full range of environmental costs. Combustion of coal and diesel fuel causes local air pollution which is harmful to public health, though the resulting costs vary considerably across countries depending, for example, on population exposure to pollution, use of emissions control technologies, and people's willingness to pay to avoid health risks (local air pollution damages from gasoline and natural gas tend to be small). More generally, use of road fuels in vehicles is indirectly associated with traffic congestion and accidents. There are more effective instruments for addressing domestic environmental problems, but reflecting environmental costs in fuel prices improves economic welfare in the interim, until these instruments have been widely implemented.[24]

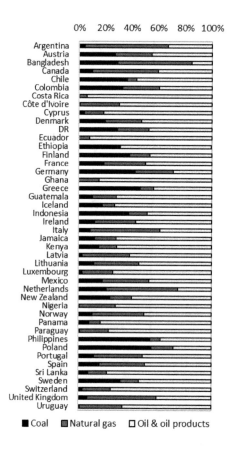

Figure 1.6   *Percent CO_2 emissions by fossil fuel, 2030 baseline*

Fossil fuels are pervasively underpriced across Coalition countries—despite high rates of road fuel excise in many cases[25]—though the degree of underpricing varies not only across countries but also across fuel types (Black and Parry 2020). For example, underpricing is generally more pronounced for coal than for natural gas, and for diesel than gasoline.

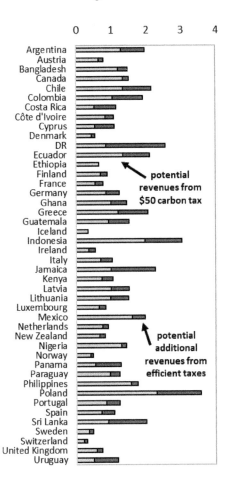

Figure 1.7   *Potential revenues in 2021 (% GDP)*

Comprehensive energy price reform to reflect broader environmental damages would yield substantial additional revenues for Coalition countries. For the most part, retail prices are equal to or greater than supply costs across fuel products and Coalition countries, so there is little scope for revenue gains from eliminating subsidies from undercharging for supply costs. A broader definition of subsidies, however, would reflect the difference between current prices and efficient prices needed to reflect supply and all environmental costs[26]—subsidy reform in this broader sense (i.e., moving from current to efficient fossil fuel prices) would, in contrast, yield large revenue gains. This can be seen in Figure 1.7 where revenues from full price reform in 2021 add, on a simple average basis, slightly more than double revenues from a $50 carbon tax. Such major reform may be unrealistic, at least in such a short time frame, but the estimates serve to underscore the ample space for reforming energy prices in an economically efficient direction while also contributing significantly to fiscal needs.

CONCLUSION

This chapter suggests that, if anything, the global economic crisis may have strengthened the case for phasing in carbon taxes as economies recover. Carbon taxes will help to ensure that climate considerations are adequately integrated into private investment decisions as the economy picks up while revenues from carbon pricing can help protect fiscal space. If fossil fuels are underpriced, that is, prices fail to fully reflect both supply and environmental costs, there is a danger that recoveries will lock in carbon-intensive capital (e.g., fossil fuel power plants) that will ultimately become stranded. Stimulus packages will need to be sustainably funded to reassure capital markets and carbon pricing can help with this by establishing a robust stream of new revenues over the medium term, helping to lower borrowing costs as countries incur greater debt. Raising funds through other sources would not contribute to environmental objectives.[27]

The chapter presents extensive cross-country analysis to help Coalition members understand the impacts of carbon taxation and trade-offs with other instruments. This analysis underscores that the economic crisis has had little effect on the need for emissions reductions and the emissions and fiscal impacts of carbon pricing.

The burden of increased energy prices on businesses and households is a critical concern, though a comprehensive reform may increase their acceptability. For most carbon pricing designs, near-term burdens of higher energy prices are not large: typically less than 1 percent of production costs for industries on average, and around 1 percent of consumption for the average household, for a $25 carbon price in 2021.[28] Carbon pricing may also be more acceptable at a time of lower energy prices—for example, carbon prices of around $65 per ton could be introduced without raising projected 2021 retail road fuel prices above 2019 price levels (though coal and natural gas prices would rise above 2019 levels). A comprehensive strategy to enhance acceptability could include extensive consultation with stakeholders and communication to the public; assistance programs for households, workers, firms, and regions vulnerable to higher energy prices; visible, equitable, and productive use of carbon pricing revenues; and complementary investments (e.g., in renewables) to enhance the credibility of reform.

The timing of carbon tax reform is also critical. For some debt-constrained countries, recovery programs can be funded through a combination of international support and domestic revenue mobilization. Carbon taxation may be a less economically depressing domestic source than broader taxes on work effort and investment. For countries able to borrow, carbon taxes can contribute to debt sustainability over the medium to long term, and their introduction might be delayed until economic recovery is well underway. Reform in some countries may need to wait, for example, if there is currently a risk of provoking social unrest or domestic energy producers have been badly hit by lower energy prices.

Beyond carbon taxation, climate considerations need to be factored into the spending side of stimulus plans. Recovery plans could be assessed on their decarbonization potential as well as their implications for short-term recovery. And public investment projects could focus on low-carbon infrastructure (e.g., renewables, smart grids), developing and adopting new technologies (e.g., batteries for storing electricity, carbon capture and storage), adaptation (e.g., more robust roads and drainage systems), while avoiding investments in carbon-intensive sectors (e.g., coal generation plants).[29]

NOTES

1. Fiscal Affairs Department, IMF. Khamal Clayton provided valuable research assistance. The authors are grateful to Kristina Åkesson, Juan Carlos Benitez, Amar Bhattacharya, Paula Suarez Buitron, James Daniel, Kurt Van Dender, Luisa Dressler, Florens Flues, Thibault Guyon, Stephane Hallegatte, Michael Keen, Joaquim Levy, Carola Maggiulli, Grzegorz Peszko, Dinar Prihardini, Jun Rentschler, Karl-Anders Stigzelius, Jonas Teusch, and Philippe Wen for very helpful comments and suggestions. The views expressed in the chapter are those of the author(s) and do not necessarily represent the views of the IMF, its Executive Board, IMF management, or members of the Coalition of Finance Ministers for Climate Action.
2. IPCC (2018). Put another way, global GHGs must rapidly fall to 50 percent below current levels by 2030 to meet the 1.5°C goal (and continue declining thereafter), or by 25 percent for the 2°C goal (UNEP 2020).
3. IEA (2020) projects global CO_2 emissions will decline by 8 percent in 2020 before rebounding with economic recovery commencing 2021.
4. UNEP (2020).
5. UN (2020).
6. See for example Pigato and others (2020).

7. The Coalition of Finance Ministers for Climate Action is a group of 52 countries (as of December 2020) whose Finance Ministers are committed to achieving the Paris Agreement's objectives. One goal of the Coalition is to help these countries assess the potential role of carbon pricing for achieving climate and revenue mobilization objectives. For more information see www.financeministersforclimate.org.
8. See Black and Parry (2020): 0.23 versus 0.41 tons of CO_2 per US$1,000 of GDP.
9. For details on the model, refer to Black and Parry (2020).
10. Alternatively, carbon taxes can be integrated into fiscal regimes for industries extracting coal, oil, and natural gas with rebates for fuel exports and taxes applied to fuel imports. See Calder (2015) for a discussion of carbon tax administration.
11. See Carl and Fedor (2016), WBG (2019b).
12. Aside from Table 1.1, all monetary values below are expressed in constant 2018 US dollars.
13. Calculated from WBG (2019a).
14. The latter provide a sliding scale of fees on products or activities with above average emission rates and a sliding scale of rebates for products or activities with below average emission rates. For example, if applied to transportation, new vehicle sales would be subject to a fee equal to the product of: (i) a CO_2 price; (ii) the difference between the vehicle's CO_2 per mile and the average CO_2 per mile of the new vehicle fleet; and (iii) the (discounted) lifetime mileage of the average vehicle. Analogous schemes could reduce emission rates from power generation and industries or increase the energy efficiency of products and capital.
15. Analysis of the distributional burden of carbon pricing across households and industries, trade effects, and sectoral employment effects, can guide the design of measures to assist groups vulnerable to higher energy prices but is beyond the scope of this chapter.
16. The tool has been used in previous cross-country reports on climate mitigation policies including IMF (2019a and b). For model details refer to Black and Parry (2020).
17. For most countries, there is little change in the CO_2 intensity of energy given that renewables as a share of total energy start from a low base and in the BAU there is no assumed change in the stringency of policies to promote renewables.
18. Mitigation pledges in NDCs typically specify targets for total GHGs rather than fossil fuel CO_2 emissions. The above calculations assume CO_2 emissions need to be reduced in the same proportion to total GHGs except for countries with large forestry and land use change contributions.
19. For example, Denmark, the EU, and the UK have recently adopted targets to cut emissions 70, 55, and 68 percent below 1990 levels by 2030, respectively.
20. The new revised GDP projections extend to 2024 and beyond that GDP is assumed to grow at the same annual average rate as in the last year of the projection period.
21. Projected (real) oil prices are $50/barrel in 2030 (compared with $66 in 2019 and a previous forecast for 2030 of $74).
22. See IMF (2019b) for a discussion of international carbon price floors and how they could equitably scale up mitigation action among large emitters.
23. The calculations above account for revenue losses from the erosion of pre-existing fuel tax bases.
24. Congestion, for example, is most efficiently addressed through peak period charges on busy roads and local air pollution though charges on emissions out of the smokestack. See Parry and others (2014) for an extensive discussion of

25. See OECD (2018) for more detail on energy taxes in different countries.
26. See Coady and others (2019) on different notions of energy subsidies.
27. See Jones and Keen (2009) for a discussion of carbon pricing reform in the context of economic recovery programs.
28. Inferred from calculations in IMF (2019b).
29. See IMF (2020).

REFERENCES

Black, Simon J., and Ian Parry, 2020. 'Implications of the Global Economic Crisis for Carbon Pricing: A Quantitative Assessment for Coalition Member Countries.' Accessed 28 January 2021 at https://www.financeministersforclimate.org/sites/cape/files/inline-files/IMF-WB%20Coalition%20Note%20-%20Implications%20of%20the%20Global%20Economic%20Crisis%20for%20Carbon%20Pricing.pdf.

Calder, Jack, 2015. 'Administration of a U.S. Carbon Tax.' In *Implementing a U.S. Carbon Tax: Challenges and Debates*, edited by I. Parry, A. Morris, and R. Williams, Routledge, New York, pp. 38–61.

Carl, Jeremy, and David Fedor, 2016. 'Tracking Global Carbon Revenues: A Survey of Carbon Taxes versus Cap-and-Trade in the Real World.' *Energy Policy* 96, 50–77.

Coady, David, Ian Parry, Nghia-Piotr Le, and Baoping Shang, 2019. 'Global Fossil Fuel Subsidies Remain Large: An Update Based on Country-Level Estimates.' Working Paper 19/89, International Monetary Fund, Washington, DC.

IEA, 2020. *Global Energy Review 2020: The Impacts of the Covid-19 Crisis on Global Energy Demand and CO_2 Emissions*. International Energy Agency, Paris, France.

IMF, 2019a. *Fiscal Policies for Paris Climate Strategies: From Principle to Practice*. International Monetary Fund, Washington, DC.

IMF, 2019b. *Fiscal Monitor: How to Mitigate Climate Change*. International Monetary Fund, Washington, DC.

IMF, 2020. *Greening the Recovery*. Special Series on Fiscal Policies to Respond to COVID-19. International Monetary Fund, Washington, DC.

IPCC, 2018. *Global Warming of 1.5 °C*. Intergovernmental Panel on Climate Change, Geneva, Switzerland.

Jones, Benjamin, and Michael Keen, 2009. *Climate Policy and the Recovery*. IMF Staff Position Note 09/28. Washington, DC.

OECD, 2018, *Effective Carbon Rates 2018: Pricing Carbon Emissions through Taxes and Emissions Trading*. OECD Publishing, Paris. https://doi.org/10.1787/9789264305304-en.

Parry, Ian W.H., Dirk Heine, Shanjun Li, and Eliza Lis, 2014. *Getting Energy Prices Right: From Principle to Practice*. International Monetary Fund, Washington, DC.

Pigato, Miria, Simon J. Black, Damien Dussaux, Zhimin Mao, Miles McKenna, Ryan Rafaty, and Simon Touboul, 2020. *Technology Transfer and Innovation for Low-Carbon Development: International Development in Focus*. World Bank, Washington, DC.

UN, 2020. *The Race to Zero Emissions, and Why the World Depends on It*. Accessed 28 January 2021 at https://news.un.org/en/story/2020/12/1078612.

UNEP, 2020. *Emissions Gap Report 2019*. United Nations Environment Programme, Nairobi, Kenya.

WBG, 2019a. *State and Trends of Carbon Pricing 2019*. World Bank Group, Washington, DC.

WBG, 2019b. *Using Carbon Tax Revenues*. World Bank Group, Washington, DC.

2. Setting a price for carbon to achieve carbon neutrality in the European Union

Alberto Majocchi[1]

1. THE REASONS BEHIND ENERGY TAXATION

In the past, environmental policy has largely relied on command-and-control measures. These generally identify maximum emissions levels or minimum efficiency standards that apply equally to every economic agent through all economic sectors. If controls are cheap and efficient, regulatory measures have, as the main advantage, the possibility to ensure that environmental targets are indeed met. Especially in cases where the achievement of the target is of crucial importance (for instance, for sanitary reasons), they may be preferable to alternative instruments. There are, however, many drawbacks associated with these regulatory instruments:

- from the point of view of static efficiency, if a standard for emission reduction is set, every firm will have to make equal reduction efforts, regardless of the fact that marginal reduction costs could differ among polluters. It would be cheaper for the economy as a whole if firms with relatively low marginal reduction costs were forced to reduce emissions more than firms with high costs, because total costs in this case would be minimised;
- from the point of view of dynamic efficiency, with direct regulations a firm is not penalised for emitting a residual amount of pollution as long as the firm complies with the standard. Therefore, firms have no incentive to use new technologies to reduce emissions below the norm set by the regulatory authority. Conversely, under a tax regime polluting firms have to pay taxes on the remaining amount of pollution. This will stimulate them to look for and adopt new reduction technologies, thereby reducing their tax burden, since firms have a cost incentive to reduce polluting emissions as much as possible, otherwise they face high tax payments.

The debate on the use of an energy tax has been reinvigorated with the growing awareness of the problems of global warming. If the aim of the envisaged policy is exclusively to cut down emissions of carbon dioxide (CO_2), the key instrument, from an economic point of view, is a pure carbon tax as opposed to an energy tax. Here, the reduction of CO_2 emissions is achieved in three ways:

- a reduction of energy usage in households and firms, induced by the higher relative prices of energy;
- rising energy prices provide an incentive to improve the efficiency of energy usage both in end-use sectors and in the production sector of secondary energies;
- fuel substitution leads to replacement of carbon-intensive fuels by low- or non-carbon-intensive alternatives, especially in electricity production where significant possibilities exist. However, this option is also available in end-use sectors (e.g. the substitution of coal for heating by natural gas).

A pure carbon tax links the tax burden on various energy products to their carbon content perfectly, through all three options described above. An energy tax leads to little fuel substitution. Hence, compared to an energy tax, a carbon tax needs a lower tax rate to reach the same target of reduction of CO_2 emissions because carbon-intensive fuels are made relatively more expensive.

2. THE ROLE OF CARBON PRICING

The problem of climate change is a global one and it currently represents one of the principal areas of concern for all mankind. CO_2 emissions are considered to be the main contributory factor to the greenhouse effect and the atmospheric concentration of CO_2 is largely of anthropogenic origin, primarily caused by the burning of fossil fuels. In this case the principle that the American biologist Hardin (1968) called 'The Tragedy of the Commons' applies: the optimal solution is a multilateral agreement, but – unfortunately – for everyone it is convenient to behave like a free rider.

While global warming is a worldwide problem, the main responsibility lies with industrialised countries. In 2018, world emissions of CO_2 reached 36,573 million tonnes.[2] The EU contribution to global emissions is only 8.38%, compared to 14.8% for the US, 3.17% for Japan, 27.5% for China, 4.67% for Russia and 7.25% for India. In the near future policy measures needed for curbing CO_2 emissions should especially be implemented in Northern industrialised countries. But, with the expected economic growth of developing countries, their CO_2 emissions could increase dramatically, since energy efficiency is significantly at a lower level. An effective policy for addressing the global warming problem should therefore provide the right economic incentives to industrialised countries for increasing energy efficiency and shifting to renewable energy sources, but at the same time it should warrant adequate incentives for curbing emissions in less developed countries as well.

A unilateral action by the European Union would not solve the greenhouse problem, whose nature is global. But with the adoption of the Convention on Climate Change at the United Nations Conference on Environment and Development (UNCED) Earth Summit held in Rio in June 1992 and, afterwards, with the approval of the Kyoto Protocol and the Agreement reached within the COP21 (held in December 2015 in Paris), a worldwide commitment to cope with the problem of global warming has been taken. It is within this framework that the best instruments to achieve the goal in the most cost-effective way should be chosen.

Even if at an international level there seems to be a widespread consensus on the need to curb climate-altering gas emissions, there is a lack of concrete initiatives to encourage behaviour consistent with these objectives. In literature, the imposition of a price on carbon is considered the best tool to get prices right, that is, to balance the damages resulting from the pollution generated by CO_2 emissions from the combustion of fossil fuels, and to curb the use of polluting energy sources, thus promoting the achievement of the Kyoto targets.

In 'Economists' Statement on Carbon Dividends',[3] published in the *Wall Street Journal* on 17 January 2019 and signed by 3,589 American economists, 4 former Federal Reserve Presidents, 27 Nobel Prize laureates, 15 former Presidents of the Council of Economic Advisers and two former Secretaries of the US Treasury Department, it is stressed that the carbon tax is the most efficient instrument for reducing CO_2 emissions. It is emphasised that it is not a question of imposing a new levy, but of correcting a market failure by providing a price signal to steer the behaviour of producers and consumers in the direction of a carbon-free economy. The 'Economists' Statement on Carbon Pricing',[4] promoted by the EAERE (European Association of Environmental and Resource Economists), expresses itself in the same way. The EAERE Statement has already reached 1,752 subscriptions.

3. THE EUROPEAN STRATEGY FOR CURBING CO_2 EMISSIONS

In 1992, in preparation for the UNCED Earth Summit to be held in Rio, the European Community put forward a Draft Directive introducing a carbon-energy tax,[5] with the double goal of promoting energy saving – through the share of the tax linked to the quantity of energy used; and fuel switching – through the tax rate linked to the carbon content of each fossil fuel. However, after the failed attempt to introduce a carbon-energy tax, the EU

Council decided to follow a different path and finally approved a Directive[6] introducing an Emissions Trading System (ETS).

In the ETS, companies receive or purchase emission permits which they can trade on the market. The overall volume of greenhouse gases (GHGs) that can be emitted each year by the power plants, factories and other companies covered by the system is subject to the cap set at the EU level that, from 2013 onwards, is reduced by 1.74% each year (as of 2021, the EU ETS as an investment driver will be strengthened by increasing the pace of annual reductions in allowances to 2.2%). The allowances will be progressively allocated through an auctioning mechanism – with a phasing out of free allocation of allowances – with additional revenues which could be allocated to the EU budget.

The ETS adopts a cap-and-trade method. The activities covered by the scheme include combustion installations with a thermal input exceeding 20 Megawatt (MW): power and heat generation, energy-intensive industry sectors including oil refineries, steel works and production of iron, aluminium, metals, cement, lime, glass, ceramics, pulp, paper, cardboard, acids and bulk organic chemicals, commercial aviation (until the end of 2023 the ETS will apply only to flights between airports located in the European Economic Area), totalling about 11,000 installations, representing 43% of total emissions. The number of permits to be allocated is defined through national allocation plans, as there are differences between the commitments to be made by Member States under the European Burden Sharing Agreement and the Kyoto Protocol. The allocation of permits takes place before the trading period begins, since the ETS requires that polluters hold an entitlement to emit a given quantity of pollution, and covers CO_2 emissions from installations listed in Annex 1 of the Directive. Each allowance gives the holder the right to emit 1 tonne of CO_2. Allowances can be used only once since companies have to surrender allowances for every tonne of CO_2 that they emitted in the previous year.

The transition to carbon neutrality that, according to the Guidelines presented to the European Parliament in July 2019 by the Presidential candidate von der Leyen,[7] must be achieved by 2050 gives a central role to energy, which today is responsible for 75% of CO_2 emissions. They envisage a package of measures: reform of the ETS, national constraints to reduce emissions, legislation to maintain carbon sinks in soils and forests, energy efficiency targets for renewable energy, ad hoc legislation to improve the efficiency of cars and trucks. These measures should reduce emissions by 45% in 2030 and around 60% in 2050. But carbon neutrality requires an additional effort.

The European Union, which is responsible for 8.4% of global CO_2 emissions, has a leading role in the transition to a carbon-free economy. Already in 2009 it set itself the target of reducing GHG emissions by 80–95% in 2050 and, in her State of the Union Address 2020,[8] the President of the Commission, after stressing that the Union has already achieved decoupling because 'while emissions dropped 25% since 1990, our economy grew by more than 60%', stresses that 'the European Commission is proposing to increase the 2030 target for emission reduction to at least 55% compared to 1990'.

It is in this perspective that the hypothesis of proposing the introduction of a carbon price for the use of fossil fuels that emit CO_2 during the combustion process has re-emerged. The tax base for carbon pricing should not include sectors that are already part of the ETS, whose allowances will be progressively allocated through an auctioning mechanism – with a phasing out of free allocation of allowances – with additional revenues which should be allocated to the EU budget.

4. THE LEVEL OF THE CARBON PRICE

Theoretically, the carbon price should be equal to the social costs of CO_2 emissions (Metcalf, 2020). But in the literature, given the difficulty of correctly measuring the social costs of CO_2 emissions (Espagne, 2017), different estimates have been put forward.

The carbon price should be high enough to give a signal to the market and to promote a progressive change in the structure of consumption and production methods. The simplest method for deriving a price on carbon is a second-best approach, starting from fixing the reduction in the quantity of energy used needed to reach the goal of emission decrease to be achieved. Given the elasticity of demand $\eta = \Delta Q/Q \, (P/\Delta P)$, the percentage increase in prices due to the introduction of a carbon price, required to bring about the percentage change in the quantity of energy demanded that allows the wanted reduction of CO_2 emissions, could be estimated as $(dP/P) = \Delta Q/Q/\eta$.

A Report of the High-Level Commission on Carbon Pricing, chaired by J. Stiglitz and N. Stern, on behalf of the Carbon Pricing Leadership Coalition[9] clearly highlights the fact that 'a well-designed carbon price is an indispensable part of a strategy for reducing emissions in an efficient way'. And,

> based on industry and policy experience, and the literature reviewed, this Commission concludes that the explicit carbon-price level consistent with achieving the Paris temperature target (at COP21 in Paris, in December 2015, nearly 200 countries agreed to hold the increase in the global average temperature to well below 2°C above pre-industrial levels) is at least US\$40–80/tCO_2 [tonneCO_2] by 2020 and US\$50–100/tCO_2 by 2030.

At the current exchange rate the price in 2020 is around €34/€68, reaching the level of €42.5/€85 in 2030. To assess this level, it is useful to bear in mind that the price of emission permits under the ETS is already around €30. The price suggested by Stiglitz and Stern therefore appears to be near to what has already been achieved in Europe.

In the Quinet Commission Report (2019), 'on the basis of the models used, the Commission proposes to define a target value for climate action of €250 in 2030, €500 in 2040 and €775 in 2050'. These values are therefore higher than those calculated in previous studies. The initial value is close to a recent estimate from a study carried out at the University of Berkeley (Diaz and Moore, 2017), where the conclusion is reached that the social cost of carbon is not $37 per tonne, as previously estimated, but $220 per tonne.

Finally, according to a European Citizen Initiative,[10] the carbon price, which could initially be set at €50 per tonnes of CO_2 emitted, should then be gradually increased to the level necessary to put the EU economy on the path to an effective reduction in polluting emissions (e.g. €100 within 5 years). Since the emission of 1 tCO_2 corresponds to the use of 2.7 barrels of oil, equivalent to 429 litres, a tax of €50 would therefore affect each litre's price by €0.116, an increase of 7.6% (assuming a petrol price of €1.5).

The response of consumers and producers to a new price on carbon depends on two main factors: the elasticity of demand – that increases over time – and the availability of efficient and cheap alternatives. In the short-term there will be a behavioural change that will produce energy saving, that is, consuming less in response to higher prices (e.g. reduced indoor temperature). This change will be moderate given the low price elasticity.[11] In the long term changes in investment behaviour will follow, with a fuel switching, that is, buying less carbon-intensive equipment (e.g. more efficient boilers). The change will be more significant if an alternative is readily available.

If it is assumed – as it has been upheld by President von der Leyen in her State of the Union Address 2020[12] – that the required reduction of CO_2 emissions will have to be 55% in 2030, a calculation 'on the back of the envelope' suggests that the price of petrol, if initially set at €1.5/litre, should rise to €2.56. Given the long term elasticity of demand $\eta = [\Delta Q/Q].(P/\Delta P)$, it follows $\Delta P = P_0[\Delta Q/Q/\eta]$. If $\Delta Q/Q = 0.55$, $\eta = 0.773$ and $P_0 = €1.5$, then $\Delta P/P = 71.15\%$ and $P_1 = €2.56$ with $\Delta P = €1.06$, equivalent to a carbon tax of €455/tCO_2 since the emission of 1 tCO_2 corresponds to the use of 429 litres of petrol. Clearly, this rise in the rate of the carbon tax or in the floor price of emission allowances will be needed if no improvement in energy efficiency or no gradually increasing effect of fuel switching is contemplated.[13]

5. CARBON DIVIDEND AND FISCAL REFORM

Setting a carbon price could provide a significant amount of additional revenue to finance the expenditures that are essential for the ecological transition and to support a tax reform that shifts the burden of taxation from a good – labour – to an evil – GHG emissions. The tax base of carbon pricing is represented by coal, gas and mineral oils, and the levy should be commensurate to the carbon content of each energy source. Given the fixed ratio between carbon inputs and quantity of emissions, introducing a price on energy sources based on carbon content is equivalent to directly taxing CO_2 emissions.

Within the European Union total CO_2 emissions in 2018 amounted to 3.9 billion tonnes, of which 2.2 billion tonnes were in sectors excluded from the ETS. With a price per tCO_2 of €50, the carbon dividend would therefore amount to around €195 billion if the carbon price were applied to all emissions. If a carbon price of €50 per tonne of CO_2 were also imposed on imported products, since per capita CO_2 emissions amounted to 7 tonnes in 2018, of which 1 tonne was linked to imports, for a total amount of imported emissions of 446.1 million, the revenue from the compensatory right levied at the border would amount to €22.3 billion and would flow directly to the EU budget, with an increase in revenue of around 15% (the EU budget in 2019 is €148 billion).

These numbers should be evaluated with considerable caution In some countries, such as Sweden, where the current price imposed on carbon is already higher – €110 (SEK 1,190) per tCO_2 – than the (envisaged) European price level, it is unlikely that there will be an increase in revenue from this source. In other countries, such as Italy, where the revenue from excise duties on mineral oils is already high, there will be probably a reshaping of the tax base which will, at least partially, be commensurate with the carbon content of the various fossil fuels. It is therefore difficult to predict *ex ante* what the actual amount of the carbon dividend will be. However, it is indisputable that, beyond the actual amount of additional revenue that will be obtained through carbon pricing, *the revenue estimated above represents in any case a global price differential between traditional and renewable sources.*

The carbon dividend could be used to promote a tax reform aimed at ensuring redistribution in favour of the most disadvantaged income groups, countering the regressive effects of an energy tax, to combat the inequalities generated by the globalisation process, to foster an economically efficient and socially sustainable ecological transition, with support for the production of renewable energy (already favoured by the negative price differential against traditional energies), to ensure the creation of the necessary infrastructure for the production and transport of renewable energy.

6. BORDER CARBON ADJUSTMENT

In the ETS there are two main limits to be exceeded. The first limit – 57% of emissions do not pay a price in sectors excluded from the system – could be overcome if carbon pricing is extended to the four sectors that are now excluded from the ETS: agriculture, transport, building and small to medium-sized enterprises. The second limit – European carbon pricing can encourage carbon leakages and the loss of competitiveness of European companies – requires a fiscal adjustment at the European borders.

An effective design of carbon pricing – introduced as a complement to the ETS – requires that a tax be levied on total carbon consumption, including the taxation of imports of energy-intensive goods. Then, the carbon tax should combine a levy on domestic consumption and a fiscal adjustment at the border. If the domestic tax is complemented by a border carbon adjustment (BCA) levied on imports from countries that do not set a carbon price, the competitiveness of European companies is safeguarded and the risk of carbon leakages avoided, while respecting World Trade Organization (WTO) rules. This choice is crucial to ensure the political acceptability of carbon taxation within the European Union, preventing serious distortions to the detriment of European production.

The adoption of the BCA is sometimes rejected as contrary to WTO rules. A level playing field is not excluded by fair competition rules at the international level and a BCA is essential to prevent the risk of a loss of competitiveness for domestic firms that could make the adoption of a domestic carbon price difficult. The concept underlying a BCA is the destination principle, according to which goods are taxed where they are consumed, not where they are produced. The border charge on imports should be equivalent to the tax on the corresponding domestic product since, according to the WTO rules, a state shall not discriminate between domestic and foreign goods. Even if a BCA were considered a border enforcement of EU domestic tax, it cannot treat imported products less favourably than *like* domestic products. Basing the tax on the carbon content of the imported goods should ensure that a BCA is compatible with Article I, according to which the European Union cannot discriminate against an import based on its origin.

A General Agreement on Tariffs and Trade (GATT) Report[14] reached a negative conclusion on fiscal adjustments at the border, rejecting the principle of a level playing field and noting that 'there is no difference between the competitive implications of the type raised by different environmental standards and the competitive consequences of many other policy differences ...'. But the possibility of adjustments at the border for environmental levies on goods, when these goods are used as inputs into the production process of other products, was not rejected by a GATT Panel[15] when the European Community – together with Canada – challenged the US Superfund Amendments and Reauthorization Act of 1986 (the Superfund Act). The amount of the tax on any of the imported substances was equal in principle to the amount of the tax which would have been imposed under the Superfund Act on the chemicals used as materials in the production of the imported substance if the taxable chemicals had been sold in the United States for use in the production of the imported substances.

The Panel concluded that, to the extent that the tax on imported substances was equivalent to the tax borne by like domestic substances, the tax met the national treatment requirement of Article III:2, first sentence, of the GATT. It remains to be checked if the ruling of the Superfund case could be applied if BCAs are related to products using a large amount of energy not as a raw material, but as a combustion fuel consumed during the production process. It should be proved that the tax is levied on a product (the fuel utilised during the production process) and not on the process as such – to avoid the ban of trade measures with extra-jurisdictional effects emphasised by the Tuna Panel Report.[16]

Importers were required to provide sufficient information regarding the chemicals inputs of taxable imported substances to enable the tax authorities to determine the amount of the tax to be imposed. If the importer failed to furnish such information a tax could be imposed equivalent to 5% of the appraised value of the product at the time it was entering into the United States for consumption, use or warehousing. As a matter of fact, a crucial element in the implementation of a BCA is the methodology used to collect the information needed to determine the carbon footprint of each imported good, that could be ensured by requiring imported products to be accompanied by certification or labelling of relevant aspects of their production process and the related carbon emissions created during their production.

7. THE EXTENSION OF THE ETS WITHIN THE EUROPEAN UNION

The European Commission is interested in extending the EU ETS with the aim of accelerating the reduction in emissions realised in the road transport and buildings sectors. According to Cambridge Econometrics (2020), introducing an extended ETS which includes road transport and buildings alongside existing ETS sectors, leads to some further emission reductions, although neither sector achieves the envisaged reduction target for 2030, placing greater weight on the existing ETS sectors. Because there is a hard cap on emissions, and road transport and buildings do not deliver their share of emissions reductions, greater reductions must be achieved in other sectors. A lower ETS price for road transport and buildings is required to achieve the same emissions reduction when some of the revenues are used to invest in energy efficiency and low-carbon technologies, as in the low-carbon investment variant, where 10% of the revenues are diverted away from tax cuts – 9% being used to realise energy savings, and 1% for direct subsidies of low-carbon technologies, while the remaining 90% is used for tax cuts. The best way to decarbonise (through electrification) transport and buildings has to be played by the ETS in driving decarbonisation of the electricity sector.

On 29 November 2019, the two Houses of the German Parliament approved a decision to introduce a carbon price of €10 per tCO_2 for the transport and domestic heating sector, which together account for 32% of GHG emissions in Germany. Under pressure from the Green Party during the negotiations between the Bundestag and the Bundesrat, this price was raised from €10 to €25 per tCO_2 as of 2021, which entails an increase in the final price of 7 cents per litre on petrol, 8 cents on diesel and fuel oil and 0.5 cents per kilowatt-hour (kWh) of energy. Under this mechanism, companies selling fossil fuels will be required to purchase emission trading allowances, the price of which will rise gradually from €25 per tCO_2 in 2021 to €55 by 2025. Subsequently, as of 2026, the price will be determined by the market, although it cannot deviate from a price corridor set between €55 and €65 per tCO_2.

The German emissions allowance system for transport (excluding air transport) and domestic heating (methane emissions in intensive livestock farming still remain excluded) will develop in parallel with the EU ETS and cover most non-ETS GHG emissions. The price will be levied on fuels such as petrol, diesel, natural gas and coal. It will not be paid directly by the carbon emitters, but rather by the companies that sell to end users, or by refiners (*upstream approach*). Germany's decision enables the controversial choice to be avoided between adopting a system where emission levels are fixed *ex ante* as happens in the ETS, and the imposition of a carbon pricing system where emission levels depend on the elasticity in demand for fossil fuels.

Emission permits will be auctioned as of 2026 and would have to be acquired by those who market fossil fuels, and their relative cost would then be passed on – if market conditions allow for forward shifting – to the sale price for end consumers. Ultimately, by adopting this upstream approach, the instrument chosen is similar to the introduction of an excise duty such as the carbon tax, but has the advantage of being part of an existing mechanism, such as the ETS. The price corridor envisaged for the allowances auctioned on the market will represent a potential benchmark for pricing European CO_2 emissions.

8. THE EUROPEAN RECOVERY PLAN

The positive decision on the proposal of a European Recovery Plan by the European Council in the 17–21 July 2020 meeting,[17] focusing on a new instrument called Next Generation EU (NGEU), introduces a number of important elements into the European political landscape, including from an institutional perspective. The ban on the use of bonds to finance public expenditure in the Union is no longer in force. With the possibility of financing investments and reforms by raising funds on the market (which is currently valid until 31 December 2026), the *golden rule* is finally being applied in Europe too, whereby investments, normally lasting several years, can be financed with debt. Fundraising on the financial markets will help to spread over time the financing costs of the instrument designed to relaunch the European economy.

The funds borrowed may be used for loans up to an amount of €360 billion in 2018 prices and for grants up to an amount of €390 billion. Together with the three important safety nets endorsed by the European Council on 23 April 2020 (SURE – Support to mitigate Unemployment Risks,[18] ESM (European Stability Mechanism) Pandemic Crisis Support,[19] EIB (European Investment Bank) Guarantee Fund for Workers and Businesses[20]) amounting to a package worth €540 billion, these exceptional measures taken at the EU level would reach €1,290 billion of targeted and front-loaded support to Europe's recovery.

The amount of the own resources ceiling shall be temporarily increased by 0.6 percentage points for the sole purpose of covering all liabilities of the Union resulting from its borrowing to address the consequences of the COVID-19 crisis, until all these liabilities have ceased to exist, and at the latest until 31 December 2058. The Multiannual Financial Framework (MFF) 2021–27 was approved in the same meeting of the Council. The overall amount for commitments is €1,074.3 billion. Applying conservative estimates of the leverage effect of the MFF and Next Generation EU, the total investment that could be generated by this package of measures amounts to €3.1 trillion.

To the funds channelled through the budget should be added the liquidity provided by the European Central Bank (ECB) through the pandemic emergency purchase programme (PEPP) with a total envelope of €1,350 billion. Net purchases under the ECB asset purchase programme (APP) will continue at a monthly pace of €20 billion, together with the purchases under the additional €120 billion temporary envelope until the end of 2020. The monetary policy measures that have been taken since early March 2020 are providing crucial support to underpin the recovery of the euro area economy and to safeguard medium-term price stability.

The NGEU amounts channelled through the EU budget for expenditure shall constitute external assigned revenues. The recovery and resilience plans of each Member State shall be assessed by the Commission within two months of the submission. Effective contribution to the green and digital transitions shall be a prerequisite for a positive assessment. The assessment of the recovery and resilience plans shall be approved by the Council, by qualified majority on a Commission proposal. An overall target will apply to the total amount of climate expenditures from the NFF and NGEU and be reflected in appropriate targets in sectoral legislation.

The twin transitions to a green and digital Europe remain the defining challenges of the 2019–24 European legislature. Investing in a large scale renovation wave, in renewable energies and clean hydrogen solutions, clean transport, sustainable food and a smart circular economy has enormous potential to get Europe's economy growing. Support should be consistent with the Union's climate and environmental objectives. Investing in digital infrastructure and skills will help boost competitiveness and technological sovereignty. Investing in resilience to future health challenges and strategic autonomy will make the Union better prepared for future crises.

The Union will over the coming years work towards reforming the own resources system and introduce new own resources. As a first step, a new own resource based on non-recycled plastic will be implemented with a call rate of €0.80/kg. As a basis for additional own resources, the Commission will put forward in the first semester of 2021 proposals on a carbon border adjustment mechanism and on a digital levy, with a view to their introduction at the latest by 1 January 2023. In the same spirit, the Commission will put forward a proposal on a revised ETS scheme, possibly extending it to aviation and maritime. The Union will, in the course of the next MFF, work towards the introduction of other own resources, which may include a Financial Transaction Tax.

9. INSTITUTIONAL DEVELOPMENTS

The introduction of the new taxes must go through the procedure laid down in Article 311 of the Treaty on the Functioning of the European Union (TFEU), with the unanimous approval of the Council and ratification by the 27 Member States. Only the BCA can be introduced under the ordinary legislative procedure since Article 3 TFEU provides that the Union has exclusive competence as regards the common commercial policy and Article 207(2) explicitly provides that 'the European Parliament and the Council, acting by means of regulations in accordance with the ordinary legislative procedure, shall adopt the measures defining the framework for implementing the common commercial policy'.

The BCA, being a custom duty, is an own resource directly allocated to the Union budget. This decision to impose a BCA, which is essential for the implementation of the Green Deal, would make it possible, albeit of modest financial size, to take a first step towards fiscal autonomy for the Union. Further measures would certainly find more obstacles, since Article 311 would have to be applied. It seems reasonable to think that, taking advantage of the difficulties that will emerge on this point, a battle can be launched by the European Parliament – currently excluded from the procedure for the approval of new resources – for a reform of the Treaties involving co-decision between Parliament and the Council by majority vote, without national ratifications, as currently required by Article 311.

A further push towards a constitutional development in a federal direction can come from the Green Deal as the central point for achieving carbon neutrality concerns the energy problem, that is, initially the shift from mineral oils to natural gas and, then, to renewable energies. The decisive instrument for achieving this objective is certainly the setting of a carbon price, but relations with Russia and the countries of Saharan Africa are also at stake. Searching for a solution to these issues, the European Parliament can be expected to find the strength to promote a reform of the Treaties (including the Euratom Treaty given its competence in the field of energy), which will guarantee the Union the characteristics of a federal democracy, as well as in the field of taxation.

NOTES

1. Emeritus Professor of Public Finance at the University of Pavia (Italy).
2. The reported data can be found on: globalcarbonatlas.org/en/CO2-emissions (accessed 1 May 2021).
3. See econstatement.org.
4. See eaere.org.
5. The Draft Directive on carbon-energy tax (European Commission, *Proposal for a Council Directive introducing a tax on carbon dioxide emissions and energy* (COM(92)226, 30 June 1992) was presented by the Commission, but it was never approved by the Council. On this proposal see: A. Majocchi, 'Therationale behind energy taxation: The European Commission's proposal of an energy-carbon tax', in International Fiscal Association (IFA), Environmental Taxes and Charges, Florence, 1993, pp. 27–44.
6. European Commission, Directive 2003/87/EC establishing a scheme for greenhouse gas emissions allowance trading within the Community, 13 October 2003.
7. U. von der Leyen, *A Union that strives for more: My agenda for Europe – Political Guidelines for the next European Commission 2019–2024*, European Commission Directorate-General for Communication, 9 October 2019, accessed 1 May 2021 at https://op.europa.eu/en/publication-detail/-/publication/43a17056-ebf1-11e9-9c4e-01aa75ed71a1.
8. U. von der Leyen, *State of the Union 2020*, Address by the President at the European Parliament Plenary, Brussels, 16 September 2020, accessed 1 May 2021 at ec.europa.eu/commission/presscorner/detail/ov/SPEECH_20_1655.
9. See *carbonpricingleadership.org/report-of-the-highlevel-commission-on-carbon-prices* (accessed 20 May 2021).
10. Stop Global Warming.EU – The European Citizens' Initiative, *A EU carbon pricing for a socially sustainable ecological transition*, accessed 1 May 2021 at eumans.eu/CARBON PRICING.
11. For electricity the elasticity of demand rises from -0.126 in the short term to -0.365 in the long term; for natural gas from -0.180 to -0.684 and for gasoline from -0.293 to -0.773 (J. Rosenow, *Carbon pricing: the right tool to decarbonise buildings?*, The Regulatory Assistance Project, Brussels, 2020).
12. U. von der Leyen, *State of the Union 2020*, Address by the President at the European Parliament Plenary, Brussels, 16 September 2020, accessed 1 May 2021 at ec.europa.eu/commission/presscorner/detail/ov/SPEECH_20_1655.
13. Other GHG emitting sectors such as agriculture and waste are not considered and would need to be reflected in further research. Another point that should be taken into account is if it could be expected that a carbon price will be able to drive radical technological change. See for instance M. Hourihan and R.D. Atkinson (2011). For a more positive view see McKinsey (2020), p. 58.

14. GATT, *Dunkel report on trade and environment*, 11 February 1992.
15. GATT, *United States taxes on petroleum and certain imported substances (Superfund)*, Report of the Panel, 17 June 1987 (L6175 – 34S/136): 'To the extent that the tax on certain imported substances was equivalent to the tax borne by the like domestic substances as a result of the tax on certain chemicals, the tax met the national treatment requirement of Article III:2 …'.
16. United States, *Restrictions on the imports of tuna*, Report of the Panel, 3 September 1991.
17. European Council, *Special meeting of the European Council (17, 18, 19, 20 and 21 July 2020): Conclusions*, accessed 1 May 2021 at data.consilium.europa.eu/doc/document/ST-10-2020-INIT/en/pdf.
18. Council Regulation (EU) 2020/672 of 19 May 2020 on the establishment of a European instrument for temporary support to mitigate unemployment risks in an emergency (SURE) following the COVID-19 outbreak, accessed 1 May 2021 at data.europa.eu/eli/reg/2020/672/oj.
19. See esm.europa.eu/content/europe-response-corona-crisis (accessed 1 May 2021).
20. See eif.org/what_we_do/egf/index.htm (accessed 1 May 2021).

REFERENCES

Cambridge Econometrics, *Decarbonising European transport and heating fuels: Is the EU ETS the right tool?*, European Climate Foundation, June 2020.

D. Diaz and F. Moore, *Quantifying the economic risks of climate change*, Nature Climate Change, 2017, (7), 774–82.

E. Espagne, *The social cost of carbon: A review*, Carbon Pricing Leadership Coalition, 28 May 2017.

G. Hardin, *The tragedy of the commons*, Science, New Series, 1968, 162 (3859), 1243–8.

M.M. Hourihan and R.D. Atkinson, *Inducing innovation: What a carbon price can do and can't do*, Information Technology and Innovation Foundation (ITIF), 23 March 2011.

A. Majocchi, 'The rationale behind energy taxation: The European Commission's proposal of an energy-carbon tax', in International Fiscal Association (IFA), *Environmental Taxes and Charges*, Florence, 1993, pp. 27–44.

G. Metcalf, *How to set a price on carbon pollution: A smart combination of math and policy choices can determine a practical tax that will cut CO_2 emissions*. Scientific American, 2020, 29 (3s).

McKinsey, *How the European Union could achieve net-zero emissions at net-zero cost*, Report, 3 December 2020.

Quinet Commission Report, *La valeur de l'action pour le climat*, France Strategie, Février 2019.

3. The Green New Dividend: a cost neutral market-based alternative to the Green New Deal

Russell Mendell

INTRODUCTION

Passing comprehensive climate legislation has eluded lawmakers since the climate crisis first came into public view more than 30 years ago. New pressures from the Covid-19 pandemic and increasing climate related damages have further complicated prospects for passing comprehensive climate legislation. Climate policy faces political resistance to big spending in the wake of pandemic relief. At the same time there is a need for strong, swift action that would put the US in a position to meet Paris climate targets.

The preferred framework of many policymakers is a revenue neutral carbon tax. This emissions reduction technique taxes greenhouse gas (GHG) emissions and returns the generated revenue to the public by way of dividends or tax reductions. It is viewed as a cost-effective method for reducing emissions. However, a market-based approach to carbon pricing relies on behavioral shifts and the effects can be gradual. Some climate advocates are wary of these kinds of proposals because scientists have called for more rapid emissions reductions than models would suggest this kind of policy can achieve.

Recently, an alternative has emerged in the political discourse, known as the Green New Deal, which 80% of US presidential hopefuls endorsed during the 2020 Democratic primary. The concept builds on the success of the FDR era New Deal, which spurred investment in public infrastructure and helped lift the US out of the Great Depression. The Green New Deal similarly promises to employ millions in transitioning to a carbon neutral future through investments in green technologies and infrastructure. The challenge to implementing Green New Deal legislation is the expense, with many plans costing trillions to implement.

This chapter explores a third approach which combines a revenue neutral carbon tax with Green New Deal-style investment. This policy framework would allocate a portion of the tax revenues to be managed and invested by green banks. The green banks would utilize green bonds and green loans to finance infrastructure and technological innovation. The funds invested would be repaid to the public when the bonds mature. The policy would be revenue neutral in the long term and increase zero-carbon investments in the short term. This approach is called the 'Green New Dividend.'

This chapter is intended to explore primarily the revenue side of the Green New Dividend, which could be generated using a variety of carbon pricing schemes including cap and trade or a carbon tax. The focus is on creating a framework for an equitable emissions reduction policy that is both effective and politically feasible. Further research is needed to address questions related to implementation, procedural barriers and detailed financial analysis. This chapter intends to assist policymakers in evaluating viable alternative strategies to address the threat of climate change.

PART 1: IMPEDIMENTS TO CLIMATE ACTION

By January of 2021 the US federal government had already spent upwards of $5 trillion on a pandemic response, making it the costliest relief effort in modern history.[1] After passing an additional $1.9 trillion Covid relief package, President Biden proposed a $2.3 trillion infrastructure plan that includes spending for climate.[2] The proposed package lacks bipartisan support and a climate infrastructure bill would likely need to be passed through budget reconciliation along party lines.

At the same time pressure is increasing for federal action on climate change as more severe disasters impact the US at an increasing rate. Scientists believe climate change likely played a role in record heat waves and droughts throughout the Western US that led to the largest and most destructive wildfire season in history.[3] With many wildfires still expanding, a record 4 million acres have already burned in California with five of the six worst wildfires in history occurring in 2020.[4] In its wake the fires have left thousands of buildings destroyed, billions in damages and a polluted red sky. The fires are far from the only extreme weather event of 2020, which has already seen 15 others totaling over a billion dollars in damages, also the most in history.[5]

The increasing toll of rising temperatures has shifted public opinion with 60% of Americans now believing that 'global climate change is a major threat to the well-being of the United States,' up from 40% in 2013.[6] A total of 68% of voters now say climate change is an important issue to them in the 2020 election. Opinion on the importance of climate action still falls largely along partisan lines, with 91% of Biden supporters saying climate change is important to their vote in the 2020 election while just 40% of Trump voters say the same.[7]

The polarization of the climate issue has been and remains one of the single greatest impediments to climate action. The Waxman-Markey climate bill was the closest the US has come to climate legislation becoming law. The bill titled the American Clean Energy and Securities Act, a modest cap and trade bill, passed the House in 2009 with 219 votes, 211 from Democrats.[8]

Public opinion shifted quickly after the 2008 presidential election. A Harris poll on climate change captured a 20% drop in Americans who believe that 'the release of carbon dioxide and other gases will lead to global warming' in just a 2-year span. From November of 2007 to November of 2009 the percentage of the population who agreed with scientific consensus on climate change plummeted from 71% to just 51%.[9] Scott Keeter of the Pew Research Center called the rapid change in opinion on climate change in the US 'among the largest shifts over a short period of time seen in recent public opinion history ...'[10]

An ABC/Washington Post poll found that the change in public opinion regarding climate science from pre to post the Obama election was almost entirely partisan. From July 2008 to November 2009, Democratic opinion on climate science was nearly unchanged, while Republican belief in climate science dropped by nearly 20%.[11] A further breakdown found that those who support cap and trade policy had virtually no change in their view about global warming, while belief in climate science fell by 13% among those who opposed cap and trade.[12]

A study conducted by Duke University on the subject of 'solution aversion' supported the idea that the solutions and not the problems were fueling climate denial. The study found that Republicans were more than two times more likely to agree with climate science when presented with a market solution than when they were presented with a regulatory solution, while Democrats' belief in the science was unaffected by the solutions proposed.[13] One possible explanation is that conservative views on economics guide their view of climate change more than their view of environmental issues.

Former Republican congressman Bob Inglis, who currently heads the conservative environmental organization RepublicEn, summed up the idea, 'It's solution aversion that's caused conservatives to doubt the existence of the problem ... but if those on the "eco-right" show Republicans a solution that fits with our deeply held conservative values, then I think we'll see many embrace this exciting, free enterprise opportunity.'[14]

Overall, political momentum for climate action appears to be growing. With Democrats taking control of the White House, Senate and retaining the House of Representatives, many will argue the 2020 election represents a significant mandate for climate action. However, with the Senate evenly split between Republicans and Democrats, climate legislation will likely need to address spending concerns of the Senate's more moderate members to have any chance of passing both chambers in regular order.

PART 2: THE GREEN NEW DEAL

In the wake of the 2018 midterm election the Green New Deal became the rallying cry for progressive climate action. Modeled off The New Deal, which helped lift the US out of the Great Depression, the policy embodies the progressive approach to societal shifts. Rather than embracing the market, the Green New Deal models itself after large, ambitious government programs that would rebuild infrastructure and directly employ millions of Americans in building a zero-carbon economy. The plan not only aims for net zero emissions by 2030, but also states a purpose of promoting justice and equity for historically marginalized people.[15]

The Green New Deal started with strong bipartisan support, utilizing the popular messaging of green jobs. The first survey conducted by Yale Program on Climate Change Communication and George Mason Center for Climate Change Communication found that 81% of all registered voters supported the Green New Deal, with 93% of Democrats and 64% of Republicans approving.[16] Four months later public opinion had shifted dramatically as conservative media outlets, like Fox News, targeted the plan. By April, 80% of Republicans and 90% of Fox News viewers strongly opposed the Green New Deal, as Fox News covered the proposal more than CNN and MSNBC combined.[17]

The network claimed the plan would cost $93 trillion.[18] Bernie Sanders' presidential campaign has drafted a policy proposal for implementation that has been widely praised on the left and has a price tag of $16 trillion.[19] Proponents of the resolution have not shied away from the cost of the proposal, noting that the future costs of climate damage are likely to far outweigh even the hefty price tag.

While this message has resonated with those on the left, it is precisely the kind of policy that conservatives are wary of. The Green New Deal represents a large expansion of government. It is the antithesis of Ronald Reagan's famous line from his first inaugural address, 'government is not the solution to the problem; government is the problem.'[20]

The Green New Deal nevertheless maintains strong support among Democratic voters and elected Democrats. The non-binding resolution introduced by Congresswoman Ocasio-Cortez and Senator Markey has attracted more than 100 cosponsors and support from the majority of candidates running in the Democratic presidential primary.[21]

However, there are no Republican cosponsors and when Mitch McConnell introduced the resolution on the Senate floor it was defeated 57–0,[22] The vote was seen as disingenuous by Senate Democrats, as the bill was not going to be debated on the floor. In protest 42 Democrats voted present.[23] Four senators who caucused with the Democrats voted against the resolution along with all Senate Republicans.[24]

While the Green New Deal's popularity is largely split along partisan lines, the principles of the resolution are largely popular. A recent poll found that 70% of Americans support upgrading all federal buildings for energy efficiency and 69% support a shift to 100% zero-emission energy in 10 years. The cost of such an undertaking is what lacks public support. According to the same poll just 30% of Americans support spending trillions to implement the Green New Deal.[25] With historic spending focused on alleviating the economic damage of the coronavirus pandemic, a multi-trillion-dollar bill focused solely on mitigating the damage from climate change is likely to have trouble passing a divided Senate.

PART 3: REVENUE NEUTRAL PRICE ON CARBON

The approach to climate action that is most accepted by economists is a market-based pricing scheme that would account for the negative externalities of GHG emissions. In many mainstream approaches to a carbon price, the revenue would be recycled in the form of tax relief and dividends to make the policy revenue neutral. This approach may temper conservative fears that federal solutions to the climate crisis would serve to expand the size and scale of government.

One model that has gained popularity in the US is the fee and dividend policy. The framework applies a fee for carbon emissions, and then returns the revenue through per capita dividends back to the American public. It is an approach that has been embraced by both grassroots organizations like the Citizens Climate Lobby (CCL) and business lobbies like the Climate Leadership Council (CLC). While CCL is a citizens lobbying network featuring 561 grassroots chapters,[26] CLC was co-founded with some of the largest corporations in the world including fossil fuel giants like ExxonMobil, BP and Shell.[27] Their approach is slightly different. CLC identifies as a conservative organization and CCL identifies as nonpartisan, but the two organizations are strategic partners and their policy framework is remarkably similar. A version of CCL's plan was introduced to the House as the Energy Innovation and Carbon Dividend Act of 2019 as H.R. 763 (EICDA).

The fee and dividend proposal is based on a simple economic concept. Currently the costs of GHG pollution from fossil fuels are being socialized, because they are not accounted for in the cost of goods and services. By attaching a price to GHG emissions, the economic instrument accounts for a failure of markets to incorporate the cost of carbon into the price the consumer pays. By increasing market efficiency, the policy incentivizes less polluting human behavior, so the costs of GHG emissions are not passed on to the public. A key question is whether the price on carbon is enough to shift a society that is so heavily reliant on fossil fuels to carbon neutrality.

A 2019 study conducted by Columbia University and the Rhodium Group projected that if EICDA were signed into law that same year, US emissions would drop to 36–38% below 2005 levels by 2030.[28] This is compared with a baseline of 15–17% below 2005 by 2030 with current policy.[29] The 2005 levels are often used as a baseline following the precedent the US set when signing the Paris Climate Accord in 2015.

The International Panel on Climate Change (IPCC) issued a Special Report on Climate Change in 2018 that helped set the barometer for needed emission reductions. The report called for a 45% reduction in global GHG from 2010 levels by 2030 (emissions in 2010 were roughly 6% below 2005 levels) to avoid hitting potentially catastrophic tipping points for climate change and net neutral by 2050.[30] The EICDA has a target to reduce emissions by 90% by 2050, however, the study shows after 2030 emissions reductions would no longer be on course to meet 2050 targets.[31] This modeling shows that EICDA may require supplementary policy to reach an ambitious 2050 target.

The likely reason for the limited impact after the first 10 years is that some emissions reduction is more difficult with current infrastructure. The modeling in the Columbia study shows that only the electricity sector would experience a dramatic drop in emissions with EICDA, but those emissions also begin to flatline around 2030. The analysis sees coal electricity generation being virtually eliminated, renewable electricity would power 44% of the grid, while nuclear and natural gas would make up the rest.[32]

Getting to 100% renewable energy by 2050 has become a rallying cry for the environmental movement across the country. Sierra Club's Ready for 100 campaign reports that 166 cities and six states are committed to 100% renewable by 2050. Sierra Club boasts that one in four Americans live in a community committed to 100% renewable energy by 2050.[33] Stanford scientist Mark Jacobson's organization The Solutions Project has mapped out how every state and country could get to 100% renewable energy by 2050, using current technology.[34]

For this transformation to take place advances in utility scale storage and transmission are needed to address the intermittency of resources like wind and solar for power generation. The grid needs 12-hour storage to keep from blackouts when demand is high but the wind is not blowing and the sun is not shining. Transmission is also critical because the places with the greatest capacity to generate wind energy tend to be places with smaller populations and thus less demand. Transmission lines can take the excess wind energy from the middle of the country and distribute it to the cities on the coasts.

In the US, 28% of GHG emissions come from electricity, while the rest comes from other sectors such as transportation, industry, agriculture, commercial and residential.[35] Sectors other than electricity would only fall 6–9% below 2005 levels with EICDA according to the Columbia study.[36] Agriculture and waste were both exempted from EICDA.[37]

Transportation has the largest emissions footprint by sector in the US,[38] and needs a massive infrastructural shift to significantly reduce emissions. Upgrades will be needed across the board from greater access to public transportation, bike and carpool lanes to the electrification of America's vehicle fleet, the latter of which will require mass installations of electric charging stations across the country.

The lack of federal funding for infrastructure is where EICDA and other similar policy proposals come up short. Carbon pricing is an efficient tool to reduce emissions within the current system, yet it is unlikely to encourage the kind of system transformation needed for deep decarbonization. According to the 2018 IPCC report, meeting the Paris climate targets will require 'rapid, far-reaching and unprecedented changes in all aspects of society.'[39] Given the short time frame to overhaul domestic energy systems, correcting market failures in accounting for GHG emissions is only a part of the solution.

PART 4: THE GREEN NEW DIVIDEND

Legislators concerned with confronting the climate crisis are faced with a challenge to enact a policy solution that is as effective as the Green New Deal and as politically palatable as a market-based solution. The Green New Dividend may be such a solution, by transforming the fee and dividend into a revenue neutral style Green New Deal. A portion of revenue from the fee would be invested for a prescribed period before being returned to the public in a per capita dividend once the investment had matured and produced a return. This approach would have the climate mitigation and job creation benefits of a Green New Deal and the cost neutral political advantage of a fee and dividend.

The revenue would be managed by green or climate banks either on the state level or on the federal level. Green banks in Connecticut and New York already exist and operate as semi-public non-profit institutions that finance projects to reduce emissions and create jobs. The state level green banks have generated $3.40 in private investment for every dollar invested.[40] In 2019 a bill was introduced into the Senate to establish a National Climate Bank, with an initial public investment of $35 billion. An analysis by the Coalition of Green Capital estimates that the $35 billion of initial investment would drive as much as $1 trillion in climate related investment.[41]

Revenue from carbon pricing can vary because it is often based on the socialized cost of carbon or tailored to change behavior. The Obama administration estimated that the socialized cost is equal to about $50 per ton of $CO2e$[42] with increases of 2% every year.[43] The US Treasury estimates that price would raise approximately $2.2 trillion of revenue over a 10-year period.[44] If 75% is returned immediately in the form of dividends to every American, the remaining 25% would amount to $550 billion over 10 years to be invested in green banks. On an annual basis that would average $55 billion invested by green banks spurring hundreds of billions more in private sector investments. The additional market instrument of a price on carbon would further accelerate a rapid shift of capital from polluting industry to sustainable innovation.

In many energy sectors green bonds and other forms of green finance are already contributing to change, but not at the speed required to build the infrastructure for a zero-carbon energy system. For instance, to provide for an increased electric vehicle (EV) market the National Renewable Energy Laboratory estimates that the US would have to add a minimum of 8,000 fast charging stations.[45] Financing is needed to build out this infrastructure, and Rocky Mountain Institute's plan to meet the need of EV charging calls for 'patient capital' such as green bonds.[46]

Green banks managing the revenue generated by the policy would seek opportunities that are on the verge of profitability, but not yet capitalized on by private investors. By providing financing for these opportunities through public investment, the policy can drive the market toward job creating green innovation. For instance, long duration energy storage could help address the variability of wind and solar, which would allow for the displacement traditional fossil fuel powerplants. Some technologies like compressed air, flow batteries and new kinds of pumped hydro may be profitable investments in the near future and substantial investment from green bonds could create an economy of scale to drive down costs and spur private investment.

In many areas of the country, converting buildings to zero emissions has not yet been profitable in all cases. However, recent innovations in the cost of solar panels, with Tesla dropping the panel price from $3 a watt to $2 a watt for residential,[47] would make most zero-carbon building conversions feasible. Adding a price on carbon would make these investments more attractive as the cost of carbon based fuel increases. The revenue generated by the policy could finance a fuel switch to zero-emission buildings and tip the scales to spur widespread private investment.

On the grid scale there is tremendous potential for energy utilities to issue green bonds to finance an energy transition away from conventional fossil fuels. As the price of renewables falls, much of the old fossil fuel infrastructure is becoming uneconomic. Of the $788 billion of green bonds issued in 2019, just $10 billion were issued by energy utilities, while Boston University estimates there is the opportunity for as much as $500 billion in additional transition bonds.[48] Investments into utility green bonds could mobilize private capital to finance the stranding of utility owned fossil fuel assets that are no longer profitable.

Green banks have the advantage of being non-profits so they can lend money at lower interest rates than commercial banks. This allows green banks to make more attractive loans to finance infrastructure and technology projects. The financing in turn makes these green sectors more profitable and attractive to private lenders. The combined effect of incubating private finance in key areas of the energy transition along with the increasing cost of carbon pollution would make it more probable that the US could reach emission reduction targets in the necessary time frame.

PART 5: ADDRESSING EQUITY

One of the principle goals of the Green New Deal, as stated in the resolution before Congress, is 'to promote justice and equity.' How climate policy impacts inequality and historically oppressed communities is an important consideration of any proposal. Carbon taxes are, by their nature, regressive because a higher percentage of low income household spending goes into necessities that create emissions than those in higher income brackets. This makes the rebate part of a fee and dividend policy crucial, because wealthier households pay a significantly higher absolute percentage of tax.[49]

Rebating the tax immediately on a per capita basis will mean the vast majority of low income households receive a larger dividend than the carbon tax they paid. The percentage of the tax that is rebated immediately instead of deferred for future dividends should be calculated to ensure the policy does not affect low income households negatively. One approach is to provide a full dividend to low income households immediately, while deferring the dividends of higher income households that can afford to wait while the investments mature.

A full equity analysis of the policy should extend beyond class to examine how the policy would affect people based on race, gender and geographic region. Green banks should prioritize equity when financing projects, taking into account where projects are located and the makeup of the workforce. In 2019 black workers represented 13% of the workforce, but less than 8% of jobs in the solar industry.[50] According to a 2019 study, black and Hispanic majority neighborhoods are less likely to have installed solar photovoltaics than majority white neighborhoods.[51]

One challenge to address is the lack of participation in the green economy by renters. There is a split incentive when it comes to green investments because, in a traditional arrangement, property owners pay the cost of a zero-carbon transition while tenants receive the benefits. One way to address this is by having investments target property adjusted clean energy financing, which allows property owners and renters to share in the benefits.

Financing through the Green New Dividend should be evaluated through the lens of sustainability bonds, which is a subset of green bonds that accounts for justice and equity along with green credentials. Current financing of green projects has tended to leave out low income and racial minority communities and climate policy should work to provide greater opportunity for communities that have been left out in the past. Investments should also take into account the makeup of the workforce and prioritize companies that hire historically marginalized people.

While historic and economic equity consideration are key for the policy to be a part of a just transition, it is equally important to account for displaced jobs as the conventional fossil fuel economy is phased out. It is estimated that renewables can supply 50% more jobs at similar pay to fossil fuels per energy unit produced,[52] but there are still nearly a million Americans currently working in fossil fuel jobs. A portion of the interest on investments should be allocated to helping workers transition through training, placement and severance pay.

CONCLUSION

Modern climate policy is faced with a difficult challenge. It must meet the ambitious timeline of the Paris Climate Accord, while adhering to the fiscal demands of a country in economic recovery with a split Senate. With these parameters it would be helpful to look to a hybrid solution that can simultaneously meet economic and social needs, while transitioning to a low carbon economy. The Green New Dividend is a pathway to maximize the potential for emissions reduction in a cost neutral climate policy by combining several already existing policy frameworks.

Further research is needed to understand the full range of opportunities and limitations of the Green New Dividend. More detailed analysis is required to determine whether the symbiotic relationship between strategic green financing and carbon pricing could accelerate emission reductions in accordance with Paris climate targets. The macroeconomic impact of the policy should be explored including projected job creation. Studying the impacts on equity is critical for evaluating what form a potential policy should take.

There is no easy solution to transitioning the US to a low carbon economy. The scientific community has made it clear that action cannot wait. The Covid-19 pandemic creates challenges to implementing the kind of policy that can put the US in a position to meet the emissions reduction targets set out in the Paris Climate Accord. The Green New Dividend provides the basis for a policy that can bring climate concerned parties from the left and right together to create millions of American jobs while drastically reducing emissions.

NOTES

1. Peter Whoriskey, Douglass MacMillan and Johnathan O'Connell, *'Doomed to fail': Why a $4 trillion bailout couldn't revive the American economy*, The Washington Post (Oct. 5, 2020), accessed 10 October 2020 at https://www.washingtonpost.com/graphics/2020/business/coronavirus-bailout-spending/ https://www.washingtonpost.com/graphics/2020/business/coronavirus-bailout-spending.
2. The Whitehouse, Fact Sheet: The American Jobs Plan, (Mar. 31, 2021), accessed September 2021 at https://www.whitehouse.gov/briefing-room/statements-releases/2021/03/31/fact-sheet-the-american-jobs-plan/.
3. Umair Irfan, *Why we're more confident than ever that climate change is driving disasters*, Vox (Sep. 30, 2020), accessed 1 October 2020 at https://www.vox.com/21452781/zogg-fire-glass-wildfire-california-climate-change-hurricanes-attribution-2020-debate.
4. Kristina Dahl, *5 of California's 6 largest fires on record are burning now*, Clean Technica (Oct. 9, 2020), accessed 1 October 2020 at https://cleantechnica.com/2020/10/09/5-of-californias-6-largest-fires-on-record-are-burning-now/.
5. NOAA National Centers for Environmental Information, *Billion dollar weather and climate disasters: Overview* (2020), accessed 21 September 2020 at https://www.ncdc.noaa.gov/billions.
6. Brian Kennedy, *U.S. concern about climate change is rising, but mainly among Democrats*, Pew Research Center (Apr. 16, 2020), accessed 21 September 2020 at https://www.pewresearch.org/fact-tank/2020/04/16/u-s-concern-about-climate-change-is-rising-but-mainly-among-democrats.
7. Alec Tyson, *How important is climate change to voters in the 2020 election?*, Pew Research Center (Oct. 6, 2020), accessed 21 September 2020 at https://www.pewresearch.org/fact-tank/2020/10/06/how-important-is-climate-change-to-voters-in-the-2020-election.
8. H.R. 2524, 111th Cong. (2009).
9. *Big drop in those who believe global warming is coming* (Dec. 2, 2009), The Harris Poll, accessed 15 May 2020 at https://theharrispoll.com/big-drop-in-those-who-believe-that-global-warming-is-coming-12-02-2009.
10. Naomi Klein, *This Changes Everything: Capitalism vs the Climate*, New York: Simon and Schuster (2014).
11. *Conservatives, Republicans move away from belief that the Earth is warming*, ABC News/Washington Post Poll (Nov. 24, 2009), accessed 24 May 2020 at https://abcnews.go.com/images/PollingUnit/1096a7GlobalWarming.pdf.
12. Id.
13. Troy H. Campbell and Aaron C. Kay, *Solution aversion: On the relation between ideology and motivated disbelief*, Journal of Personality and Social Psychology, 107 (5), 809–24.
14. Michael Greshko, *US conservatives unveil plan to fight climate change*, National Geographic (Feb. 11, 2017), accessed 24 May 2020 at https://www.nationalgeographic.com/news/2017/02/conservatives-unveil-plan-to-fight-climate-change.

15. H.R. 109, 116th Congress (2019–20).
16. Abel Gustafon, Seth Rosenthal, Anthony Leiserowitz, Edward Maibach, John Kotcher, Matthew Ballew and Matthew Goldberg, *The Green New Deal has strong bipartisan support*, Yale Program on Climate Change Communication (Dec. 14, 2018), accessed 24 May 2020 at https://climatecommunication.yale.edu/publications/the-green-new-deal-has-strong-bipartisan-support.
17. David Roberts, *Fox News has united the right against the Green New Deal: The left remains divided*, Vox (Apr. 22, 2019), accessed 24 May 2020 at https://www.vox.com/energy-and-environment/2019/4/22/18510518/green-new-deal-fox-news-poll.
18. Gregg Re, *Green New Deal would cost $93 trillion, or $600G per household, study says*, Fox News (Feb. 25, 2019), accessed 24 May 2020 at https://www.foxnews.com/politics/green-new-deal-would-cost-93-trillion-or-600g-per-household-study-says.
19. *The Green New Deal* (2019), BernieSanders.com, accessed 24 May 2020 at https://berniesanders.com/en/issues/green-new-deal.
20. Ronald Reagan, First Inaugural Address (Jan. 20, 1981), accessed 25 May 2021 at https://avalon.law.yale.edu/20th_century/reagan1.asp.
21. The Sunrise Movement, *The Green New Deal* (2019), accessed 26 May 2020 at https://www.sunrisemovement.org/green-new-deal.
22. Guardian Staff, *Green New Deal: Senate defeats proposal as Democrats unite in protest*, The Guardian (Mar. 26, 2019), accessed 25 May 2020 at https://www.theguardian.com/us-news/2019/mar/26/green-new-deal-senate-democrats-protest-republicans.
23. Id.
24. Robinson Meyer, *The 3 Democrats who voted against the Green New Deal*, The Atlantic (Mar. 26, 2019), accessed 29 May 2020 at https://www.theatlantic.com/science/archive/2019/03/climate-change-which-democrats-oppose-green-new-deal/585802.
25. Dino Grandoni and Scott Clement, *Americans like the Green New Deal's goals but, they reject paying trillions to reach them*, Washington Post (Nov. 27, 2019), accessed 1 June 2020 at https://www.washingtonpost.com/climate-environment/2019/11/27/americans-like-green-new-deals-goals-they-reject-paying-trillions-reach-them.
26. Citizens Climate Lobby, *Chapters* (2019), accessed 24 November 2019 at https://citizensclimatelobby.org/about-ccl/chapters.
27. Climate Leadership Council, *Founding Members* (2019), accessed 24 November 2019 at https://clcouncil.org/founding-members.
28. Dr. Noah Kaufman, John Larsen, Peter Marsters, Hannah Kolus and Shashan Mohan, *An assessment of the Energy Innovation and Carbon Dividend Act*, Columbia Center on Global Energy Policy (Nov. 6, 2019), accessed 25 November 2019 at https://www.energypolicy.columbia.edu/research/report/assessment-energy-innovation-and-carbon-dividend-act.
29. Id. Using 2005 levels as a baseline is a bit misleading, because that was when US GHG emissions peaked and by 2017 US GHG had fallen to 13% below 2005 levels.
30. *Summary for policy makers of special report on global warming of 1.5°C approved by governments*, IPCC (Oct. 10, 2018).
31. Dr. Noah Kaufman John Larsen, Peter Marsters, Hannah Kolus and Shashan Mohan, *An assessment of the Energy Innovation and Carbon Dividend Act*,

Columbia Center on Global Energy Policy (Nov. 6, 2019), accessed 25 November 2019 at https://www.energypolicy.columbia.edu/research/report/assessment-energy-innovation-and-carbon-dividend-act.
32. Id.
33. Sierra Club, *Ready for 100* (2019), accessed 1 April 2020 at https://www.sierraclub.org/ready-for-100.
34. The Solutions Project, *Our 100% Clean Energy Vision* (2019), accessed 2 December 2019 at https://thesolutionsproject.org/why-clean-energy/#/map/countries/location/USA.
35. EPA, *Inventory of U.S. greenhouse gas emissions and sinks* (2017), accessed 26 November 2019 at https://www.epa.gov/ghgemissions/inventory-us-greenhouse-gas-emissions-and-sinks.
36. Dr. Noah Kaufman, John Larsen, Peter Marsters, Hannah Kolus and Shashan Mohan, *An assessment of the Energy Innovation and Carbon Dividend Act*, Columbia Center on Global Energy Policy (Nov. 6, 2019), accessed 25 November 2019 at https://www.energypolicy.columbia.edu/research/report/assessment-energy-innovation-and-carbon-dividend-act.
37. H.R. 763, 116th Cong. (2019).
38. EPA, *Inventory of U.S. greenhouse gas emissions and sinks* (2017), accessed 27 November 2019 at https://www.epa.gov/ghgemissions/inventory-us-greenhouse-gas-emissions-and-sinks.
39. *Summary for Policy Makers of Special Report on Global Warming of 1.5°C Approved by Governments*, IPCC, (Oct. 10, 2018).
40. Coalition for Green Capital, *Mobilizing $1 trillion towards climate action: An analysis of a National Climate Bank* (Sep. 2019), accessed 1 December 2019 at http://coalitionforgreencapital.com/wp-content/uploads/2019/09/1T-investment-white-paper.pdf.
41. Id.
42. CO2e stands for carbon dioxide equivalent.
43. Interagency Working Group on Social Cost of Greenhouse Gases, *Technical update for the social cost of carbon for regulatory impact analysis*, United States Government (Aug, 2016).
44. John Horowitz, Julie-Ann Cronin, Hannah Hawkins, Laura Konda and Alex Yuskavage, *Methodology for analyzing a carbon tax*, The Department of Treasury (Jan, 2017).
45. Eric Wood, Clément Rames, Matteo Muratori, Sesha Raghavan and Marc Melaina, *National plug-in electric vehicle infrastructure analysis* (Sep, 2017), accessed 2 December 2019 at https://www.nrel.gov/docs/fy17osti/69031.pdf.
46. Garrett Fitzgerald and Chris Nelder, *From gas to grid* (2017), accessed 3 December 2019 at https://rmi.org/wp-content/uploads/2017/10/RMI-From-Gas-To-Grid.pdf.
47. Cristian Roselund, *How is Tesla selling residential solar for less than $2 a watt*, PV Magazine (May 2019).
48. Tan Lan, Peter Fox-Penner and Jennifer Hatch, *Assessing the potential for US utility green bonds*, Boston University Institute for Sustainable Energy (May, 2019).
49. Joseph Rosenberg, Eric Toder and Chenxi Lu, *Distributional implications of a carbon tax*, Columbia Center on Global Energy Policy (Jul. 17, 2018), accessed 1 December 2019 at https://www.energypolicy.columbia.edu/research/report/distributional-implications-carbon-tax.

50. The Solar Foundation, *US solar industry diversity study 2019* (2019), accessed 29 November 2019 at https://www.thesolarfoundation.org/wp-content/uploads/2019/05/Solar-Industry-Diversity-Study-2019-2.pdf.
51. Deborah A. Sunter, Sergio Castellanos and Daniel M. Kammen, *Disparities in rooftop photovoltaics deployment in the United States by race and ethnicity*, Nature Sustainability (Jan. 10, 2019).
52. Max Wei, Shana Patadia and Daniel M. Kammen, *Putting renewables and energy efficiency to work: How many jobs can the energy industry generate in the US?*, Energy Policy, vol. 38 (Oct. 19, 2009), accessed October 2020 at http://rael.berkeley.edu/old_drupal/sites/default/files/WeiPatadiaKammen_CleanEnergyJobs_EPolicy2010.pdf.

PART II

COVID-19 and EU-wide tax policies

4. 100 years of externalities
Astrid Ladefoged and Mirka Janda

INTRODUCTION

A hundred years ago Arthur C. Pigou told us to put a price on externalities.[1] Since then we have been discussing the theory and, more challengingly, how we can put it into practice and internalise environmental external costs. Despite this, we have not managed to apply the polluter-pays principle fully and drive a real change of price signals.

Universities and business schools across the world teach students that, in a free market economy, prices determine the efficient distribution of goods and resources throughout the economy. Prices provide a standard of measure of value throughout the world. Prices act as a signal to which producers and consumers will respond. The degree to which market prices reflect all available, relevant information determines market efficiency.

A market failure (unless corrected, for example, by regulation) leads to an inefficient distribution of goods and services. It can occur due to a variety of reasons, such as monopoly, public goods and/or externalities. Externalities come in many forms; they can be both positive and negative. With positive externalities, the benefit to society is greater than the personal benefit.

The concept of negative externalities is, though, the dominant frame in environmental policies. They occur when production and/or consumption imposes external costs on third parties outside of the market for which no appropriate compensation is paid. Many examples exist. A classic one is pollution – external costs from polluting production or consumption might occur because of injuries to human health, reduced property values, destruction of wildlife habitats, reduction of recreation possibilities, or because of other negative impacts. Failure to consider those external costs in prices results in a market failure.

The largest ever market failure is climate change, as Lord Stern and others have said.[2] Others argue that this is not about failures at all, but rather about absences. Markets do not deal with externalities, whether positive or negative, because as that word externality implies, they are outside markets.[3]

However, if the market cannot capture the cost of pollution without outside intervention, then it has failed.

WHY GOING GREEN COSTS MONEY?

Green products are often more expensive than traditional products. Why? Well, it is not easy to make a product that has minimal impact on the environment – and extra costs come with a higher degree of difficulty.

There are many reasons why green production can be costlier. If you take agriculture, a common practice of organic farming is to avoid chemicals. By reducing the use of chemicals, farms will have to either accept lower productivity or compensate by employing more labour for tasks like weeding or reparation of pest damage. Labour is expensive, in particular if 'green' means 'sustainable' in a broader sense, and thus covers also fair labour/employment terms. On the other hand, farmers using pesticides are not made to compensate for the damage their use may cause beyond the farm into water or ecosystems and so on.

Sometimes, the burden to show that a product is different also brings extra costs, such as fees for (third-party) certificates or labels. Green production may also be small and local. This does not allow for economies of scale, and the fixed cost per unit of a product is high. This leads to a higher price and a Catch 22 situation – as the price is high, the demand is lower, the supply will not increase and thus the price will not go down. Similar reasoning (and constraints) would apply to other green/sustainable products or services.

Prices send a signal to both producers and consumers. The (often) higher price of the green products sends a signal to consumers to think about their purchases more carefully, and means that markets are not efficient. Prices also send a signal to investors in financial markets, where stocks and shares are sold based on the market prices.

Of course, green products are not always more expensive. The Porter Hypothesis[4] suggesting that strict environmental regulations can induce efficiency and encourage innovations that help improve commercial competitiveness holds in some cases, and means that green production can be cheaper over time.

WHAT SHOULD THE POLLUTER PAY?

Prices should reflect the 'polluter-pays'[5] and, in some cases, the 'user-pays'[6] principles. The European Union (EU) has the 'polluter-pays principle' embedded in its Treaties,[7] which then translates into different policies and legislation.

Indeed, the polluter should pay for the external costs (s)he causes. The aim of internalisation of external costs is to maximise society's welfare. Internalisation can be achieved with various policy measures, including market-based instruments (such as taxes, charges and tradable permits), regulatory instruments (emission standards, restrictions, caps, etc.) and voluntary instruments (e.g. voluntary commitments, voluntary agreements) and/or their combination.

The general principle for internalisation of external costs is 'social marginal cost charging', whereby prices should correspond to the additional short-term cost generated by one extra unit/product, ensuring fair treatment of both the buyers of the product and society in terms of the consequences of the production and use of the product.

So, in theory the price that captures the real costs of an environmentally damaging product and does not ignore the externalities should be higher than the price for a green product. However, the problem comes with the availability of information, measurement and application.

Markets do not internalise externalities often due to poorly defined property rights. This is the principle set out in Hardin's 1968 paper 'The Tragedy of the Commons'.[8] In 2015, Mark Carney, at the time Governor of the Bank of England, explained in his famous speech 'Breaking the Tragedy of the Horizon: change and financial stability' that 'Climate change is the Tragedy of the Horizon' and that 'once climate change becomes a defining issue for financial stability, it may already be too late'.[9] He pointed out three risks through which financial stability can be affected because of climate change: the physical risk, the liability risk and the transition risk. However, he finishes by explaining that: 'By managing what gets measured, we can break the Tragedy of the Horizon. With better information as a foundation, we can build a virtuous circle of better understanding of tomorrow's risks, better pricing for investors, better decisions by policymakers, and a smoother transition to a lower-carbon economy.'[10]

Ensuring measurement has been a keen European priority over the last decade – and legislation has been built up to ensure data and information availability.[11]

HOW DO WE KNOW WHAT IS GREEN?

Investors tell us that they cannot manoeuvre in a financial market with price signals that do not reflect the real value of their potential investments. We have seen an increased interest from so-called 'impact investors' in better understanding how to balance financial return with positive social and environmental impacts, taking into account both positive and negative externalities, and ensuring the outcome leads to a fairer, more sustainable society.[12] Hence, a major effort is taking place in the EU to help provide that information via what is called the taxonomy.[13]

The Taxonomy Regulation[14] entered in force in July 2020. It creates consistent, well-founded definitions of which activities are green or, to be precise, within each economic activity (e.g. steel manufacturing, new building construction, electricity generation, etc.) which activities make a substantial contribution to meeting the climate and environmental policy objectives.[15] This is complemented by a 'do no significant harm' concept, so we do not, for example, promote the production and use of biofuels in a way that damages biodiversity.

To specify the requirements set by the Regulation for the individual objectives, the European Commission will adopt delegated acts. A delegated act on the climate objectives was due by 31 December 2020 and will enter into force in December 2021.[16] A second delegated act on the environmental objectives beyond climate change should be adopted by 31 December 2021 and enter into force in December 2022.

The sustainable finance taxonomy and related delegated acts will provide a common framework to identify investment opportunities that align with our environmental ambition and that support a green recovery. But this is not all.[17]

EU law also requires large companies to disclose certain information on the way they operate and manage social and environmental challenges. The Non-Financial Reporting Directive (NFRD)[18] lays down the rules on disclosure of non-financial and diversity information by large companies. This helps investors, consumers, policymakers and other stakeholders to evaluate the non-financial performance of large companies and encourages these companies to develop a responsible approach to business.

As announced in the European Green Deal,[19] the Commission has launched a review of the reporting obligations of businesses under the Directive, with a view to improving the quality and scope of non-financial disclosures, including on environmental aspects.[20] The direction of travel is likely to require companies to increase disclosure on their sustainable activities, and to require adequate reliable information on sustainability risks and opportunities.

The reporting obligations under the NFRD, the 2019 'Guidelines on non-financial reporting: Supplement on reporting climate-related information'[21] and the Taxonomy Regulation are interlinked. This will be underpinned by the Commission supporting a business-led initiative to develop environmental accounting principles which potentially can complement financial data with data on environmental impacts on natural capital such as water, air, land and biodiversity as well as data on environmental performance, for example as regards the circular economy.

To ensure environmental and social interests are fully embedded into business strategies, the Commission will put forward a new initiative in 2021 on sustainable corporate governance.[22]

WHAT DOES THE THEORY SAY ABOUT INTERNALISATION OF EXTERNAL COSTS?

In 2020 we celebrated 100 years since Arthur Pigou introduced the concept of what became known as a 'Pigovian tax'. The Pigovian tax is a tax on any market activity that generates negative externalities (costs not included in the market price). The tax should correct an undesirable or inefficient market outcome by being set equal to the social cost of the negative externalities and thus could be seen as a legitimate policy means to enforce the polluters-pay principle.[23]

Over time, different approaches to internalisation of external costs evolved, based on different theoretical or methodological approaches. Common to them all is the economic rationale for using environmental taxes or other market-based instruments, which is that they have the ability to correct market failures in a cost-effective way, based on market signals, and so contribute to the achievement of the environmental objectives.

The 'double-dividend' literature emphasises the value of the revenues derived from Pigovian taxes, which can reduce the need for revenues from other tax instruments. Hence, such taxes may then be set with multiple objectives in mind – alleviating externality distortions and contributing to efficient revenue-raising with the possibility for lowering other distortive taxes. Yet most literature seems to focus on one side or the other.

William Jack Baumol, some 50 years after Pigou, wrote: 'It is ironic that just at the moment when the Pigouvian tradition has some hope of acceptance in application it should find itself under a cloud in the theoretical literature.'[24] He went on to defend the conclusions of the Pigovian tradition and suggest how to make use of both taxation and subsidies. Subsidies are widely used and few people question whether they are absolutely correctly and precisely allocated. Some of them are even environmentally harmful.

As David Pearce wrote with a certain optimism at the beginning of this century: 'In the cases of environmental taxes and tradable permits, what was essentially a theoretical literature a few decades ago has now become practical policy. Environmental taxes are extensive in OECD countries and are emerging fairly fast in middle-income and even low-income countries.'[25] However, this has not been the path most governments have walked down.

WHAT IS THE SITUATION?

While both taxes and direct regulation can be used to discourage behaviour that gives rise to externalities, in the EU we have favoured regulatory instruments when it comes to tackling environmental problems. Many have led to successful environmental outcomes.

Nevertheless, according to the European Environment Agency (EEA)'s 'European environment: state and outlook 2020' report,[26] while European environmental and climate policies have driven improvements in the environment over recent decades, Europe is not making enough progress and the outlook in the coming decade is not positive. Achieving Europe's goals will require better implementation and improved coordination between current policies. It will also need additional policy actions to achieve fundamental change in the key systems of production and consumption that underpin our modern lifestyles, such as food, energy and mobility, which have substantial environmental impacts. The report also stresses that achieving change will require investing in a sustainable future and stopping using public funds to subsidise environmentally damaging activities. Europe will gain immensely from such a change in investment priorities because of the economic and social opportunities that it can create.

In 2020 for the first time in the history of the Global Risks Perception Survey,[27] environmental concerns dominate the top long-term risks by likelihood among members of the World Economic Forum's multi-stakeholder community; three of the top five risks by impact are environmental.

WHAT ABOUT ENVIRONMENTAL TAXATION?

According to the Eurostat data (2018), total environmental tax[28] revenue in the EU amounted to €324.6 billion, representing 2.4% of EU gross domestic product (GDP) and 6.0% of total EU government revenue from taxes and social contributions, with huge variations across the EU Member States. A very large portion of the environmental tax revenue – 77.7% – comes from energy taxes. The share of transport taxes is 19.1%. Taxes on pollution and resources together represent only 3.3%, with some countries not taxing resources and pollution at all.[29] These numbers have been largely stable over the last decade, in spite of the numerous calls for environmental tax reforms.

The OECD reports in the 'Tax Policy Reforms 2020'[30] that taxes on energy use in 2017 accounted for more than 50% of total environmentally related tax revenues in the 40 countries covered by the report,[31] except China (48%), with huge variations across the countries. On average, energy use taxes yielded 72% of environmentally related tax revenues. Motor vehicle taxes and other taxes on transport were the second largest component of environmentally related tax revenues (on average 24% of environmentally related tax revenues).

According to the above OECD report:

> environmentally related tax reforms have continued at a slow pace in 2020. While the number of measures adopted increased compared to 2019, reforms were concentrated in a few countries and their scope remained generally limited. Most of the reforms were related to the taxation of energy use, but unlike in previous years, transport fuels were not the main focus. Instead, changes were made to carbon taxes and taxes on electricity consumption. Tax reforms in the transport sector, aside from energy use, were limited to adjustments to vehicle registration taxes and tax reductions for vehicles running on alternative fuels. There was an increase in reforms related to other environmental tax bases (e.g. plastic and waste), but their overall number remained limited.[32]

In Africa, we observe interesting trends where the recent legislative changes are raising the tax burden borne by mining companies. The mining sector is an important contributor to tax revenues in many African countries. In 2015, the extractive sector accounted for more than 20% of the total revenues of nine countries on the continent, according to the Extractive Industry Transparency Initiative. Mining tax systems must then both attract investors and ensure sufficient revenues for governments. Following the increase in commodity prices in the second half of the 2000s, most African countries reformed their mining laws in order to capture a larger share of the rent generated by mining companies. This trend continues: mining royalty rates are rising, mineral resource rent taxes are reappearing and free equity for the state is becoming more and more common.[33] Still, there is an underexplored potential for environmental taxes to contribute to more progressive and sustainable tax systems and more equitable societies, while decreasing state dependence on aid and debt financing.

In response to the COVID-19 crisis, many countries took unprecedented steps and introduced broad fiscal measures to keep the economy alive. The OECD reports that 'while the size of fiscal packages in response to the COVID-19 crisis has varied across countries, most have been significant, and many countries have taken unprecedented action'.[34] It also points out that most countries have adopted a phased approach to COVID-19, gradually adapting their fiscal packages as the crisis has unfolded. Initial government responses focused on providing income support to households and liquidity to businesses to help them stay afloat. As the crisis has continued, many countries expanded their initial response packages.[35] The most recent measures and discussions suggest that the recovery phase will be supported by expansionary fiscal policy in a number of countries. Once recovery is well underway, governments should shift from crisis management to more structural tax reforms. 'Right now, the focus should be on the economic recovery. Once the recovery is firmly in place, rather than simply returning to business as usual, governments should seize the opportunity to build a greener, more inclusive and more resilient economy,' said Pascal Saint-Amans, Director of the OECD Centre for Tax Policy and Administration. 'One path that should be urgently prioritised is environmental tax reform and tax policies to tackle inequalities.'[36]

We could not agree more.

WHY DO WE NEED TAX REFORM?

Revenues from labour tax and social contributions account for more than 50% of total tax revenues in the EU 27 Member States. In comparison, environmental taxation represents a fraction (EU average around 6% with variations across Member States).[37] Looking ahead this will be problematic not only because of the impacts of the coronavirus crisis, but also due to the challenges brought about by the ageing of population and the transformation of the labour markets due to digitalisation, robotisation and globalisation. This will create further substantial fiscal pressure on national budgets.

It is expected that by 2070, the cohort of 65+ year olds will correspond to 42.1% of the EU population and the old-age dependency ratio (people aged 65+ relative to those aged 15 to 64) will increase from the current 29.9% to 52.2%.[38] Obviously, this has direct consequences for the revenue side of the budget. The ageing of the population will, however, also affect the expenditure side of the budget with higher public sector transfers for pensions, health care and long-term care. Public expenditure on health and pensions in OECD countries already nowadays accounts for one-third to one-half of primary expenditure.

On top of that, labour taxes affect employment decisions. High payroll costs can be an incentive to minimise the number of employees, outsourcing to lower income countries, lowering investment in human capital (education) or replacement of human labour by automation. They affect the business model companies will take. In general, a lower tax burden on labour should benefit all sectors, and in particular those that rely heavily on human resources such as research, health care or education.

The digital era and globalisation will increase competition at the international level, resulting in increased labour and income tax competition between different countries. The complexity of the globalised world also opens the door for new ways for tax avoidance and tax evasion.

IS THERE A DOUBLE DIVIDEND?

The 'double-dividend hypothesis'[39] proposes that a revenue-neutral substitution of environmental taxes for revenue-raising taxes might offer two benefits. The first dividend is the welfare gain resulting from an improvement in the environment (less pollution), and the second dividend is due to a reduction in the distortions of the revenue-raising tax system, which also produces an improvement in welfare. In other words, environmental taxes can improve the environment and increase economic efficiency simultaneously.

Either motivation can legitimately support a tax reform. The first dividend intuitively makes sense: decreasing pollutant emissions improves the environment. The European Commission has examined in various studies the costs associated with the gaps in implementing the EU environmental acquis and thereby meeting our environmental objectives. These costs relate to many impacts – in particular, potential environmental benefits are not realised, but also impacts such as uncertainty for business and infringement costs and health costs. The costs are not easy to quantify but, as an indicative estimate, the costs and foregone benefits for the EU are estimated to be around €55 billion per year from not achieving the environmental targets specified in the EU environmental legislation.[40]

The second dividend relates to improvement in economic efficiency and results from a shift away from distorting taxes such as the income tax. In the context of the earlier mentioned socio-economic megatrends, this is an important element to consider when looking at fiscal sustainability.

An introduction of environmental taxes often raises concerns about impacts on income inequalities. In practice, there are many policy options available to alleviate the impact on low-income households. These can take the form of exemptions, tax credits, allowances or deductions. Green taxes can also be made more progressive by applying, for example, higher rates for higher use or a tax-free threshold (e.g. a certain amount of energy or water can remain untaxed). They should go hand in hand with reduction of labour taxation. Note also that existing inequalities are further worsened by market failures not being properly addressed by sustainable fiscal systems. Groups of lower socio-economic status (the unemployed, those on low incomes or with lower levels of education) tend to be more negatively affected by environmental health hazards, as a result of their greater exposure and higher vulnerability.[41]

In many developing countries, increasing the amount of revenues raised through environmental taxation has the potential to reduce state dependence on aid and debt financing, and to facilitate the mobilisation of domestic resources for public services. As environmental taxes are harder to evade than, for example, corporate or personal income taxes, they also have the potential to strengthen state accountability, improve tax morale and enhance fiscal governance.

So why is it so that the share of environmentally related tax revenue has stayed stable for the last two decades at around the above mentioned 5–6% of the total tax revenues in the EU?

WHY IS IT SO?

The importance of environmental taxation in the last hundred years' academic literature – this chapter included – includes many researchers' work to explain the positive feedbacks between environmental tax reforms and the economy – and potentially social objectives. Yet in the media and in public discourse, such positive benefits are still highly debated. The failure of environmental tax experts to convince means that Pigou has largely remained relevant for debates by scholars.

In the EU, competences in the taxation field generally remain with Member States. Taxation is the last EU policy area where decision-making relies on unanimity. This makes EU level coordination a lengthy and not always successful process. To date, EU tax policies have mainly focused on targeted deliverables responding to specific problems. There is no common and holistic vision for EU tax policies shared by all Member States. Coordination is even harder when we move to the global level.

Fiscal frameworks in the individual Member States have been in place for decades. A comprehensive tax reform is likely to face strong political challenges. While the public often does not understand how the fiscal framework exactly works and why it would need a reform, it might have very strong opinions on individual taxes to be introduced. Past experience shows that a buy-in of a reform by different stakeholder groups and citizens is key to a successful reform (e.g. charges on plastic bags, landfill levies, energy taxes, etc.).

Politicians are more likely to focus on prominent tax issues, rather than approaching fiscal frameworks in a comprehensive way. It takes time and sometimes longer than a political cycle, hence policymakers may shy away from addressing the issues in a systematic way. In general, politicians face an incentive to enact reforms whose gains are visible at the time of the next election – and, if possible, whose costs are not.[42] Environmental improvements may take time to become visible. Fiscal reforms therefore tend to take a piecemeal approach, instead of addressing the whole system.

However, the challenges we face are also of an unprecedented scale; they are essentially connected in processes of rapid, dynamic change; they are fundamentally systemic and often linked to mankind's interference with nature and climate and planetary boundaries being crossed. Major disease outbreaks such as the current one have originated from viruses spreading from wildlife to humans. We have learned from experience that we cannot sustainably manage such complex, connected systemic issues through ad hoc, short-term, sectoral interventions. Singular short-term oriented measures without proper alignment with long-term policy objectives might be efficient in the short run, but more often than not will fail to stimulate sustainable investment and to substantially improve the foundations of society.

What is required is a systems approach[43] to incorporate the non-linearities, evolution, interlinkages, tipping points, emergence, trade-offs, synergies and other characteristics of the systems we inhabit. This would be a paradigm shift in economic thought towards a systems-based approach. Perhaps the most important lesson from the crisis is that our socio-economic system is evolving fast and becoming more and more distant from our old basic economic model. The old economy was one that primarily expressed itself in a language of prices and GDP. Despite us all knowing for 100 years that those prices did not reflect the true cost for society, we nevertheless used this language every day to inform most of our decisions. Since the 1960s the international statistical community has tried to find ways to correct or accompany GDP measurement by addressing social accounting issues and the environmental problems that were not captured within the indicator. However, GDP is still often taken as a measure of the welfare of a country. These misinterpretations lead to serious political consequences, as decisions can be based on inadequate evidence and a biased reading of the facts.[44]

These challenges need to be addressed through systemic reforms rather than addressing different issues in isolation. Such reform(s) need to take into consideration the need to support the transition to a green economy, ensuring sustainability of tax revenues, social justice for citizens and competitiveness for business. Shifting taxation from labour and business to unsustainable consumption and pollution has a potential to address all these aspects, in particular if coordinated at EU and international level.

Obviously changing the dynamics of sometimes complex and well-established administrative tax systems is not easy. The many interlinkages within and between complex systems mean that there are often strong economic, social and psychological incentives that lock society into particular ways of meeting its needs. As explained in much of the EEA's work, radically altering these systems is likely to disrupt established investments, jobs, consumption patterns and behaviours, knowledge and values, inevitably provoking resistance from affected industries, regions or consumers. Such resistance constrains governments in their ability to, for example, impose environmental taxes that are consistent with long-term environmental goals.[45]

'It always seems impossible until it's done.' – Nelson Mandela is quoted as having said.

WHAT SHOULD BE DONE?

When faced with large complex problems we have all learned to break them down into smaller pieces to solve them bit by bit; but with a systemic approach, we need to keep an eye on all the pieces. The pieces are often strongly interlinked and mutually reinforcing, hence careful attention will have to be paid when there are potential trade-offs between economic, environmental and social objectives. That is the essence of sustainability or sustainable development.

Following this approach, the European Commission has set out a European Green Deal for the EU and its citizens. The Green Deal is an integral part of this Commission's strategy to implement the United Nation's 2030 Agenda and the sustainable development goals. The Green Deal resets the European Commission's commitment to tackling climate and environment-related challenges that is this generation's defining task. It is a new growth strategy that aims to transform the EU into a fair and prosperous society, with a modern, resource-efficient and competitive economy where there are no net emissions of greenhouse gases in 2050 and where economic growth is decoupled from resource use. It also aims to protect, conserve and enhance the EU's natural capital, and protect the health and well-being of citizens from environment-related risks and impacts. At the same time, this transition must be just and inclusive.

Part of our response to the economic crisis therefore needs to look at taxation in a systemic and structural way. Future-proof tax systems need to address current and emerging challenges.

Public spending, funded by debt, will increase significantly, and some of the companies best placed to weather the economic storm will be global or digital companies, who are hardest to tax. For the recovery, it is important that fiscal consolidation is used also as an occasion to rationalise the tax systems by revenue-neutral reforms to enhance its efficiency and remove distortions harmful to growth. This would imply shifting taxation towards growth enhancing tax bases (away from labour towards consumption, property and environment), and improving tax governance. Design needs to ensure that revenues remain relatively stable even when the behavioural change diminishes the tax base and brings positive environmental impacts. Broadening tax bases, indexation to inflation and increases of the tax rate over time can be part of the solution.

Hence the European Green Deal calls for well-designed tax reforms to boost economic growth and resilience, provide the right incentives for sustainable behaviour by producers, users and consumers. This was also followed up by similar text in 2020's European Semester about the need to shift the tax burden from labour to pollution. The European Commission will be looking for proposals on sustainable tax reforms in the National Recovery Plans in response to the COVID-19 crisis. The work taken forward by the European Commission in relation to the Energy Taxation Directive,[46] a Carbon Border Adjustment Mechanism[47] as well as any changes that might be made to the

Emission Trading Scheme[48] are steps forward. However, carbon pricing is just one element of a much broader reform agenda that needs to happen.

There is a popular perception that the regressive effects make environmental taxes undesirable despite their environmental benefits. Despite the perception of regressivity, if properly designed, the negative effect of reforms on the poor can be offset by using the revenue for redistributive expenditure, similar to other taxes.

It is in the strong interest of Europe to support and cooperate with our international partners on taking forward the necessary sustainable fiscal reforms outside Europe. The European Commission in its dialogue with third countries will also put emphasis on the 'polluter-pays principle', which calls for pricing the negative externalities of polluting or other damaging activities. There is also an underexplored potential for environmental taxes to contribute to more progressive and sustainable tax systems and more equitable societies in developing countries.

As European Commission President Ursula von der Leyen said in her State of the Union Address 2020: 'A virus a thousand times smaller than a grain of sand exposed how delicate life can be. It laid bare the strains on our health systems and the limits of a model that values wealth above wellbeing.'[49]

Prices need to reflect what we value and ensure that the polluter pays. If we want to build back better, we will also need a lot of money – both public and private. National governments are responsible for raising taxes and setting tax rates. Some EU countries manage to raise 10% or more of their total tax revenues from environmental tax measures. Imagine how high this number could become if all governments across the world adopted best practices. If we wait another 100 years, it will be too late.

NOTES

1. Arthur Cecil Pigou, *The Economics of Welfare* (Macmillan 1920).
2. See Nicholas Stern, 'The Economics of Climate Change' (2008) 98 (2) *The American Economic Review* 1 <https://www.jstor.org/stable/29729990> accessed 14 January 2021.
3. Tim Worstall, 'Sure, There Is Such a Thing as Market Failure' (*Adam Smith Institute*, 14 September 2016) <https://www.adamsmith.org/blog/sure-theres-such-a-thing-as-market-failure> accessed 14 January 2021.
4. Michael Porter, 'America's Green Strategy' (1991) 264 (4) *Scientific American* 168.
5. '**Polluter-pays Principle:** principle according to which the polluter should bear the cost of measures to reduce pollution according to the extent of either the damage done to society or the exceeding of an acceptable level (standard) of pollution.' Department for Economic and Social Information and Policy Analysis, Statistics Division, *Studies in Methods Series F, No. 67 Glossary of Environment*

Statistics (United Nations 1997) <https://unstats.un.org/unsd/publication/seriesf/seriesf_67e.pdf> accessed 14 January 2021.
6. '**User-pays Principle:** variation of the polluter-pays principle that calls upon the user of a natural resource to bear the cost of running down natural capital.' Ibid 75.
7. Consolidated versions of the Treaty on European Union and the Treaty on the Functioning of the European Union (TFEU) [2012] OJ C326/01, art 191 (2) <https://eur-lex.europa.eu/legal-content/EN/TXT/?uri=CELEX%3A12012E191> accessed 14 January 2021.
8. Garrett Hardin, 'The Tragedy of the Commons' (1968) 162 (3859) *Science* 1243.
9. Mark Carney, former Governor of the Bank of England and former Chairman of the Financial Stability Board, 'Breaking the Tragedy of the Horizon: Climate Change and Financial Stability' (Speech at Lloyd's of London, London, 29 September 2015) <https://www.bankofengland.co.uk/-/media/boe/files/speech/2015/breaking-the-tragedy-of-the-horizon-climate-change-and-financial-stability.pdf?la=en&hash=7C67E785651862457D99511147C7424FF5EA0C1A> accessed 14 January 2021.
10. Ibid.
11. See *Better Regulation* <https://ec.europa.eu/commission/priorities/democratic-change/better-regulation_en> accessed 14 January 2021.
12. See e.g. Ladislas de Guerre, 'How can Impact Investors Balance the Green Energy Equation?' (*World Economic Forum*, 28 August 2020) <https://www.weforum.org/agenda/2020/08/how-can-impact-investors-balance-the-green-energy-equation> accessed 14 January 2021.
13. See *EU Taxonomy for Sustainable Activities* <https://ec.europa.eu/info/business-economy-euro/banking-and-finance/sustainable-finance/eu-taxonomy-sustainable-activities_en> accessed 14 January 2021.
14. Regulation (EU) 2020/852 of the European Parliament and of the Council of 18 June 2020 on the establishment of a framework to facilitate sustainable investment, and amending Regulation (EU) 2019/2088 [2020] OJ L198/13 <https://eur-lex.europa.eu/legal-content/EN/TXT/?uri=CELEX:32020R0852> accessed 14 January 2021.
15. The Regulation covers the following policy objectives: climate change mitigation; climate change adaptation; the sustainable use and protection of water and marine resources; the transition to a circular economy; pollution prevention and control; and the protection and restoration of biodiversity and ecosystems.
16. For further information on the delegated act on climate objectives see <https://ec.europa.eu/info/law/better-regulation/have-your-say/initiatives/12302-Climate-change-mitigation-and-adaptation-taxonomy#ISC_WORKFLOW> accessed 14 January 2021.
17. See Commission, 'Commission Work Programme 2021: A Union of Vitality in a World of Fragility' (Communication) COM/2020/690 final <https://ec.europa.eu/info/publications/2021-commission-work-programme-key-documents_en> accessed 14 January 2021 and also Commission, 'The European Green Deal' (Communication) COM/2019/640 final <https://eur-lex.europa.eu/legal-content/EN/TXT/?qid=1576150542719&uri=COM%3A2019%3A640%3AFIN> accessed 14 January 2021.
18. Directive 2014/95/EU of the European Parliament and of the Council of 22 October 2014 amending Directive 2013/34/EU as regards disclosure of non-financial and diversity information by certain large undertakings and groups [2014] OJ L330/01 <https://ec.europa.eu/info/business-economy-euro/company-reporting-and

-auditing/company-reporting/non-financial-reporting_en> accessed 14 January 2021.
19. Commission, 'The European Green Deal' (Communication) COM/2019/640 final <https://eur-lex.europa.eu/legal-content/EN/TXT/?qid=1576150542719&uri=COM%3A2019%3A640%3AFIN> accessed 14 January 2021; see also <https://ec.europa.eu/info/strategy/priorities-2019-2024/european-green-deal_en> accessed 14 January 2021.
20. For further information on the revision of the NFRD-Directive see <https://ec.europa.eu/info/law/better-regulation/have-your-say/initiatives/12129-Revision-of-Non-Financial-Reporting-Directive/public-consultation> accessed 14 January 2021.
21. European Commission, Directorate-General for Financial Stability, Financial Services and Capital Markets Union, *Guidelines on Reporting Climate-Related Information* (European Commission 2019) <https://ec.europa.eu/finance/docs/policy/190618-climate-related-information-reporting-guidelines_en.pdf> accessed 14 January 2021.
22. For further information on sustainable corporate governance see <https://ec.europa.eu/info/law/better-regulation/have-your-say/initiatives/12548-Sustainable-corporate-governance> accessed 14 January 2021.
23. See also Laurent Franckx and Athanasios Kampas, 'On the Regulatory Choice of Refunding Rules to Reconcile the "Polluter Pays Principle" and Pigovian Taxation: An Application' (2005) 23 (1) *Environment and Planning C: Government and Policy* 141.
24. William Jack Baumol, 'On Taxation and the Control of Externalities' (1972) 62 (3) *The American Economic Review* 307 <https://www.jstor.org/stable/1803378?seq=1#metadata_info_tab_contents> accessed 14 January 2021.
25. David Pearce, 'An Intellectual History of Environmental Economics' [2002] 27 *Annual Review of Energy and the Environment* 57, 75 <https://www.cepal.org/ilpes/noticias/paginas/1/35691/ja_histofenvecon.pdf> accessed 14 January 2021.
26. European Environment Agency, *The European Environment: State and Outlook 2020 – Knowledge for Transition to a Sustainable Europe* (EEA 2019) <https://www.eea.europa.eu/soer> accessed 14 January 2021.
27. The Annual Global Risks Perception Survey is completed by approximately 800 members of the World Economic Forum's communities; see *The Global Risks Report 2020* <https://www.weforum.org/reports/the-global-risks-report-2020> accessed 14 January 2021.
28. According to Regulation (EU) No 691/2011 of the European Parliament and of the Council of 6 July 2011 on European environmental economic accounts [2011] OJ L192/11, art 2 (2), an 'environmentally related tax' is a tax whose tax base is a physical unit (or a proxy of it) of something that has a proven, specific negative impact on the environment and which is defined in the ESA 95 (European system of accounts) as a tax. European statistics distinguish four different categories of environmental taxes relating to energy, transport, pollution and resources. Regulation (EU) No 691/2011 <https://eur-lex.europa.eu/legal-content/EN/ALL/?uri=CELEX%3A02011R0691-20140616> accessed 14 January 2021.
29. ESTAT – Environmental tax statistics <https://ec.europa.eu/eurostat/statistics-explained/index.php/Environmental_tax_statistics> accessed 14 January 2021.
30. OECD, *Tax Policy Reforms 2020: OECD and Selected Partner Economies* (OECD Publishing 2020) <https://www.oecd-ilibrary.org/docserver/7af51916

-en.pdf?expires=1600354455&id=id&accname=oid031827&checksum=36 FF48E5BE43C4E5EEFCEF206C727864> accessed 14 January 2021.
31. The Tax Policy Reforms 2020 report covers 40 countries including all OECD countries (with the exception of Colombia, which became a member of the OECD after the primary data collection exercise had been completed), as well as Argentina, China, Indonesia and South Africa.
32. OECD *supra* note 30, 11.
33. Yannick Bouterige, Céline de Quatrebarbes and Bertrand Laporte, 'Analysis: Mining Taxes Are on the Rise in Africa' (*Intergovernmental Forum in Mining, Minerals, Metals and Sustainable Development*, 8 July 2020) <https://www.igfmining.org/en-fr-analysis-mining-taxes-are-on-the-rise-in-africa/> accessed 14 January 2021.
34. OECD *supra* note 30.
35. OECD *supra* note 30.
36. OECD, *Countries Have Responded Decisively to the COVID-19 Crisis, but Face Significant Fiscal Challenges Ahead*, <http://www.oecd.org/tax/tax-policy/countries-have-responded-decisively-to-the-covid-19-crisis-but-face-significant-fiscal-challenges-ahead.htm?utm_source=Adestra&utm_medium=email&utm_content=Press%20release&utm_campaign=Tax%20News%20Alert%2003-09-2020&utm>accessed 14 January 2021.
37. European Commission, *Data on Taxation*, <https://ec.europa.eu/taxation_customs/business/economic-analysis-taxation/data-taxation_en> accessed 14 January 2021.
38. European Commission, Directorate-General for Economic and Financial Affairs, *The 2018 Ageing Report Economic and Budgetary Projections for the EU Member States (2016–2070)* (European Commission 2018) <https://ec.europa.eu/info/sites/info/files/economy-finance/ip079_en.pdf> accessed 14 January 2021.
39. Arij Lans Bovenberg, 'Environmental Taxation and the Double Dividend' (1998) 25 (1) *Empirica* 15.
40. European Commission, Directorate-General for Environment E.2, *Study: The Costs of not Implementing EU Environmental Law – Final Report* (European Commission 2019) <https://ec.europa.eu/environment/eir/pdf/study_costs_not_implementing_env_law.pdf>accessed 14 January 2021.
41. European Environment Agency, *EEA Report No 22/2018: Unequal Exposure and Unequal Impacts – Social Vulnerability to Air Pollution, Noise and Extreme Temperatures in Europe* (European Environment Agency 2018) 6 <https://www.eea.europa.eu/publications/unequal-exposure-and-unequal-impacts> accessed 14 January 2021.
42. European Commission, Directorate-General for Economic and Financial Affairs, *Political Economy of Tax Reforms: Workshop Proceedings* (European Economy Discussion Papers, European Union 2016) 21 <https://ec.europa.eu/info/sites/info/files/dp025_en.pdf> accessed 14 January 2021.
43. OECD, *Systemic Thinking for Policy Making: The Potential of Systems Analysis for Addressing Global Policy Challenges in the 21st Century* (OECD 2019) 3 <https://www.oecd.org/naec/averting-systemic-collapse/SG-NAEC(2019)4_IIASA-OECD_Systems_Thinking_Report.pdf> accessed 14 January 2021.
44. SWD(2013) 303 final, Commission Staff Working Document, *Progress on 'GDP and Beyond' Actions – Annexes* <https://ec.europa.eu/environment/enveco/pdf/SWD_2013_303_annexes.pdf> accessed 14 January 2021.

45. European Environment Agency, *EEA Report No 09/2019: Sustainability Transitions – Policy and Practice* (European Environment Agency 2019) 25 <https://www.eea.europa.eu/publications/sustainability-transitions-policy-and-practice> accessed 14 January 2021.
46. Directive 2012/27/EU of the European Parliament and of the Council of 25 October 2012 on energy efficiency, amending Directives 2009/125/EC and 2010/30/EU and repealing Directives 2004/8/EC and 2006/32/EC, Text with EEA relevance, OJ L 315, 14 November 2012, pp. 1–56 <https://eur-lex.europa.eu/legal-content/EN/TXT/?uri=celex%3A32012L0027> accessed 20 May 2021.
47. A proposal to be tabled in June 2021, inception impact assessment available at <https://ec.europa.eu/info/law/better-regulation/have-your-say/initiatives/12228-Carbon-Border-Adjustment-Mechanism> accessed 20 May 2021.
48. Directive 2003/87/EC of the European Parliament and of the Council of 13 October 2003 establishing a scheme for greenhouse gas emission allowance trading within the Community and amending Council Directive 96/61/EC, Text with EEA relevance, OJ L 275, 25 October 2003, pp. 32–46 <https://eur-lex.europa.eu/legal-content/EN/TXT/?uri=CELEX%3A32003L0087> accessed 20 May 2021.
49. Ursula von der Leyen, 'State of the Union Address 2020' <https://ec.europa.eu/info/sites/default/files/soteu_2020_en.pdf> accessed 20 May 2021.

5. Promoting a green economic recovery from the Corona crisis

Holger Bär, Matthias Runkel and Kai Schlegelmilch[1]

1. INTRODUCTION

Aligning economic recovery with climate mitigation needs has been a key topic throughout 2020 in many countries as well as in the EU. The underlying challenges are similar in all countries and the examples discussed in this chapter serve as illustrations of *how* to think about the design of economic recovery policies – they are not a 'prescription' of what recovery policies should look like. The goal is rather to point out some key issues for a green recovery and to enable readers from different countries to use this framework on how to build back better on their own.

2. CRISIS AS OPPORTUNITY – FOR ECONOMIC RECOVERY AND THE CLIMATE

2.1 2020 as a Crossroads

Throughout 2020, the corona crisis has sent the global economy into a downturn and many countries into recession. Hopes for a quick, V-shaped recovery seem valid for some countries, while others are heading for a second downturn and prolonged crisis. The global nature and dimension are of historic proportions. Public life and the economy are at a standstill in some areas. In addition to the major challenges for our health care system, short-time work, redundancies, liquidity bottlenecks, insolvencies and many other problems are looming. While short-term support measures should focus on health needs and provide security for employees and companies that were hit the hardest, we must not repeat the mistakes of past economic crises and consider the way we respond to the crisis not just in the short term, but also long term. Under the pressure of the crisis, far-reaching decisions are being made at a rapid pace and massive public expenditures are being outlined that will have an effect for many years and decades to come. At best, they can accelerate the modernisation of the economy – at worst, they can reinforce the dominance of fossil-fuel based technologies and business models 'saving' them from necessary structural changes, further delay the decarbonisation in crucial sectors, lead to stranded investments while draining government's ability to finance necessary investments in urgently needed areas[2] and contribute to not meeting the Paris Agreement.

2.2   A 'Historic Opportunity' for Sustainable Development

How *should* the economic crisis be addressed then if one wanted to address the economic downturn while advancing sustainable development? Fatih Birol was one of the first to name the dangers of the crisis as well as the 'historic opportunity' to address several challenges *simultaneously*: by using large-scale investments in clean energy and energy efficiency to secure jobs *and* advance climate goals (Birol 2020). Soon thereafter, a number of discussion papers and articles carried on the debate, further aligning crisis response and climate policy.[3]

Historical evidence from past crises suggests that crises *can* support the modernisation and decarbonisation of economies – but they do not do so by default. Historical examples of Eastern European states (particularly Lithuania, Latvia, Estonia, Romania and Slovakia) after the collapse in 1990 as well as Southern European states (particularly Greece and Portugal) after the financial crisis in 2008 showed that recovery can go hand in hand with lower CO_2-intensity – but only if recovery policies are used to advance structural changes (Lilliestam 2020).

2.3   The German 2008 Crisis Response as a Lesson

In the German response to the 2008 financial crisis, climate protection and other long-term goals were pushed into the background, while short-term economic recovery dominated the political agenda. While climate change was widely debated between 2006 and 2008, its presence in debates in the German federal parliament sharply declined with the 2008 financial crisis and remained low for many years. Only in 2018/19, the topic returned to a similar presence in debates, as shown by a keyword analysis of the speeches in parliament.[4]

This absence in debates was also reflected in the recovery policies adopted. Crises are a *breeding ground for new ideas* – good and bad ones and a catalyst for their dissemination. The 'scrapping premium' (officially: environmental bonus) was conceived in Germany as a stimulus measure with little consideration of its ecological effects and was copied in many countries (Schmidt et al. 2009; Schweinfurth 2009). As a result, old vehicles that could have been used for many more years were scrapped and replaced. Assessments of the ecological effects show mixed results and point to low cost-effectiveness (see e.g. Leisinger and Rösel (2020) and OECD (n.d.)), especially when taking into account real-world emissions rather than type-approval emission values (ICCT 2020). In contrast, the American Recovery Act of 2009 promoted the creation of almost one million clean energy jobs in the wind and solar industries in the following years (Lashof 2020).

Another lesson is that some stimulus measures run the risk of preventing structural change. One example from the 2008 financial crisis is the so-called 'zombie banks', which were only kept alive by public subsidies and liquidity injections. The danger of repeating such unintended consequences still exists today – for example, if fundamental structural changes in business models and technological changes (particularly in decarbonizing the economy) are effectively being halted by the way economic support is given. In responding to the 2020 crisis, we should learn from the lessons of the past and avoid repeating mistakes. Looking at the timetable for getting on track to meet the Paris climate goals, there is no time for postponing the decarbonisation of the economy. Economic recovery and climate protection can – and must – go hand in hand this time.

3. HOW TO APPROACH THE ECONOMIC RESPONSE TO THE CRISIS

The Hippocratic Oath says: 'primum non nocere – first do not harm', followed by: 'secundum cavere, tertium sanare – secondly be careful, thirdly heal'. The approach is also useful when thinking about how to address the economic crisis. A sensible approach thinks of short- and long-term challenges together: when dealing with the acute challenges not to lose sight of the long-term transformation tasks and to find potential synergies between the different objectives:

1. Managing the public health crisis: through measures to reduce new infections and strengthen the health care system;
2. Emergency aid for employees and companies: by providing support for employees, households and companies to cushion social hardship during the economic downturn;
3. Decarbonisation and structural change: by promoting sustainable investments in solutions to long-term challenges.

Worldwide, unprecedented amounts of capital have been mobilised by national governments, the European Union and international organisations to combat the crisis (see also section 4). Given these huge levers, we should design them very carefully and beware of short-sighted crisis management that ignores long-term goals. Instead, we should implement measures that combine the short-term (public health and recovery) with the long-term perspective (energy system transformation, decarbonisation, digitisation, etc.). Translating this into specific recovery measures could create synergies between investments and win-win situations.

3.1   What Is Needed in the Short Term: Focus on Hardship

The focus of fiscal and monetary policy measures in the short term must provide support for those most affected. The central focus is on bridging the temporary loss of wages and income and providing short-term, temporary support to affected companies in order to minimise the economic consequences of the current exceptional situation – in other words: 'first, focus on hardship, not G.D.P.' (Krugman 2020). Personal and business insolvencies due to the temporary economic standstill must be prevented as much as possible in order to facilitate a quick return to normal business operations. As a matter of principle, these measures should be speedy, substantial and sustained (Schemmel et al. 2020). They must act quickly, address those affected and be limited to the time of the crisis.

3.2   Avoiding the 'Wrong Things'

'Primum non nocere – first, do not harm' is part of the Hippocratic Oath. The same goes for the economy. Otherwise, there is a danger that fighting the short-term crisis will lead us to postpone urgent tasks and thus take us one step forward and two steps back. Thöne (2020) correctly notes: 'The corona crisis relativizes the other problems, but their absolute size does not diminish. Rather, an additional, very large and acute problem has come on top of it'.

Naturally, economic policy debates are heavily influenced by competing interests. In the spring of 2020, in the German as well as the European debate, there had been various calls for either postponing or temporarily suspending environmental policies put forward in the guise of 'support the economy'. Examples are calls for the abolition of EU emissions trading (Barteczko 2020), softening the CO_2 targets for EU car manufacturers (Mortsiefer 2020) and putting the European Green Deal 'on hold' (Simon 2020); postponing the introduction of the German CO_2 price and the fertiliser ordinance (ntv 2020) as well as the increase of the air transport tax (Kiani-Kreß 2020; RND 2020). Such calls – including the long debate on a renewal of the scrappage premium for cars with combustion engines – have largely been unsuccessful in Europe. However, the Trump administration, for example, used the policy window created by the initial downturn to advance the roll-back of several environmental policies, such as in oil and gas regulation as well as car mileage standards (InfluenceMap 2020).

A related question is 'green' requirements for bailouts for airlines. It is necessary in the short term to provide liquidity to secure airlines and their employees. However, countries have used very different approaches with Germany and the United States providing billions of financial support to airlines with few conditions related to the industry's climate impact or employment protection – while in other countries (e.g. France, Netherlands and Austria) bailouts were connected to green strings. Such conditions (e.g. increased investment in climate-friendly technologies or R&D on alternative fuels, etc.) could lead to synergies in the long term. Unconditional support can run the risk of inhibiting and delaying necessary reforms in the sector.

The current crisis differs from typical economic crises in that it is both a supply and demand crisis (Bofinger et al. 2020). Therefore, such unconditional support would not only delay the decarbonisation of the economy, but also have little economic impact in the current situation. Further, it slows down the necessary structural change towards a low-carbon economy and unsettles actors who have set their sights on long-term decisions (e.g., investors in renewable energies or companies investing in their decarbonisation). Especially in a crisis, 'directional stability' (e.g., towards the Paris Agreement and Sustainable Development Goals) is important and an internationally coordinated economic policy has great advantages over an approach in which each country sets different priorities in national economic stimulus packages (OECD 2020). Additionally, the long-term costs of unabated or 'postponed' climate mitigation exceed the investments required for the necessary decarbonisation. This insight should be common sense since the Stern Review (Stern et al. 2006).

3.3 Doing the 'Right Things': Public Health, Emergency Aid and Investments in Structural Change

So, how to 'heal' the economy? Synergies with long-term climate and sustainable development goals can be found in investing and accelerating structural change. A sustainable structural policy does not attempt to 'prevent' structural change, but is used to achieve societal goals through it (cf. Bär and Jacob 2013). Public spending that addresses both economic recovery and long-term goals should be considered as *investments in the future* and be used to prepare companies and employees for structural change, to accelerate these transitions and thus combine economic opportunities and climate mitigation[5] (cf. Fischedick and Schneidewind 2020). Opportunities can be found in many different sectors. The following examples serve as illustrations of how to find synergies between short- and long-term goals. They are not meant to outline what should be done, but how to identify good policies that provide synergies.

3.3.1 Urban transport: enabling win-wins for health and environment

A major challenge in times of a global pandemic is safe urban mobility. It is true that relying on cars likely lowers the rate of infections. However, for low-income households this option is often not affordable and it would further increase traffic congestion in larger cities. Goods and passenger transport must be maintained despite the health risks. A *short-term* contribution to solving this problem could be investments in health security, for example, by disinfecting buses and trains. Role models could be cities with experience in managing pandemics in densely populated areas, such as Hong Kong or Singapore.

Many cities have recorded increased bike use throughout 2020. Offers for bike sharing and cargo bikes are already being expanded. In Bogotá, to lower the risk of infection, roads have been temporarily converted to bicycle lanes to facilitate the mobility of people (Walker 2020). This example has been copied in many European cities, such as Brussels, Vienna, Barcelona, London or Berlin. Investing in the use of bicycles and public transport makes sense in the *long term* as it also reduces negative external effects from urban car traffic (above all noise, pollutant emissions and traffic congestion).

3.3.2 'Energiewende': removing obstacles for investments in renewable energies

Short-term investments in small and medium-sized photovoltaic (PV) plants can support the economy and secure employment. In Germany, investments in PV expansion were discouraged due to a cap on total solar capacity. While the government had declared its intention to lift the cap since the fall of 2019, it only did so in the summer of 2020. While there were some concerns about supply-side bottlenecks for PV during the first lockdown period in the spring of 2020, these did not materialise as Asian supply chains for PV and electricity storage recovered quickly (Wood Mackenzie 2020).

In the *long term* and from a global perspective, it is important that investments in renewable energies do not come to a standstill, but that governments use this opportunity to accelerate the global transformation of energy systems (Birol 2020). Next to the expanding power production from wind and solar, investment opportunities and needs particularly lie in the field of power storage as the share of renewable sources in power grids is rising. The latest data on renewable power suggests that 2020 has brought a record expansion of renewable power sources globally with high growth expected to continue in the next years (IEA 2020).

3.3.3 Energy-efficient buildings: win-win for the construction industry and climate protection

Short-term investments in energy-related building refurbishment or replacing oil heating systems contribute to stabilising the economic situation and have positive long-term climate effects. Investments in energy efficiency in particular can have a strong impact on employment (cf. Umweltbundesamt 2019). Therefore, it would be important to examine which specific measures can be implemented quickly. In the *long term*, higher public and private investments are needed to reduce the energy demand of the building sector in order to meet the sector's 2030 climate mitigation targets.

3.3.4 Work: from the short-term 'need to work from home' to more digital collaboration and fewer business trips

In the *short term*, mobile working from home is a public health necessity and offers several advantages: people do not pose a risk of infection for others while continuing to work from home and care for their children; also, there is less commuting and environmental pollution.[6] In the short term, there is enormous growth potential for applications that improve digital collaboration and digital education in order to enable people to work productively from home.

From an ecological point of view, the *long-term* perspective promises opportunities for less commuting and less business travel because of the digital alternatives. Additional research is needed in order to tap the environmental and social opportunities associated with enabling more people to work independently of location.[7]

3.3.5 Further education: using the short-term slowdown to get fit for the demands of tomorrow

For some employees and companies, the crisis offers *short-term* opportunities to use for further training and up-skilling. Through 'green skills' opportunities, employees can train themselves specifically for the broad structural change of tomorrow. An important question is whether and how conventional face-to-face training can be digitised so that those interested in further training can take advantage of these opportunities.

In the *long term*, these considerations are important as to how we can use the time of the crisis for further training in order to make individual employees (and their companies) fit for the coming structural changes in their sectors – in order to guarantee long-term employment with good working conditions in Germany.

3.4 Employment and Climate Opportunities from a Green Recovery

A recent study outlines the opportunities for employment and climate in a green recovery. The policy package for Germany consisted of a range of recovery measures in different sectors. In the study, 50€ billion of public funds leverage a similar amount of private investments between 2020 and 2024, would create an additional 365,000 jobs – more than making up for the jobs due to the downturn – and reduce CO_2 emissions by up to 56 million tons of CO_2 equivalent per year (FÖS and DIW 2020).

3.5 The Social Dimension of Recovery Policies

Economic policies aiming at securing jobs and providing stability to companies in various sectors have distributional impacts and, depending on their specific design, benefit one group or another. Therefore, they can run the risk of exacerbating already existing and rising inequalities of income, wealth and influence and endangering public support for such measures. This is true for both interpersonal inequality as well as differences between sectors of the economy, such as sectors heavily hit by the crisis that enjoy little political influence like the hospitality and health care sectors, while examples from many different countries underscore the ability of fossil-fuel companies to receive extensive support without (green) conditions. Generally, state aid for large companies should not be given without conditions (see e.g. Lazonick et al. 2020) and the preservation of jobs must be clearly prioritised over shareholder value.

Fairness and distributional questions are also important in the long term and a transformation towards greater sustainability. Inequality between rich and poor groups within our societies and in the international context has risen sharply: while the world's richest 1% receive more than 20% of global income, the poorest 50% receive less than 10% (WID 2018). Economic research also shows that the amount of assets now 'hidden' in offshore tax havens has grown to 10% of global gross domestic product (GDP) over the last four decades and belongs to only the richest part of the richest 1% (Alstadsæter et al. 2018). The fact that huge assets can be 'hidden' offshore from tax authorities harms us all, limits the ability of our communities to act (e.g., to finance health care systems) and polarises our societies.

3.6 The Financing of Recovery Policies

In the short term, recovery policies must be financed through government expenditure with corresponding public debt. Directly related to the question of who benefits from recovery policies is the question of who pays for these expenditures in the long term. Linked to this is the question of how to design a fairer tax system that offers new answers to growing inequality. As a general rule, tax revenues should be reformed and financed more strongly through environmental taxes (FÖS 2019) in order to reduce the tax burden on labour. Environmental taxes, particularly a price on carbon, can impact low-income households more than high-income groups. This can be and has been addressed in several countries by the way revenues are used and (at least partly) returned to citizens.[8] Revenue recycling can, if designed properly, lead to a situation in which those polluting less become net beneficiaries, while those members of society polluting more, pay more than the average (in line with the polluter-pays-principle). Reforming the tax structure in a way that provides incentives for climate mitigation and efficient use of resources is key for ensuring our societies' ability to transform and become more sustainable. Another important source of finance is the dismantling of environmentally harmful subsidies that could free billions of Euros, while at the same time helping society to move away from fossil energy (Coady et al. 2019). The currently low crude oil prices both pose a risk for a reduction in energy efficiency efforts (Birol 2020) as well as an opportunity to tackle the $160 billion of environmentally and climate-damaging subsidies for oil worldwide and to give new impetus to stalled international processes to abolish such subsidies (see OECD-IEA 2020). Crisis situations like this offer a policy window to gather enough political will for reforms of subsidies and energy taxes (Abdallah et al. 2020; Bär et al. 2011).

4. RECOVERY MEASURES SO FAR (ANALYTICAL PART)

Over the course of the year 2020, the economic crisis has impacted most countries in the world – albeit to different degrees. A study by McKinsey concludes that more than ten trillion USD have been adopted in support measures – more than four trillion in the European Union alone (Cassim et al. 2020). The extent of support is vastly higher than in the economic crisis in 2008 (see Figure 5.1). The type of policy measures adopted varies widely between countries. An overview on types of policies is included in the study by Cassim et al. (2020). With regard to the crucial question whether the trillion are spent on structural changes or support existing fossil-fuel based economic structures and business models, the initiative Energy Policy Tracker[10] provides an overview on specific energy policy measures adopted in G20 countries. The analysis suggests that more than half of the spending supports fossil fuels (52%), while only a third (35%) is devoted to clean energy (see Figure 5.2).[11]

Promoting a green economic recovery from the Corona crisis 75

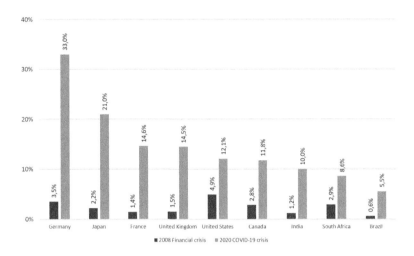

Source: Own figure based on data by Cassim et al. (2020)[9]

Figure 5.1   Size of economic aid measures (relative to GDP) for the 2020 COVID crisis, compared to spending in the 2008 financial crisis

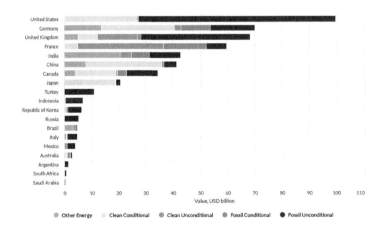

Source: Energy Policy Tracker, public support commitments to various categories of energy in recovery packages, USD billion, as of 23 December 2020

Figure 5.2   Size of public energy finance in G20 countries and how much of the spending is devoted to fossil or clean energy

5. CONCLUSION

The corona crisis has led to an economic crisis in many countries. In designing economic recovery policies, policymakers should avoid past mistakes and instead of creating trade-offs between short- and long-term goals, find synergies between them. The decarbonisation of the economy is shared by all countries and provides investment opportunities in many sectors in order to secure employment and advance both economic recovery as well as climate mitigation. While current public expenditures are financed by debt, government should look towards environmental taxes and the removal of environmentally harmful subsidies as a source of financing as well as support for a low-carbon economy. The analysis of recovery policies so far suggests that many countries are still missing out on the economic and environmental opportunities associated with a green recovery.

NOTES

1. A first version of this chapter was published in March 2020 as an input to the debate on the German economic recovery package and has been updated since (Bär and Runkel 2020). Holger Bär and Matthias Runkel are research fellows and Kai Schlegelmilch is one of the founding members and chairman of the supervisory board of Green Budget Germany. They thank Swantje Fiedler, Ann-Cathrin Beermann, Florian Zerzawy, Leonard Müller, Tobias Austrup and Maximilian Köster for many helpful comments on various versions of the chapter.
2. For example, a 2019 study calculated the level of additional public sector investments needed in Germany over the course of the next decade. It concluded that more than 450€ billion (over 10 years) were needed for investments in infrastructure, education, public housing and the public's share in spending on decarbonisation and digitisation (Bardt et al. 2019).
3. Among them were, for example, the papers by Bär and Runkel (2020) and Fischedick and Schneidewind (2020) as inputs on the debate in Germany and Europe, but also articles in *The Economist* (2020) as well as by the UN Secretary-General (Guterres 2020).
4. *Die Zeit* features a search engine for keywords in parliamentary debates, see: <https://www.zeit.de/politik/deutschland/2019-09/bundestag-jubilaeum-70-jahre-parlament-reden-woerter-sprache-wandel#s=klimawandel%2Cfinanzkrise> (accessed 1 May 2021).
5. This is precisely what Fischedick and Schneidewind (2020) call 'targeted exploitation of synergy potential for urgently needed investments in the future'.
6. We acknowledge the many hardships for (particularly low-income) families this necessary situation brings about as well as that mobile working is not per se associated with ecological advantages (if additional equipment needs to be procured, etc.).
7. The question has not only an ecological, but also a social dimension: if villages manage to provide people with the necessary infrastructure for remote work, this

can bring location-independent jobs from the cities to the countryside while reducing rent increases in the cities.
8. Scientific literature suggests that there is no 'single way' of returning revenues to the public, but rather several lessons of good and not-so-good practice (cp. Baranzini and Carattini 2017; Carattini et al. 2017, 2018, 2019; Kallbekken and Aasen 2010).
9. The GDP for 2019 was taken into account for values related to the COVID-19 crisis. 2008 data published by International Monetary Fund in March 2009; includes discretionary measures announced for 2008–10. Sources: Global economic policies and prospects, International Monetary Fund, March 2009, imf.org; government sources; IHS Market; IMF; press search; The state of public finances: Outlook and medium-term policies after the 2008 crisis, IMF, March 2009, imf.org.
10. See <https://www.energypolicytracker.org/>. The web site is a collaboration by many different organisations, including FÖS.
11. The remaining 13% cannot be attributed to either category.

LITERATURE

Abdallah, C., Coady, D., and Le, N. (2020): The time is right! Reforming fuel product pricing under low oil prices. IMF Special Series on COVID-19. Accessed 1 May 2021 at: <https://www.imf.org/~/media/Files/Publications/covid19-special-notes/enspecial-series-on-covid19the-time-is-right-reforming-fuel-product-pricing-under-low-oil-prices.ashx?la=en>.

Alstadsæter, A., Johannesen, N., and Zucman, G. (2018): Who owns the wealth in tax havens? Macro evidence and implications for global inequality. *Journal of Public Economics*, 162, June, 89–100. Accessed 1 May 2021 at: <https://www.sciencedirect.com/science/article/abs/pii/S0047272718300082>

Bär, H., and Jacob, K. (2013): Nachhaltige sektorale Strukturpolitik. In: von Hauff, M., and Nguyen, T. (eds.): *Nachhaltige Wirtschaftspolitik*. Baden-Baden: Nomos. pp. 253–76.

Bär, H., and Runkel, M. (2020): Wie notwendige Wirtschaftshilfen die Corona-Krise abfedern und die ökologische Transformation beschleunigen können. FÖS Policy Brief, 2020, 03. Accessed 1 May 2021 at: German version: <https://foes.de/publikationen/2020/2020-03-FOES-Wirtschaftshilfen-Corona-Krise.pdf>; English version: <https://foes.de/publikationen/2020/200330_FOES_Economic_support_measures_corona_crisis_v10_en.pdf>.

Bär, H., Jacob, K., Meyer, E., and Schlegelmilch, K. (2011): Wege zum Abbau umweltschädlicher Subventionen. Accessed 1 May 2021 at: <http://www.foes.de/pdf/Studie Subventionsabbau fin.pdf>.

Baranzini, A., and Carattini, S. (2017): Effectiveness, earmarking and labeling: Testing the acceptability of carbon taxes with survey data. *Environmental Economics and Policy Studies*, 19, 1, 197–227.

Bardt, H., Dullien, S., Hüther, M., and Rietzler, K. (2019): Für eine solide Finanzpolitik: Investitionen ermöglichen! (November). Accessed 1 May 2021 at: <https://www.dgb.de/presse/++co++c4b7acfc-09d5-11ea-97b8-52540088cada>.

Barteczko, A. (2020): EU should scrap emissions trading scheme, Polish official says. Reuters. Accessed 1 May 2021 at: <https://www.reuters.com/article/us-health-coronavirus-poland-ets-idUSKBN2141RC>.

Birol, F. (2020): Put clean energy at the heart of stimulus plans to counter the coronavirus crisis: Analysis. Accessed 1 May 2021 at: <https://www.iea.org/commentaries/put-clean-energy-at-the-heart-of-stimulus-plans-to-counter-the-coronavirus-crisis>.

Bofinger, P., Dullien, S., Felbermayr, G., Fuest, C., Hüther, M., Südekum, J., and Weder di Mauro, B. (2020): Wirtschaftliche Implikationen der Corona-Krise und wirtschaftspolitische Maßnahmen. Accessed 1 May 2021 at: <https://www.iwkoeln.de/fileadmin/user_upload/Studien/policy_papers/PDF/2020/IW-Policy-Paper_2020-COVID.pdf>.

Carattini, S., Carvalho, M., and Fankhauser, S. (2018): Overcoming public resistance to carbon taxes. *Wiley Interdisciplinary Reviews: Climate Change*, 9, 5, e531.

Carattini, S., Kallbekken, S., and Orlov, A. (2019): How to win public support for a global carbon tax. *Nature*. Accessed 1 May 2021 at: <https://www.nature.com/articles/d41586-019-00124-x>.

Carattini, S., Baranzini, A., Thalmann, P., Varone, F., and Vöhringer, F. (2017): Green taxes in a post-Paris world: Are millions of nays inevitable? *Environmental and Resource Economics*, 68, 1, 97–128.

Cassim, Z., Handjiski, B., Schubert, J., and Zouaoui, Y. (2020): The $10 trillion rescue: How governments can deliver impact. *McKinsey & Company* (June), 13. Accessed 1 May 2021 at: <https://www.mckinsey.com/~/media/McKinsey/Industries/Public%20Sector/Our%20Insights/The%2010%20trillion%20dollar%20rescue%20How%20governments%20can%20deliver%20impact/The-10-trillion-dollar-rescue-How-governments-can-deliver-impact-vF.pdf>.

Coady, D., Parry, I., Le, N.-P., and Shang, B. (2019): Global fossil fuel subsidies remain large: An update based on country-level estimates. IMF Working Paper, 19, 89. Accessed 1 May 2021 at: <https://www.imf.org/en/Publications/WP/Issues/2019/05/02/Global-Fossil-Fuel-Subsidies-Remain-Large-An-Update-Based-on-Country-Level-Estimates-46509>.

Fischedick, M., and Schneidewind, U. (2020): Folgen der Corona-Krise und Klimaschutz: Langfristige Zukunftsgestaltung im Blick behalten (March). Accessed 1 May 2021 at: <https://wupperinst.org/a/wi/a/s/ad/7264>.

FÖS (2019): Die Finanzierung Deutschlands über Steuern auf Arbeit, Kapital und Umweltverschmutzung. Berlin. Forum Ökologisch-Soziale Markwirtschaft, 2019. Accessed 1 May 2021 at: <http://www.foes.de/pdf/2019-10_FOES_Steuerstruktur-2019.pdf>.

FÖS and DIW (2020): Der Neun-Punkte-Plan: Beschäftigungs- und Klimaschutzeffekte eines grünen Konjunkturprogramms. Accessed 1 May 2021 at: <https://foes.de/publikationen/2020/2020-06_DIW-FOES_Der-Neun-Punkte-Plan.pdf>.

Guterres, António (2020): Opinion: A time to save the sick and rescue the planet. *The New York Times*, 28 April. Accessed 1 May 2021 at: <https://www.nytimes.com/2020/04/28/opinion/coronavirus-climate-antonio-guterres.html>.

ICCT (2020): Aus alt mach neu: Über den (Un-)Sinn einer Kaufprämie für Neufahrzeuge. International Council on Clean Transportation, 2020. Accessed 1 May 2021 at: <https://theicct.org/blog/staff/aus-alt-mach-neu-%E2%80%93-%C3%BCber-den-un-sinn-einer-kaufpr%C3%A4mie-f%C3%BCr-neufahrzeuge>.

IEA (2020): Renewables 2020. International Energy Agency, 2020. Accessed 1 May 2021 at: <https://www.iea.org/reports/renewables-2020>.

InfluenceMap (2020): The COVID-19 crisis and climate lobbying. Accessed 1 May 2021 at: <https://influencemap.org/report/The-Coronavirus-Crisis-and-Climate-Lobbying-23249d39450ff19b441090a6a50174eb>.

Kallbekken, S., and Aasen, M. (2010): The demand for earmarking: Results from a focus group study. *Special Section: Payments for Ecosystem Services – From Local to Global*, 69, 11, 2183–90.

Kiani-Kreß, R. (2020): Höhere Luftverkehr-Steuer trotz Corona? 'Nicht die am stärksten betroffene Branche abkassieren'. Accessed 1 May 2021 at: <https://www.wiwo.de/my/unternehmen/dienstleister/hoehere-luftverkehr-steuer-trotz-corona-nicht-die-am-staerksten-betroffene-branche-abkassieren/25613896.html>.

Krugman, P. (2020): 3 rules for the Trump pandemic. Accessed 01 May 2021 at: <https://www.nytimes.com/2020/03/19/opinion/trump-coronavirus.html>.

Lashof, D. (2020): US coronavirus response: 3 principles for sustainable economic stimulus. Accessed 1 May 2021 at: <https://www.wri.org/blog/2020/03/coronavirus-US-economic-stimulus>.

Lazonick, W., Hopkins, M., Jacobson, K., Palladino, L., Erdem Sakinç, M., and Tulum, Ö. (2020): 4 ways to eradicate the corporate disease that is worsening the Covid-19 pandemic. Accessed 1 May 2021 at: <https://www.ineteconomics.org/perspectives/blog/4-ways-to-eradicate-the-corporate-disease-that-is-worsening-the-covid-19-pandemic>.

Leisinger, C., and Rösel, F. (2020): Kaum mehr als ein Strohfeuer. Evaluationsstudien zu Abwrackprämien im Überblick, 2020. Accessed 1 May 2021 at: <https://www.ifo.de/DocDL/ifoDD_20-03_25-27_Leisinger.pdf>.

Lilliestam, J. (2020): Crises as climate catalysts. *Behavioural and Social Sciences at Nature Research*, 22. April 2020. Accessed 1 May 2021 at: <http://socialsciences.nature.com/users/341377-johan-lilliestam/posts/66603-crises-as-climate-catalysts>.

Mortsiefer, H. (2020): Corona löst Kettenreaktion in der Autoindustrie aus: Tagesspiegel Background. Accessed 1 May 2021at: <https://background.tagesspiegel.de/mobilitaet-transport/corona-loest-kettenreaktion-in-der-autoindustrie-aus>.

ntv (2020): Wirtschaftskrise wegen Corona: FDP befürwortet Pause bei Umweltgesetzen. n-tv.de. Accessed 1 May 2021 at: <https://www.n-tv.de/wirtschaft/FDP-befuerwortet-Pause-bei-Umweltgesetzen-article21653378.html>.

OECD (n.d.): Car scrapping schemes. Accessed 1 May 2021 at: <https://www.oecd.org/greengrowth/greening-transport/car-scrapping.htm>.

OECD (2020): *Coronavirus: The World Economy at Risk*. Paris. Accessed 1 May 2021 at: <https://www.oecd.org/berlin/publikationen/Interim-Economic-Assessment-2-March-2020.pdf>.

OECD-IEA (2020): Analysis of fossil fuels support. Accessed 1 May 2021 at: <https://www.oecd.org/fossil-fuels/publication/>.

RND (2020): FDP fordert Aufschub der Steuererhöhung für Flugtickets. Accessed 1 May 2021 at: <https://www.rnd.de/politik/fdp-fordert-aufschub-der-steuererhohung-fur-flugtickets-RS7P5HLI64UIJW2ACN3RA7SPKY.html>.

Schemmel, J.P., and Schumacher, K., principal authors (2020): Zukunftsfähige Konjunkturimpulse zur Bewältigung der wirtschaftlichen Folgen der Corona-Krise. Berlin: Öko-Institut, 2020. Accessed 1 May 2021 at: <https://www.oeko.de/fileadmin/oekodoc/Zukunftsfaehige-Konjunkturimpulse.pdf>.

Schmidt, S., Prange, F., Schlegelmilch, K., Cottrell, J., Görres, A. (2009): Sind die deutschen Konjunkturpakete nachhaltig? FÖS: Berlin. Accessed 1 May 2021 at: <https://foes.de/publikationen/2009/2009-06-FOES-Konjunkturpaket.pdf>.

Schweinfurth, A. (2009): Car-scrapping schemes: An effective economic rescue policy? IISD Policy Brief. GSI and IISD, 2009. Accessed 1 May 2021 at: <https://www.iisd.org/gsi/sites/default/files/pb2_carscrap.pdf>.

Simon, F. (2020): Green Deal facing delays due to coronavirus, EU admits. Accessed 1 May 2021 at: <https://www.euractiv.com/section/energy-environment/news/green-deal-facing-delays-due-to-coronavirus-eu-admits/>.

Stern, N.H., Britain, G., and H.M. Treasury (2006): Stern Review: The economics of climate change. Accessed 1 May 2021 at: <http://www.hm-treasury.gov.uk/d/bowes_1.pdf>.

The Economist (2020): The epidemic provides a chance to do good by the climate. *The Economist*, 2020. Accessed 1 May 2021 at: <https://www.economist.com/science-and-technology/2020/03/26/the-epidemic-provides-a-chance-to-do-good-by-the-climate>.

Thöne, M. (2020): Von der Schwierigkeit, tragfähig in die Zukunft zu investieren: Und wie es doch zu schaffen ist Plus Nachbemerkung – Zukunftsinvestitionen in Zeiten der Corona-Pandemie. Accessed 1 May 2021 at: <http://www.fifo-koeln.org/images/stories/fifo-dp%2020-02%20thne%20zukunftsinvestitionen-corona.pdf>.

Umweltbundesamt (2019): Ökonomische Indikatoren von Maßnahmen zur Steigerung der Energieeffizienz: Investitionen, Umsätze und Beschäftigung in ausgewählten Bereichen. Dessau-Roßlau; Berlin. Accessed 1 May 2021 at: <https://www.umweltbundesamt.de/sites/default/files/medien/1410/publikationen/2019-06-13_uib_02-2019_indikatoren-energieeffizienz.pdf>.

Walker, P. (2020): Why not encourage cycling during the coronavirus lockdown? Accessed 1 May 2021 at: <https://www.theguardian.com/environment/bike-blog/2020/mar/20/why-not-encourage-cycling-during-the-coronavirus-lockdown>.

WID (2018): World Inequality Report 2018. Accessed 1 May 2021 at: <https://wir2018.wid.world/>.

Wood Mackenzie (2020): Coronavirus impact update: Week of March 16 – Report brochure and key takeaways. Accessed 1 May 2021 at: <https://www.woodmac.com/news/opinion/how-italys-lockdown-is-affecting-power-demand/>.

6. Reconciling EU tax and environmental policies: VAT as a vehicle to boost green consumerism under the EU Green Deal

Francesco Cannas and Matteo Fermeglia

1. INTRODUCTION

In 2019, the European Commission launched the European Green Deal (EGD) as the cornerstone of its policy agenda.[1] Amidst the COVID-19 pandemic outbreak, the same Commission has leveraged the emergency to reinvigorate the economy in accordance with the key pillars of the EGD and with the key objective of the UN 2030 Sustainable Development Goals. While the EGD comprises a comprehensive array of policies and unfolds wide-ranging measures to transition to a low-carbon economy, however, one of the most controversial issues pertains to the alignment of the newly embraced environmental and climate objectives with an ambitious and far-reaching EU tax policy. In fact, a lingering misalignment lies between the EU's environmental objectives and the key tenets of its tax policy. In this regard, the value added tax (VAT) as one of the most comprehensive EU harmonized interventions in Member States' tax policies can prove to be a suitable instrument to drive green consumerism and, therefore, contribute to the achievement of the EGD objectives while ensuring a sustainable path to the post-COVID-19 recovery.[2] Yet, to achieve this, environmental underpinnings pursued by VAT should be duly reconciled with its inherent revenue-oriented nature. In fact, according to well-established case law of the Court of Justice of the European Union (CJEU), the revenue purposes of VAT have consistently prevailed over environmental ones.

This chapter thus aims to overcome the above policy conundrum by offering a proposal for a consumption-based indirect taxation model linked to the carbon emission intensity of production chains with a view to fostering the potential environmental impacts of VAT. In sum, this contribution advocates the use of carbon labeling techniques as one of the underlying elements to benchmark VAT rates in order to influence consumers' behaviors towards sustainable, low-carbon products.

The contribution is structured as follows. Part 2 summarizes the main features of the existing VAT's 'environmental-tax paradox' by providing a comprehensive overview of the most relevant judgments in the CJEU jurisprudence. Part 3 charts the newly developed policy background for VAT within the context of the EGD, moreover highlighting the European Commission's striving towards better coordination between the EU's tax and environmental objectives. Part 4 describes two appealing models developed to apply a full life-cycle thinking throughout the supply chain of different products with regard to their greenhouse gases (GHG) emissions, as assessed through their *Carbon Emission Intensity* (CEI). Part 5 appraises the implications of embedding such life-cycle thinking models into VAT's rates structure. Part 6 concludes.

2. VAT IN THE EU'S ENVIRONMENT-TAX POLICY PARADOX: A PRIMER

The EU has long attempted to ensure complete coordination of its tax policy with its (increasingly) ambitious environmental and climate objectives. Such a major gap has been widely appraised considering the institutional hurdles that have traditionally hampered the harmonization of indirect taxes in order to deploy an EU-wide environmental tax consistently with the integration principle under Article 11 of the Treaty on the Functioning of the European Union (TFEU) and Article 37 of the European Charter of Fundamental Rights.[3]

One of the outstanding examples of the above-mentioned policy gap can be found in the realm of indirect taxation, and in particular with regard to the functioning mechanisms of VAT as implemented by Member States. The paradox unfolded in several CJEU judgments that minimized environmentally-friendly VAT implementation in some Member States. In *Commission v France*,[4] for instance, the Court upheld the Commission's view that the total abolition by France of the right to deduct VAT on diesel fuel constituted a failure in the transposition and implementation of the so-called Sixth Directive.[5] Ever since its entry into force in the late 1970s, VAT legislation allowed Member States to retain certain exclusions provided for under their domestic law when the Directive came into force, which France did on diesel fuel.[6] When, after a number of amendments,[7] the right to deduct VAT on diesel was abolished completely in 1998, the Commission brought an action alleging that a subsequent reintroduction of a total exclusion from the right to deduct VAT on certain expenses was contrary to VAT legislation.[8] Relevantly, the CJEU explicitly rejected the argument brought by the French Government that the legislative amendment at issue was made for environmental reasons and stated that it 'cannot justify legislation which breaches the Sixth Directive'.[9]

Although formally correct, the reasoning of the Court clearly highlights that domestic environmentally-friendly divergences regarding the harmonized VAT legislation are not justifiable unless explicitly provided for with the consequence that, in most cases, revenue objectives shall always prevail over environmental policies.

On a similar note, in the 2015 *Commission v United Kingdom* case,[10] the CJEU stated that, by applying a reduced VAT rate to supplies of services of installing energy-saving materials, the United Kingdom (UK) failed in implementing the VAT Directive.[11] The case originates from an action brought by the Commission which disputed the transposition of Annex III of the Directive in the British legislation under the Value Added Tax Act 1994. In particular, the Commission held the view that the reference to the 'provision, construction, renovation and alteration of housing, as part of a social policy' can encompass the application of reduced rates on 'supplies of services of installing energy-saving materials in (a) residential accommodation; or (b) a building intended for use solely for a relevant charitable purpose'.[12] Accordingly, the mentioned statutory terminology should have been interpreted in the context that it is only the supply of housing in itself that must be considered as part of a social policy with the consequence that the promotion of energy-saving materials in the general housing stock does not constitute such a social policy.

For what is relevant herein, it has to be emphasized that the CJEU considered that the reduced rate at issue was adopted by the UK not exclusively on the grounds of social interest or, at least, for reasons of principally social interest (i.e. improving the quality of housing and protecting the health of the residents), but to serve environmental or energy policy objectives.[13] Nevertheless, the Court ultimately set aside the piece of UK legislation at issue on the basis that: (i) the extension of the scope of the reduced rate of VAT at issue to all residential accommodation cannot be described as essentially social,[14] and that (ii) goods and services having social or cultural objectives may be subject to a reduced rate of VAT provided those goods or services pose little or no risk of distortion to competition.[15] In this case, despite the formal correctness of the CJEU's reasoning, the situation is witnessed when environmentally-oriented VAT policies are overridden by other objectives, specifically, the preservation of a *perfect competition* within the single market.

3. TURNING THE TIDE IN VAT'S ENVIRONMENTAL-TAX POLICY PARADOX?

The Commission is fully aware that the current legal framework of indirect taxation may hinder the achievement of its environmental and climate objectives. In a working document released in January 2018 accompanying the proposal for amendments of VAT rates, it explicitly states that VAT rate differentiation may, in general, be utilized to help achieve social policy objectives other than revenue raising.[16] Even if VAT is not *sensu strictu* a regulatory tax aimed at influencing behaviors or correcting market failures, it can play a role in achieving objectives that are not necessarily – or not primarily – related to the generation of public revenue. The Commission has also made clear that the shaping of the definitive European VAT system shall foremost pursue a proper balance between the increase in Member States' leeway on reduced rates and any negative impact on the functioning of the single market.[17]

To strike such a balance, however, is all but an easy task in the context of VAT. The Commission working document hence outlines two broad policy solutions in this regard.[18] The first provides for the establishment of a mechanism of constant review of Annex III of the VAT Directive, which contains the list of supplies entitled to reduced VAT rates and should, therefore, regularly be aligned with the evolving environmental and climate policy objectives of the EU. The second solution requires reversing the current principle informing Annex III by introducing a 'negative' supply list. Accordingly, reduced VAT rates may only be introduced if not specifically excluded under the same Annex III.

Importantly, such an approach would not have made it necessary to go to the European Court of Justice in the cases presented above.

Furthermore, the tide towards green consumerism seems to be revived due to the fundamental commitments embraced by the Von der Leyen Commission.[19] Stepping-up the EU's environmental and climate objectives has been put at the forefront of the Commission's agenda. Such ambition is reflected in the EGD, adopted by the Commission in late 2019 as the flagship of its upcoming action. The EGD lays down the roadmap and priorities for a more harmonized, comprehensive, and effective response to tackle climate change and drive the transition to a low-carbon economy in the EU. Notably, one of the major aims of the EGD in this regard is to further harmonize existing EU policy silos in order to enhance their mutually reinforcing dimensions. The EGD thus highlights the potential for tax policies to leverage behavioral change and steer the transformational path to net-zero carbon in the EU's economy while also recognizing the urge for reform. In particular, in the EGD, the design of tax reforms should fully reconcile economic growth, resilience to climate shocks, and distributional impacts. In the Commission's perspective, taxes 'play a direct role by sending the right price signals and providing the right incentives for sustainable behaviour by producers, users and consumers'.[20] In this regard, the EGD stresses the importance of a more targeted use of VAT rates 'to reflect increased environmental ambitions', for example, by supporting less GHG-intensive products.[21] Therefore, the EGD envisages a redesign of VAT in order to foster sustainability of product manufacturing in accordance with a common, circular design and approach with a view to supporting business models that are more sustainable and drive the market towards less environmental and climate impactful products. Furthermore, in 2020, the European Commission adopted its action plan for fair and simple taxation.[22] The action plan is aimed at redesigning the EU's tax system in order to both achieve the objectives of the EGD and support the EU's post-COVID-19 recovery strategy. Importantly, the action plan acknowledges the importance of taxation to 'reach climate neutrality by 2050 as well as the other environmental objectives of the European Green Deal'.[23]

4. GREENING VAT THROUGH A CONSUMPTION-BASED INDIRECT TAXATION MODEL LINKED TO THE CEI OF PRODUCTION CHAINS

The 'greening-up' of VAT does not constitute a novel exercise and is a priority that has already been identified by legal scholars.[24] Although VAT is not per se (and should not become) an environmental tax, the focus on VAT within the broader policy context of spurring green consumerism is justified on manifold grounds.

First, VAT is a well-established mechanism encompassing local and cross-border transactions as well as a broad range of products and services – unlike other forms of harmonized forms of taxation. Second, the VAT rate structure is influential for the decisions of consumers seeking to reduce their expenditures and thus it can be used as an effective lever to either decrease the price of 'merit-goods' or increase those of 'unmeritorious-goods' thus obstructing their dissemination.[25] Third, VAT has high revenue-raising potential for both EU Member States and the EU's own resources. This is important in light of the commitment adopted by the European Commission to finance the overarching COVID-19 Recovery Plan (Next Generation EU) also through its own resources.[26] While a large share of these resources is expected to be drawn from higher EU Emissions Trading System (EU ETS) prices and the future Carbon Border Adjustment Mechanism, VAT could nevertheless meaningfully contribute in this score. In this vein, collected revenues can be used for research and development of low-carbon technologies and recovery of socially depressed areas as a result of de-carbonization of the economy. Moreover, revenues generated from such measures can be used to finance reductions in other pre-existing, revenue-driven taxes thus lowering economic distortions arising therefrom ('double-dividend' theory).[27] It is relevant that the context of the transition to a low-carbon economy precisely paves the way for tax swaps in order to enhance public welfare by both compensating for environmental and climate externalities and providing public goods.

Furthermore, and importantly, environmental (and climate) impacts of VAT differentiation should be appraised throughout the product's entire life cycle, also in order to fully take into account any indirect effects.[28] Hence, a reform of VAT rates is advocated, in order to better align it with the actual climate change impact of product manufacturing in terms of GHG intensity throughout the supply chain while steering consumers' behaviors towards sustainable products. This can be essentially achieved by drawing from existing GHG emissions products' labeling systems.[29] More specifically, CEI ratios as underpinnings of carbon labeling could and should inform the applicable VAT rates. This would subsequently strongly link consumers' expenditures to the carbon emissions generated throughout different products' production and supply chain.

Carbon labeling mechanisms have been extensively developed and applied within and outside Europe as a quantitative tool to reduce GHG emissions in industrial sectors.[30] The assessment of climate impacts in carbon labeling systems conceptually draws from a *Life Cycle Assessment* (LCA) thinking. LCA is now increasingly used to quantify the environmental impacts of products or services by including all processes along their supply chains. The scope of LCA (system boundary) and, therefore, of carbon labeling analysis, includes all processes along the value chain with significant GHG emissions – including, for instance, upstream processes of extraction or biomass production and end-of-life processes. LCA system boundaries can assess the total GHG emissions from the extraction of raw materials to product manufacture up to the factory gate (cradle-to-gate); this is mostly the case for business-to-business (B2B) products. Alternatively, they can assess the total GHG emissions from the extraction of raw materials to the product's manufacture, distribution, use, and eventual disposal (cradle-to-grave); this is mostly used for business-to-consumer (B2C) products.

Carbon labeling programs rely on different models.[31] Among them, the most appealing for application to consumption-based taxation are those aimed to calculate products' CEI ratios rather than their absolute emissions. CEI relates to the amount of GHGs emitted (all relevant GHGs, not only CO_2) either by production unit (e.g., tonnes of CO_2 per tonne of product produced) or economic unit (e.g., tonnes of CO_2 per thousand pounds worth of product produced).

The first model analysed in this chapter is that developed by Zhao et al.[32] Notably, it presents a four-step, dimensionless system based extensively on available inputs from existing public and easily accessible data (e.g., on gross domestic product and national greenhouse emissions levels from the World Bank databases). This methodology first calculates the basic indicator defined as CEI. CEI is obtained by putting the GHG emissions of the product derived

LCA (in kg per functional unit) as the nominator and placing the retail price of the product at that year as the denominator.

Second, a baseline dimensionless indicator, the *National Carbon Emissions Intensity* (NCEI), is developed as the ratio between the national GHG direct emissions (nominator) and the same country's gross domestic product (GDP) over the same year (denominator). The NCEI allows to forego fluctuations in retail prices (e.g., due to inflation while assessing different products' CEI). In addition, The NCEI facilitates comparison of CEI between like products over a specific timeframe.

Third, the *Carbon Emission Intensity Ratio* (CEIR) is calculated as the ratio between the CEI (nominator) and the NCEI (denominator). Since the NCEI would remain constant for successive years, any variation in the CEIR indicator would be accounted for primarily by changes in carbon emissions per product unit for the given product. A mean value (μ) is then calculated by summing up the CEIR values of all products analysed and dividing them by the number of the same measured products. A standard deviation of GHG intensity ratio for each product is also calculated in order to fully reflect the discrepancies between a specific product's CEIR and the mean.

Fourth, the CEIRs of the different products are clustered along five different ranges of deviation from μ according to their specific carbon emissions intensity ratio: Extremely low; Low; Medium; High; Extremely high.

The second model to appraise products' CEI is that developed by Meinrenken et al.[33] This model allows calculating the carbon intensity of a wide variety of products and sectors from 50 countries – including the United States, Canada, the EU (23 Member States, except Bulgaria, Croatia, Slovakia, and Slovenia), and Japan – as broken down in each main step of the value chain: (i) *Upstream*, that is, the supply chain (e.g., acquisition and pre-processing of raw materials); (ii) The reporting company's own *direct operations* (e.g., factory energy consumption while assembling the product); and (iii) *Downstream* (e.g., energy consumption during the product's use). The method is based on available data of products' carbon footprints as reported by 145 companies in relation to each step of the LCA assessment through the Carbon Disclosure Project (CDP) questionnaires for the years 2013–17.[34] Based on this data, the CEI of each product (in kg CO2eq) is defined to enable comparisons across products of similar weight and size. Next, all identified CEI values are mapped and grouped into a set of overarching industrial sectors to ensure statistically robust sample sizes and similarity between analysed products. Moreover, in this step, each product's CEI is mapped into the threefold cycle stages (i.e., upstream, direct operations, and downstream), plus some stand-alone life-cycle stages, namely transport and end-life. Last, any reported changes in products' carbon intensity vis-à-vis previous reporting due to modifications in the overall product's life cycle or in the applied LCA model is accounted for to fine tune the final carbon intensity calculations.

5. APPLICATION OF LCA-BASED CARBON INTENSITY MODELS TO VAT: CRITICAL REMARKS

Both of the above models are primarily conceptualized to inform packaging of products or to be applied within the context of broader labeling processes (e.g., the Ecolabel scheme under Regulation no. 66/2010/EU). Nonetheless, this chapter argues that such models should be leveraged to also inform VAT rates. Theoretically, this could be achieved by aligning VAT's rate structure with the key indicators of the carbon intensity models. More specifically, two options for reform of the VAT system can be deployed accordingly.

First, the standard VAT rate could be applied by Member States to products with high CEI ratios pursuant to Article 96 of the VAT Directive, also in combination with an additional penalizing increased rate under the same article (amended for this purpose). All key elements of the benchmarking model should be established in a specific Annex to the VAT Directive, in order to ensure coherence in its application by Member States for the purposes of VAT rate setting. This can be achieved under three key conditions. First, the conceived penalizing mechanism should be applicable to B2C transactions only. This would stimulate a gradual change in the market direction towards green products and production chains without discrimination between businesses as opposed to, for instance, the introduction of non-deductibility of the input tax paid by taxable persons. Second, such a mechanism should be devised so as to not negatively affect businesses already adopting sustainable production process (e.g., with substantial energy savings or recovery as certified under the EMAS/ISO 14001 systems) or bearing extremely small dimensions. Third, the mechanism should duly reconcile its B2C scope of application with the adequate allocation of compliance costs to the actual polluter, that is, the producers. An option in this regard could be to selectively pre-empt some of those businesses and industries from the mechanism that are merely involved in the very downstream process of the supply chain or that buy and sell their products locally (e.g., a homemade ice cream manufacturer selling its products in two shops located in the same town) and thus are not involved in GHG-intensive activities. The second model presented in Part 4, by breaking down GHG intensity ratios for each main step of the production chain, might be advantageous in this regard.

Second, the model could inform the application of reduced VAT rates to a specific group of targeted products with low CEI ratios under Article 98 of the VAT Directive. More specifically, within the context of the proposed roadmap for the definitive VAT system, this could be achieved by regularly updating the list of products included in Annex III of the VAT Directive according to the results of the CEIR model. Alternatively, all key elements of the benchmarking model should be laid down in a specific Annex to the VAT Directive and coordinated with both Annex III and Article 98 of the same VAT Directive in order to allow for the application of lower rates on products with a low CEI ratio.

As pointed out by the same European Commission, however, to steadily apply reduced VAT rates can result in perverse or contradictory effects.[35] VAT rates are deemed as a poor distributive tool as financially advantaged households tend to benefit more in absolute terms from VAT reduced rates. The authors are aware of such a potential distortive effect as an inherent consequence of reducing VAT rates. Moreover, it is evident that such modification of the VAT rate structure may also imply higher administrative and compliance costs.[36] Yet, reduced VAT rates as designed in the proposed model would provide for significant environmental benefits for a wide array of product categories (e.g., central heating boilers, appliances, construction materials, etc.), that would ultimately outweigh the above-mentioned pitfalls. In addition, to expand the scope of reduced VAT rates might imply an overall loss of public revenues. This can be balanced by an increase in the standard VAT rate and other fiscal or budgetary measures.

Both of the above-mentioned amendments to standard and reduced rates under the VAT Directive could also be designed to target inherent GHG-intensive products' characteristics and components through their production chain as preconditions for mandatory CEI assessment. For example, the CEI assessment could be deemed mandatory for all products for which manufacturing entails raw material extraction activities (e.g., aluminum) or requires long and highly energy-intensive production processes. This should be calibrated, however, in order to minimize arbitrary distinctions between production chains that are key to low-carbon technologies. For example, the production of batteries and solar panels that entails rather significant energy and raw material-intensive production processes for their production are nevertheless crucial to foster renewable energy generation.[37]

At the same time, however, any such reform must not come to the detriment of VAT's inherent neutrality and result in increased public and private transaction costs.[38] Due to its overall neutrality throughout the supply chain, VAT alone bears a limited impact in fostering investments (e.g., in low-carbon technologies) even if doing so would be socially beneficial.[39] An effective policy to achieve distributional objectives should hence rely on an amalgamation of solutions that combines standard and/or reduced VAT rates when possible and measures that are directly targeted at specific goals (e.g., direct subsidies, income tax credits, etc.).[40]

From a purely economic standpoint, such a conceptual model raises a number of crucial issues. First, it must be noted that any carbon emission indicator can be accurate only inasmuch as the inputs from which it draws are accurate. In this regard, the national GHG emissions data used to benchmark the CEI value are likely to vary significantly among Member States. Since it is hardly possible to devise a process-specific ratio for the application of the model, a certain degree of universalization is inevitable. The higher the degree of universalization, the more likely that the VAT rates' design results in unduly disadvantageous taxation on certain products. Moreover, price fluctuation is often only minimally taken into account in these models. This might bias the choice of products to be levied and hence undermine the application of the mechanism.

Next, more in general, the mechanism incites some core questions of governance and legitimacy. On the one hand, to adopt an EU-wide, centralized system would increase the risk of over-universalization as outlined above. On the other hand, to mandate national tax administrations with the calculation and application of the carbon intensity ratio for the purposes of VAT levy might ultimately undermine the entire regime's administrative feasibility. Additionally, Member States may well, when allowed, opt out for some products on these grounds, insofar as such differential treatment is objective in relation to the subject matter and main purpose of the rules to be applied.[41] This has already been the case, for example, regarding the scope of application of the EU ETS.[42] In this scope, the EU's 2020 action plan for fair and simple taxation envisages a more prominent and executive role for the VAT Committee.[43] Accordingly, the Committee should forego its traditional advisory role to become a full-fledged 'comitology' body that would maintain oversight of implementation and administrative coordination of the VAT system as pursued by the Commission. While the reform process of the VAT Committee is still in its infancy, it could be argued that such stronger EU-centered VAT governance could enhance efficiency, lower the overall administrative burden on Member States, and ensure consistency with the internal market (also concerning state aid rules) as well as addressing potential negative spillover effects of national measures at the EU level.

Regarding the legitimacy of this system, it must be noted that the proper functioning of this system lies extensively on data reliability. Most of the data to be used for CEI calculations are found in existing repositories of international organizations and private bodies or should come from the same taxed industries (as happens, to some extent, with regard to the EU ETS). Thus, in order for the system to work correctly, a strong pattern of collaboration between the owner and generators of data (either public or private), public administrations, and a central government is required. Concerning the figures on the economic performance of the different countries collected by international organizations such as, for example, those on GDP made available by the World Bank, issues on the democratic accountability of these organizations could be raised if the data are used as grounds for the levy of taxes. It would be necessary to equip the Eurostat or the European Environmental Agency for this purpose or, alternatively, to rely on the data made available by national institutes of statistics but increasing the risk of an uncoordinated application of the model.

Last, such a system could open the gate for new forms of 'aggressive tax optimization'. Since the model takes into account the functional units of the products, companies might move highly polluting industrial activities as part of the production chain outside the EU, in order for the information on certain production chains to be difficult to access by tax administrations. This should be duly addressed, for example, by providing for cross-border cooperation and by enhancing coordination of the mechanism with other existing or future instruments such as the Carbon Border Adjustment Mechanism regarding imports of goods under the umbrella of Articles 207 and 191 TFEU.

6. CONCLUSIONS

This chapter has argued that a more comprehensive LCA approach should conceptually drive the future design and application of VAT rates in the EU. Importantly, such an approach would reconcile the EU's tax policy with its environmental and climate objectives as laid down in the EGD, moreover heralding demand-driven technological innovation in GHG-intensive industrial processes that still account for 19% of total GHG emissions EU-wide and increasing revenues to foster the recovery in the wake of the COVID-19 pandemic.[44] This contribution draws from the assumption that VAT is a suitable tool to direct consumers' behavior being an already established mechanism covering an extremely large spectrum of supplies to final consumers. In particular, this chapter argues that VAT rates should be designed to duly reflect the GHG emissions intensity of different production chains as enshrined in existing models already applied for products' carbon labeling. This conceptual model constitutes an appealing option in several respects as it relies on extensive reliable sector-specific (if not process-specific) data that can well be extrapolated from existing LCA databases. This contribution aims at being a catalyst for a legal conceptual analysis and thus further economic and more technical appraisal of the proposed model is needed. This chapter hence deals neither with the economic arguments on the unpredictable impacts that a change in the treatment of B2C supplies may have on the intermediate links in the production chain nor with proposals to green-up other taxes (such as excise duties) that are apt to meaningfully contribute to solving the EU's long-standing environmental-tax policy paradox. Furthermore, this chapter acknowledges that several remarkable legal, institutional, and economic hurdles hinder the adoption of such a mechanism, and the urged ongoing process of harmonization of the EU VAT system will face fierce resistance as sovereignty will remain the battle horse of many Member States.

NOTES

1. Commission, 'The European Green Deal' COM (2019) 640 final.
2. Commission, 'Annual Sustainable Growth Strategy 2021' COM (2020) 575 final.
3. A Pirlot, 'Exploring the impact of EU law on energy and environmental taxation' in CHJI Panayi, W Haslehner and E Traversa (eds), *Research Handbook in European Union Taxation Law* (Edward Elgar 2020) pp. 361–88; S Speck, 'The design of carbon and broad-based energy taxes in European countries' (2008) 10 *Vermont Journal of Environmental Law* 31–59, 33–4. For some critics of the lack of environmental considerations in the EU energy taxation directive by legal scholars, who argue that further harmonization is needed so as to align the Directive with the EU commitments in terms of climate change, see A Di Pietro, *La fiscalità ambientale in Europa e per l'Europa* (Cacucci Editore 2016) 20; M Villar Ezcurra, 'State aids and taxation in the energy sector: Looking for a new approach' in M Villar Ezcurra (ed), *State Aids, Taxation and the Energy Sector* (Thomson Reuters Aranzadi 2017) pp. 37–55, at 45–8. For some general considerations, see J van Eijndthoven, 'Energy taxation at the European level: What does it do for the environment and sustainability?' (2011) 6 *EC Tax Review* 283–90.
4. Case C-40/00 *Commission v France* [2001] ECLI:EU:C:2001:338.
5. Council Directive (EEC) 77/388 on the harmonization of the laws of the Member States relating to turnover taxes: Common system of value added tax – uniform basis of assessment [1977] OJ L145/1.
6. ibid art 17(6).
7. Case C-40/00 (n 4) paras 5–6.
8. In particular, the Commission affirmed that it is 'not covered by the derogation provided for by Article 17(6) of the Sixth Directive and is in breach of Article 17(2) of that directive': see case C-40/00 (n 4) para 13.
9. Case C-40/00 (n 4) para 21.
10. Case C-161/14 *Commission v United Kingdom* [2015] ECLI:EU:C:2015:355.
11. Council Directive (EC) 2006/112 on the common system of value added tax [2006] OJ L347/1.
12. See Section 29A of the Value Added Tax Act 1994 and Part 2 of Schedule 7A to that Act, Group 2, headed '*Installation of energy-saving materials*'.
13. See case C-161/14 (n 10) para 14.
14. ibid para 30.
15. ibid para 25.
16. Commission, 'Impact Assessment accompanying the document Proposal for a Council Directive amending Directive 2006/112/EC as regards rates of value added tax' SWD (2018) 7 final.
17. See ibid 14, where it is recalled that the legal framework restricting Member States' autonomy in setting VAT rates was consistent with the objective of achieving a VAT system based on the origin principle, which is no longer current. This explains why the Commission is taking initiatives in this field.
18. ibid 31ff.

19. Ursula von der Leyen, 'Political guidelines for the next European Commission 2019–2024: A Union that strives for more – My agenda for Europe' <https://ec.europa.eu/commission/sites/beta-political/files/political-guidelines-next-commission_en.pdf> accessed 21 September 2020. See also A Šemeta, 'EU tax policy in support of the EU 2020 growth strategy' (The FEE Tax Day 2011, Brussels, 11 October 2011, SPEECH/11/650) <http://europa.eu/rapid/press-release_SPEECH-11-650_en.htm?locale=EN> accessed 3 October 2020: 'taxation, beyond its primary role in raising fair and legitimate revenues to finance public goods, is an appropriate market based instrument to contribute to achieving specific policy objectives. [...] [E]nvironmental taxation can support environmentally sustainable growth [...]'.
20. See Commission (n 1) 17.
21. ibid.
22. Commission, 'An action plan for fair and simple taxation supporting the recovery strategy' COM (2020) 312 final.
23. ibid 1–2.
24. See, among others, Pirlot (n 3); CA Herbain, 'Should VAT be the next environmental policy tool?' (2020) 31 *International VAT Monitor* 69–73; C De Camillis and M Goralczyk, 'Towards stronger measures for sustainable consumption and production policies: Proposal of a new fiscal framework based on a life cycle approach' (2013) 18 *International Journal of Life Cycle Assessment* 263–72; H Kogels, 'Would VAT be an effective instrument for supporting the environment?' (2012) 23 *International VAT Monitor* 172–3; CE McLure, 'Could VAT techniques be used to implement border carbon adjustments? Illustration of VATs and VATCATs – Expanded version' (2012) 66 *Bulletin for International Taxation*, 1–19.
25. For example, the Commission used this premise as a basis in its action plan as appended to its 2007 White Paper on Sport: 'Given the important societal role of sport and its strong local anchoring, the Commission will defend maintaining the existing possibilities of reduced VAT rates for sport'. See Commission, 'White Paper on Sport' COM (2007) 391.
26. Council Conclusions 21 July 2020, EUCO 10/20.
27. See WK Jaeger, 'The double dividend debate' in JE Milne and MS Andersen (eds), *Handbook of Research on Environmental Taxation* (Edward Elgar 2012) pp. 211–29.
28. Institute for Environmental Studies, 'The use of differential VAT rates to promote changes in consumption and innovation, Institute for Environmental Studies', Final Report commissioned by the Commission, DG Environment (Amsterdam 2008) <https://ec.europa.eu/environment/enveco/taxation/pdf/vat_final.pdf> accessed 9 October 2020.
29. See, among others, R Zhao, P Deutz, G Neighbour and M McGuire, 'Carbon emissions intensity ratio: An indicator for an improved carbon labelling scheme' (2012) 7 Env Res Lett 014014, 1–9.
30. See M Canavari and S Coderoni, 'Consumer stated preferences for dairy products with carbon footprint labels in Italy' (2020) 8 *Agricultural and Food Economics* 1–16 <https://doi.org/10.1186/s40100-019-0149-1> accessed 5 October 2020; T Kim, S Lee, C Chae, H Jang and K Lee, 'Development of the CO2 emission evaluation tool for the life cycle assessment of concrete' (2017) 9 *Sustainability* 2116, 1–14.

31. For a general overview, see S Zidoniene and J Kruopiene, 'Life cycle assessment in environmental impact assessment of industrial projects: towards the improvement' (2015) 106 *Journal of Cleaner Production* 533–40.
32. Zhao et al (n 29).
33. CJ Meinrenken, D Chen, RA Esparza, V Iyer, SP Paridis, A Prasad and E Whillas, 'Carbon emissions embodied in product value chains and the role of life cycle assessment in curbing them' (2020) 10 Sci Rep, 1–12.
34. The CDP emission dataset is available at <https://www.cdp.net/en/investor/ghg-emissions-dataset> accessed 3 October 2020.
35. Copenhagen Economics, 'Study on reduced VAT applied to goods and services in the Member States of the European Union' Final Report (Copenhagen, 21 June 2007) <https://ec.europa.eu/taxation_customs/sites/taxation/files/resources/documents/taxation/vat/how_vat_works/rates/study_reduced_vat.pdf> accessed 25 September 2020.
36. OECD, 'Consumption tax trends 2018: VAT/GST and excise rates, trends and policy issues, consumption tax trends' (Paris 2018) <https://doi.org/10.1787/ctt-2018-en> accessed 10 September 2020.
37. S Carrara, P Alves Dias, B Plazzotta and C Pavel, 'Raw materials demand for wind and solar PV technologies in the transition towards a decarbonised energy system', Report EUR 30095 EN (Luxembourg 2020).
38. See, among others, R de la Feria, 'Blueprint for reform of VAT rates in Europe' (2015) 43 *Intertax* 155, 154–71. More in general, see J Owens, P Battiau and A Charlet, 'VAT's next half century: Towards a single-rate system?' (2011) 284 *OECD Observer*, 20–23 <http://oecdobserver.org> accessed 15 September 2020.
39. Although it is strongly focused on distributional goals, see, among others, Institute for Fiscal Studies, 'A retrospective evaluation of elements of the EU VAT system', Final report – TAXUD/2010/DE/328 FWC – No. TAXUD/2010/CC/104 (London, 1 December 2011) 538 <https://ec.europa.eu/taxation_customs/sites/taxation/files/docs/body/report_evaluation_vat.pdf> accessed 30 September 2020, where the example of pollution reduction is proposed.
40. Institute for Environmental Studies (n 28).
41. For example, in agricultural matters the CJEU has consistently held that, in order to be comparable for the purposes of non-discrimination, two situations 'must be considered in the light of the aims of the Community agricultural system' (Case C-6/71 *Rheinmühlen Düsseldorf* [1971] ECLI:EU:C:1971:100, para 14).
42. Case C-127/07 *Société Arcelor Atlantique et Lorraine and others v Premier Ministre* [2008] ECLI:EU:C:2008:728.
43. Commission (n 22) 15.
44. European Environmental Agency, 'Total greenhouse gas emission trends and projections in Europe' (Copenhagen 2020) <https://www.eea.europa.eu/data-and-maps/indicators/greenhouse-gas-emission-trends-7/assessment> accessed 10 October 2020.

PART III

Carbon pricing in Latin America in the pandemic era

7. Carbon pricing in Perú: a matter of climate justice in the Covid-19 context

Carlos Trinidad Alvarado and Daniela Soberón Garreta[1]

INTRODUCTION TO CARBON PRICING IN PERÚ

Nowadays, the discussion around climate change has become more complex. Any climate issue needs to be approached as a social, ethical, and political problem. The impacts of climate change are global and fall with greater force affecting the most vulnerable, such as the poor, indigenous people, women, among others (UN, 2019, p. 4). Precisely, recently, taxation has joined this trend with environmental taxation, due to the incentives green taxes provide for further efficiency gains, green investment, and innovation (OECD, 2020).

In this context, carbon pricing appears as an instrument that captures the external costs of greenhouse gas (GHG) emissions and ties them to their sources through a price on the carbon dioxide (CO_2) emitted (World Bank, 2020a). Carbon pricing's main goal is to internalize environmental costs of the emissions generated by different economic activities.

Also, through the implementation of a carbon pricing policy (CP), countries comply with the international commitments assumed. For example, the Paris Agreement provides the overall framework to hold the increase in the global average temperature below 2°C, over the pre-industrial levels and to reach zero emissions by 2050.

A CP, in developing countries such as Perú, could be more than a climate instrument. It could help reduce the social and economic gaps of some countries in the region, which have been exacerbated by the Covid-19 crisis. Whether different modalities of a CP have been implemented around the world, the social, environmental, and economic conditions in Perú shape the CP types that should be prioritized, as follows: (i) a carbon tax and (ii) fossil fuel subsidies' substitution or elimination. This research aim is to present a proposal of CP to promote energy transition in Perú and to accomplish social equity in a Covid-19 context.

1. SOCIAL, ECONOMIC, AND CLIMATE CONTEXT IN PERÚ

Covid-19 appeared in a context where inequalities and deficient public services arise commonly in the country. Preexistent conditions in Perú are the key to understanding how CP could be a relevant instrument to reduce social and economic gaps, which have been strengthened by the pandemic. Therefore, to achieve both climate and social goals.

a. Peruvian GHG Emissions Profile and Climate Conditions

Peruvian geographic conditions make this country highly vulnerable to climate change. Perú has seven of the nine characteristics of vulnerability identified in the United Nations Framework Convention on Climate Change. There are low coastal areas, arid and semi-arid areas, zones susceptible to deforestation or erosion, zones susceptible to natural disasters, zones susceptible to drought and desertification, highly polluted urban areas, and fragile ecosystems (Cepal, 2014).

Also, Perú is one of the countries which differ from Latin America's emissions profile as its GHG emissions come mainly from the Land Use, Land-Use Change and Forestry (LULUCF) category (51%), followed by Energy (26%) and Agriculture (15%) (Minam, 2016, p.105). Deforestation is mainly responsible for the emissions of the LULUCF sector, which is concentrated in two anthropogenic activities: agriculture and livestock (Piotrowski, 2019, p. 11; Minam, 2016, p. 53) causing 81–93% of the deforestation rate. However, agriculture is the main cause of deforestation with 49–54% (Global Green Growth Institute, 2015, p. 14).

Moreover, the energy sector reaches almost half of the LULUCF emissions and is below the Latin American average of energy emissions, which is 46% (Cepal, 2018, p. 23). Nonetheless, the energy emissions have increased by more than 60% since 2000 (Minam, 2016, p. 71). According to the last Intergovernmental Panel on Climate Change (IPCC) report, global anthropogenic GHG emissions have increased mainly due to economic and population growth, and are now higher than ever (2015, p. 4). This tendency has also arisen in Perú (Minam, 2016, p. 22).

b. Socio-Economic Context of Climate Profile in Perú

In 2018, Perú was part of the group of Latin American countries with the second best poverty levels together with Costa Rica and Panama. Perú's approximate rates of total poverty were between 15% and 20% and extreme poverty was below 5% (Cepal, 2019, p. 99). Nevertheless, as stated by the National Household Survey, in 2019, the monetary poverty index affected 20.2% of the country's population, rural areas being the most affected. The extreme poverty line in rural areas of the highlands, coast, and Amazon is lower compared to urban areas (INEI, 2020a, p. 34).

There is a remarkable interface between the urban and rural spheres in Perú. For example, in 2017, poverty in rural areas amounted to 42.1% of its population, being three times more than in urban areas (14.4%) (INEI, 2019, p. 40). Also, the illiteracy rate in rural areas was 14.8%, while in urban areas it was 3.6% (INEI, 2016, p. 133). On the other hand, for the same year, informality in urban areas was 65% and in rural areas 95% (INEI, 2018, p. 119).

Among the reasons for poverty in these regions are the inefficiency of public policies to mitigate social gaps and the prioritization of economic interests. In 2019, only 21.4% of the population in rural areas had sewers (INEI, 2020b, p. 34).

These conditions make rural and poor populations more vulnerable to the climate change effects.

c. Market Failures and Climate Change in Perú

There are two main market failures regarding climate change that still have not been solved in Perú. According to Gutman, economic theory considers GHG emissions as a negative externality driven fundamentally from the burning of fossil fuels for industrial and energy production (Gutman, 2019, p. 68). Moreover, climate change is associated with the failure of public goods. In other words, anyone, from anywhere in the world, can freely access and enjoy the ecosystem services provided by Amazonian forests, even though their conservation involves high costs which are borne directly by rural communities and, especially, by indigenous peoples (Trinidad and Ortiz, 2019, pp. 273–4). They not only live in a condition of poverty, yet forest policies also require them to sacrifice too much to avoid deforestation: giving up agricultural, livestock, or harnessing activities within their territories and without expecting to have roads, dams, or power plants. However, this opportunity cost is not internalized by the main climate beneficiaries.

As can be seen, there is a pattern in the social and economic correlation of Peruvian emissions: while cities capture wealth and, through consumption, drive the growth of energy emissions, illegal and subsistence activities supply the Peruvian state in rural areas and are the engines of forest conversion and the extension of the agricultural frontier (Trinidad, 2020).

d. **Socio-Economic Instruments for Climate Change**

There are different measures implemented for mitigation and adaptation of climate change in Perú. Most of the tools to correct the market failures associated with environmental issues that the Peruvian government has used have been preponderantly of command-and-control instruments (OECD, 2017, p. 75). Nevertheless, some economic measures to mitigate climate change in Perú have been developed: (i) the Remuneration Mechanisms for Ecosystem Services (MRSE) and (ii) the National Program for the Conservation of Forests for the mitigation of climate change (PNCB).

According to Trinidad and Ortiz, in relation to ad hoc economic instruments, the main axis of climate policies has been the creation of green markets (2019, p. 285). Thus, through the approval of Law No. 30215 and its regulation, MRSE are the schemes, tools, instruments, and incentives to generate, channel, transfer, and invest resources, where an agreement is established between environmental communities and private companies, public entities, among others, to preserve, recover, and sustain the use of the sources of ecosystem services. Nonetheless, the main issue of this instrument is that agreements are strictly voluntary and only the Sanitation sector had successful experiences. In fact, one of its main problems is the lack of financial incentives to involve the private sector (Quintero and Pareja, 2017, p. 163).

The PNCB is an executive agency of the Ministry of Environment which was created in 2010,[2] which aims to conserve 54 million hectares of tropical forests as a contribution to climate change mitigation and sustainable development. Even if the program beneficiaries are native and peasant communities,[3] each community only receives annually S/. 10.00[4] per hectare of forest to preserve[5] (Minam, 2019). Also, there is no clear method to calculate such amount or determine whether it covers the opportunity costs of these communities. It is further noted that this amount corresponds to 1% of the Peruvian monthly minimum wage and 2.8% of the Peruvian monthly basic family provision per person (S/. 930 and S/. 352 respectively).

In conclusion, as Trinidad and Ortiz stated, the two main economic instruments used by the Peruvian state to mitigate the effects of climate change would not adequately reflect the costs arising from avoiding deforestation, especially opportunity costs (2019, p. 286).

2. EFFECTS OF COVID-19 IN PERÚ

The impacts of Covid-19 in Latin America have been severe compared with other regions in the world. Even when Perú was the first country in the region to implement sanitary and economic measures against the coronavirus, it had the highest death rate of the 20 countries most affected by the virus (BBC, 2020).

a. Socio-Economic Effects

Until 6 September 2020, there were 684 000 cases and almost 30 000 deaths from Covid-19 in Perú (PAHO, 2020). As the Peruvian population is approximately 32 million (INEI, 2020c, p. 42), the number of cases and deaths represented 2% and 0.09%, respectively. The main reasons the impact of Covid-19 in Perú has been so challenging are the current levels of informal labor and the inefficiency of the public policies undertaken. The bonds and subsidies granted by the Peruvian government have proven to be insufficient for Peruvian households and have been granted belatedly to some population groups. Additionally, people with less income have been the most affected since the majority depend on a day-to-day income. The employed population of the country is 11 million people, approximately. During the second quarter of 2020, there was a reduction of salaried workers (-40.7%), independent workers (-56.9%), and employers (-69.6%), as well as in the number of unpaid family workers (51.9%) (INEI, 2020d, p.1).

Regarding the economic performance, currently, the gross domestic product (GDP) growth projected for the year 2020 has changed from 4.5% (MEF, 2020b) to -12.0% (World Bank, 2020b, p. 86). This is explained by different reasons, like the impact on labor. In the second quarter of 2020, there was an unemployment rate of 8.8%, 5.2% points higher than the same quarter of the previous year (3.6%) (INEI, 2020d, p.23).

b. Main Impacts Regarding Nationally Determined Contribution (NDC)

As LULUCF and the energy category represent the source of most of the Peruvian GHG emissions, the impact of Covid-19 regarding these sectors is relevant to understanding if there are enabling conditions for a CP in the country. The Covid-19 pandemic has brought a unique scenario to confronting the market failures highlighted before, as energy emissions have dropped and the need to preserve the Amazon has become more evident.

Covid-19's impact has affected in different proportions diverse economic areas in Perú, such as tourism or services and trade. Regarding the LULUCF category, the suspension of economic activities represented approximately 30% of the total budget for protection and preservation of natural protected areas (Sierra, 2020), amplifying the national gap of conservation. Together with the before mentioned, the coronavirus pandemic had a negative impact on deforestation levels instead of the opposite. The latter due to illegal activities such as mining and logging that have continued in regions like Loreto, Ucayali, and Madre de Dios (MAAP, 2020).

Impacts in both categories directly affect the compromises assumed by the Peruvian government through its NDC, as reducing GHG emissions has become more difficult. The reduction in the conservation budget limits the possibility of achieving the goal of reduction for 2030, which is 1.5 million tons of carbon dioxide equivalent (MtCO2eq).

Regarding the energy category, according to the Peruvian Environmental Ministry, Perú has reduced emissions of more than 400 000 tons of GHG only in electrical energy, as it was reported that more than 1 MtCO2eq were not emitted into the atmosphere due to social distancing (El Peruano, 2020). The main GHG emissions reduction has occurred in the transportation category since the measures implemented limited vehicle movements.

The Covid-19 pandemic represents a special scenario for the energy sector, and it has become an opportunity for NDC goals. This situation has underlined the need to rethink Peruvian climate public policies in the context of Covid-19.

3. CONTEXT TO IMPLEMENT CP IN PERÚ

a. The Excise Tax (ISC)

The ISC is an indirect and specific tax levied on the sale and import of goods that generate various negative externalities for society, such as alcohol, fuel, or cigarettes. In the case of fuels, the ISC is an upstream tax applied on production or import activities. Legally, it does not tax final consumers, although there is an economic transfer to them through price. One of its characteristics is that the income collected is destined exclusively for the public treasury.

Fuel ISC revenues are minimal, representing less than 1% of the total revenue of the treasury, amounting to USD 144 million, approximately, in 2019. Although the income from ISC on fuels has decreased, the main reason is the massification of gas and its notable growth inside the Peruvian energy matrix, which has increased from 29% to 75% between 2008 and 2016.

Initially, it was conceived as a traditional oil tax, which had differentiated rates by type of fuel, and which was based on, typically, fiscal criteria. However, after a reform in 2006 (Law No 28694), an environmental criterion was incorporated into the structure of the ISC whereby the most polluting fuels should be taxed with a higher tax rate: the harmfulness index (INC, Spanish acronym).

The INC is calculated weighting the emissions of local pollutants by type of fuel,[6] considering variables such as consumption by economic activity in the country, sources of emissions, technologies available in the market, among others.

b. Problems of the ISC

The INC calculated for the ISC is based on internalizing the negative externalities of the local pollutants produced by the combustion of fossil fuels. Although the INC seeks to reflect the negative externalities produced by fuels in relation to people's health. The INC does not present a direct link with environmental costs, as it does not fall on the source of contamination (Patón García, 2016, p. 113). In this sense, according to Trinidad and Ortiz (2019, p. 299–301), the ISC presents the following limits to achieving its environmental goals:

- The ISC was created as a tax collection and its late acquisition of extra-fiscal nuances makes it ineffective to mobilize preferences.
- INC does not include the CO2 emissions. Thus, it does not reflect the value of the negative environmental externality in terms of the volume of GHG emissions from fuels.
- It does not provide effective information of/to consumers regarding the relationship between ISC and its environmental purposes.
- The policy to apply INC has not been consistent over time, insofar as certain fuels with higher pollution had a lower ISC, compared with others with lower GHG emissions.
- The establishment of the INC has not been accompanied by comprehensive energy transition policies leading to decarbonization.
- Its income belongs to the public treasury and is not distributed to finance environmental and social issues.

In addition, ISC presents a unique political framework in Perú and Latin America. In general, all tax rates are determined by the Congress of the Peruvian Republic, yet the ISC is an exception to this rule due to a special delegation of powers. The ISC rates are fixed by a regulation of lower level, namely, a Supreme Decree, which belongs to the Executive Power jurisdiction. Therefore, the ISC can be easily changed, especially, by political and economic circumstances, which explains why INC is not a solid policy at present.

c. GHG Emission Subsidies

Perú has various fuel subsidies, but the most prevalent in the national economy are: (i) tax incentives for the promotion of investment in the Amazon, (ii) Fuel Price Stabilization Fund (FEPC, Spanish acronym), and (iii) the Energy Social Inclusion Fund (FISE, Spanish acronym) (APEC, 2015). For the 2008–14 period, the first two represented on average about 0.3% of the Peruvian annual GDP and, in general, energy subsidies represented 1% of GDP for the same period (Marchán et al., 2017).

i.   **Fossil fuels**

Regarding the general panorama of fiscal subsidies for fossil fuels, the Peruvian regulation presents various tax incentives and benefits. Such tax incentives and benefits report a potential collection, which amounted at least USD 948 million for the period of 2014–19, that the Peruvian state does not record as revenue. On the other hand, regarding transportation, a refund of 53% of the ISC of the fuels consumed by the transport of passengers and cargo was approved in 2019, representing 0.1% of the GDP for the period 2021–24 (MEF, 2020a, p.231).

It is important to highlight that, according to the 2020–23 Multiannual Macroeconomic Framework, the tax expenditures of the transportation sector represent 0.05% of GDP for the year 2019, while the health sector represented less than 0.02% of the GDP for the same period (MEF, 2020b).

ii.   **Amazon**

The most important, due to their fiscal implications, are the exemptions from value added tax (VAT) and ISC to marketers or final consumers of fuels located in the Peruvian Amazon, which includes various regional jurisdictions and have been in force since 1999. This benefit generated a tax expenditure of USD 676 million for the 2014–19 period. Likewise, only concerning the ISC, this benefit represents, on average, almost 25% of the total income from the ISC to fuels for the same period.

In the case of the Amazon fuels subsidy, the most outstanding of all, to date, there is no evidence that the presence of these tax benefits has been neither effective nor efficient for the development of this area (MEF, 2019a, p.15). The roots of the subsidies in the Amazon and the fiscal cost they entail counteract the impact of the reforms operated since 2006 to internalize the social cost of environmental pollution in the ISC through the INC.

Agriculture subsidies represented in 2019 approximately 0.1% of the GDP for that year. In the period of 2014–19, agricultural subsidies in the Amazon amounted to USD 1 014 869, approximately (MEF, 2019b, p. 141–2).

4.   SHAPING A CP ACCORDING TO THE PERUVIAN CONDITIONS IN TIMES OF CRISIS

Confrontation with climate change effects in Perú necessarily implies mitigation of poverty and inequality. A proposal of a CP in this country should be consistent with energy transition and development policies. Thus, two instruments must be considered for a CP in Perú: (i) the conversion of the ISC to a CP and (ii) substitution or elimination of subsidies for goods with high levels of emissions or services such as transport and oil production.

a. Main Proposal: Transforming ISC

i. Key of the proposal

It is necessary to realign the INC based on GHG emissions, so that the degree of fuels' harm is determined, solely and exclusively, based on their emissions. In other words, the INC will not consider other criteria, as is currently the case. The INC will only limit itself to considering the contribution of carbon emissions from fuels.

In this sense, the ISC will be determined based on the GHG emissions of the fuels, incorporating in their price the monetary value of the equivalent carbon emissions. It is important to specify that the proposal seeks to reflect in the tax the value of emissions for specific fuels.

Moreover, this proposal takes advantage of the ISC institutional infrastructure to ensure the efficiency of the instrument, since the proposal would build an index within the structure of the final price of fuels. Likewise, it would maintain the upstream tax scheme, without generating an additional margin of informality or costs added to those already established. In addition, it would ensure a correct quantification of CO_2eq emissions (Pizarro et al., 2020, p. 37).

ii. Climate potential

The CO_2 emissions of the energy sector, according to the source of emissions, either mobile or stationary, are distributed as follows: (i) the stationary emissions represent 38.51% of the CO_2 emissions of the sector and 10.03% of the Peruvian emissions and (ii) mobile emissions represent 39.18% of the CO_2 emissions of the sector and 10.17% of Peruvian emissions.

This outlook restrains the options of a CP in Perú. First, a tradable emission permit could only cover emissions from stationary sources, hence its emissions reduction potential would amount to 38.51% of the energy sector emissions and 10% of the total emissions.

A downstream tax on emissions, like the Chilean tax, would follow this same pattern, because it could only cover stationary emissions.

On the contrary, an upstream tax on fuels affects the first stage of production or commercialization, therefore it ends up taxing the fuel that is destined for energy or for transportation. For this reason, the coverage of a carbon tax in Perú, based on the ISC structure, would cover both mobile and stationary sources. Hence, according to Pizarro et al. (2020, p. 41), the potential for reducing emissions by a proposal of this type would be 79% of the energy sector and 20% of total emissions in Perú.

iii. Legal requirement

The institutional framework for this proposal does not require any changes, since the same entities that participate in the approval process of the ISC and the INC participate in this proposal. Regarding the regulatory aspects, the proposal only needs a change at an infralegal level, because, to modify the INC calculation method, it is only necessary to have approval by Supreme Decree.

iv. Distributive impacts

In the first stage, the objective of this proposal is not to increase the ISC or to generate additional resources for the Peruvian treasury, but to provide a market signal on the price of carbon emissions that come from fossil fuels. In other words, make visible the relationship between the ISC charged and the use of fuels.

Since the ISC can be modified by the Executive Power, this proposal has the flexibility that the tax rate can be gradually increased by them to get closer to the international carbon pricing average. But, only after an in-depth evaluation of the social and economic conditions for such increase. For example, by analysing the presence of alternatives to fossil fuels in public passenger transport or the massification of gas in Peruvian transport.

It is important to say that there is a difference between this proposal and the current transparency of the fixed ISC on fuels. While the determination method of INC is not clear for the citizens, carbon pricing is a clear instrument that allows the citizens to understand the direct relationship of tax and emissions.

For this reason, this mechanism could help the ISC accountability for people and environmental interest groups, especially, when the Peruvian government decides to change ISC rates of fuels.

Therefore, this proposal does not affect the current price of transportation or energy in Perú and its distributional effects are minimal.

b. Complementary Measures

Despite the presence of fossil fuel subsidies in the Amazon, economic growth rates, in some of the regions, continue to be among the lowest in Perú (APEC, 2015, p. 37). That is the reason for our proposal to contemplate two options: (i) to eliminate general subsidies (agricultural and transportation) and finance gaps to mitigate Covid-19 effects and the public fund that compensates the indigenous opportunity cost and (ii) to substitute specific fuel subsidies in the Amazon and finance development for indigenous peoples and the actions of LULUCF.

According to the MEF, a percentage of the exemptions from VAT and ISC in the Peruvian Amazon would have been used to benefit illegal industries, like smuggling, and to subsidize the costs of illegal mining in the Madre de Dios and Ucayali regions by 68% and 30%, respectively (2019a, p. 5).

Also, the impact of fossil fuel subsidies in Perú usually benefits the households with higher income more than the households with lower income, since the use of fuels differs among them. The demand for liquefied petroleum gas (LPG) is lower in the lowest quintiles and higher in the highest ones.

To optimize public expenditure, social and economic gaps could be prioritized through the elimination of these types of subsidies. For example, public services, access to health insurance, and electrification in rural areas have been particularly affected in the context of Covid-19. By redirecting these incomes, climate justice could be achieved. Additionally, the allocation of these economic resources could finance an environmental payment services program for indigenous peoples. This achieves climate justice as it recognizes the opportunity cost indigenous people assume to conserve the Amazon.

There has been a successful experience of replacing inefficient subsidies for direct cash transfer in the regions. For example, the San Martín region case is distinguished. A substitution of fiscal benefits and subsidies for transfers from the public budget to a public trust to promote investments in public services was conducted. Such substitution had a direct impact on its development. Although the growth of the Peruvian Amazon decreased between 2007 and 2016, the San Martín region grew 0.3%. The difference in the development of the Peruvian Amazon and San Martín region has a direct relation with the reform in the subsidies for the region, which was requested in 2006.

Therefore, the present assessment is justified, as its purpose is to redirect these types of subsidies for social inclusion policies and promotion of the Amazon's conservation. Specifically, the resources could be destined for the PNCB or the MRSE taking into consideration a new methodology and strengthening its regulatory framework to improve the conditions of indigenous people. In this sense, the proposal will achieve not only a more efficient use of public revenue, but also will contribute to the decarbonization of the Peruvian economy, considering the national social issues.

5. FINAL CONSIDERATIONS

CP is an iconic mechanism to mitigate the effects of climate change around the world, especially burning fossil fuels' emissions. However, a CP in developing countries such as Perú may be more than a climate instrument. Our proposal links the two main categories of GHG emissions, LULUCF and energy, and also ties in urban and rural areas. It achieves climate justice by recognizing the different social and economic conditions of the Peruvian population, like the case of indigenous people who face the consequences of climate change. Therefore, people in urban areas would be charged with a carbon tax, while rural communities would receive fair compensation for the opportunity cost each community assumes to preserve the Amazon. This makes sense as indigenous people have a protagonist role in conservation. In conclusion, a CP in

Perú could be a key development tool necessary and fundamental to address both main global issues: climate change and Covid-19.

The impact of the coronavirus pandemic will leave severe consequences in all societies. However, through the implementation of comprehensive instruments that take into consideration both social and climate impacts, economies will be more resilient to future crises. According to the above, a CP in Perú could meet the climate and social objectives by redirecting its revenues to reducing social gaps, for example, and becoming a development tool.

NOTES

1. Carlos graduated in law from the Pontificia Universidad Católica del Perú, postgraduate studies in sustainable environmental management from the University of California, Berkeley, and candidate for a master's degree in business management from the Berlin School of Economics and Law. Currently, he is a Senior Researcher at the Climate Policy Institute. ORCID: 0000-0002-3339-4363. E-mail: ctrinidad@politicasclimaticas.com. Daniela graduated in law from the Universidad del Pacífico and postgraduate studies in renewable energy from the Earth University. Currently, she is a Public Policy Officer at the Climate Policy Institute. ORCID: 0000-0003-0197-5662. E-mail: dsoberon@politicasclimaticas.com.
2. Approved by Supreme Decree No 008-2010-MINAM.
3. Only if they have a property title.
4. Which equals almost USD 3.00.
5. It is conditional on the presentation, approval and compliance with an Investment Plan and compliance with forest conservation and reduction of deforestation.
6. The INC includes the following local pollutants: nitrogen oxides (NO), carbon monoxide (CO), non-methane hydrocarbons (NMHC), sulfur dioxide (SO2), and particulate matter less than 2.5 microns (PM 2.5).

REFERENCES

APEC (Asia-Pacific Economic Cooperation) (2015, July). Peer Review on Fossil Fuel Subsidy Reforms in Peru [versión Adobe Reader], pp. 36–7, 85. Accessed 28 July 2020 at: https://bit.ly/2ZJg8J0.

BBC (2020, August 28). Coronavirus en Perú: 5 factores que explican por qué es el país con la mayor tasa de mortalidad entre los más afectados por la pandemia. Accessed 28 July 2020 at: https://www.bbc.com/mundo/noticias-america-latina-53940042.

Cepal (Comisión Económica para América Latina y el Caribe) (2019). Panorama Social de América Latina, 2019 (LC/PUB.2019/22-P/Re v.1), p. 99. Santiago, 2019. Accessed 15 August 2020 at: https://repositorio.cepal.org/bitstream/handle/11362/44969/5/S1901133_es.pdf.

Cepal (2018, December). Economics of Climate Change in Latin America and the Caribbean: A Graphic View, pp.19, 23, 33. Accessed 14 August 2020 at: https://bit.ly/2ynlLil.

Cepal (2014, December 10). Climate Change in Peru Seen Affecting the Fishing, High Andes' Livestock and Agricultural Sectors the Most. Accessed 15 July 2020 at: https://bit.ly/33NMdUc.

El Peruano (2020, April 15). Perú disminuyó más de 400,000 toneladas de gases de efecto invernadero (GEI) solo en energía eléctrica. Accessed 20 June 2020 at: https://elperuano.pe/noticia/94484-peru-disminuyo-mas-de-400000-toneladas-de-gases-de-efecto-invernadero-gei-solo-en-energia-electrica.

Global Green Growth Institute (GGGI) (2015, October). Interpretación de la dinámica de la deforestación en el Perú y las lecciones aprendidas para reducirla [versión Adobe Reader]. Accessed 22 August 2020 at: http://siar.minam.gob.pe/puno/sites/default/files/archivos/public/docs/interpretacion-de-la-dinamica-de-la-deforestacion.pdf.

Gutman, V. (2019, September). Argentina: descarbonización energética y precios al carbono, p. 68. Accessed 15 July 2020 at: https://spda.org.pe/?wpfb_dl=4161.

INEI (Instituto Nacional de Estadística e Informática) (2020a, May). Evolución de la pobreza monetaria 2007–2019 [versión Adobe Reader], p. 34. Accessed 6 July 2020 at: https://www.inei.gob.pe/media/cifras_de_pobreza/informe_pobreza2019.pdf.

INEI (2020b, May). Encuesta Demográfica y de Salud Familiar – ENDES 2019, p. 34. Accessed 6 July 2020 at: https://www.inei.gob.pe/media/MenuRecursivo/publicaciones_digitales/Est/Endes2019/Libro.pdf.

INEI (2020c, n/e). Estado de la población peruana 2020, p. 42. Accessed 27 August 2020 at: https://www.inei.gob.pe/media/MenuRecursivo/publicaciones_digitales/Est/Lib1743/Libro.pdf.

INEI (2020d, August). Informe técnico N° 03 – Agosto 2020. Comportamiento de los indicadores de mercado laboral a nivel nacional. Trimestre: Abril–Mayo–Junio 2020. Año móvil: Julio 2019 – Junio 2020, p. 1. Accessed 28 August 2020 at: http://m.inei.gob.pe/media/MenuRecursivo/boletines/03-informe-tecnico-n03_empleo-nacional-abr-may-jun-2020.pdf.

INEI (2019, April). Evolución de la pobreza monetaria 2007–2018 [versión Adobe Reader]. Accessed 18 May 2020 at: https://bit.ly/2P4C4dZ.

INEI (2018, November). Producción y empleo informal en el Perú. Cuenta Satélite de la Economía informal 2007–2017, p. 45. Accessed 14 June 2020 at: https://www.inei.gob.pe/media/MenuRecursivo/publicaciones_digitales/Est/Lib1589/libro.pdf.

INEI (2016, May). Perú: Indicadores de Educación por Departamentos, 2005–2015 [versión Adobe Reader]. Accessed 7 July 2020 at: https://www.inei.gob.pe/media/MenuRecursivo/publicaciones_digitales/Est/Lib1360/index.html.

IPCC (Intergovernmental Panel of Climate Change) (2015). Climate Change 2015. Synthesis report, p. 14. Accessed 10 August 2020 at: https://archive.ipcc.ch/pdf/assessment-report/ar5/syr/SYR_AR5_FINAL_full_wcover.pdf.

Marchán, E., Espinasa, R., and Yépez-García, A. (2017, November). The Other Side of the Boom: Energy Prices and Subsidies in Latin America and the Caribbean during the Super-Cycle. Accessed 11 March 2020 at: https://bit.ly/2jZ9G1V.

Minam (Ministerio del Ambiente) (2016, April). Tercera Comunicación peruana a la Convención Marco de las Naciones Unidas sobre Cambio Climático, p. 22, 53, 71 and 105. Accessed 10 January 2020 at: https://sinia.minam.gob.pe/documentos/tercera-comunicacion-nacional-peru-convencion-marco-las-naciones.

Minam (2019). Information request regarding the PNCB: ¿Cómo el Programa de Bosques determina la subvención económica que las comunidades nativas y campesinas reciben a través de las Transferencias Directas Condicionadas (TDC) por la conservación de los bosques? Received by Cindy López (IPC) on 2 October 2019.

MEF (Ministerio de Economía y Finanzas del Perú) (2020a). Marco Macroeconómico Multianual (2021–2024), p. 231. Accessed 16 August 2020 at: https://www.mef.gob.pe/es/?option=com_content&language=es-ES&Itemid=100869&lang=es-ES&view=article&id=3731.

MEF (2020b, n/e). Proyecciones macroeconómicas. Producto Bruto Interno (Variación porcentual real anual). Accessed 16 August 2020 at: https://www.mef.gob.pe/es/proyecciones-macroeconomicas.

MEF (2019a, April). Sustitución de beneficios tributarios en la Amazonía, pp. 5 and 15. Accessed 25 April at: http://www.descentralizacion.gob.pe/wp-content/uploads/2019/04/PPT-Sustituci%C3%B3n-de-beneficios-tributarios-Amazon%C3%ADa-15abr19-1.pdf.

MEF (2019b). Marco Macroeconómico Multianual (2019–2022), pp. 141–2. Accessed 16 August at: https://www.mef.gob.pe/es/?option=com_content&language=es-ES&Itemid=100869&lang=es-ES&view=article&id=3731.

MAAP (Monitoring of the Andes Amazon Project) (2020, August). MAAP #124: Deforestation Hotspots 2020 in the Peruvian Amazon. Accessed 20 August 2020 at: https://maaproject.org/2020/hotspots-peru.

OECD (Organisation for Economic Co-operation and Development) (2020, n/e). Environmental Taxation. Accessed 25 July 2020 at: https://www.oecd.org/environment/tools-evaluation/environmentaltaxation.htm.

OECD (2017). Evaluaciones del desempeño ambiental: Perú 2017, p. 75. doi: 10.1787/9789264289000-es.

PAHO (2020, n/e). Covid-19 Information System for the Region of the Americas. Accessed 19 May 2020 at: https://paho-covid19-response-who.hub.arcgis.com.

Patón García, G. (2016). Fiscalidad ambiental, responsabilidad social y desarrollo sostenible en América Latina: Propuestas para el Perú, p. 113. Lima: Thomson Reuters.

Piotrowski, M. (2019, May). Nearing the Tipping Point: Drivers of Deforestation in the Amazon Region [versión Adobe Reader]. Accessed 7 February 2020 at: https://bit.ly/2QujwVq.

Pizarro, R., Trinidad, C., and Díaz, M. (2020). Informe preliminar de análisis de opciones de precio al carbono en el Perú. Consultoría para la elaboración de un análisis del impacto regulatorio sobre el establecimiento de un precio al carbono en el Perú. Elaborado para el Ministerio del Ambiente, pp. 38–40, 50–51.

Quintero, M. and Pareja, P. (2017). Retribución por servicios ecosistémicos en Perú: orígenes y estado de avance en la práctica y en las políticas nacionales. En Ezzine de Blas, D., Le Coq, J.F. and Guevara Sanginés, A. (coords.), Los pagos por servicios ambientales en América Latina. Gobernanza, impactos y perspectivas. Ciudad de México: Universidad Iberoamericana.

Sierra, Y. (2020, March). Áreas naturales protegidas: riesgos y beneficios del cierre por el coronavirus. Accessed 18 May 2020 at: https://es.mongabay.com/2020/03/areas-naturales-protegidas-coronavirus.

Trinidad, C. (2020, July 22). Cambio climático y pueblos indígenas en el Perú: ¿políticas ambientales o políticas de desarrollo? Accessed 25 October 2020 at: https://polemos.pe/cambio-climatico-y-pueblos-indigenas-en-el-peru-politicas-ambientales-o-politicas-de-desarrollo.

Trinidad, C. and Ortiz, E. (2019, September). Precio al carbono en América Latina: tendencias y oportunidades, pp. 273–4, 285, 299–301. Accessed 2 September 2020 at: https://spda.org.pe/wpfb-file/precio-al-carbono-en-al_digital_6nov_2-pdf.

UN (United Nations) (2019, July). Report of the Special Rapporteur on Extreme Poverty and Human Rights: Climate Change and Poverty. A/HRC/41/39. Accessed 27 July 2020 at: https://undocs.org/A/HRC/41/39.

World Bank (2020a, n/e). Carbon Pricing Dashboard. What Is Carbon Pricing? Accessed 6 July 2020 at: https://carbonpricingdashboard.worldbank.org/what-carbon-pricing.

World Bank (2020b, May). Global Economic Prospects, p. 86. June 2020. Washington, DC. doi: 10.1596/978-1-4648-1553-9. License: Creative Commons Attribution CC BY 3.0 IGO.

8. The Carbon Tax in Argentina is sick with COVID-19[1]

Rodolfo Salassa Boix

I. INTRODUCTION

The Coronavirus pandemic 2019 (COVID-19) is affecting the health and economy of the whole world with critical social consequences, and this new scenario has led many countries, including Argentina, to issue different kinds of regulations in an attempt to contain the spread of the virus and restore economic health (Urquizu Cavallé, 2020). But in many cases these legal reforms have also affected environmental taxes designed to discourage polluting behaviors within the framework of green tax reforms (Schlegelmilch and Joas, 2015).

The green tax reform in Argentina consisted more of ecological tax benefits than environmental taxes,[2] although since the end of 2017 this trend appears to have reversed with the enactment of the Carbon Tax. Leaving aside some isolated controversial cases, this is the only national tax that had an expressly environmental nature according to the lawmakers' statements (Salassa Boix, 2020, 181–204). But because of the way it has been implemented, including in-depth changes with respect to the original proposal, many doubts have arisen regarding that nature. In addition, its ecological purposes were also affected by Decree 488/2020, recently issued within the framework of the economic and social crisis generated by COVID-19.

The national Carbon Tax was implemented through Law 27430 of 2017, which carried out important general national tax reforms and had three main goals for the country: to become a member of the Organisation for Economic Co-operation and Development (OECD); to reduce the consumption of certain liquid and solid fuels; and to finance services, projects, and public works to combat climate change.

The first goal had economic purposes and was one of the main promises of former President Mauricio Macri during his term (2015–19). The other two goals had ecological purposes and were framed within the commitments assumed by Argentina when ratifying the Paris Agreement of 2016 to face climate change.[3] The Argentine government seemed to become aware of the need to address climate problems with effective legal changes, including new environmental tax measures to discourage the generation and consumption of non-renewable energy and to encourage the development and use of renewable ones.[4]

Unfortunately, almost 3 years after the Carbon Tax came into force, none of the three planned goals seem to have been reached and now, with the global pandemic and certain provisions derived from it, the outlook is even bleaker. OECD membership has not occurred yet and, despite the considerable progress made in 2018–19, the negotiations have definitely stalled under the new national government of Alberto Fernández (2019–23), among whose priorities strengthening ties to that organization does not figure.[5] However, our chapter focuses on the two ecological goals.

Considering the climate and health emergency currently affecting the world as a whole, the ecological goals pursued with the Carbon Tax in Argentina, and the economic and social goals of the recent Decree 488/2020, this chapter aims to determine, on the one hand, how effective is this tax in reducing the consumption of certain fuels and financing environmental services, projects, and public works and, on the other, how the provisions derived from COVID-19 could affect it.

For these purposes, the analysis is divided into three sections: first, we will see the Carbon Tax legal regulation to understand its legal framework, how it works, and what products are taxed; second, we will assess its effectiveness, both in reducing the consumption of certain fuels and in financing services, projects, and public works to combat climate change; and third, we will assess the implications that the recent Decree 488/2020 may have on the ecological goals of this tax. All this will lead us to the final conclusions.

II. CARBON TAX LEGAL REGULATION

II.1 Legal Context

Until 2017 Argentina had only implemented the Liquid Fuels and Natural Gas Tax, but without any explicit ecological connotation. At the end of that year, this tax was limited to liquid fuels (natural gas was excluded) and complemented with a new tax that, also through the amount of fuels purchased, attempts to levy carbon dioxide (CO_2) emissions indirectly. According to this, none of the taxes in force levied the specific tons of those polluting emissions. The new tax is regulated in Title III[6] of Law 23966 of 1991,[7] after having been modified by Law 27430 of 2017,[8] by which the general Tax Reform of 2017 was carried out.

The purpose of this Tax Reform was to examine in depth a 'program to reduce the tax burden ... in order to rationalize the tax structure, reduce taxes, and promote economic growth.'[9] But, as we see in this chapter, it was not only conceived to reduce the tax burden since, in terms of environmental protection or digital services, the idea was precisely the opposite. This initiative had five main points: (1) to encourage investment, (2) to formalize the labor market, (3) to improve competitiveness, (4) to seek equity and efficiency in the tax system, and (5) to fight tax evasion. According to the parliamentary debates of the bill, the amendments regarding the Carbon Tax were included within the fourth point, with the idea of modifying the Liquid Fuels and Natural Gas Tax to give it 'a sense of environmental protection.'[10] All this is in the same vein as the commitments assumed when ratifying the Paris Agreement and the concern about the environmental consequences derived from non-renewable energy sources.[11] But beyond the lawmakers' statement, the key is to analyse how this new tax really works.

As a consequence of all this, the Liquid Fuels and Natural Gas Tax has split into two taxes that levy the fuels in different ways.[12] On the one hand, we have the Liquid Fuels Tax, which replaces the historical Liquid Fuels and Natural Gas Tax, but no longer includes natural gas and, on the other, the Carbon Tax on liquid and solid fuels, the combustion of which involves releasing carbon into the atmosphere. Thus, Law 23699, in force throughout the national territory, currently establishes two taxes that levy fuels: Liquid Fuel Tax[13] and Carbon Tax, although only the latter had an explicitly environmental purpose.

II.2 Taxable Event

The tax affects the commercialization of the following fuels:[14] unleaded gasoline, virgin gasoline, natural gasoline, solvent, turpentine, diesel oil, kerosene oil, fuel oil, petroleum coke, and coal.[15] In this way, the tax applies to eight types of liquid fuels and two solid fuels, where the common element is the emission of CO_2 released from their combustion.[16]

Neither biofuels, biodiesel, nor bioethanol fuel are reached by the Carbon Tax when the tax has already been paid on the fuel component. Likewise, transfer of fuels for: (1) export; (2) fishing vessels and international transportation vessels and aircrafts; (3) using it as raw material in certain chemical and petrochemical processes; and (4) cabotage maritime transport, in the case of fuel oil, are all exempt from payment.[17] Definitive imports of taxed fuels are also exempt when they are used by those who import them for certain chemical, petrochemical, or industrial processes.[18]

The legislation considers that the tax is imposed on:[19]

a. those who import the taxed fuels;

b. companies that refine, produce, prepare, manufacture, or obtain liquid fuels or other derivatives, directly or through third parties;
c. those who produce or process mineral coal;
d. carriers or holders of taxed fuels that cannot prove that they have paid the tax or that they are exempt from paying it.

The tax is imposed when:[20]

a. delivering the fuels, issuance of the invoice, or equivalent act, whichever is earlier;
b. withdrawing the product for consumption;
c. verifying the possession of the levied products by the transporters or holders who cannot prove payment of the tax;
d. defining the inventory differences in the taxed fuels.[21]

The tax settlement period is monthly and is based on the tax statements that taxpayers must submit, except in the case of imported fuels.[22]

The tax has an evident international scope, since its taxable event covers not only the sale of fuels within the country, produced in the country, or abroad, but also the importation of fuels. But exportations are exempt from the payment of the tax.[23]

II.3   Settlement Process

The quantifying elements that influence the settlement process are essential to assess the purpose of the Carbon Tax and, therefore, its effectiveness. That is why we will analyse them in the next point. But we can anticipate that the calculation is based on the amounts set in local currency (Argentine pesos: $) for each type of taxed fuel, which must be updated quarterly according to the variations in the Consumer Price Index.[24] This update is justified by the severe inflationary process that Argentina has undergone over the last two decades.

The levy uses different amounts[25] for each of the taxed fuels,[26] according to the updated value by the Federal Tax Office[27] on its official website[28] through General Resolution 4257/2019:[29]

a. $1.063 per liter for gasoline in all its versions;[30]
b. $1.144 per liter for pyrolysis gasoline, solvent, and turpentine;[31]
c. $1.220 per liter for gasoil;[32]
d. $1.314 per liter for diesel oil and kerosene oil;[33]
e. $0.432 per liter for fuel oil;[34]
f. $0.464 per kilogram for petroleum coke;[35]
g. $0.357 per kilogram for coal.[36]

The legislation also empowers the national Executive Branch to increase these amounts by up to 25% for environmental or energy reasons.[37] This power is at odds with the principle of legality (Casas, 2003, 275–84) recognized by the National Constitution[38] according to which all the aspects of the tax must be set by law ('no taxation without representation').

III. EFFECTIVENESS OF THE CARBON TAX

III.1 Effectiveness of the Carbon Tax to Reduce Fuel Consumption

The effectiveness of a tax to modify polluting behaviors is related to the imposed activity in the taxable event and involves assessing whether we are dealing with an environmental or collection tax and, in the first case, whether the taxpayers are changing their behavior as a result of the tax burden. We must not forget that 'the non-fiscal purpose is based on the discouragement of certain behaviors, but not in the fact that the resources are addressed to that non-fiscal purpose' (Milne, 2011, 439). 'If this is not clear, we may be mistaken when classifying as environmental taxes those levies that are really not, since the taxable event does not fulfill any dissuasive function.' (Salassa Boix, 2018, 117).

When we analyse the taxable event, the key is to determine whether the polluting behavior is taxed and whether the tax burden is high enough to actually affect such behavior, because 'for an authentic ecological purpose, the levy must have such a tax burden that it significantly influences the alternatives of potential polluters.' (Salassa Boix, 2018, 104). All of this will help us to define the tax effectiveness to reduce the consumption of the levied fuels, by comparing the taxpayers' behavior before and after the date the tax came into force.

The Carbon Tax is levied on polluting behaviors that contribute to generating climate change, as it includes the consumption of certain liquid and solid fuels whose combustion releases CO_2 into the atmosphere.

Regarding the tax burden, if we analyse the current amounts, it is not clear that the Carbon Tax has a dissuasive role in discouraging the emission of greenhouse gases. Let us consider the case of the most consumed fuel in the country ('super gasoline'). In January 2021 the average price of 'super gasoline' in Argentina is around $71.44 (U$S3.225/gallon)[39] and the tax amount is fixed at $1.063/liter (1.48%). Thus, the percentage of the total price represented by the tax does not seem sufficient to modify the behavior of fuel consumers.

Indeed, during the fiscal years after the Carbon Tax came into force (January 2018) there was a considerable increase in the most widely consumed fuels (gasoline and diesel) compared to the previous years,[40] despite the strong economic recession that started at the end of 2018 in Argentina.[41] In Figure 8.1 we can visualize the variation in consumption of gasoline and diesel over the last

11 years, until September 2020. The key years are 2018 and 2019, because the data from the last year are not reliable to analyse the fuel consumption trend linked with the Carbon Tax, since it was affected by the government mobility restrictions adopted to contain the spread of COVID-19.

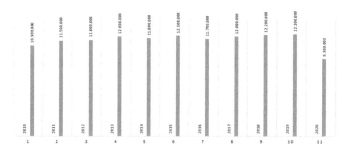

Source: Own preparation based on public information and database from the Observatorio de la Energía, Tecnología e Infraestructura para el Desarrollo (http://www.oetec.org, accessed 4 December 2020)

Figure 8.1 Consumption of gasoline and diesel (M3) – gas stations

III.2 Effectiveness of Carbon Tax to Finance Environmental Expenditures

The effectiveness of a tax to finance environmental services, projects, and public works is related to the destination of its collection and, in the first place, involves corroborating whether we are dealing with an ecological collection tax or not and, if so, whether the funds are actually allocated for that purpose. Although the environmental nature of a tax depends on the dissuasive function, we are able to 'classify the taxes according to the destination of their funds, so that we will be able to consider levies whose collection, beyond the configuration of their taxable event, has an environmental destination or not.' (Salassa Boix, 2018, 117).

In the case of the Carbon Tax, it will be necessary to check whether the regulation allocates its collection to combating climate change and, if so, whether this environmental destination is actually reached (Da Silva, 2012, 5014). To do this, we must analyse the complex legal process by which the collection of the levy is distributed between the nation and the provinces and by which the specific partial purposes are assigned to its collection.

There are two distribution systems: a general one, for the vast majority of taxed fuels, which is regulated by Law 23699,[42] and a special one, for the remaining levied fuels, which follows the rules of Law 23548.[43] In both cases, the distribution process includes two steps: a primary distribution (between nation and provinces) and a secondary distribution (among provinces).

III.2.1 General distribution system

The general distribution system applies to the collection derived from the following taxed fuels: gasoline in all its versions, solvent, turpentine, gasoil, diesel, diesel oil, and kerosene. Primary distribution is carried out as per the following percentages:[44]

a. 10.40% to the National Treasury;
b. 15.07% to the National Housing Fund;[45]
c. 10.40% to the provinces;
d. 28.69% to the Unique Social Security System;
e. 4.31% to the Water Infrastructure Trust;[46]
f. 28.58% to the Transport Infrastructure Trust;[47]
g. 2.55% to the Public Transport Compensation System.[48]

We can observe that a large part of this collection is granted to the National State, since although section (a) specifically mentions the National Treasury, sections (b), (d), (e), (f), and (g) are also intended to cover national expenses, but with specific allocations. Only a minor percentage (10.40%) is directed to the provinces.

In the secondary distribution, the province funds (10.40%) are distributed among them as follows:[49]

a. 60% for the provincial highway administrations;[50]
b. 30% to finance electrical energy infrastructure works and public works in general, according to the percentages fixed by Law 23548[51] for each province;
c. 10% for the Interior Special Electricity Development Fund, administered by the Federal Electricity Council.[52]

The general system specifies a different destination of funds for particular expenditures. Considering the part assigned to the nation in the primary distribution, a large part of the collection is applied to expenses related to housing, social security, and water and transport public works. Considering the part assigned to the provinces in the secondary distribution (10.40% of the total), everything has a specific allocation related to highway, infrastructure, and electrical development public works. We conclude then that there are no specific allocations directly linked to the environment and climate change.

The original bill provided that a generous part of the collection would be destined to finance 'programs and actions of the Executive Branch aimed at encouraging renewable and efficient energy and other specific programs related to the reduction of greenhouse gas emissions within the scope of the Ministry of Energy and Mining.'[53] Unfortunately, this point was modified in the final version due to political negotiations, affecting the ecological purpose of the Carbon Tax.

III.2.2 Special distribution system

The special distribution system applies to the collection derived from fuel oil, petroleum coke, and coal. Its collection integrates the funds that Law 23548 distributes together with the rest of the national taxes.[54]

These funds are distributed primarily among the Nation (42.34%); the provinces (54.66%); an extra amount for certain provinces (Buenos Aires, Chubut, Neuquén and Santa Cruz) that need to recover their relative level compared to the rest (2%), and the National Treasury Contribution Fund for the provinces (1%).[55] Likewise, the nation delivers 3.75% of its funds to the Autonomous City of Buenos Aires[56] and 0.7% to the Province of Tierra del Fuego,[57] since they are not included in the primary distribution.[58]

In the secondary distribution, the portion that corresponds to the provinces (54.66%) is distributed[59] according to different percentages for each one.[60] Unlike the previous regime, none of these cases reflect a specific allocation of the funds, since the provisions establish how they should be distributed, but do not determine how they should be used. Hence there are no specific allocations linked to the environment and climate change.

IV. IMPACT OF THE CARBON TAX BY DECREE 488/2020

Since the beginning of the pandemic (early March 2020), like the rest of the countries, Argentina issued numerous regulations to contain the spread of the new virus and stem its economic and social consequences.

Within this context, Decree 488/2020[61] was issued on 18 May to regulate matters related to crude oil in the local market. Among other measures, it was also provided that the last update of the Carbon Tax amounts (July 2020) does not apply to gasoline and diesel, two of the most widely consumed fuels in Argentina. Hence, although the amounts have been updated every 3 months since 2018 as the legislation ordered, everything changed with Decree 488/2020, because for certain taxed fuels the amounts set in the previous update (April 2020) remain fixed at least until the end of the year.

At first this decision would not represent a juridical problem because the Carbon Tax is still in force, except for the inflation that has affected the country over the last years, more than 30% during 2020 (INDEC, 2020b, 3–5), which includes the price of fuels. For instance, during the last 12 months (January 2020/January 2021) the price of 'super gasoline' has increased by

34% (from $53.3 to $71.44), while the tax on this fuel has only increased by 27% (from $0.837 to $1.063).

As a consequence of the recently issued Decree 965/2020 (December 1), which partially modified Decree 488/2020 in order to allow for an update in tax amounts until 15 January 2021, the current year began with a slight tax increase of 13% for the aforementioned fuels: from $0.936[62] to $1.063/liter (gasoline) and from $1.074[63] to $1.220/liter (diesel). As of April 2020, the tax amount for the other fuels increased around 23%, almost twice as much as the other two.

The Decree 488/2020 has economic and social goals. The aim is to lighten the tax burden that levies the purchase of the most widely consumed fuels for the transportation of people and goods and, in this way, to protect the regional economies and the oil industry sector. Despite this, the measure being analysed was unable to prevent poverty in Argentina from reaching 41% of the population (INDEC, 2020a, 3).

Furthermore, the government seems to have failed to consider the negative effects that the outdated amounts of Carbon Tax imply for public spending in relation to its collection (housing, social security, water and transport public works, highway infrastructure, and electric development public works), which is also important to protect the Argentine regional economies and the oil industry sector. Nor does it seem to be concerned about the negative economic effects that CO_2 emissions and climate change generate for the country. In fact, nowadays there are not even any updated official data on greenhouse gas emissions.

Besides these economic implications, this measure has also negative ecological consequences, since it further reduced the meager tax burden of the Carbon Tax on the most widely consumed fuels in Argentina. In January 2018, when the Carbon Tax came into force, 'super gasoline' cost around $23/liter (U$S4.60/gallon) and the tax was $0.412/liter. As a result, the tax burden was 1.8% of the total price. But today, with Decree 488/2020 still in force,[64] the average market price of 'super gasoline' is around $71.44/liter[65] and the amount of the tax is $1.063/liter. As a result, the tax burden of the tax currently represents only 1.48%, that is, it even fell by more than 0.3% compared to the original amounts, despite the increase in the price of gasoline.[66] In Table 8.1 we visualize this comparison.

Table 8.1   Super gasoline's price comparison (2018 and 2021)

Period	Price of 'Super Gasoline'	Carbon Tax Amount	Percentage
January 2018	$23.00/liter	$0.412	1.80%
January 2021	$71.44/liter	$1.063	1.48%

Source: Prepared by the author

The decrees issued during 2020 and the lack of public explanation of them indicate that there is no medium- or long-term plan for fixing the Carbon Tax amounts and that the tax burden will not be updated every 3 months, let alone increased in absolute terms, as expected in 2017. Indeed, updates were initially suspended for 3 months (Decree 488/2020), then for a further 2 more months (Decree 783/2020) and, finally, in December there was a minimal update, implemented at the beginning of January (Decree 965/2020), which will be reviewed at the end of this month.

Although the Carbon Tax, implemented by the former government, does not convince the current government, there is no interest in abrogating it because the revenue is necessary for the state budget, even when its amounts are less than it raised months ago because the updates were suspended. But then nor is the government interested in applying it for the environmental purpose for which it was initially devised. Considering this, its fiscal purpose is becoming more and more evident over the years. If we add to this the lack of updated official data on CO_2 emissions, to monitor the effectiveness of environmental measures, we must conclude that this issue is not a priority for the current government.

Even the original bill of the Carbon Tax presented by the former government was much more ambitious than the final version of the law enacted by the National Congress by the end of 2017. First, higher amounts were intended than those that were finally approved.[67] As an example, gasoline in all its variants was intended to be taxed at the beginning of 2018 with $1.030/liter, but finally $0.412/liter was applied, and fuel oil with $1.297/liter, but finally $0.519/liter was applied. Second, the bill also included natural gas, liquefied natural gas, liquefied petroleum gas, and aero-kerosene, but these were finally removed from the tax. Lastly, the idea was not only to update the amounts to account for inflation, but also to increase them in real terms so that the tax burden would be more effective in modifying behaviors over the years. But the latter did not happen either and, indeed, certain fuels are no longer even being updated, as established by the new decree analysed herein. These latest modifications, which diminish the environmental goal of the tax, derived from the parliamentary negotiations with opposition parties. Without these legal adjustments, the Carbon Tax might not even have been approved.

V.   CONCLUSIONS

Considering the climate and health emergency affecting the world as a whole, the ecological goals pursued with the Carbon Tax in Argentina, and the economic and social goals of the recent Decree 488/2020, this chapter aimed to determine, on one hand, how effective is this tax in reducing the consumption of certain fuels and financing environmental services, projects, and public works and, on the other, how the provisions derived from COVID-19 could affect it.

Regarding its effectiveness, we verify, on one hand, that although the taxable event of the Carbon Tax levies polluting behaviors that contribute to climate change (fuel consumption), its tax burden is insufficient to generate an authentic change of taxpayers' behaviors, since there is no reduction in fuel consumption directly linked to this tax. On the other hand, we also verify that the legislation does not allocate any part of the collection to fight climate change and protect the environment.

Regarding the impact of Decree 488/2020, although it is too early to know whether it will be efficient and useful in reaching its economic and social goals, the latest economic data and reports are not very encouraging. What we do know, however, is that it will affect the environmental goals of the Carbon Tax even more and, therefore, the fulfillment of the commitments assumed by Argentina in the Paris Agreement.

Although the Carbon Tax represented a great advance for the Argentine tax system to face climate change and protect the environment, as there was no such type of tax until 2018, this purpose was met only halfway. At the time of its birth, the political debate in Congress in December 2017 modified the original (and more ambitious) proposal and strongly weakened its environmental characteristics. In addition to this, the recent decree of May 2020, issued because of the pandemic, destroyed any ecological vestige of this levy. As a result of its Article 6 the tax burden of the Argentine Carbon Tax for the most consumed fuels in the country (gasoline and diesel) represents only 1.48% of the total fuel price, which is insufficient to encourage taxpayers to reduce the consumption of such fuels.

In order to reverse this situation, we propose to abrogate or modify the provisions of Decree 488/2020 related to the immutability of the tax amounts, to increase the tax burden in order to guarantee its dissuasive function, to update the tax amounts through legal provisions to respect the principle of legality, and to destine some percentage of the tax collection to face climate change thus giving it greater public acceptance.

The year 2020 will be remembered as the year of COVID-19, a year in which, unfortunately, many people died, companies folded, and jobs were lost. Many legal systems around the world were modified because of this. We hope it will not be also remembered as the year in which the pandemic fatally wounded environmental taxes.

NOTES

1. This chapter has been written within the conclusiones of the research project entitled: 'Derecho Aduanero y medio ambiente: una alternativa sustentable para enfrentar la vulnerabilidad originada por el cambio climático' (2020–21), directed by Rodolfo Salassa Boix and funded by Fundación Séneca of Murcia. Professor in Tax and Public Finance Law (Serra Húnter), Pompeu Fabra University of Barcelona. ORCID ID: 0000-0001-9371-339X. Emails: rodolfo.salassaboix@upf .edu – rodolfoboix@gmail.com.
2. There have been numerous legal cases of ecological tax benefits in Argentina, especially since 2006. The complexity of listing them exceeds the scope of this chapter.
3. This Agreement was ratified by more than 100 countries, among them Argentina with Law 27270 of 2016.
4. Examples are Decree 134/2015, which recognized the emergency of the national electricity sector due to pollution issues and energy shortages; Decree 531/2016, which regulated Law 27191 of 2015 that fixed the second stage of the National Development Regime for the Use of Renewable Sources of Energy for the Production of Electric Power; Law 27270 of 2016, which ratified the Paris Agreement; Law 27424 of 2017, which established the National Regime for the Promotion of Distributed Generation of Renewable Energy Integrated into the Electricity Grid; Decree 986/2018, which regulated the previous law; Law 27430 of 2017, which established the Carbon Tax; and Law 27520, which sets the minimum standards for the adaptation and mitigation to global climate change. All these regulations, except for Law 27430 that creates a new tax, recognize several ecological tax benefits to combat climate change. All this shows that Argentina has not been immune to this problem or to the need to resort to environmental tax measures to face its consequences.
5. It is important to remember that the current president, Alberto Fernández, belongs to a political force (Justicialismo) ideologically opposed to the former president, Mauricio Macri (Cambiemos)
6. Approved by Article 7 of Law 23966.
7. Articles 10 to 13 of Article 7 (Tit. III) of Law 23966.
8. Articles 139 to 145 of Law 27430.
9. This is the statement of Deputy Laspina when explaining the main points of the Tax Reform Bill during the Chamber of Deputies' debate (19 December 2017). A similar statement came from Senator Blas in the debate held in the Argentine Chamber of Senators (27 December 2017).
10. *Idem.*
11. In the future, Argentina should seriously rethink its livestock activity, although it will not be easy at all because it is one of the most important productive activities in the country. Current studies show that 'livestock is responsible for the emission of 14.5% of Greenhouse Gases (GHG), a percentage equivalent to the transport sector. Among the gases emitted is CO_2, but especially methane and nitrous oxide,

two much more powerful greenhouse gases than CO_2' (García de Pablos, 2019, 12).
12. Despite the critical point of view of their detractors, these types of taxes favor the energy independence of oil-exporting countries and promote the development of new industries related to alternative energies (Montes Nebreda, 2019, 51–2).
13. In order to compare this tax, when it was the only tax on fuels in Argentina, with other similar ones from that time in countries such as Brazil and the United States, we suggest the paper by Salassa Boix, 2016 (262–93).
14. Article 10 of Article 7 (Tit. III) of Law 23966.
15. General Resolutions 4233/2018 and 4234/2018 of AFIP (Argentine Federal Tax Office).
16. In the same vein as the Spanish Hydrocarbon Tax, it can be said that 'taking into account the proportional relationship between the CO_2 emissions and the carbon content of fossil fuels, if the structure of tax rates is defined depending on the carbon content of fuels, the special Spanish Hydrocarbon Tax would be equivalent to a tax on carbon emissions' (Jiménez Vargas, 2016, 11).
17. Article 13.II of Article 7 (Tit. III) of Law 23966.
18. Article 8 of the Annex of Decree 501/2018.
19. Article 12 of Article 7 (Tit. III) of Law 23966.
20. Article 13 of Article 7 (Tit. III) of Law 23966.
21. Article 13 of Article 7 (Tit. III) of Law 23966.
22. Article 14 of Article 7 (Tit. III) of Law 23966.
23. Article 13bis of Article 7 (Tit. III) of Law 23966.
24. Article 11 of Article 7 (Tit. III) of Law 23966.
25. Article 11 of Article 7 (Tit. III) of Law 23966.
26. These amounts are applied to the total of the measurement unit included in the invoice or the import destination request (art. 6, Annex, Decr. 501/2018).
27. 'Administración Federal de Ingresos Públicos' (AFIP), in English: Federal Administration of Public Incomes.
28. Article 4 of General Resolution 4257 of AFIP; Article 7 of the Annex of Decree 501/2018, and Article 11, second paragraph, of Article 7 (Tit. III) of Law 23699.
29. See http://biblioteca.afip.gob.ar/cuadroslegislativos/getAdjunto.aspx?i=11619 (accessed 4 January 2021).
30. The starting value (at the end of 2017) was $0.412 (Argentine pesos).
31. The starting value (at the end of 2017) was $0.412 (Argentine pesos).
32. The starting value (at the end of 2017) was $0.473 (Argentine pesos).
33. The starting value (at the end of 2017) was $0.473 (Argentine pesos).
34. The starting value (at the end of 2017) was $0.519 (Argentine pesos).
35. The starting value (at the end of 2017) was $0.557 (Argentine pesos).
36. The starting value (at the end of 2017) was $0.429 (Argentine pesos).
37. Article 11 of Article 7 (Tit. III) of Law 23966.
38. Articles 4, 17, 52, 75.1 and 2, 99.3 of the National Constitution.
39. See https://es.globalpetrolprices.com/Argentina/gasoline_prices/ (accessed 4 January 2021).
40. According to the Observatory of Energy, Technology and Infrastructure for Development: http://www.oetec.org/nota.php?id=4963&area=1 (accessed 4 December 2020).
41. According to Management Solutions and OECD reports: https://www.managementsolutions.com/sites/default/files/publicaciones/esp/Informe-Macro-Argentina.pdf (accessed 4 January 2021) and OECD (2019).

42. Articles 19 to 23 of Article 7 (Tit. III) of Law 23966.
43. Article 23bis of Article 7 (Tit. III) of Law 23966.
44. Article 19 of Article 7 (Tit. III) of Law 23966.
45. Established by Law 21581 of 1977.
46. Established by Decree 1381/2001.
47. Established by Decree 976/2001.
48. Established by Decree 652/2002.
49. Article 20 of Article 7 (Tit. III) of Law 23966.
50. Percentages fixed by the Federal Transport Council according to the provisions of Article 23 of Decree-Law 505/5.8.
51. Articles 3.c) and 4 of Law 23548.
52. According to Article 33 of Law 15336 of 1960 (Electric Energy Law).
53. See https://www4.hcdn.gob.ar/dependencias/dsecretaria/Periodo2017/PDF2017/TP2017/0020-PE-2017.pdf (accessed 4 January 2021).
54. Article 2 of Law 23548.
55. Article 3 of Law 23548.
56. Article 1 of Decree 194/2016.
57. Article 1 of Decree 2456/90.
58. Article 8 of Law 23548.
59. Article 4 of Law 23548.
60. Buenos Aires 19.93%, Catamarca 2.86%, Córdoba 9.22%, Corrientes 3.86%, Chaco 5.18%, Chubut 1.38%, Entre Ríos 5.07%, Formosa 3.78%, Jujuy 2.95%, La Pampa 1.95%, La Rioja 2.15%, Mendoza 4.33%, Misiones 3.43%, Neuquén 1.54%, Rio Negro 2.62%, Salta 3.98%, San Juan 3.51%, San Luis 2.37%, Santa Cruz 1.38%, Santa Fe 9.28%, Santiago del Estero 4.29%, and Tucumán 4.94%.
61. Modified (1 October) by Decree 783/2020.
62. See http://biblioteca.afip.gob.ar/cuadroslegislativos/getAdjunto.aspx?i=10623 (accessed 21 May 2021).
63. See http://biblioteca.afip.gob.ar/cuadroslegislativos/getAdjunto.aspx?i=10623 (accessed 21 May 2021).
64. Modified (1 December) by Decree 956/2020.
65. See https://es.globalpetrolprices.com/Argentina/gasoline_prices/ (accessed 4 January 2021).
66. In provinces like Córdoba, Jujuy, and Salta the price is $76/liter, so the Carbon Tax represents only 1.39%.
67. See https://www4.hcdn.gob.ar/dependencias/dsecretaria/Periodo2017/PDF2017/TP2017/0020-PE-2017.pdf(accessed 4 January 2021).

REFERENCES

Casas, J. (2003). Principios jurídicos de la tributación. In H. García Belsunce (Dir.). *Tratado de Tributación: Derecho tributario. Tomo I. Volumen 1* (275–84). Astrea, Buenos Aires: Astrea.

Da Silva, D. (2012). Tributos verdes: ¿proteção ambiental ou uma nova roupagem para antigas finalidades? *Revista Instituto de Derecho Brasilero*, 1 (8), 5001–19.

García De Pablos, J.F. (2019). El aumento de tributación sobre el consumo de carne. *Quincena fiscal*, 21, 29–50.

INDEC (2020a). Índice de la pobreza y la indigencia. *Informes técnicos*, 4 (181), 1–18.

INDEC (2020b). Índice de precios. *Informes técnicos*, 4 (225), 1–20.

Jiménez Vargas, P.J. (2016). Fiscalidad ambiental en España y su armonización europea. *Quincena fiscal*, 1/2, 1–28.

Milne, J. (2011). Environmental taxation in the United States: the long view. *Lewis & Clark Law Review*, 15 (2), 418–46.

Montes Nebreda, A. (2019). Imposición al carbono, Derecho comparado y propuestas para España. *Documentos de Trabajo del Instituto de Estudios Fiscales*, 1, 1–69.

OECD/OCDE (2019). *Estudios Económicos de la OCDE: Argentina 2019*. Paris: OECD Publishing.

Salassa Boix, R. (2016). Fiscalidad y petróleo: un análisis tributario-ambiental a partir de gravámenes concretos. *Revista de Derecho de la Universidad del Norte*, 45, 262–93.

Salassa Boix, R. (2018). *Tributación y medio ambiente: una alternativa sustentable*. San José de Costa Rica: Editorial Jurídica Continental.

Salassa Boix, R. (2020). La naturaleza jurídica del impuesto al dióxido de carbono en Argentina y su comparación con el impuesto a los combustibles líquidos, *Nueva Fiscalidad*, 2, 181–204.

Schlegelmilch, K. and Joas, A. (2015). *Fiscal Considerations in the Design of Green Tax Reforms*. Venice: Green Growth Knowledge Platform GGKP.

Urquizu Cavallé, À. (2020). Medidas tributarias para el control y el tratamiento de una pandemia, *Quincena fiscal*, 15/16, 9–45.

9. Public finance, taxation, and environment post-Covid-19: perspectives for Brazil

Daniel Giotti de Paula and Lígia Barroso Fabri

1. INTRODUCTION

The pandemic caused by Covid-19 has had a profound impact on all sectors of society. Brazil was already struggling to balance the federal budget when it was overwhelmed by the devastating effect of the new coronavirus, which has already claimed the lives of over 117,000 Brazilians and has drastically affected the country's 210 million inhabitants' routine.

With the onset of the health crisis, the public authority has been under pressure to review its fiscal priorities for 2020, readjusting its budget and strategic planning and, therefore, increasing public spending to meet urgent demands arising from the pandemic. Such spending increase is mostly related to healthcare (expenses with medicines, equipment, field hospitals and the professionals involved), the creation of an emergency financial assistance for the most vulnerable population (informal workers, unemployed and self-employed people) and subsidies to private institutions in general, to foster the economy and safeguard employability.

Brazil will have to deal with several delicate problems post-Covid-19, highlighting the matter of economic recovery and job creation, while fighting inequalities aggravated by the pandemic, in addition to all the factors inherent to the condition of a developing country. To this end, a series of structural reforms is being planned by the federal government, including tax reform, which could boost this subsequent economic recovery phase.

The health crisis rekindled the debate on how countries are dealing with the environmental agenda internally. From this perspective, we consider that this is an opportune time for the environmental protection measures to leave the abstract and prospective fields and be definitively incorporated in the political agenda so that the strategies of economic recovery must necessarily interconnect with the protection of the environment.

After these general considerations, we analyse the preliminary fiscal measures adopted by Brazil, their connection with environmental fiscal policies that have already been adopted over time and reflect on what to expect for the post-pandemic scenario.

2. MAIN FISCAL MEASURES ADOPTED BY BRAZIL TO MITIGATE THE IMPACTS OF COVID-19

The fiscal stimulus package presented by Brazil to mitigate the effects of the new coronavirus stands out in the international scenario when compared to measures adopted by other nations, mainly among those that fall into the category of emerging countries, once the country has invested about 11.8% of its Gross Domestic Product (GDP).[1]

Despite the massive investments made, healthcare experts say that the country's response was slow, fragmented and poorly coordinated,[2] which may have contributed decisively to the limited effectiveness and the high mortality rate[3] in the national territory.

One of the major obstacles pointed out by the study was the lack of coordination in the federal government and the tension between the head of the federal government and the heads of state and municipal governments, the latter being in favor of adopting stricter social isolation measures. Despite the deadlock, several regulatory acts were published at state and municipal levels restricting economic activities considered to be non-essential to a determined period, following the guidelines of public health authorities. Those guidelines recommended to reduce the circulation of people and, consequently, reduce the spread of the new coronavirus and the collapse of the public health system.

From a legal point of view, the Supreme Federal Court (STF) ruled that there would be competing competences between states, the federal district, municipalities and the federal government in the combat against Covid-19, because, based on article 23 of the Constitution of the Republic, second paragraph, all of them can legislate on public health.[4]

In fact, in addition to the restrictive actions, the Brazilian government managed to approve – with the National Congress' intervention – a series of rules easing fiscal ties, allowing for an increase in public spending. Through Legislative Decree no. 06/2020, published on 20 March 2020, the National Congress declared a state of public calamity in Brazil, recognizing that the country would need to invest far beyond what was foreseen and approved in the 2020 budget law (Law no. 13898/2019), thus exempting compliance with the fiscal target for the current year. Constitutional amendment no. 106/2020 also came into force, which instituted the 'Extraordinary Tax, Financial and Procurement Regime', also known as the 'war budget', which allowed the segregation of expenditures made by the federal government to combat the pandemic from those referring to the federal budget. Besides that, it exempted the government from complying with the so-called 'golden rule', which prevents the government from indebting itself with operational expenses.

The Supreme Court also granted a precautionary measure, in Direct Action of Unconstitutionality (ADI) no. 6357, interpreting it according to the Fiscal Responsibility Act (LRF) provisions, to allow that the increase in expenses and the waiver of revenues could be made without observing the need for compensatory measures to the budgetary impact. It was eventually endorsed by the 'war budget'.[5]

In the meantime, the Ministry of Economy released, on 7 February 2020, a balance containing fiscal measures that sought to mitigate the effects of the pandemic,[6] which reached R$ 521.3 billion of primary impact in 2020 (R$ 508.5 billion in expenses and R$ 12.8 billion in revenue waivers).

Among the current expenditures of the federal government, almost half of them are directed to emergency financial assistance, totaling R$ 254.2 billion, consisting of the transfer of R$ 600.00 per month to those most vulnerable citizens, who meet the criteria established in regulatory acts (provisional measures no. 937, 956, 970, 988/2020 and Law no. 13982/2020). Such social subsidy is critical to ensure minimum conditions of survival for the most economically vulnerable population, given the high rate of informal work and the significant increase in the unemployment rate because of the pandemic.[7]

The aforementioned report also mentions expenses with the so-called 'Federative Emergency Financial Aid', aiming at providing financial support to states, the federal district and municipalities, according to Provisional Measure no. 978 and complementary law no. 173/2020, involving direct fund transfers and suspension of debts of subnational entities.

The third large group of expenditures is formed by resources earmarked for the 'Emergency Benefit for Supporting Employment and Income', which go up to R$ 51.6 billion invested until July 2020 (provisional measures no. 935 and 936 of 2020). It has two main goals: (i) granting financial relief to companies whose activities have been reduced or suspended due to the pandemic, and (ii) ensuring the maintenance of jobs in this time of turmoil. This program allows a temporary suspension of the employment contract, and proportional reduction of hours and wages, which can be of 25%, 50% or 75%. Both the suspension and the reduction of working hours are established for a determined period, granting the worker, at the end of the period, provisional stability for an equal period. If the company joins the program, the federal government will pay a percentage of the unemployment insurance amount to which the employee would be entitled.

Resources are also destined to equip the health sector better (procurement of personal protective equipment, respirators, medical and hospital supplies, Covid-19 tests, among others) and to expand assistance programs, such as 'Bolsa Família'. Besides these, they fund emergency programs to facilitate access to credit by companies, in which the federal government invests resources to certain guarantee funds. All other expenses are duly identified in the report made available by the Ministry of Finance, on the federal government's official website.

About the reduction in revenues, based on the aforementioned report released on 7 February 2020, the federal government gave up collecting approximately R$ 12.8 billion, due to the reduction of the tax burden on products aimed at combating the new coronavirus, including the reduction to zero of import tax rates on medical and hospital supplies, Tax on Manufactured Products (IPI) exemption for items necessary to combat Covid-19, temporary reduction of the Tax on Financial Operations (IOF) and credit or temporary exemption on PIS and COFINS, which are Brazilian social contributions involving import and sale operations in the domestic market of zinc sulfate for medicines. In the exemption package, the rates of social security contributions payable to the so-called 'S System' were also reduced.

Following a worldwide trend, the federal government also granted a tax moratorium by extending the payment of a series of taxes, either for companies subject to the real profit and estimated profit regimes or in order to benefit companies included in the special tax regime (Simples Nacional). The goal was to support their cash flow, which was seriously affected by the paralysis of their activities.

The following measures can also be mentioned: (i) deferral of the period for meeting certain ancillary obligations, (ii) extension of the expiration date of certificates of tax compliance, (iii) suspension of collection and inspection acts by the tax authorities for a certain period, and (iv) drafting of a law regulating the negotiation of tax debt, implementing the so-called 'tax transaction' (Law no. 13988/2020) and subsequent infra-legal regulations that granted favorable payment and installment terms involving debts recorded as outstanding debts to be collected.

Other fiscal measures were implemented, not only by the federal government but also by states and municipalities. We focus on the actions carried out at the federal level, considering their greater scope and economic impact when compared to the fiscal actions adopted by the states and municipalities, which are managing emergency health claims, such as maintaining and managing the demands of hospitals and health professionals, since they are the authorities that are closer to the demands of the population.

In a way, considering that Latin America was one of the last regions to be affected by the pandemic, it can be inferred that the fiscal policy adopted by

Brazil was influenced by international experiences and is partially in line with the recommendations of the report provided by the Organisation for Economic Co-operation and Development (OECD), about 'tax and fiscal policy in response to the coronavirus crisis'.[8] The document defines four phases caused by the health crisis and the possible fiscal responses presented by countries according to their peculiarities.

At first, given the virus' outbreak, it is recommended that countries adopt fiscal relief measures aimed at protecting companies and families, safeguarding the maintenance of productive activities. In phase '2', companies must show economic resilience and might need to rely on government assistance to avoid insolvency due to the maintenance of restrictive measures. In phase '3' it is estimated that businesses will be the target of fiscal and tax incentives, especially those sectors most affected by partial shutdowns, such as travel agencies, sports and the music industry, which may need continuous liquidity and solvency support. The last phase shall focus on the recovery of public finance, an opportunity for the countries to focus on the means to overcome the deficits resulting from the measures adopted.

However, as indicated in the report, each country will have its particularities while managing the crisis and must evaluate fiscal measures according to their level of economic development, with no standard solution. The document points out that emerging countries will suffer more from the crisis due to their big informal markets, currency devaluation, increased fiscal deficit, and dependence on consumption taxes.

3. ENVIRONMENTALLY-ORIENTED TAX POLICIES AND THEIR ROLE IN ECONOMIC RECOVERY

It was seen that the government tax measures adopted are, to a certain extent, in line with the guidelines presented by the OECD for the initial phases, and consist of the extension of the payment deadline for certain taxes, the postponement of the deadline for meeting ancillary obligations and some focal exemptions, especially targeting the products used by health professionals to combat the pandemic.[9]

Before experiencing the most severe effects of the global pandemic, the political class was working on a series of structural reforms to boost the country's economic growth, including tax reform aimed at reformulating taxes levied on goods and services, which are marked by complexity,[10] regressiveness and several distortions.[11]

With the onset of the pandemic, the work of the National Congress joint commission, formed to deal with tax reform issues, was initially halted. Until then, two proposals were mostly discussed in the Brazilian parliament:

a constitutional amendment proposal – PEC 45/2019, presented by the House of Representatives, and PEC 110/2019, initiated by the Senate. Despite their specificities, both proposals are focused on simplifying the taxation levied on goods and services through the removal of a series of taxes, providing for the replacement of these taxes by either a Value Added Tax (IVA) or a dual tax, or a Tax on Goods and Services (IBS), inspired by the most successful cases abroad.

At the end of July, the federal government decided to contribute by forwarding the first part of the text regarding the tax system's reform, Bill no. 3887/2020, which foresees the creation of a tax called Social Contribution on Transactions with Assets and Services (CBS), aiming at replacing PIS and COFINS, a project that will be incorporated into the processing of the two proposals mentioned above.[12]

A few months after the implementation of measures to restrict economic activities, in a stage where they are already becoming more flexible, allowing the gradual resumption of non-essential activities, it is clear that the agenda involving tax reform has returned to the center of public debate, including the return of the activities of the joint committee of the National Congress.

What stands out in the existing formal proposals is that almost nothing has been discussed about the sustainable function of taxes and environmental tax policies, which are still incipient in the national tax system. It cannot be forgotten that taxation is an extremely relevant instrument in the scope of public policies and a factor that interferes and guides certain market behaviors, even though this is not the purpose of taxes for revenue collection.

As an important public policy instrument, 'the taxation system needs to operate as a key tool for the internalization of negative externalities, the effective protection of socio-environmental assets and the transition, in due time, to long-lasting development, in a strong sense'.[13] Therefore, taxation must operate as a factor of socio-environmental protection, linked to other economic instruments, due to constitutional principles, in particular article 170, VI, which establishes that the economic order must be founded, among other principles, in defense of the environment, and article 225 of the Federal Constitution of 1988, which states the universal right to a balanced environment, and it is the public authority's duty, alongside the community, to defend and preserve it for present and future generations.

The Brazilian tax system, however, is far from satisfying such imperatives and has counted, for the time being, on specific green initiatives, such as the ecological ICMS, which is a tax on consumption collected by the Brazilian states,[14] tax incentives for renewable energies,[15] green IPTU, which is a local tax on urban estates,[16] and CIDE-fuel, which is an economic regulatory charge.[17]

Although the approach regarding the strategies and instruments that may be adopted by the public authority to afford the post-pandemic fiscal costs is relevant, the country is in line with the roadmap presented in the OECD's report mentioned above, since the phase that aims at the recovery of public revenues should only be prioritized after the subduing of the most critical phases. In such critical phases, the objective should be centered on helping families and companies, supporting them from the health crisis' most immediate effects, considering that Brazil has a large market of 'informal' jobs.

The country will have to deal with the increase in public debt and, consequently, will have difficulties in the macroeconomic context post-Covid-19. Although there are no safe projections, there are forecasts that the economic downturn will be up to 6%, even though the impacts are quite heterogeneous, depending on the sector. Despite the scenario of simultaneous challenges, the moment is of potential inflection, so that the country can resume the development process soon, which should be marked by sustainability. In this sense, 'public policy proposals and robust and objective evidence are critical inputs to guide government action in the short, medium, and long term'.[18]

Thus, the tax reform will undoubtedly be a strategic agenda in the phase of economic recovery. Moreover, following this approach, if well inserted, environmental fiscal policies may have a positive impact on economic growth. In addition to all the arguments that advocate the adoption of certain environmental tax policies, there are also economic arguments that cannot be disregarded for the country to invest in sustainable taxes, especially intending to promote ecologically-oriented activities, which are in line with the proposals of the United Nations Agenda 2030 – Sustainable Development Goals (ODS) – and with the commitments made by Brazil in the Paris Agreement.

In the manifesto 'Convergência pelo Brasil', announced on 14 July 2020, with the consent of former Economy Ministers of different theoretical lines and party colors, it is proposed that the economic recovery involves reducing regional inequalities, creating a redistributive, inclusive and low-carbon-based economy, plus environmental protection and regeneration.[19]

New guidelines have been incorporated into the corporate and investment environment, possibly because of the constant evolution of society's expectations regarding companies, linked to the new demands of consumers and investors who are increasingly concerned about environmental sustainability. Such criteria are known in the corporate environment by the acronym ESG (environmental, social and governance), an indicator that is usually used for investors to assess whether the companies they intend to invest in are environmentally, socially and economically sustainable. It seems that this business analysis practice is gaining more and more space, which justifies the constant inspection by investment companies.[20]

A good example of how such issues are assuming a prominent role in the economic environment can be extracted from the international pressure on the Brazilian government, so that there are effective actions in favor of the environment, in order to combat deforestation and the effects of climate change. As reported at the beginning of the year, a series of wildfires started in the Amazon region at the same time that the World Economic Forum was held in Davos, which adopted the slogan 'Committed to the Improvement of the World'. On one occasion, the Minister of Economy, who represented Brazil at the event, was questioned by external investors about the actions that were being taken in order to safeguard environmental preservation.[21]

Therefore, nowadays, the changes that have occurred in the business environment, which are increasingly aligned with sustainable practices and the influence of foreign capital as an instrument to propel national growth, should influence government decisions in the formulation of post-pandemic macroeconomic strategies. It happens because the state, as an intervener in the economic order, must present proposals aligned with the sustainable use of the environment, under penalty of the country having to deal with the adverse effects of bad choices, among them a possible mass foreign capital flight.

4. POSSIBLE PROGNOSIS OF POST-PANDEMIC FISCAL MEASURES AND THEIR INTERACTION WITH GREEN INITIATIVES

Amid the gradual resumption of discussions involving changes in tax legislation, the federal government's economic team signaled that it is studying the institution of the 'green tax' on carbon emissions, (even though details on the project have not been specified, covering what would be the taxation targets and the collection forecast, for example). Besides that, it was advanced that this proposition would be included in the scope of the 'selective tax', which must be presented for a second time by the economic team, replacing the current Tax on Manufactured Products (IPI).[22]

As previously mentioned, no matter how the tax reform proposals present their specificities and distinct scope (PEC 45/2019 and PEC 110/2019, in addition to the federal government proposal), they all seek to provide greater rationality and simplification of the taxes levied on the consumption of goods and services, whose main objective is to favor the country's economic growth potential.

Currently, the taxable base on goods and services is fragmented and shared between the three levels of the federation, so that the federal government is competent for the PIS and COFINS contributions, which are levied on revenues, and for the IPI, which focuses on transactions with manufactured products. In turn, the states collect and manage the ICMS, a tax levied on the circulation of goods (including electricity) and the provision of interstate and intercity transport and communication services. Finally, the municipality is competent for ISS, which is a local tax on consumption collected by the municipalities.

The proposals seek to unify those taxes, which will be replaced by a single tax (IBS), which collection will be shared between the federal government, states and municipalities.[23] In addition to the IBS, the proposals provide for the creation of a selective tax to be levied on transactions involving certain goods, services or rights.

The big issue that arises is that, up to the present moment, there are no environmental tax instruments in the pending projects in the temporary joint tax reform committee aimed at the transition from a 'brown economy' to a 'green economy'. Having noted this gap, some members of the parliament, with the support of third sector institutions, recently launched a movement in favor of implementing a 'green tax reform',[24] thus forcing the Congress to appreciate the issue.

In this sense, a set of nine proposals for sustainable tax reform was presented to be added to the proposals under discussion in the National Congress, developed within the scope of a working group formed by a set of 12 civil society organizations coordinated within the scope of the Collaborative Advocacy Network (RAC), associated with the work of some parliamentary fronts such as the environmentalist, green economy, ODS, indigenous rights and other fronts related to sustainability and economics. The proposals are summarized as follows:[25]

1: TO GUARANTEE SOCIO-ENVIRONMENTAL PRINCIPLES IN THE TAX REGIME
To ensure that the currently debated reform of the National Tax System is in line with sustainable socio-environmental principles and with the constitutional provisions already established in this regard. The principles to be integrated are prevention, 'polluter pays', and 'protector-receiver'. Harmonization between them occurs through differentiated tax treatment according to the environmental and climatic impact.

2: TO IMPROVE LOCAL CLIMATE AND SOCIO-ENVIRONMENTAL GOVERNANCE – ECOLOGICAL IBS
To create a mechanism within the scope of resources raised by the tax on goods and services for compensation and financial transfer to Municipalities (inspired by the Ecological ICMS) that stimulates good results in local climate and socio-environmental governance considering biodiversity indicators (indigenous lands, conservation units and the remnant of native vegetation), improvements in sanitation and solid waste management indicators and performance in management, mitigation, and adaptation to climate change.

3: TO FOSTER 'SUSTAINABLE' REGIONAL DEVELOPMENT
To create a fund that encourages sustainable regional development, fight against social and regional inequalities and national integration through direct promotion

of productive activities or investments in sustainable economic infrastructure that converge with the national climate change policy, and benefit indigenous peoples, traditional local populations, small and micro-entrepreneurs and family farmers.

4: TO GUARANTEE THE FULL MUNICIPALIZATION OF ITR AND TO ENCOURAGE THE PRODUCTIVE AND SUSTAINABLE USE OF THE LAND WITH CIDE-USE OF SOIL

To adapt the current ITR [Rural Territorial Property Tax] by giving it a fundraising function for municipalities and instituting CIDE-use of soil, with an extra-fiscal function (without revenue generation function) to discourage the unproductive and unsustainable use of rural soil.

5: TO TRANSFORM CIDE-FUEL INTO CIDE-CARBON OR CIDE-ENVIRONMENTAL

To improve the scope, incidence, and effectiveness of CIDE, aiming to combat the emission of pollutants, defend the environment and ensure climate stability, in compliance with item VI of article 170 and article 225 of the Constitution.

6: TO SPECIFY ENVIRONMENTAL EXTERNALITIES FOR SELECTIVE TAX COLLECTION

To improve the Federal Selective Tax proposal, explaining the impact on environmental externalities. Thus, the law that will regulate the tax can guarantee its selective impact on products and services that, measurably, either harm the health, the well-being of the population, the climate, or the ecologically balanced environment.

7: TO COMPENSATE TAXATION ON GREEN ECONOMIC ACTIVITIES

To ensure that different treatment is given to producers and service providers that effectively contribute to the climate and sustainability in Brazil, through the partial return of the IBS paid for activities considered, in law regulation, as 'green' or sustainable (with the creation of a National Register of Green Activities – 'CNAE Verde').

8: TO FORBID BENEFIT CONCESSIONS TO HEAVY-POLLUTING INDUSTRIES

To ensure the premise that tax benefits and subsidies will not be granted to Brazil's huge carbon-emitting industries, by expressly forbidding it according to the Constitution.

9: TO DIFFERENTIATE THE GRADUAL ELIMINATION OF SUBSIDIES

To eliminate, with differentiated and progressive terms, the incentives granted to sectors in line with national and international forestry, climate, and socio-environmental policies. In other words, those less intensive in carbon emissions.

The aforementioned initiatives enrich the debate on tax reform proposals, which did not expressly aggregate environmental tax instruments until then. Such an undertaking is commendable and deserves to be appreciated with zeal and gravity by the members of the parliament. Several of these proposals have been debated for a long time in the academic environment, but, so far, only by a very restricted circle. Their rise to the center of public debate at an opportune moment to address environmental issues leads to the belief that, although such initiatives are not entirely accepted, since they depend on an interdisciplinary analysis, if observed the impacts of their adoption on the economy and its adverse effects, they will bring some practical contribution.[26]

As a whole, civil society should be invited to give its opinion on the feasibility of adopting environmental tax measures. It can be seen that, following the division presented by the specialized doctrine, the proposals revolve around two groups: on the one hand, the forecast of the implementation of environmental taxes, which make certain polluting activities more costly, and, on the other, the incentives for activities that effectively favor climate and sustainability.

The insertion of environmental fiscal policies may help the country to face economic adversities, considering the international experience, by boosting investment in sustainable activities that have special tax treatment, such as companies that operate in the renewable energy sector.[27]

5.   FINAL CONSIDERATIONS

The search for economic recovery based on sustainability will undoubtedly be a remarkable feature in the post-pandemic scenario.

From a brown economy, founded on pollution and the pursuit of profit at any cost, we have moved on to a somber economy, in which the death of people and the closing of businesses appear as social evils. The pandemic caused by the new coronavirus comes out, therefore, as a global alert, so that ecological issues are definitively incorporated into public policies, which in addition to tying the conduct of the public sector, has a fundamental role in the choices made in the private sector, leading to certain behaviors.

Therefore, given the signs presented by economic agents and the well-known warnings presented by scientists regarding climate change impacts, there is no doubt that policies aimed at the environment will play a fundamental role in the economic recovery process. In this sense, although the interdisciplinary debate is indispensable, with the affected stakeholders being called to the center of the debate, we conclude that the current moment is opportune to appreciate in good faith proposals for the incorporation of environmental tax instruments.

Amid sadness and fear, something new can be built, a truly green economy. In order to demonstrate its commitment to this project, we hope Brazil will carry out the structural tax reform it actually needs!

NOTES

1. According to a survey based on International Monetary Fund (IMF) data. Available at: http://web.boun.edu.tr/elgin/COVID.htm(accessed: 20 August 2020).
2. Researchers from Osvaldo Cruz Foudation (FIOCRUZ) carried out a comparative analysis, looking into the results presented by the following Latin American countries: Brazil, Argentina, Chile, Colombia and Peru, regarding the content and the response time to the pandemic. The study provides tables and comparative data between countries, indicating the initiatives and investments in social protection

adopted by governments concerning the spread of the disease in their territories, until 24 April 2020. They assumed that the effectiveness of measures could only be assessed indirectly through the number of confirmed cases and deaths, considering that the measures' effectiveness deserves to be better explored. From the data analysed, they concluded that, among the five countries evaluated, Chile and Argentina showed better performance in the face of the health crisis, despite some negative factors, such as a large elderly population. In turn, Brazil and Mexico stand out for presenting negative results, when considering the contagion and mortality rate curve. The study concludes that 'in a crisis that grows exponentially, the response time seems to be relevant to the success of public policies' (Tavares, Amarílis Busch, Silveira, Fabrício and Paes-Sousa, Rômulo. Social Protection and COVID-19: the policy response of Brazil and largest economies in Latin America. May/October 2020. Available at: https://socialprotection.org/discover/publications/prote%C3%A7%C3%A3o-social-e-covid-19-resposta-do-brasil-e-das-maiores-economias-da (accessed: 21 August 2020)).

3. According to data presented by Johns Hopkins University. Available at: https://coronavirus.jhu.edu/data/mortality (accessed: 20 August 2020).
4. BRASIL, STF, Pleno, ADI 6341, Rel. Min. Marco Aurélio, j. on 15 April 2020. Available at: http://portal.stf.jus.br/processos/detalhe.asp?incidente=5880765 (accessed: 21 August 2020).
5. STF, BRASIL, ADI 6357-MC, Rel. Min. Alexandre de Moraes, j. on 29 March 2020, DJe on: 31 March 2020. Available at: http://portal.stf.jus.br/processos/downloadPeca.asp?id=15342780618&ext=pdf (accessed: 21 August 2020).
6. Available at: https://www.gov.br/economia/pt-br/centrais-de-conteudo/apresentacoes/2020/julho/2020-07-02-transparencia.pdf/view (accessed: 21 August 2020).
7. According to the data retrieved from the weekly edition of the National Household Sample Survey (PNAD) Covid-19, released on 14 August 2020 by the Brazilian Institute of Geography and Statistics (IBGE), 3 million people lost their jobs in the past 4 months, so that the unemployment rate reached 13.7%, which corresponds to 12.9 million people. Available at: https://agenciabrasil.ebc.com.br/economia/noticia/2020-08/desemprego-na-pandemia-continua-subindo-e-chega-137#:~:text=Desemprego%20na%20pandemia%20continua%20subindo,13%2C7%25%20%7C%20Ag%C3%AAncia%20Brasil (accessed: 26 August 2020).
8. OECD. Tax and Fiscal Policy in Response to the Coronavirus Crisis: strengthening confidence and resilience. 19 May 2020. Available at: https://read.oecd-ilibrary.org/view/?ref=128_128575-o6raktc0aa&title=Tax-and-Fiscal-Policy-in-Response-to-the-Coronavirus-Crisis (accessed: 25 August 2020).
9. For a more comprehensive view of how Brazil has implemented tax measures to deal with the pandemic and proposals for paths to follow, especially in the last phase, post-pandemic, see the report prepared by the legislative consultancy team at: de Barros Correia Neto, Celso, Evande Carvalho Araujo, José, and Calderari da Silveira e Palos, Lucíola. Taxation in Pandemic Times. June 2020. Available at https://bd.camara.leg.br/bd/bitstream/handle/bdcamara/40012/tribute% C3% A7% C3% A3o_pandemia_CorreiaNeto.pdf?sequence=4 (accessed: 25 August 2020).
10. On the complexity of tax law, worldwide and especially in Brazil, see Paula, Daniel Giotti de. *A crescente hipercomplexidade tributária brasileira: uma categoria necessária.* In: Revista Justiça Fiscal, Brasília, January/April 2008, pp. 37–40.

11. The distortions in the tax system are so great that many refer to it as a 'tax madhouse'. We can mention the high degree of regressiveness, complexity and incoherence involving taxation on goods and services, poor distribution of the tax burden levied on taxation on income, dysfunctions and legal uncertainty in taxation on payroll and the lack of control and consistency of tax benefits and incentives granted to specific sectors. For more details on the Brazilian tax landscape and the need for tax reform, with analysis of some guidelines, see the study prepared by researchers from the Institute for Applied Economic Research (IPEA), Orair, Rodrigo and Wulff Gobetti, Sergio. Tax Reform in Brazil: guiding principles and proposals under debate. May 2019. Available at: https://ipcig.org/pub/eng/WP182_Tax_reform_in_Brazil_guiding_principles_and_proposals_under_debate.pdf (accessed: 23 August 2020).
12. Available at: https://www12.senado.leg.br/noticias/materias/2020/07/21/congresso-recebe-primeira-parte-da-reforma-tributaria-do-governo (accessed: 24 August 2020).
13. Freitas, Juarez. Função sustentável dos tributos. Tributação ambiental e energias renováveis. Paulo Caliendo; Denise Lucena Cavalcante (Orgs). Porto Alegre, Editora Fi, 2016, p. 225.
14. Mechanism that allows municipalities to receive resources higher than they would be entitled to receive from the transfer of ICMS funds (state tax which collection is shared with municipal entities), due to meeting certain environmental criteria provided for in the respective state laws.
15. As, for example, the 'exemption from ICMS on operations with equipment and components for the use of solar and wind energy' provided for in the CONFAZ (national farm policy council, is a collegiate formed by the Secretaries of Finance or Taxation of the States and the Federal District, responsible for issuing normative acts and agreements) Agreement 101/1997 and the reduction to zero of the import tax rates involving solar energy equipment (photovoltaic modules, inverters and other accessories), as ex-tariffs (Resolution No. 69 and 70, of 16 July 2020, of the Chamber of Foreign Trade (CAMEX)).
16. A type of tax benefit instituted by some municipalities, which grants a reduction in the value of IPTU to the taxpayer who adopts certain sustainable measures.
17. Part of the funds raised is used to finance environmental projects related to the oil and gas industry (art. 177, § 4°, II, 'b', if Constitution of 88 c/c Law no. 10636/2002.
18. Institute of Applied Economic Research. Post-Covid Brazil: contributions from Institute of Applied Economic Research. July 2020. Available at: https://www.ipea.gov.br/portal/index.php?option=com_content&view=article&id=36143 (accessed: 26 August 2020).
19. See 'Carta da Convergência pelo Brasil'. Available at: https://convergenciapelobrasil.org.br/leia-a-carta-na-integra (accessed: 24 August 2020).
20. For further details on this corporate standard, see: https://www.investopedia.com/terms/e/environmental-social-and-governance-esg-criteria.asp#citation-1 (accessed: 24 August 2020).
21. Gregório, Rafael. Davos 'Fits' Brazil for Environmental Reasons, and the Government Moves so as Not to Lose Trillions. January 2020. Available at: https://valorinveste.globo.com/blogs/rafael-gregorio/post/2020/01/davos-enquadra-o-brasil-por-questao-ambiental-e-governo-se-mexe-para-nao-perder-trilhoes.ghtml (accessed: 24 August 2020). More recently, we can also quote the letter sent in August 2020 to Brazilian embassies by 29 funds that manage R$ 20 trillion in

assets in the country, signaling concern about deforestation in the Amazon and indicating uncertainty about the conditions for investing and providing financial resources to Brazil. Available at: https://www1.folha.uol.com.br/mercado/2020/06/investidores-e-deputados-da-ue-elevam-pressao-contra-desmatamento-no-brasil.shtml (accessed: 24 August 2020).
22. Gregorio, Rafael. Davos 'Fits' Brazil for Environmental Reasons, and the Government Moves so as Not to Lose Trillions. January 2020. Available at: https://g1.globo.com/economia/noticia/2020/08/15/reforma-tributaria-governo-estuda-criacao-de-imposto-verde.ghtml (accessed: 24 August 2020).
23. PEC 110 is more comprehensive and also provides for the replacement of IOF (Tax on Financial Operations), PASEP (is a type of social contribution), CIDE-fuel (which is an economic regulatory charge) and the Education Payroll Tax, besides other matters. The comparison can be seen from the information compiled by the House of Representatives, available at: https://www2.camara.leg.br/atividade-legislativa/estudos-e-notas-tecnicas/publicacoes-da-consultoria-legislativa/fiquePorDentro/temas/sistema-tributario-nacional-jun-2019/reforma-tributaria-comparativo-das-pecs-em-tramitacao-2019#:~:text=PEC%20110%3A%20s% (accessed: 26 August 2020).
24. Available at: https://istoe.com.br/congresso-quer-reforma-tributaria-verde (accessed: 26 August 2020).
25. Available at: http://estafaltandoverde.org.br (accessed: 26 August 2020).
26. To enrich the debate, such initiatives can be analysed in parallel with the proposals contained in the OECD Environmental Performance Assessment Report – 2015. OECD – Organisation for Economic Co-operation and Development. Environmental performance assessments: Brazil 2015. Brazil: OECD, 2016. Available at: https://repositorio.cepal.org/bitstream/handle/11362/40895/1/S1700018_pt.pdf (accessed: 26 August 2020).
27. It is worth mentioning a survey presented in the study carried out by the legislative consultancy of the House of Representatives that points out that there was a growth of eco-industry in countries where tax reform was adopted (growth of 8.3% per year between 2004 and 2008. Also, tax reform, together with specific regulations, is considered the most effective environmental innovation approach. Jänicke, Martin and Zieschank, Roland. ETR and the environmental industry. In: Ekins, P. and Speck, S. (org.). Environmental Tax Reform (ETR): a policy for green growth. New York: Oxford University Press, 2011, pp. 321, 324 as cited in Soares, Murilo Rodrigues da Cunha and Juras, Lídia da Ascenção Garrido Martins. Desafios da tributação ambiental. Consultoria Legislativa da Câmara dos Deputados, 2015, p. 261.

10. Tax incentives for electric vehicles and biofuels: a Brazilian case study
Rafaela Cristina Oliari, Carlos Araújo Leonetti and Elena Aydos[1]

INTRODUCTION

Reducing greenhouse gas emissions by the transport sector depends on switching from the use of fossil fuels to low carbon alternatives that are mainly connected to biofuels or electric vehicles. Both technologies can tackle climate change, but they also carry their own positive and negative effects. Most countries in the world rely on the technological development of electric vehicles. This policy is not being followed by Brazil.

In 2017 and 2018, Brazil launched two important regulations regarding greenhouse gas emissions by the transport sector: (i) the RenovaBio Programme that aims to encourage the use of biofuels, and (ii) the Rota 2030 Programme, the successor of the Inovar-Auto Programme, which intends to develop the automotive sector, boost the export of vehicles and auto parts and incentivize research and development (R&D) activities. This chapter examines the incentives provided by both programmes, as well as the previous public policies, to investigate the Brazilian choice to encourage biofuels instead of electric vehicles and the risks associated with this course of action.

The chapter is divided as follows: the first part presents the current data concerning Brazil's greenhouse gas emissions from the transport sector; the second part describes the Rota 2030 Programme, comparing it with its predecessor, the Inovar-Auto Programme, in order to analyse changes in public policy following the resolution of a dispute over that programme before the World Trade Organization (WTO); the third part describes the RenovaBio Programme and the Decarbonization Credit; the fourth part critically scrutinizes the Brazilian choice to encourage biofuels rather than electric vehicles.

GREENHOUSE GAS EMISSIONS FROM TRANSPORT

According to the International Energy Agency (IEA),[2] 'transportation is still responsible for 24% of direct CO2 emissions from fuel combustion. Road vehicles – cars, trucks, buses and two- and three-wheelers – account for nearly three-quarters of transport CO2 emissions, and emissions from aviation and shipping continue to rise'.

The statistics above reflect the emissions in 2019, and it is important to highlight the impacts of the current Covid-19 crisis in all forms of transport. As pointed out by IEA,[3] 'the changing in human behaviour, due to the restrictions put in place, has had huge knock-off effects for oil consumptions, contributing to a 5% decrease in demand in the first quarter of 2020'. The unanswered question that arises from the pandemic is 'whether changes to transport behaviours may result in a permanent change in behaviour (and transport energy use) or if transport patterns will revert to "business as usual" when the crisis ends'.[4]

In comparison with world statistics, Brazil has a different trajectory regarding greenhouse gas emissions. In 2018, the transportation sector was responsible for approximately 10.3% of emissions, while agriculture, forestry, and other land use (AFOLU) accounted for 69% of emissions.[5] Furthermore, Brazil has an overall clean energy matrix, represented by the fact that 45% of the energy and 18% of the fuels consumed derive from renewable sources.[6]

Brazil has pledged to reduce greenhouse gas emissions by 37% below the 2005 levels by 2025, in the context of the Paris Agreement. Brazil's Intended Nationally Determined Contribution (iNDC) corresponds to an estimated reduction of 66% in terms of greenhouse gas emissions per unit of gross domestic product by 2025 and of 75% in terms of emissions intensity by 2030, both in relation to 2005.[7]

According to studies released at the end of 2019,[8] Brazil was targeting an average annual economic growth per capita of 2.55% between 2019 and 2030. However, due to the Covid-19 pandemic the projections for economic growth have changed and there is a high level of uncertainty at this point.

Despite the unclear consequences of Covid-19 for the world, national socioeconomic indicators are still relatively distant from those in the developed countries. For this reason, the Brazilian Energy Research Company (EPE) stated that the main challenge for Brazil, unlike the iNDCs of other countries, is not to increase the renewability of its energy matrix, but to maintain the high proportion of renewable energies, with greater inclusion of the so-called 'new renewables', in a context of growing energy consumption by 2030.[9]

Considering the above and the commitment established in the Brazilian iNDC, Brazil has a long and challenging path towards reducing anthropogenic greenhouse gas emissions. The necessary transition to meet those goals must be driven by a coherent and coordinated set of policies and broad incentives for technological development. In the transport sector, the measures that would be taken by public policies revolve around managing travel, improving the energy efficiency of vehicles, and increasing the availability and use of sustainable, low carbon fuels.[10] The Organisation for Economic Co-operation and Development (OECD) anticipates that transport volumes for non-OECD countries, including Brazil, will 'grow more than twice as fast as in the OECD with 4% annual growth for passenger and 5% for freight transport'.[11]

As far as energy efficiency in the transport sector is concerned, two technologies play a key role in environmental and sustainable objectives: electric vehicles and biofuels. Biofuels are leading, as reported by IEA, 'renewables energy met around 3.7% of transport fuel demand in 2018, with around 4 exajoules (EJ) of consumption. Biofuels provided 93% of all renewable energy, the remainder being renewable electricity'.[12] However, it is expected that the electric car fleet will expand quickly considering that, to date, 2020, '17 countries have announced 100% zero-emission vehicle targets or the phase-out of internal combustion engine vehicles through 2050'.[13]

Historically, Brazil has incentivized the use and production of biofuels, especially ethanol from sugar cane. Over the last decade, however, Brazil launched policies that also intended to foster the technological development of the automotive sector, seemingly in order to incentivize the electric vehicles market. Currently, two Brazilian public policies aiming at the reduction of the greenhouse gas emissions in the transport sector are in place: (i) Rota 2030 that intends to incentivize the technological development of the automotive industry, and (ii) RenovaBio that intends to stimulate the use, production and technological development of biofuels.

On the one hand, Rota 2030 is an industrial public policy, linked to the Ministry of Economy. RenovaBio, on the other hand, is an energy public policy, developed by the Ministry of Mines and Energy. Whereas these policies have different origins, it is important to investigate whether they are coherent with each other and whether they are able to incentivize not only biofuels but also the development of the electric vehicles market in Brazil.

The IEA Special Report concluded that 'innovation policy and energy policy need to be considered together, and that clean energy technology innovation should be seen as a core element in energy policy decision making'.[14] Thus, in order to assess the main Brazilian innovation and energy policies for the transport sector, this chapter analyses the so-called Rota 2030 and RenovaBio programmes.

THE ROTA 2030 PROGRAMME

The automotive sector has been a permanent client of Brazilian public policies.[15] From 1950 to 2017, this industrial field experienced a repetitive and permanent cycle: a *sector crisis* that created a *political pressure*, resulting in *tax incentives*.[16]

The first cycle occurred between the years 1950 and 1980, when the import substitution policy[17] was widely used. The second and third cycles were represented by the establishment of sectoral meetings in the early 1990s, which aimed at a 22% reduction in vehicle prices, and by a new public policy, named New Automotive Regime, in the late 1990s, which encouraged local production. The last cycle started in 2012, with the Inovar-Auto Programme, which provided local content requirements and tax reductions and exemptions. Over time, the industrial policies adopted by Brazil became protectionist and demanded few returns of its beneficiaries.[18] These peculiarities became internationally well known when the European Union (EU) challenged the Inovar-Auto Programme in a dispute before the WTO, which was ultimately decided in favour of the EU and against Brazil.[19]

The Inovar-Auto Programme, introduced by Law n. 12.715/2012, attempted to attract new investments to Brazil, and improve industrial production standards, promoting the energy efficiency of vehicles.[20]

> The programme has provided a reduction of the IPI[21] tax (an indirect federal tax) burden on certain motor vehicles (i) either through presumed IPI tax credits granted to accredited companies; (ii) or through reduced IPI tax rates on the importation of vehicles originating in certain countries, as well as on certain domestic vehicles.[22]

The Appellate Body of the WTO noted that:

> it is undisputed that, in order for companies to obtain any sort of accreditation that entitles them to accrue and use presumed IPI tax credits, they must either be located and operate in Brazil, in the case of domestic manufacturers and importers/distributors, or be in the process of establishing in the country as a domestic manufacturers, in the case of investors.

For this reason, the WTO Appellate Body concluded that the conditions for accreditation in order to receive presumed tax credits accorded less favourable treatment to import products than that accorded to like domestic products, policies which were inconsistent with Articles III:2 and III:4 of the GATT 1994 and Article 2.1 of the Agreement on Trade-Related Investment Measures (TRIMs) Agreement.[23]

Despite the fact that the Panel[24] found that the tax reductions through presumed tax credits granted under the Inovar-Auto Programme were prohibited subsidies, within the meaning of the Agreement on Subsidies and Countervailling Measures (SCM Agreement), the Appellate Body reversed some of the Panel's findings considering that the Brazilian requirements were not contingent within the meaning of 3.1(b) of the SCM Agreement.

Besides the legal controversies of Inovar-Auto, from the economic perspective, the programme was a resounding failure. The Inovar-Auto Programme: (i) did not generate relevant innovations nor increase exports of vehicles and auto parts, (ii) created an enormous excess of industrial installed capacity, (iii) instead of stimulating specialization in models with domestic demand and growth potential, led to the widespread production of the most varied categories and models of vehicles, some of which had ridiculously low and clearly unsustainable demand, and (iv) transferred an average of BRL 1.5 billion to the automotive industry with few offsets related to innovation and Brazilian insertion in global value chains.[25]

In this puzzling political scenario, after months of negotiation between the Brazilian government and the representatives of the industrial sector, the successor of the Inovar-Auto Programme was introduced by Law n. 13.755, on 10 December 2018, named the Rota 2030 Programme. The Rota 2030 – Logistics and Mobility Programme aims to foster the automotive sector, supporting technological development, competitiveness, innovation, vehicle safety, protection of the environment, energy efficiency, and to improve the quality of vehicles, including trucks, buses, and other vehicles with chassis, engines, and auto parts.

Law 13.755/2018 is entirely designed for the automotive sector, and is divided into three different parts: (i) the mandatory requirements for selling and importing vehicles in Brazil, (ii) the set-up of the Rota 2030 Programme, and (iii) the establishment of a special tax regime for imported parts and components (where no national equivalent is available) to be used in the manufacturing of automotive products.

In its first part, Law 13.755/2018 provides the mandatory requirements for selling and importing new vehicles related to labelling, energy efficiency, and performance of driver assistance technologies. According to its provisions, the Brazilian government could reduce up to 2% of the IPI on vehicles that meet certain requirements related to energy efficiency, and 1% on vehicles that meet certain requirements related to driver assistance technologies. Such reductions are limited to 2%, except for the hybrid vehicles with flexible fuel engines that should have a *minimum* reduction of 3% of the IPI. Expressly, Law 13.755/2018 demands that the requirements for the sale and import of vehicles should be designed in such a way that the imported goods do not receive less favourable treatment than to like domestic products. This provision is a direct result of the WTO dispute and resolution.

In its second part, Law 13.755/2018 establishes the Rota 2030 Programme, which basically consists of a corporate income tax deduction for R&D expenditures, equal to 34% of 30% to 45% of R&D expenditures incurred in Brazil. Companies that manufacture vehicles and their parts and components, and that have technological production development projects in Brazil are eligible. The R&D expenditures may be applied to research, development and innovation projects, and priority programmes to support industrial and technological development for the automotive sector and its chain, jointly with Brazilian private and public institutions that promote R&D projects.

In its third part, Law 13.755/2018 institutes the exemption of the import tax for imported parts and components to be used in the manufacturing of automotive products, if no national equivalent is available. In light of the above, it is possible to observe several differences between Inovar-Auto and Rota 2030. Firstly, the tax scheme of Rota 2030 is less complicated than Inovar-Auto. As pointed out by Schapiro,[26] the complex logics of the presumed credit of IPI provided in the Inovar-Auto Programme was used to hide prohibited local content requirements. Secondly, the consumption tax incentives (IPI) provided in Rota 2030 concern both national and imported vehicles. Thirdly, Rota 2030 incentivizes the entire automotive chain, not only the manufacturers.

Furthermore, the protectionism opposed by the WTO was avoided under the new legislation. In the Inovar-Auto Programme, imported products received less favourable treatment than national products, and vehicles were subsidized through a complex tax scheme that granted presumed IPI credit. In the Rota 2030 Programme, companies that perform R&D in Brazil are entitled to a deduction of the respective expenditure against the Brazilian corporate tax. Thus, the tax incentive shifts from product to producer, from consumption tax to corporate tax.

It is certainly not possible to ensure that the tax incentive promoted by Rota 2030 would not be challenged by the WTO rules, especially in relation to the SCM Agreement provisions. The change in the tax scheme structure, in comparison with the Inovar-Auto Programme, allows for the interpretation that there are no apparent local content requirements. However, as Luca Rubini demonstrated, 'the general scenario with respect to the status of subsidies for renewable energy under WTO subsidy disciplines is one of significant legal uncertainty and even conflict between legal requirements and policy prescription'.[27]

Regardless of issues about WTO subsidy discipline, the question that arises is whether the Rota 2030 effectively spurs the electric vehicles market. Until 2018, electric and hybrid vehicles were overtaxed in comparison with vehicles with a combustion engine. The launch of Rota 2030 in 2018 was followed by the IPI reduction announcement for electric and hybrid vehicles[28] to give electric and hybrid vehicles the same treatment, with the same rate, as vehicles with a combustion engine.

Although Rota 2030 provides a large IPI reduction for hybrid vehicles with a flexible fuel engine and encourages technological development in the field of energy efficiency, it does not do so for electric vehicles in one particular way. In other words, there is no specific tax reduction for electric vehicles; the large tax reduction is for cars equipped with a fuel engine.

EPE, a public agency that provides services to the Ministry of Mines and Energy in the area of studies and research aimed at subsidizing the planning of the energy sector, covering electricity, oil, and natural gas and their derivatives and biofuels, prepared an extensive study regarding Brazilian electromobility. According to the EPE, in Brazil, there will be a long energy transition related to light vehicles, the so-called 'hybridization process'. This means that combustion vehicles will coexist with electric and hybrid vehicles for a long period, with advantages for the former at the lowest price. EPE does not consider electric vehicles' penetration in the Brazilian market until 2030 as statistically relevant. The study reveals that by 2050 (i) electric vehicles will only have 11% of the market, (ii) hybrids will comprise 61%, and (iii) conventional combustion engines will retain a significant portion of the market at 28%.[29]

THE RENOVABIO PROGRAMME

As described by the International Council on Clean Transportation (ICCT), 'Brazil is one of the world's leading biofuel markets, producing nearly 40 billion liters of biofuels in 2018'.[30] Brazil's biodiesel industry has expanded in recent years as a result of increases in the mandated blend for diesel fuel.

Historically, ethanol production from sugar cane in Brazil was boosted by Decree n. 19,717 of 1931 which required the mixing of 5% of anhydrous ethanol with gasoline. In the 1970s, as a response to the oil crisis, the government instituted the National Alcohol Program (Proalcool), that provided incentives and subsidies for the sector, and determined the mandatory blending between gasoline and ethanol.[31]

Since the establishment of the Proalcool programme, the ethanol mandate has increased from a 4.5% blend in 1977 to 27% in 2015.[32] Besides the mandatory blending, 88.5% of the total vehicles sold in Brazil are flexible fuel vehicles with an internal combustion engine designed to run with gasoline blended with ethanol or pure ethanol.[33]

Given the particular strength of its biofuels programme, Brazil realized that it could develop a policy that would fulfil the pledge at the Paris Agreement by promoting mechanisms that would improve the price stability of biofuels and thus their economic attractiveness.[34] On 26 December 2017, the National Biofuel Policy was launched, called RenovaBio.

The provisions of RenovaBio aim for Brazil to (i) comply with the commitments established under the Paris Agreement, (ii) contribute to establishing the proper relation between energy efficiency and reduction of greenhouse gas emissions, (iii) promote the production and use of biofuels in the national mix, and (iv) collaborate in a predictable way for the competitive participation of biofuels in the Brazilian market. However, the main innovation of RenovaBio is the creation of a market instrument, rather than a tax scheme, to incentivize and operationalize the programme.

As explained by Grassi and Pereira:

> Brazilian authorities set a reduction target of 10.1% to be achieved in 10 years, equivalent to a reduction of emissions of 591 million tonnes of fossil CO2. To achieve those numbers, individual carbon intensity targets were defined and applied for fuel distributors. In order to achieve these goals, the distributors will need to acquire bonds equivalent to carbon credits, called CBIOs, on the Stock Exchange. Each CBIO corresponds to one tonne of CO2 that is no longer emitted, and it is generated from the production of biofuel.[35]

The Decarbonization Credit (CBIO) is issued by the biofuel producer, which must be certified by an accredited agency and comply with several environmental requirements linked to efficiency, land use, and others established in a specific regulation. The CBIOs are traded at B3 – Brazil Stock Exchange and may be acquired by regulated parties, the fuel distributors, and non-regulated parties, any third party such as a natural person or company.

The first CBIOs began trading on B3, the Brazilian Stock Exchange, in April this year (2020).[36] However, due to the Covid-19 pandemic and the delay of the Brazilian government in publishing the final regulation of the programme, many uncertainties have arisen. For example, the taxation of CBIOs is unclear. The relationship between the individual targets of the distributors and the CBIOs for the year 2020 has not been clarified. So far, 3 million CBIOs have been issued, but the authorities established an original sales target of 28.7 million CBIOs.

Despite the lack of certainty, expectations for RenovaBio are high. According to the report issued by the Netherlands Enterprise Agency:[37]

> Brazil aspires to have the RenovaBio program fully operational in 2020. The ministry of Mines & Energy (MME) expects that the program will eventually generate around 1 million jobs along the total value chain (from feedstock production to fuel distribution). The Brazilian consultant Datagro estimates that RenovaBio is able to increase domestic demand for bioethanol to 40 billion liters in 2030.

In addition to the domestic efforts to boost biofuel production, the Brazilian government leads the international initiative named 'Biofuture Platform' that congregates 20 countries, including China, the United States, Argentina and the United Kingdom. As stated on the website of the international initiative:

> In light to the fact that low carbon transport fuels are the fastest alternative to reduce the carbon intensity of the transport sector without waiting for fleet and infrastructure changes, the Biofuture Platform aims to help filling that attention gap, promoting policy coordination and raising the issue in the global agenda.[38]

THE BRAZILIAN CHOICE

After analysing Rota 2030 and RenovaBio, it can be said that the Brazilian government has made a clear choice for incentivizing biofuels as a path to decarbonization in the transport sector, at least for the near future. Rota 2030 propels energy efficiency improvements through any technology that replaces fossil fuels. In this sense, electric, hybrid, and flexible fuel vehicles receive the same treatment, except when hybrid and flexible fuel are combined. In this scenario, there is a major reduction of the IPI tax.

The tax incentive for a hybrid flexible fuel vehicle and the evident orientation towards biofuels will shape the Brazilian market for the next 10 years. Public authorities and representatives of the private sector are endorsing the idea that Brazil has a natural vocation for biofuels and will be the world leader in hybrid flexible fuel vehicles technology.

For example, Mr Luis Henrique Guimarães, CEO at Cosan (one of the largest economic groups in Brazil), said in February 2019 that:

> We have to make the country grow more in biofuels, regardless of the discussion of the electric or non-electric vehicle. This is a fortress, a comparative advantage of Brazil, we cannot surrender this leadership to other countries. Brazil cannot fall into temptation, sorry for the word, as a mongrel, we are ashamed of what we are good at, and we are really good at biofuels and agriculture.[39]

In the same direction, Mr Marcos Clement, from the Automotive Engineering Association, has suggested that the future of the Brazilian vehicular matrix is *bioelectrification*,[40] a new term to indicate the coexistence of engines with electric components in vehicles. In addition, Aneel, the Brazilian Electricity Regulatory Agency, estimates that the fleet of electric vehicles in Brazil will reach 360,000 in 2026, which represents only 2.5% of the total fleet,[41] confirming the EPE projection that electric vehicles' penetration in the Brazilian market by 2030 will be statistically irrelevant .

As a result, Toyota has launched the first hybrid vehicle equipped with a flexible fuel internal combustion engine. According to the company website, the price of the car is BRL 136,890.00, which is very expensive for Brazilian standards.[42] Therefore, Rota 2030 and RenovaBio are coherent policies in the sense that they both work to prioritize the use of biofuels. However, there is no direct and exclusive incentive for the development of the electric vehicles market.

Some Brazilian states grant exemptions or reductions for a state tax, the so-called Imposto sobre a Propriedade de Veículos Automotores (IPVA), for hybrid and electric cars. However, considering that only a small portion of the Brazilian population can afford the high price of vehicles, it is difficult to assess whether this kind of incentive is effective in fostering the market of hybrid and electric cars.

Even if there are great opportunities for Brazil to incentivize biofuels, it is also important to point out some risks that arise from the biofuel policies on the environment and the vehicle fleet. As reported by the ICCT, '*RenovaBio*, as currently implemented, provides a weak incentive for non-food fuels and is likely insufficient to support the production of more sustainable but costly advanced fuels'.[43,44] It is important to note that Brazil produces ethanol mainly from sugar cane crops that are also used for food and feed. This type of biofuel is called a first generation biofuel and raises concerns about the impact on the price of food, as well as the potential increase of greenhouse gas emissions due to the indirect land use change (ILUC).

In addition to the regular issues related to ILUC, Brazil has an extra challenge, represented by the revocation, at the end of 2019, of the decree that regulated the expansion and production of sugar cane in areas of the Amazon, Pantanal, and Cerrado. As a result, it is possible that with more available areas for the production of sugar cane, the interest of producers in investing and developing second-generation biofuels (from non-food biomass) will decrease.

Although RenovaBio is a good, well-intentioned, and sophisticated programme that intends to put Brazil on a sustainable path, its environmental success is linked to the proper use of land. However, current Brazilian public policy has dramatically curtailed government support to tackle deforestation,[45] represented, for example, by the cut in the transfer of funds to environmental protection agencies and the suspension of the collection of fines due to non-compliance with the environmental legislation, causing the devastation in the Amazon forest to reach the highest rate in 12 years, according to data released in November 2020.[46] Consequently, the expectations around reducing greenhouse gas emissions from the transport sector may not be fulfilled.

CONCLUSION

The two main Brazilian public policies aiming to reduce greenhouse gas emissions in the transport sector are the Rota 2030 and RenovaBio programmes. Rota 2030 aims to foster the automotive sector generally, supporting technological development, competitiveness, innovation, vehicle safety, protection of the environment, energy efficiency, and the quality of vehicles, including trucks, buses, and other vehicles comprised of a chassis with an engine and auto parts. In contrast with its predecessor, the Inovar-Auto Programme, Rota 2030 is not protectionist as defined under the WTO ancillary agreements, and its tax incentives are mainly linked to the corporate tax deduction for R&D expenditures. Besides that, although Rota 2030 provides a large IPI reduction for hybrid vehicles with a flexible fuel engine and encourages technological development in the field of energy efficiency, it does not give any particular incentive for electric vehicles.

On the other hand, the provisions of RenovaBio aim to (i) comply with the commitments established under the Paris Agreement, (ii) contribute to the proper relation between energy efficiency and reduction of greenhouse gas emissions, (iii) promote the production and use of biofuels in the national mix, and (iv) collaborate in a predictable way for the competitive participation of biofuels in the Brazilian market. The main innovation of RenovaBio is the creation of a market instrument, the CBIOs, to incentivize the development and production of biofuels.

By dissecting both policies, Rota 2030 and RenovaBio, it became clear that the Brazilian government has made a choice for incentivizing biofuels as a path to decarbonization in the transport sector, as least for the near future. The combined policies are shaping the Brazilian market to the development of the *hybrid flexible fuel* technology.

It is early to assess the impact of the public policies. However, the expectation that biofuels will aid in reducing greenhouse gas emissions from the transport sector will depend on the Brazilian policies for controlling the use of land, tackling deforestation, and encouraging the development of the next generation of biofuels to assure net emissions reductions while accounting for land use changes.

NOTES

1. Msc Rafaela Cristina Oliari, PhD student, Federal University of Santa Catarina, rafaelaoliari@gmail.com; Dr Carlos Araújo Leonetti, Professor, Federal University of Santa Catarina, cleonetti37@gmail.com; Dr Elena Aydos, Senior Lecturer, University of Newcastle, elena.aydos@newcastle.edu.au.
2. IEA. Tracking transport 2020 <https://www.iea.org/reports/tracking-transport-2020> accessed 7 August 2020.
3. IEA. Changes in transport behaviour during the Covid-19 crisis <https://www.iea.org/articles/changes-in-transport-behaviour-during-the-covid-19-crisis> accessed 7 August 2020.
4. Ibid.
5. SEEG. Análise das emissões brasileiras de gases de efeito estufa e suas implicações para as metas do Brasil <http://www.observatoriodoclima.eco.br/wp

-content/uploads/2019/11/OC_SEEG_Relatorio_2019pdf.pdf> p. 6 accessed 8 August 2020.
6. ANP. Biocombustíveis <http://www.anp.gov.br/biocombustiveis> accessed 6 August 2020.
7. See <https://www.mma.gov.br/images/arquivos/clima/convencao/indc/BRAZIL_iNDC_english.pdf> accessed 9 August 2020.
8. IPEA. Cadernos ODS <https://www.ipea.gov.br/portal/images/stories/PDFs/livros/livros/190920_cadernos_ODS_objetivo_8.pdf> p. 18 accessed 7 January 2021.
9. EPE. O compromisso do Brasil no combate às mudanças climáticas: produção e uso de energia <https://www.epe.gov.br/sites-pt/sala-de-imprensa/noticias/Documents/NT%20COP21%20iNDC.pdf> p. 21 accessed 5 January 2021.
10. IEA. Changes in transport behaviour during the Covid-19 crisis <https://www.iea.org/articles/changes-in-transport-behaviour-during-the-covid-19-crisis> accessed 7 August 2020.
11. ITF. Decarbonising transport in emerging economies <https://www.itf-oecd.org/dtee> accessed 7 August 2020.
12. IEA. Transport <https://www.iea.org/reports/renewables-2019/transport#abstract> accessed 10 August 2020.
13. IEA. Global EV outlook 2020 <https://www.iea.org/reports/global-ev-outlook-2020> accessed 10 August 2020.
14. IEA. Energy technology perspectives: special report on clean energy innovation. <https://www.iea.org/reports/clean-energy-innovation> p. 143 accessed 20 August 2020.
15. Schapiro, Mario. O estado pastor e os incentivos tributários no setor automotivo. Revista de Economia Política, vol. 37, n. 2 (147), pp. 437–55, abril-junho/2017. p. 440.
16. Ibid., p. 441.
17. Import substitution policy is an attempt by economically less-developed countries to break out of the world division of labour which has emerged in the nineteenth century and the early part of the twentieth century. Under this division, Latin America (and most areas of Asia and Africa) specialized in the export of food and raw materials, while importing manufactured goods from Europe and the United States. Import substitution consists of establishing domestic production facilities to manufacture goods which were formerly imported (<http://www.jstor.org/stable/2502457> accessed 22 August 2020).
18. Coronel, Daniel A.; Azevedo, André F.Z., and Campos, Atônio C. Política Industrial e desenvolvimento econômico: a reatualização de um debate histórico. Revista de Economia Política, vol. 34, n. 1 (134), pp. 103–19, janeiro-março/2014. p. 116.
19. WTO. Brazil: certain measures concerning taxation and charges <https://www.wto.org/english/tratop_e/dispu_e/cases_e/ds497_e.htm> accessed 20 August 2020.
20. Feriato, Juliana M.F. and Leonetti, Carlos A. Os Programas Automotivos do Brasil e as Regras de Proibição de Subsídio da OMC. EALR, vol. 10, n. 1, pp. 25–40, Jan–Abr, 2019. Universidade Católica de Brasília – UCB. p. 31.
21. IPI (*imposto sobre produtos industrializados*) is a tax on import and industrialized goods, a federal consumption tax.
22. Panel Report. Brazil: certain measures concerning taxation and charges, *supra* note 19.

23. Appellate Body. Brazil: certain measures concerning taxation and charges, *supra* note 19.
24. Panel Report. Brazil: certain measures concerning taxation and charges, *supra* note 19.
25. Ferreira, Pedro and Fragelli, Renato. Inovar-Auto: ineficaz, caro e regressivo. 20 December 2017. Valor Econômico.
26. Schapiro, *supra* note 15, p. 449.
27. Rubini, Luca. Ain't wastin' time no more: subsidies for renewable energy, the SCM agreement, policy space and law reform. Journal of International Economic Law, vol. 15, n. 2, pp. 525–79, June 2012. p. 577.
28. ABVE. Associação Brasileira Veículo Elétrico <http://www.abve.org.br/governo-anuncia-rota-2030-e-corta-ipi-para-eletricos> accessed 21 August 2020.
29. EPE. Eletromobilidade e Biocombustíveis. Documento de apoio ao PNE 2050. Dezembro de 2018. p. 25
30. Pavlenko, Nikita and Araujo, Carmen. Opportunities and risks for continued biofuel expansion in Brazil. The International Council on Clean Transportation. 2019. <https://theicct.org/publications/biofuel-expansion-Brazil> accessed 25 August 2020.
31. Grassi, M.C.B. and Pereira, G.A.G., Energy-can and RenovaBio: Brazilian vector to boost the development of biofuels. Industrial Crops & Products, vol. 129, March, pp. 201–5, 2019. p. 202.
32. Pavlenko, *supra* note 30.
33. Automotive Business, Carro flex chega aos 15 anos com 30,5 milhões de unidades <https://www.automotivebusiness.com.br/inovacao/56/carro-flex-chega-aos-15-anos-com-305-milhoes-de-unidades> accessed 25 August 2020.
34. Grassi, *supra* note 31, p. 203.
35. Grassi, *supra* note 31, p. 203.
36. B3. CBIO. <https://www.google.com/url?sa=t&rct=j&q=&esrc=s&source=web&cd=&ved=2ahUKEwj_4sv097TrAhVhLLkGHfaRBY0QFjADegQICBAB&url=http%3A%2F%2Fwww.b3.com.br%2Flumis%2Fportal%2Ffile%2FfileDownload.jsp%3FfileId%3D8AE490CA70EC15FC0171AD50E47742FC&usg=AOvVaw2e4xa6hLWguf3N> accessed 26 August 2020.
37. Netherlands Enterprise Agency. Brazil determined to increase role of biofuels <https://www.rvo.nl/sites/default/files/2018/01/brazil-determined-to-increase-role-of-biofuels.pdf> accessed 25 August 2020.
38. Biofutre <http://www.biofutureplatform.org/about> accessed 23 August 2020.
39. Instituto Combustível Legal. Carro elétrico e biocombustível: seminário da ANP aponta soluções pra o futuro <https://www.combustivellegal.com.br/carro-eletrico-e-a-biocombustivel-seminario-da-anp-aponta-solucoes-para-o-futuro> accessed 23 August 2020.
40. ANP. Futuro da matriz veicular no Brasil <http://www.anp.gov.br/images/Palestras/Matriz-Veicular-2019/14-apresentacao-marcos-clemente-aea.pdf> accessed 24 August 2020.
41. ANEEL. Mobilildade elétrica: tecnologias limpas e sustentáveis <https://www.aneel.gov.br/mobilidade-eletrica> accessed 23 August 2020.
42. TOYOTA. New Corolla <https://www.toyota.com.br/modelos/corolla> accessed 28 August 2020.
43. Advanced biofuels, also known as second-generation biofuels, are fuels that can be produced from several types of non-food biomass.

44. Pavlenko, *supra* note 30, p. 2.
45. SEEG, *supra* note 5, p. 22.
46. Observatório do Clima. Plano de Bolsonaro funciona e desmatamento tem nova alta <http://www.observatoriodoclima.eco.br/plano-de-bolsonaro-funciona-e-desmatamento-tem-nova-alta> accessed 11 January 2021.

PART IV

European national case studies

11. Environmental taxation in an age of COVID-19: an Italian approach
Alberto Comelli[1]

1. INTRODUCTORY CONSIDERATIONS: TAX LEGISLATION IN ITALY AT THE TIME OF THE PANDEMIC AND THE NEED FOR A WIDE AND COMPREHENSIVE TAX REFORM

In the first months since the outbreak of the pandemic, a series of decree-laws were adopted in Italy, providing for a wide range of often piecemeal sectoral provisions drafted in a fairly loose way. In tax matters, they largely drew their inspiration from the measures adopted in the case of natural disasters, such as earthquakes. In fact, the suspension of the terms for some tax and social security payments and obligations was provided for, subject to specific selective criteria of a subjective, geographical, quantitative and time nature.

Besides the suspension of terms, new tax reliefs were provided for indiscriminately in the form of tax cuts, rebates, deductions and tax credits and an increase in short-term liquidity in favour of companies and households was fostered. The emergency legislation and regulations that emerged, aimed at supporting internal demand, and hence consumption, in an anti-cyclical perspective, are particularly complex and unsystematic.[2]

The aim of this chapter is to selectively analyse – from an Italian perspective – the major topical issues related to environmental taxation, in the current specific context characterized by the COVID-19 pandemic.

Before the outbreak of the pandemic, two important tax reforms were already at an advanced stage of discussion in Italy but, for the time being, their adoption does not appear imminent. They were, on the one hand, the reform of the personal income tax (IRPEF), from the viewpoint of its debated progressivity, and, on the other, the reform of the legal status of tax judges. In fact, also in tax matters, the emergency logic prevailed over the introduction of structural reforms, whose need in Italy has long been widely shared and called for by the sectoral legislation and regulations.

In tax literature, however, the guidelines to which a broad reform of the Italian tax system should be inspired are very different. It does not seem that the enlargement and/or strengthening of environmental taxation, as a possible pivot around which to build the reform, is a real priority, at least for most of the scholars who hope for a structural reform of the system.

Certainly many States shall impose and collect additional taxes in order to cope with the significant increase in public debt. At the end of 2021, Italy is expected to record a public debt compared to gross domestic product of approximately 160%. This is probably one of the highest increases forecast for all EU Member States.

There is no doubt that this huge public debt, which is even higher as a result of the health emergency triggered by the COVID-19 pandemic, has an impact on the tax system, thus creating the conditions for a higher tax burden, although currently this (certainly unpopular) issue does not appear at the top of the agenda of the political forces that support the government majority, at least in Italy.

In this respect, a wide and comprehensive reform of environmental taxation is not planned, at least for the time being, as taxes related to the environment and its protection are not primarily justified by increased tax revenue. With a view to increasing tax revenue more quickly, it would be necessary to take action in other areas of taxation and not – at least in principle – in environmental taxation in its various forms. If anything, it should be rationalized, as it certainly contributes to total revenue, but it should not be raised solely to increase tax revenue.

Unless a partial shift of taxation, as a whole, from labour to environmental protection is envisaged, in a circular and fully sustainable dimension. In this case, I believe that an increase in environmental taxation would be fully justified, in terms of increased revenue, but with a simultaneous reduction in taxation on labour income. In this way, the higher taxation (resulting from environmental taxes) would be balanced against the lower taxation on labour income.

The current phase, characterized by the state of need arising from the very severe economic crisis, is an opportunity not to be missed, that is, an excellent opportunity to rethink the tax system and plan its reform, going well beyond the current economic situation and projecting onto a much more lasting and, hopefully, stable time dimension,[3] thus favouring – at the same time – both the recovery of internal investment and consumption, as well as technological innovation.[4]

2. ENVIRONMENTAL TAXATION PROVISIONS IN THE CONTEXT OF EMERGENCY LEGISLATION: THE DEFERRAL OF THE TAX ON SINGLE-USE PLASTICS TO 1 JULY 2021 AND OF THE TAX ON THE CONSUMPTION OF SWEETENED BEVERAGES TO 1 JANUARY 2022

There is no doubt that, during the health emergency, the legislation and regulations on environmental taxation were not placed at the top of the lawmakers' agenda. Nevertheless, I wish to mention some significant provisions.

The plastics tax, introduced by the 2020 Budget Law[5] with a view to boosting the green economy, should have entered into force on 1 July 2020. It was decided to postpone it until 1 July 2021.[6] It is a tax on the consumption of disposable manufactured goods, even partially made with the use of plastics (the so-called plastics tax). In principle, these products are relevant for tax purposes, if they are intended for the containment, protection, handling or delivery of goods or foodstuffs. The single-use products may take the form of sheets, films or strips.

Tax obligations arise at the time of production,[7] definitive importation into the State territory[8] or introduction into the same territory from other EU Member States.[9] The tax becomes payable when the products are released for consumption in the State territory[10] and is set at 0.45 euros per kilogram of plastics.

However, the tax shall not be payable on plastics from recycling processes.

The entry into force of the tax on the consumption of soft drinks, manufactured with the addition of sweeteners, intended for human consumption (the so-called sugar tax), was postponed to 1 January 2022.[11] This tax was also introduced by the 2020 Budget Law.[12]

For the purposes of its implementation, by sweeteners we mean any natural or synthetic substance that can give a sweet taste to beverages. Tax obligations arise and the tax becomes payable considering three different cases.

Firstly, when sweetened beverages are supplied by a national manufacturer[13] to consumers in Italy or to national traders who resell them. The second case considers the relevance of the purchaser's receiving the sweetened beverages, when the products come from EU Member States. In the third case, the final importation into Italian territory is relevant, when the sweetened beverages are imported from third countries. In the three different cases, the parties liable to pay are (a) the national manufacturer,[14] (b) the purchaser and (c) the importer, respectively.

For finished products the tax amounts to 10.00 euros per hectolitre, and, for the products prepared to be used after dilution, to 0.25 euros per kilogram.[15]

The tax shall not apply to sweetened beverages supplied directly by a national manufacturer[16] for consumption in other EU Member States or intended for export by the national manufacturer.[17] The ways and arrangements for implementing this tax shall be laid down by a decree of the Minister of Economy and Finance, which has not yet been issued.

The plastics tax and the tax on sweetened beverages were simultaneously introduced by the 2020 Budget Law in view of orienting lifestyles towards the production and consumption of goods compatible with both environmental sustainability and the protection of human health. With specific reference to the first tax, the goal of significantly reducing the impact caused to the environment by the production and consumption of single-use plastic products is very clear.

Moreover, the plastics tax provisions introduced a tax bonus, as an incentive for the production of biodegradable plastics, in the form of a tax credit granted to companies active in the plastics sector and manufacturing single-use products, intended to perform the function of containment, protection, handling or delivery of goods or foodstuffs. The tax credit is set at 10% of the expenses incurred in the period from 1 January to 31 December 2020, with a maximum amount of 20,000.00 euros for each beneficiary, for the purpose of technological adjustment, aimed at the production of compostable products.

It should be underlined that the plastics tax was introduced in Italy in the wake of Directive (EU) 2019/904 of the European Parliament and of the Council of 5 June 2019, whose transposition by Member States is expected by 3 July 2021,[18] on 'reducing the impact of certain plastic products on the environment'. The Directive acknowledges the significant negative impact of certain plastic products on the environment, health and the economy,[19] with waste dispersion in the environment, in particular the marine one, by promoting reuse, repair, recycling and, more generally, more efficient and sustainable production and consumption patterns and the circular economy, in particular, in terms of plastics' life cycle.

The primary aim of the Directive is to reduce the amount of waste generated by promoting circular approaches that favour sustainable and non-toxic reusable products and systems,[20] with a view to achieving goal No. 12 of the UN Agenda 2030 for sustainable development,[21] so as to ensure sustainable production and consumption patterns. The Directive also aims at pursuing goal No. 14 of the Agenda, that is, to preserve and sustainably use the oceans, seas and marine resources for sustainable development.

Moreover, a tax credit recently introduced by Law No. 178/2020 should be mentioned,[22] designed to 'rationalizing the use of water and reducing the use of plastic containers for drinking water'. This is a tax measure that complements the plastics tax and aims to further limit 'the use of plastic containers', with a view to improving the quality of water for human consumption supplied by aqueducts. This tax credit is in force from 1 January 2021 to 31 December 2022 and is granted to all natural persons and to legal persons carrying out business activities, arts or professions, as well as non-commercial entities. This credit amounts to 50% of the expenses incurred for the purchase and installation of the systems for filtering, mineralization, cooling and addition of food carbon dioxide.[23]

3. INCENTIVES FOR ENERGY EFFICIENCY, FOR THE REDUCTION OF SEISMIC RISK, FOR THE INSTALLATION OF PHOTOVOLTAIC SYSTEMS AND FOR INFRASTRUCTURE FOR CHARGING ELECTRIC VEHICLES: THE DEDUCTION FOR IRPEF PURPOSES AND THE TRANSFERABILITY OF THE TAX CREDIT

Another interesting provision envisaged in the context of the emergency legislation is Article 119 of Decree-Law No. 34/2020.[24] This provision lays down some incentives for specific interventions aimed at improving energy efficiency, reducing the seismic risk, the installation of photovoltaic systems and infrastructure for recharging electric vehicles in buildings.

In particular, a 110% deduction for IRPEF purposes is envisaged for natural persons or for co-owners with regard to expenses incurred and documented for works carried out on real estate units from 1 July 2020 until 30 June 2022. Natural persons who carry out business activities, arts or professions are excluded. Article 119 provides for the distribution of the incentive (among the beneficiaries) in five equal annual instalments (four equal annual instalments for the expenses incurred in 2022) and it does not appear that the number of instalments can be increased or decreased. Moreover, these incentives are allowed within the spending limits provided for in Article 119.

The expenses that entitle citizens to a 110% deduction for IRPEF purposes include the main works and additional (or secondary) ones. The latter consist of certain types of expenses incurred for additional works carried out in conjunction with at least one of the main ones.

The main works include some expenses incurred for the replacement of air conditioning systems in buildings, as well as for thermal insulation and reduction of seismic risk. The additional ones include some expenses for energy efficiency systems, for the installation of solar photovoltaic systems and infrastructure for charging electric vehicles.

Instead of the deduction for IRPEF purposes, the beneficiary may opt (electronically) for the transfer of a tax credit of the same amount to the suppliers of goods and services needed for implementing the measures and interventions, as well as to banks or other financial intermediaries. This credit may subsequently be transferred to other subjects.[25]

A first consideration concerns the amount of the deduction, which makes it possible to exceed – by an amount equal to 10%, the expenses actually incurred by the natural persons (or the co-owners) (and borne by them). In fact, the deduction amounts to 110%, with a lower tax which, overall, exceeds, by 10%, the expenses actually incurred. The advantage from a tax viewpoint is fairly clear and it can be reasonably expected that this incentive will be widely used.

A second consideration concerns the transfer of an equal tax credit as the amount of the deduction being considered. This provision, too, will certainly contribute to the presumable use of this incentive on a large scale. However, the transfer of the tax credit shall be subject to steady and targeted checks by the Inland Revenue Agency, especially where there is a sequence of transfers, involving also subjects other than banks and financial intermediaries, without particular (but necessary) precautions.

More generally, the provision under consideration further confirms that, during the health emergency and the resulting severe economic crisis, legislation in Italy has been dominated by the introduction of various tax credits and tax incentives. The usefulness of this regulatory proliferation is far from obvious and, at a closer look, makes the Italian tax system even more unsystematic.

4. THE ATTENTION PAID BY THE OECD AND THE EUROPEAN UNION ON ENERGY TAXATION: IS THE 2019–2020 TWO-YEAR PERIOD A TURNING POINT FROM THE ENVIRONMENTAL VIEWPOINT OR IS IT A MESSAGE IN THE BOTTLE THROWN INTO THE SEA FOR POSTERITY?

In 2019, the Organisation for Economic Co-operation and Development (OECD) drafted an important document entitled *Taxing Energy Use*, accompanied by the related summary document.[26] In that document the OECD included the guidelines that should orient energy tax policies, with a view to gradually curbing carbon dioxide emissions and climate change, thus promoting access to clean energy, also through tax instruments.

With reference to the legislation of the States considered in the document, it shows that the level of taxation on coal is limited and there would be significant room for manoeuvre to increase it, thus acquiring the difference, as higher revenue, in favour of the use of clean and sustainable energies, whose level of taxation should be kept very low. Moreover, in many of the States considered, the taxation of polluting emissions is particularly low, if not zero, in the international air and maritime transport sectors. This fact further confirms the unbalanced taxation which, to date, characterizes the energy products sector, at least with reference to the States examined in the document.

What is highlighted above calls for the States' renewed sensitivity and interest in combating climate change, in the same way as the Paris Agreement,[27] with a view to limiting global warming as much as possible and encouraging – from a tax viewpoint – the use of cleaner and more sustainable energy sources, for example in the hydroelectric, wind and solar energy sectors.

From a different perspective, in 2019 the European Commission was very active in the field of environmental protection and on 11 December of that year it issued an important Communication entitled 'The European Green Deal'.[28] It is an ambitious project aimed at making the economy in the Union more sustainable and turning environmental issues into real opportunities in all sectors of the economy and particularly in industry, transport, major infrastructure, agriculture, construction and taxation. The Communication has an annex with a very ambitious table in terms of timing, with the indication of a series of 'key actions', including the proposed revision of Council Directive 2003/96/EC on energy taxation[29] by June 2021.

More generally, the Commission's Communication is in line with the above-mentioned OECD document and the UN Agenda 2030 and aims at promoting a circular and clean economy that creates the factual and legal conditions for improving and, in the future, for definitively overcoming a series of problems related to climate change, which still characterize the planet's current climate. Going well beyond the mere description of problems, already known to a large extent, the Commission has built a pathway consisting of a series of proposals on this issue and on dates by which the proposals will tentatively be submitted, by safeguarding the sustainability of the economy and the competitiveness of European companies.

This will be done by also considering the (public and private) investment that will inevitably be needed to implement this fundamental European project. It should put the Union at the world forefront in the fight against climate change, which is devastating many sectors of the natural environment, often irreversibly: just think about the melting glaciers linked to the increase in average temperatures.

Considering the above, tax measures are a key aspect of the Green Deal. In fact, according to the Commission, taxation must be aligned with climate and environmental goals. For example, it proposes a review and revision of the tax exemptions currently in force in some Member States for fossil fuels and for those used in air and maritime transport.

Furthermore, the Commission underlines that the Green Deal will create the conditions for far-reaching tax reforms, with a view not only to stimulating economic growth, but also to 'reducing the tax burden on labour and shifting it onto pollution'.[30]

In this respect, the proposal to amend Council Directive 2003/96/EC could be adopted by qualified majority voting, rather than unanimously by Member States, thus overcoming the risk of veto by a single Member State, which, hypothetically, would be against the proposal under consideration. This approach to the use of the legislative procedure with qualified majority voting is very positive, as it avoids a dangerous situation of deadlock and forced inaction, where tax discipline is a very important and even essential financial piece of the complex mosaic described in the European Green Deal.

More generally, it can be noted that the goals proposed in this Communication can broadly be shared, in terms of the need to protect the environment, thus preserving it as much as possible for future generations, but, at the same time, they probably seem too ambitious. In fact, they call for a qualitative leap forward in terms of culture and approach of Member States' policies (including tax policies) in many crucial sectors for their economies, which can only be achieved in a few years' time by means of a genuine 'cultural revolution', making it possible to place climate change and environmental sustainability at the core of government policies and actions by all Member States, with the operational coordination of the European Commission, which would play an active and valuable role in promoting and ensuring compliance with the commitments made.

More recently, the Communication from the Commission to the European Parliament and the Council COM(2020) 312 final[31] has set out the tax action plan to support economic recovery in the current pandemic crisis. The plan includes 25 actions that the Commission has identified in principle in the document, which it commits itself to proposing and implementing by 2024. On the whole, it is a very ambitious initiative which covers – by way of example – income taxation, indirect taxation, the charter of taxpayers' rights, transfer pricing and the settlement of tax disputes.

The Communication reaffirms the need for sustainable, climate-friendly investment in order to overcome the economic crisis, by ensuring compliance with the 'polluter pays' principle. In line with the European Green Deal, whose objectives are briefly reaffirmed, the Communication reiterates the need to amend the above-mentioned Directive on the taxation of energy products and electricity. It also calls for wide-ranging national tax reforms removing fossil fuel 'subsidies' and above all shifting the tax burden from labour to pollution,[32] provided that the necessary public revenues are ensured to 'provide an adequate level of social protection'.

In this regard, it is underlined it is appropriate to reduce the tax burden 'in other areas, e.g. on labour', at the above-mentioned condition, from the viewpoint of social protection. Based on the wording of the document, it seems that labour is not the only 'sector' in which the tax burden could be reduced, by shifting the burden onto polluters, since labour is only one of the 'sectors' that could be affected by this tax burden shift. Nevertheless, and in apparent contradiction, note No. 2 of the Communication clearly calls for a national tax reform designed to shift 'the tax burden from labour' (and not from other 'sectors') 'to pollution', without neglecting 'social considerations'.

Hence this important proposal is conveyed very clearly and is not drafted by the Commission in a dubitative way, but rather precisely indicating a desirable course of action that should characterize the national tax reform. The Commission also stresses that environmental taxes are particularly important, where they allow to design incentives to promote less polluting consumption and sustainable economic growth.

5. CAN CUSTOMS DUTIES BE USED AS ENVIRONMENTAL TAXES (AND TO WHAT EXTENT)?

The starting point for analysing customs duties is that carbon dioxide emissions are to a large extent produced by some States which are much less sensitive, compared to the EU Member States, to climate change-related matters and, more generally, to environmental protection and preservation. It is undeniable that the efforts made and the costs incurred by the latter are ineffective if the former do not feel in any way – or are scarcely – committed and involved in the front line – also from a tax viewpoint – in the fight against pollution, in all its possible forms – hence also with reference to the emission of a large quantity of carbon dioxide into the atmosphere, which, according to a considerable number of scientists, would be the main factor responsible for the climate changes taking place on our planet.

In this regard, a very serious problem arises, that is, climate change is a global phenomenon defying borders, in the sense that it affects all continents and all States, while the power to legislate – also on tax matters – is closely linked to the individual States' tax sovereignty, even where the latter is eroded or, in some way, limited, as a result of international, bilateral or multilateral agreements. But while the problem of the excessive emissions of carbon dioxide into the atmosphere is global, a unilateral tax measure would be clearly insufficient, as it would be fully inadequate and partial.

If we assume that there is a significant amount of carbon dioxide emissions in Asia, it would be completely inadequate to tackle this problem by providing for a very advanced legislation on environmental protection, also at tax level, by EU Member States alone. The efforts in terms of higher investment costs that the latter should bear would be frustrated if they were not shared by the other States, especially the non-European ones.

Undoubtedly a satisfactory response to this difficult problem can come from international agreements involving the largest number of States in the world. In this respect, the Paris Multilateral Agreement and the UN Agenda 2030 for sustainable development play and will continue to play a very important role in the relations between States.

From a different perspective, while a large quantity of harmful emissions is generated in States with very low or even non-existent environmental taxation, this aspect poses many problems – to say the least – for unfair competition from the companies that incur lower costs resulting from environmental taxation to the detriment of companies based in States where environmental taxation creates and imposes significant burdens. The solution to this problem is primarily entrusted to international agreements, firstly with the EU neighbouring States, but also with China and the other Asian States and gradually with all the other States, including developing countries, which must be fully involved and responsible for the global solution to problems which are global by nature. In this respect, the Union could actually take on and maintain the role of world leader, as called for in the Commission's document on the European Green Deal, by promoting and implementing 'ambitious environmental, climate and energy policies worldwide'.[33]

In this respect, bilateral and multilateral diplomatic channels will play a decisive role, also within international organizations. Alongside the diplomatic instruments, a fundamental role will be played by the financial instruments that the Union can use to support the environmental policies of some States that find it more difficult to bear the cost of public and private investment, albeit necessary from an environmental viewpoint, as is the case with developing countries, for example.

Nevertheless, a problem arises when a State signatory to one or more international cooperation agreements on environmental protection does not adopt tax provisions consistent with its commitments. This issue is far from theoretical and it is a matter of determining with which legal instruments a State can be persuaded to take action along these lines, within a reasonable lapse of time.

Customs duties are an old, but effective instrument among the possible ones to be used. In fact, these can be used, at best, for a certain period of time to increase import prices and hence discourage the consumption of goods coming from certain States, thus favouring goods of the same type (or similar non-polluting ones) manufactured within the European Union. If the exporting State did not apply an environmental protection policy according to the standards identified by the Union and the international community, the reaction could be as indicated above.[34]

This criterion would be very effective to put pressure on the States that do not commit themselves to drastically reducing the carbon dioxide emissions into the atmosphere in their territory, while remaining largely insensitive to the current issue of climate change. As is well known, there is a customs union in the European Union and the related tariff is not determined by the individual Member States, but rather collectively at EU level.

In this perspective, duties on imported goods could be increased in a calibrated way, with reference to those having an environmental impact, in order to offset the higher costs incurred by companies that produce the same (or similar) goods in the Union by incurring higher costs to comply with environmental obligations. This would restore fair tax competition between exporting and producing companies within the Union, which would otherwise be disadvantaged. The Carbon Border Tax recently proposed by the President of the European Commission, Ursula von der Leyen, seems to be a step in this direction.[35]

Therefore, the use of customs duties in the European Union, with a view to protecting the environment, must not be considered a taboo or, worse, a monster to be avoided at all costs. Customs duties are not the result of an ideology to be used against other ideologies. They can, however, be used wisely and sensibly to persuade the exporting States that do not comply with basic environmental rules to orient their economic and legal systems towards more careful awareness of the importance of the climate change underway and of the need for greater efforts and commitments by the international community as a whole in this regard.

6. FINAL CONSIDERATIONS: THE EUROPEAN GREEN DEAL, THE COMMISSION'S AMBITIOUS ACTION PLAN AND THE NEED TO TURN THE ECONOMIC CRISIS INTO AN OPPORTUNITY TO RETHINK SOME OF THE FUNDAMENTAL PRINCIPLES OF THE TAX SYSTEM

In Italy and, more generally, within the European Union, there is certainly growing awareness of the importance of environmental protection and preservation to the benefit of future generations, also from a tax viewpoint, as demonstrated by the European Green Deal and, more recently, by the Carbon Border Tax proposal put forward (also) by the President of the Commission, Ursula von der Leyen. Sustainable development, which is at the heart of the UN Agenda 2030, cannot do without a tax instrument capable of supporting – possibly at global and not only regional level or, worse, at unilateral level by some States – initiatives designed to supporting the necessary climate and environmental measures, without relinquishing the competitiveness of companies that shall bear higher costs to make the necessary investment.

In this context, the European Union can take on and maintain a leading role in the world, provided that its investment in technology, scientific research and artificial intelligence is much higher than the current one. Otherwise, the Union will be bound to become increasingly marginal, to the benefit of the countries that are already oriented to invest many resources in that direction, particularly compared to the United States and China.

From a different perspective, the economic crisis caused by the pandemic is an excellent opportunity to rethink some fundamental principles of the national tax system, so far considered stable and long-established. The States, and not just the EU Member States, need to turn this crisis into an opportunity to seize. The Union seems to have risen up to the economic and legal challenge that is already in the offing, as shown by the ambitious action plan submitted by the Commission on 15 July 2020.

Nevertheless, at least in Italy, the courage to plan and design an overall reform of the system, fully enhancing environmental taxation, has been lacking so far. The measures largely discussed in Italy during the pandemic, in the specific area of environmental taxation, are those described above in parts 2 and 3 of this chapter. This is too little. Greater courage and farsightedness are needed, thus governing the transition of the national tax system (but not only it) towards a regulatory system capable of ensuring fully sustainable development in its various forms.

NOTES

1. Alberto Comelli (alberto.comelli@unipr.it) is Full Professor of Tax Law at University of Parma, Italy.
2. See E. Della Valle, *Alcune coordinate dell'emergenza nell'ordinamento tributario*, in *Fisco*, 2020, p. 1513 *et seq.*
3. For example, the carry-back of tax losses could be envisaged for income tax purposes, where the Italian system currently provides only for the carry-forward mechanism for corporate income tax, with the exclusion of the regional tax on productive activities (IRAP).
4. For example, through the introduction of a specific tax credit for taxable persons (for IRPEF and corporate income tax purposes) who invest in technological innovation.
5. The tax was introduced by Article 1, paragraph 634 *et seq.* of Law No. 160 of 27 December 2019, as amended by Article 1, paragraph 1084, of Law No. 178 of 30 December 2020.
6. The deferral was provided for by Article 133 of Decree-Law No. 34 of 19 May 2020, converted with amendments by Law No. 77 of 17 July 2020 and, subsequently, by Article 1, paragraph 1084, sub-paragraph i) of Law No. 178/2020.
7. In this case, the person liable to pay is the manufacturer, provided that the manufactured goods are made in the State territory, or the subject (resident or not in Italy) that intends to sell these manufactured goods (to other national subjects and traders), provided they are obtained on his behalf in a processing plant.

8. In this case, the person liable to pay is the importer.
9. In this case, the person liable to pay is the one who buys the manufactured goods in the exercise of economic activity, or the transferor in the case when the manufactured goods are purchased by a private consumer.
10. This is provided for by Article 1, paragraph 636 of Law No. 160 of 27 December 2019.
11. As in the case of the plastics tax, also, this deferral was provided for by Article 133 of Decree-Law No. 34 of 19 May 2020, converted with amendments by Law No. 77 of 17 July 2020 and, subsequently, by Article 1, paragraph 1086, sub-paragraph e) of Law No. 178/2020.
12. The tax was introduced by Article 1, paragraph 661 *et seq.*, of Law No. 160 of 27 December 2019.
13. Or, if different, by the national subject making the so-called 'processing', or by the subject (resident or not in Italy) on whose behalf the beverages are obtained from the manufacturer, or from the operator of the processing plant.
14. Or the national subject making the so-called 'processing', or the subject (resident or not in Italy) on whose behalf the beverages are obtained from the manufacturer, or from the operator of the processing plant.
15. In principle and without considering more technical notions, the overall content of sweeteners in beverages is determined in relation to the sweetening power of each substance.
16. Or by the national subject who carries out the 'processing activity', or by the subject (resident or not in Italy) on whose behalf the beverages are obtained from the manufacturer, or from the operator of the processing plant.
17. Or by the subjects mentioned in the note above.
18. Although with some exceptions listed in Article 17, paragraph 1, of the Directive related to Articles 5, 6, paragraph 1, 7, paragraph 1 and 8.
19. See the first 'recital' of Directive 2019/904.
20. As provided for in the second 'recital' of Directive 2019/904.
21. The Agenda was adopted by the Heads of State and Government at the UN Summit on Sustainable Development held on 25–27 September 2015 and identified 17 objectives and 169 targets.
22. Specifically, by Article 1, paragraphs 1087 and 1088, of Law No. 178/2020.
23. This tax credit cannot exceed 1,000 euros per property unit in the case of natural persons not carrying out business or economic activities, and 5,000 euros per each property unit used for commercial or institutional purposes, in the case of the other subjects. The regulations governing the implementation and use of this tax credit are adopted by order of the Director of the Inland Revenue Service.
24. Converted, with amendments, by Law No. 77/2020, as amended by Article 1, paragraph 66, of Law No. 178 of 30 December 2020.
25. The unassigned tax credit can be used to offset tax liabilities. However, the portion of the tax credit not used in the year cannot be used in the subsequent years and cannot be claimed back.
26. The summary document bears the same title as the document and both were published in Paris in 2019.
27. The Paris Agreement is the first universal and legally binding agreement on climate change, adopted at the Paris Climate Conference (COP21) in December 2015. The European Union and its Member States are among the 190 parties to the Agreement and the Union also formally ratified the Agreement on 5 October 2016, thus enabling it to enter into force on 4 November 2016.

28. It is the Communication to the European Parliament, the Council, the European Economic and Social Committee and the Committee of the Regions, COM(2019) 640 final. It states that the Green Deal is intended for the Union and its citizens and places 'the Commission's commitment to tackling climate and environmental-related challenges on new bases'.
29. The Directive, still in force, 'restructures the Community framework for the taxation of energy products and electricity' and is dated 27 October 2003. There is no doubt on the necessary radical change of the Directive being examined, considering that, since its entry into force a long time ago, there have been profound changes in energy production technologies. The European Commission considered the possibility to significantly amend the Council Directive 2003/96/EC by means of the proposal for a Council Directive of 13 April 2011, COM(2011) 0169 final, 2011/0092 (CNS), but Member States did not find political agreement for its adoption and the proposal was subsequently withdrawn.
30. The Communication on the Green Deal adds that it is desirable that the Commission's proposal on VAT rates is adopted with a view to enabling Member States to make more targeted use of the various tax rates, taking into account environmental protection goals, 'for example by supporting organic fruit and vegetables'. The reference is to the proposal for a Council Directive on VAT rates COM(2018) 20 final of 18 January 2018. The proposal is still being examined by the Council.
31. The Communication is dated 15 July 2020.
32. The proposed reform is set out both in the text of the Communication and in note No. 2.
33. This is stated in point 3 of the Commission's Communication on the European Green Deal COM(2019) 640 final.
34. Consistently with the applicable rules on international trade, with specific reference to the General Agreement on Tariffs and Trade (GATT), which, however, should not be conceived as immutable over time and should, if anything, be adapted to the need to promote environmental sustainability.
35. See Ursula von der Leyen, *A Union that strives for more: My agenda for Europe. Political Guidelines for the next European Commission 2019–2024*, paragraph 1, accessed 24 May 2021 at https://ec.europa.eu/info/sites/default/files/political-guidelines-next-commission_en_0.pdf. In this paragraph devoted to the European Green Deal, the President states that 'to ensure that our companies can compete on a level playing field, I will introduce a Carbon Border Tax to avoid carbon leakage. This should be fully compliant with World Trade Organization rules. It will start with a number of selected sectors and be gradually extended. I will also review the Energy Taxation Directive'.

12. COVID-19 and urban mobility: has the time come for a paradigmatic shift? The potential of environmental tax policies in the pandemic age

Marina Bisogno

1. NEW CHALLENGES FOR URBAN MOBILITY

COVID-19 has rapidly turned a health crisis into a global economic crisis that is completely reshaping priorities for policymakers and economic operators. However, the urgency of climate change mitigation has not disappeared from the European agenda. The annual average carbon dioxide (CO_2) concentrations increased throughout 2020, even though emissions fell. Across the whole year, data estimated that CO_2 levels would rise by 2.48 parts per million (ppm). This increase is 0.32ppm smaller than if there had been no lockdown. This means that, although global emissions are smaller, they are continuing, just at a slower rate.

Although now the priority is the pandemic, seven in ten consider climate change as serious a crisis as COVID-19. According to a report published by Ipsos MORI, two-thirds globally support a green economic recovery from the pandemic.[1] For some years the World Health Organization has been affirming the close link between health and the environment,[2] which is even more evident today especially given the emerging evidence of links between COVID-19 vulnerability and environmental stressors like air pollution.[3]

The COVID-19 crisis has caused an unprecedented shock in travel demand, raising questions about the future of transport in the short and long term. Particularly, lockdown measures stopped transport activity in urban areas worldwide in recent months.

As stated by the OECD, past experience suggests that, as the crisis subsides, the amount of travel that takes place in urban areas will gradually return to pre-crisis levels.[4] Following the SARS outbreak in 2003, transport activity returned to previous levels in less than a year. Preliminary figures show that transport activity is indeed recovering in areas that have lifted lockdown measures. Road traffic in Wuhan,[5] for example, appears to be returning to pre-pandemic levels and levels of pollution in France[6] are higher than before COVID-19. Nevertheless, until everyone is given a vaccine,[7] the pandemic will open new challenges for urban mobility.

In light of the social distancing measures that have been put into place, public transport may have to be rethought. In the short term, public transport will necessarily feature less prominently among citizens. It is likely that people will find it dangerous to share confined spaces, physical contact and surfaces with other people, making the recovery for public transport services uncertain for some years. Starting from this consideration, new mobility services are required to tackle the urban mobility challenge in the COVID-19 age and taxation could play an important role to support the transition towards more sustainable transport habits.

The aim of this chapter is to assess, firstly, how COVID-19 is changing general urban mobility patterns and, secondly, to investigate the role that taxation can play in the COVID-19 crisis concerning the mobility sector.

2. HOW THE PANDEMIC IS CHANGING URBAN TRANSPORT HABITS

In the transport sector, the pandemic could trigger a number of effects, including behavioural changes. Some of these new habits can benefit the environment while others can harm it. For example, teleworking and teleconferencing reduce the use of transport and therefore the emissions from it. However, teleworking concerns only a few workers, which absorbs only a marginal portion of the total number of journeys. While working on strengthening digital infrastructures to improve the spreading of teleworking, attention must nevertheless be directed towards the reorganization of traditional forms of urban mobility.

Boston Consulting Group (BCG) conducted a survey on travel choices during the first lockdowns[8] concerning 5,000 residents of major cities in the US, China and Western Europe (France, Germany, Italy, Spain and the UK).[9] The results show that almost all transport demand fell, with the exception of bikes and e-scooters.

In the post lockdown period,[10] the positive trend of the massive use of bikes and scooters continued but the survey also revealed the spread of a negative trend that implied an increase in the use of private cars. People turned to private car use to reduce the risk of contracting the virus, encouraged by low oil prices and aggressive marketing by car manufacturers in the wake of the crisis, significantly increasing emissions. The net environmental impacts of these shifts remain uncertain for now but, in conclusion, it can be argued that the pandemic is triggering behavioural changes in urban mobility. Some of these new travel options are green but others can make environmental pollution worse and national governments must prevent the establishment of environmentally harmful habits and encourage the development of new green transport habits through tax policies.

3. TAX POLICIES TO TACKLE SUSTAINABLE TRANSPORT IN URBAN AREAS

3.1 The Role of Fiscal Policy in the Pandemic Age Concerning the Transport Sector

The Organisation for Economic Co-operation and Development (OECD) identified four phases of the pandemic, which correspond to four different types of policies.[11] In the first phase of the pandemic, countries confronted with a virus outbreak took containment and mitigation measures, whose aim was to halt the outbreak. This was followed by mitigation policies, where the goal was to slow down the spreading of COVID-19 (Phase 2). Containment and mitigation measures were followed by a potentially long transition phase during which governments had to support economic recovery (Phase 3). Finally, probably after the distribution of a vaccine, an ultimate challenge will be to rethink the economic and social system to strengthen its resilience (Phase 4).

Concerning fiscal policy, in Phase 1 tax systems played a key role in quickly delivering financial support to businesses and households. Short-term fiscal, monetary and financial policies have focused on maintaining business liquidity and supporting household income.

In Phase 2, as containment and mitigation persisted, broader and more sustained tax policy responses were required. Tax policy had to continue to focus on limiting hardship and maintaining the ability for a rebound. This phase called for expanding the set of policies already implemented.

During Phase 3, the recovery had to be supported through fiscal incentives to investments and consumptions. The OECD provides evidence that the implementation of sufficiently large, timely and properly designed green stimulus measures, which are well embedded in domestic policy settings, can deliver economic and environmental benefits.[12] During the global financial crisis, over 16% of all fiscal stimuli (totalling over half a trillion USD) were directed at green activities.[13] Mundaca and Richter[14] state that the American Recovery and Reinvestment Act of 2009[15] has been an important component of green growth in the US regarding the renewable energy sector. There is evidence that renewable energy capacity was increased, as well as the number of green patents. Positive employment effects are observed in the number and higher quality of jobs related to clean energy programmes.

In Phase 4, tax policy might be used to help the restoration of public finances. The financial strain on governments resulting from the support measures provided to businesses and households in the earlier phases may be considerable. Once economies have recovered, countries may need to consider ways of raising revenues to restore long-term fiscal sustainability and fund public investments to strengthen the resilience of the economic system.

Aforementioned data demonstrated that the fear of contagion created new green transport habits but it is possible that these alternatives are temporary and will finish with the end of the pandemic. To translate these green habits into a cultural shift, governments can use fiscal policies. In fact, they can be crucial to catalyse a paradigmatic shift in transport habits. Taxation can affect transport habits because of its regulatory dimension[16] and fiscal incentives in the phase of the economic recovery could support the implementation of green and safe alternatives in the urban mobility sector. Furthermore, while the priority is rightly on providing urgent relief to impacted businesses and individuals, a careful screening of the environmental impacts of stimulus measures introduced would be necessary. This control would significantly add coherence[17] to policies and avoid creating perverse and unintended environmental consequences that might damage the future resilience and environmental health of societies.[18] The pandemic could be a unique opportunity for national governments to foster the shift towards more sustainable transport and fiscal policy can be the right way to address this challenge.

3.2   Future Perspectives for Urban Mobility and Tax Policies

A clear paradigm shift is needed to initiate the transition from fossil fuel-based vehicles to mobility based on renewable resources, towards electrification of transport through mass market take-up of battery electric vehicles. The time is right to eliminate fossil fuel subsidies and to accelerate electrification through alternative fuels.[19] However, there are several technological burdens that need to be solved first, such as limited range and lifetime of electric vehicle (EV) batteries, price of vehicles driving on renewable energy sources,[20] technology readiness level and density of charging/fuelling spots. It will take another 5–7 years from 2020 before these limitations are really solved to become competitive with internal combustion engine vehicles. Hence, the potential of fiscal policies to fill in the gap and support the transition towards more sustainable transport habits identifying short(er)-term solutions. The International Transport Forum (ITF) suggests that the longer-term outlook for the EV market is likely to remain positive if clean mobility remains a policy priority and economic stimulus packages reflect the role of e-mobility as a driver for innovation[21] but, in the meanwhile, it is necessary to focus attention on short-term solutions.

Many cities have recognized the potential of fiscal policy, providing incentives to support the spread of green and safe alternatives like soft and micro-mobility.

Soft mobility includes any non-motorized transport. According to data above mentioned, COVID-19 has boosted pedestrian and bike mobility. Worldwide, the lockdown has driven new citywide policies. One major result is an increased focus on bicycle lanes. Milan has announced that 35 kilometres of street previously used by cars will be transitioned to walking and cycling lanes after the lockdown is lifted. Paris will convert 50 kilometres of lanes usually reserved for cars to bicycle lanes. It also plans to invest €325 million to update its bicycle network. Brussels is turning 40 kilometres of car lanes into cycle paths. Seattle permanently closed 30 kilometres of street to most vehicles, providing more space for people to walk and bike following the lockdown. Montreal announced the creation of more than 320 kilometres of new pedestrian and bicycle paths across the city.

Partly inspired by the Dutch model,[22] in 2020 the Mayor of London announced a plan to make the city more cyclist- and pedestrian-friendly.[23] The English plan included bike repair vouchers, investments to make cycling and walking safer and easier by transforming three outer London boroughs into cycling hubs, creating temporary cycle lanes and wider pavements.

Yet as lockdowns ease, more lasting changes will be needed to ensure that people continue cycling. This could include physically separating cycles from cars and the introduction of fiscal instruments to make the use of bikes cheaper and more attractive. Tax instruments to support the use of bikes are in force only in a few countries like the UK,[24] Belgium[25] and the Netherlands.[26] Following these experiences, national governments could consider introducing some tax benefits like the cycling mileage allowance to encourage the use of the bike to go to work also after the end of the pandemic.

In addition to bicycles, all micro-mobility vehicles can play a fundamental role in the COVID-19 age. Micro-mobility refers to lightweight transportations designed for individual use including e-scooters and e-bikes, segways, electric skateboards, water bikes and hover boards.

The current situation does not provide a legal framework regarding micro-mobility; there is no international or European definition and it is not clear whether these means of transport are subject to ordinary vehicle taxes. Definitions, classifications and regulatory frameworks for micro-mobility vary across the world. In some cases, they are classified as toys, hence not allowed to circulate on public streets, in other cases these devices are classified with cars (Korea) or as a new vehicle category called 'personal mobility device' (Singapore).[27] European Union regulation n. 168/2013 established the L-category vehicles as a reference for member states but this concept does not include all soft and micro-mobility vehicles. This category excludes human-powered vehicles, such as bicycles, skates and kick scooters, some bicycles with pedal assistance up to 25 km/h and with an auxiliary electric motor having a maximum continuous rated power of up to 250 watts and vehicles not equipped with a seat (i.e. standing scooters).

In the current pandemic context, which reverses the trend from public transport to private mobility, enhancing micro-mobility could be of strategic importance. Micro-mobility is considered less risky[28] than other modes of transportation and it is expected to make a strong post-pandemic recovery.

It seems appropriate to recognize that lockdown periods penalized bike and scooter sharing too. As pointed out by the ITF, the economic pressure on operators caused by the precipitous drop in demand in some markets has sometimes been amplified by poorly designed or unfair regulations and charges levied on electric scooter and bike operators.[29] Their situation improved after the first lockdown period (summer 2020), in which business models like Lime or Bird[30] showed an increase of their use in metropolises like New York and Rome.[31] To support the relaunch of shared mobility services, it would be important to make them more competitive and inclusive. The ITF has shown for some years that there is a gender gap in the use of shared mobility services. Sharing mobility does not have the same appeal for women. They are the principal users of public transport because they do not consider shared mobility a sufficiently safe alternative. To encourage the use of shared transport among women it is necessary to make them safer.[32]

Finally, in a long-term perspective, COVID-19 has shown that is crucial to accelerate the financing of innovations and infrastructures to realize multimodal transport[33] to shape mobility as a service. Some European cities such as Lyon, Geneva and Grenoble have already started implementing multimodality strategies since 2015[34] and many others are starting pilot programmes in the pandemic age. For example, Turin is the first Italian city to have a single public multimodal info-mobility service since September 2020.[35] In Turin around 100 people will have mobility vouchers for a year to move around the city, using different mobility services with a low environmental impact on just one platform.

In addition to the carrot approach, tax legislators could apply the stick one as well: while incentives are considered rewards for developing virtuous behaviours, taxes are punishments to discourage harmful ones.

In this framework, while many urban areas have made significant advances in incentivizing walking and cycling, fewer have taken steps to strengthen disincentives for private car use. Policies to discourage car travel include those that increase the cost of their ownership (e.g. registration and ownership taxes) and use (e.g. congestion levies to access to city centres[36]), as well as vehicle access regulations. The need to restart commercial and service activities concentrated in urban centres quickly has led some cities to propose the suspension of limitations on access to restricted traffic areas and pedestrian areas, as well as the suspension or reduction of parking charges. Reducing the restrictions on car traffic would, however, only lead to an acceleration of congestion with a consequent increase in the pollution threshold. It is very important not to give conflicting signals so as not to jeopardize the outcome of other policies committed to decarbonizing transport. Creating urban environments that are not car friendly will be crucial in supporting the spread of more sustainable transport systems.

3.3 The Italian Experience

The number of passengers on public transport decreased by 95% due to the emergency measures adopted by the Italian government in the first phase of the COVID-19 pandemic.[37] Once quarantine was over, according to the provisions of the Prime Ministerial Decree of 26 April 2020, a distance of at least 1 metre between passengers was required, effectively causing a net reduction of 70% in transport capacity. Even in December 2020, and probably also for 2021, suburban buses and long distance and high speed trains still have to seat passengers with spacing.

The Italian government set a series of measures to tackle the challenges of urban transport in the pandemic age.

Firstly, the implementation of a bike infrastructure was announced. Legislative Decree no. 34 of 19 May 2020 established the financing of projects for the creation, extension, modernization and compliance of cycle lanes, in addition to or as an alternative to those reserved for local public transport.[38] With the pandemic, the City of Milan has started to redraw the road markings of many streets to reserve more space for the so-called soft mobility, be it on foot, by bike, electric scooter or scooter. In December 2020, the Dutch company Swapfiets, which was created in 2014 and launched an innovative long-term bike rental formula, also arrived in Milan.

Secondly, Legislative Decree no. 34 of 19 May 2020 and Law no. 77 of 17 July 2020 amended the ecobonus regulation entered into force in 2019, increasing the bonus for the purchase of new, less pollutant cars or motorcycles.[39] The range of low emission M1 vehicles[40] for which it is possible to apply for a contribution has been extended. In fact, the range of vehicles with emissions of CO_2 61/110 g/km, belonging to the environmental class Euro 6 with a list price not exceeding €40,000, has been added.[41] For motorbikes, the contribution will be 30% of the purchase price, up to a maximum of €3,000, or 40%, up to a maximum of €4,000 in the case of scrapping. Moreover, Law no. 126 of 13 October 2020 introduced two additional contributions to stimulate the conversion of vehicles to electric ones: a contribution of 60% of the cost incurred for the requalification of the vehicle (up to a maximum of €3,500) and a contribution of 60% of the costs associated with vehicle tax.

Thirdly, the Italian government provides a mobility bonus to support the purchase of soft and micro-mobility transport.

The mobility bonus is a contribution of 60% of the costs incurred, up to a maximum of €500 for the purchase of bicycles and powered bicycles, as well as other electric vehicles for personal mobility (e.g. scooters, hover boards and segways) and shared mobility services for individual use, excluding cars. This bonus had already been introduced by art. 2 of Legislative Decree no. 111 of 14 October 2019 and was amended by Legislative Decree no. 34 of 19 May 2020 (Relaunch Decree) providing:

1. For 2020, the provision of mobility vouchers for purchases made from 4 May 2020 to 31 December 2020 without scrapping old vehicles;
2. From 1 January 2021, the provision of mobility vouchers on the scrapping of old vehicles. The vouchers can be used up until 31 December 2024.

The mobility bonus can only be requested by residents of the regional capitals, provincial capitals, metropolitan cities or towns with a population of over 50,000 inhabitants.

The Italian decision to place micro-mobility at the centre of urban mobility is welcomed; however, this contribution appears to be a propitious occasion to discuss this controversial measure. The spread of micro-mobility opens several problems from a legal and tax perspective.

The Ministry of the Environment announced in December 2020 that 558,725 purchases of bicycles and scooters were subsidized by the Italian mobility bonus. From an economic point of view, the National Association of Bicycles and Motorcycles considers that there has been a 60% sales growth compared to 2019. It should be noted that this sales explosion was not restricted to bicycles, but also, for example, to scooters. Whether the increase in sales is due to the introduction of the bonus is not clear. Nevertheless, international data and the high number of sales in Italy clearly demonstrate people's interest in soft and micro-mobility. This is the crucial point that causes some problems from a legal point of view. Firstly, it is important to understand if it is really necessary to encourage already widespread behaviours. Perhaps yes, if it is taken into consideration that the spread of soft and micro-mobility is due principally to the pandemic crisis and consequently it might be only temporary. If we want to consolidate these green options, incentives for these kinds of vehicles should be considered appropriate in the first phase of the economic recovery. After having established that the theoretical introduction of tax incentives to support micro-mobility is reasonable, it is necessary to assess the legality of the mobility bonus and in particular to investigate whether the design of this measure complies with the State Aid provision. To accelerate the transition to more sustainable transport, national governments can use tax instruments, but they must be temporary and limited to what is necessary so as not to violate the European State Aid legislation. The European logic allows incentives solely to stimulate investments, purchases or social behaviour that citizens would not otherwise have undertaken. The mobility bonus is provided to every resident in urban areas and there are some doubts that this criterion is adequate to guarantee the incentive effect. In order to safeguard the incentive effect, the Italian legislators could have reduced the number of recipients by placing an income limit to avail of the bonus. The income parameter could reduce the distributional effects linked to this instrument and support the purchase of bikes and e-scooters by middle- and low-income families. Moreover, it is doubtful that this bonus is really capable of creating new urban mobility habits. To overcome this objection it would be better to support the use rather than solely the purchase of new green vehicles, otherwise the risk of increasing the number of vehicles, even if less pollutant, without affecting travelling habits remains high.[42]

From a tax perspective, e-scooters are also exempt from registration and ownership tax in Italy. They are not considered mopeds, which, by contrast, are subject to ownership tax only from the sixth year and with a very low rate.

Finally, a consideration about the future and sustainability of vehicle tax system revenues is necessary. In the current vehicle tax system, it is the ownership of a vehicle that is taxed rather that its use, but the spread of shared transport and new mobility alternatives require a deep reflection on the updating of the vehicle taxation system to prevent an erosion of national revenues from vehicle taxation.[43] After the recovery phase, national governments will have to address the challenge of the debt repayment and revenue concerns will be placed at the centre of their political priorities.

4. CONCLUDING REMARKS

The COVID-19 pandemic is creating damage that is still difficult to calculate, from a health, social and economic point of view, but it can also have effects of positive acceleration of processes towards a just transition to environmentally sustainable economies and societies.

Cities could become smarter in their transport systems, complying with the UN 2030 Agenda goals and the European Commission agenda. The change has already started, because the need to distance and not gather people is changing urban mobility. To reach this aim national governments have a useful tool. They can use tax instruments to support new urban transport alternatives. For example, in the phase of economic recovery the implementation of tax credits to buy or, even better, to use soft and micro-mobility vehicles could generate economic growth and benefit the environment if properly designed. However, governments should define clear policy objectives and introduce *ex ante* and in particular, *ex post* assessment mechanisms to monitor their efficiency. The environmental evaluation is important to avoid tax incentives encouraging negative practices for the environment, prevent rebound effects and limit market distortion.

The COVID-19 pandemic has clearly shown that our lifestyle, including transport habits, is not sustainable. Until now, efficiency, that is, the reduction of costs and the maximization of value, was favoured over resilience. Today everyone is asking for a more sustainable transport system and, more generally, for a more resilient economic system. But rather than resilience, we should resort to Nassim Taleb's antifragility concept: something resilient resists shocks but remains the same as before, antifragility gives rise to a better thing.[44]

Green recovery is crucial to give economic support to businesses and consumers, but it is not enough. Because of COVID-19, many people are recognizing that there is actually another way to live, work and move and consequently the pandemic could be an opportunity to accelerate the green transition. The whole transport sector should be rethought so as not to go back to the previous situation. If there were ever a possibility to change the current urban mobility situation, this is the moment. Fiscal incentives must be shaped in the direction of supporting safer, greener and smarter mobility services, taking digital opportunities and environmental concerns into consideration. To foster this change, a review of the vehicle tax principles is necessary and the transition ownership versus use is at the top of this challenge. Tax policies that will be adopted in 2021 at all levels of government – municipalities, regions, states and the European Union – will determine decisively the consolidation of the unsustainability of the transport system or, instead, if the pandemic will act as a catalyst for a just transition to more sustainable urban transport patterns. It seems that the time has come for a paradigmatic shift.

NOTES

1. Ipsos Mori, Earth Day 2020, *How does the world view climate change and Covid-19?* April 2020, accessed 10 August 2020 at https://www.ipsos.com/sites/default/files/ct/news/documents/2020-04/earth-day-2020-ipsos.pdf.
2. The World Health Organization (WHO) states that 23% of all deaths could be prevented through healthier environments. See WHO, *Healthy environments for healthier populations: Why do they matter, and what can we do?*, 2019; The World Health Organization, *Preventing disease through healthy environments: A global assessment of the burden of disease from environmental risks*, 2016.
3. A study from Harvard Chan School of Public Health suggested that breathing more polluted air over many years may itself worsen the effects of COVID-19.

The Harvard study is one of several that have now suggested that air pollution is affecting COVID-19 mortality. Researchers analysing 120 cities in China found a significant relationship between air pollution and COVID-19 infection, and of the coronavirus deaths across 66 regions in Italy, Spain and Germany, 78% of them occurred in five of the most polluted regions. See Z. Yongjian, X. Jingui, H. Fengming and C. Liqing, *Association between short-term exposure to air pollution and COVID-19 infection: Evidence from China*, Science of the Total Environment, 2020, vol. 727, 138704; Y. Ogen, *Assessing nitrogen dioxide (NO2) levels as a contributing factor to coronavirus (COVID-19) fatality*, Science of the Total Environment, 2020, vol. 726, 138605.

4. OECD Environment Focus, *The challenges of greening urban mobility in the post-pandemic era*, 24 July 2020, accessed 3 August .2020 at https://oecd-environment-focus.blog/2020/07/24/the-challenges-of-greening-urban-mobility-in-the-post-pandemic-era/.
5. Data from TomTom traffic index 2020. It is a global online traffic index web platform that generates traffic congestion calculations by collecting and analysing GPS data to monitor vehicles on roads.
6. Airparif announced an increase in the level of air pollution in the Paris region in June 2020. Airparif is a non-profit organization accredited by the Ministry of Environment to monitor the air quality in Paris and in the Ile de France region.
7. There are currently more than 50 COVID-19 vaccine candidates in trials. The EU has already authorized four vaccines but its distribution will take time.
8. In the spring period 2020.
9. Boston Consulting Group, *How Covid-19 will shape urban mobility*, June 2020.
10. In the summer period 2020.
11. OECD, *Tax and fiscal policy in response to the coronavirus crisis: Strengthening confidence and resilience*, May 2020, 9.
12. S. Agrawala, D. Dussaux and N. Monti, *What policies for greening the crisis response and economic recovery? Lessons learned from past green stimulus measures and implications for the COVID-19 crisis*, Environment Working Paper no. 164, OECD, 2020, 6.
13. Strand and Toman identified different categories of stimulus concerning renewable energy generation, energy efficiency in buildings, scrappage payments for vehicles with low fuel efficiency, clean technology development support, nature conservation and water resource management and they studied their expected effect on growth, greenhouse gas (GHG) emission reduction and other environmental benefits. See J. Strand and M. Toman, *'Green stimulus' economic recovery, and long-term sustainable development*, The World Bank, 2010. Many of these measures are also being proposed in the context of greening the COVID-19 recovery.
14. L. Mundaca and J.L. Richter, *Assessing 'green energy economy' stimulus packages: Evidence from the U.S. programs targeting renewable energy*, Renewable and Sustainable Energy Reviews, 2015, vol. 42, issue C, 1174–86.
15. It was made up of production and investment tax credits, research projects and cash grants to foster innovation.
16. The regulatory dimension of taxation has been known since the Roman Age. Taxation has always been used to influence behaviours. We can refer to '*ultro tributa*' set up by Cato the Censor. As pointed out by Neumark, the great potential of tax instruments lies in leaving individuals free to choose, see F. Neumark, *Impôt et société*, Bulletin de l'Institut de Science Économique Appliquée, 1969, n.

3, 477. In tax literature Avi-Yonah supported the idea of three goals of taxation: to raise revenue, redistribute income and regulate private sector activities in the directions desired by governments, see R.S. Avi-Yonah, *The three goals of taxation*, Tax Law Review, 2006, vol. 60, n.1, 1–28. This feature of taxation is internationally accepted (see e.g. OECD, *Tackling environmental problems with the help of behavioural insights*, 2017; J.E. Milne and M.S. Andersen, *Introduction to environmental taxation concepts and research*, in J.E. Milne and M.S. Andersen (eds), Handbook of Research on Environmental Taxation, Edward Elgar Publishing, 2012, pp. 15–32) and recognized at a national level with different concepts. In France there is the concept of '*fiscalité incitative*' or '*fiscalité comportementale*', whereas in Italy and Spain there are the concepts respectively of '*extrafiscalità*' or '*extrafiscalidad*'.

17. OECD, *Building a coherent response for a sustainable post-COVID-19 recovery*, November 2020.
18. The *ex post* evaluation of green incentives introduced during the big financial crisis showed that proper policy design is critical to prevent rebound effects and limit market distortion, see S. Agrawala, D. Dussaux and N. Monti, *What policies for greening the crisis response and economic recovery? Lessons learned from past green stimulus measures and implications for the COVID-19 crisis*, Environment Working Paper no. 164, OECD, 2020, p. 6.
19. The International Transport Forum recently published a report to highlight the negative impact that subsidies, also in the form of tax reduction, have on the transition towards the electrification of the fleet, see International Transport Forum, *Company cars: How European governments are subsidising pollution and climate change*, October 2020.
20. For the EU energy mix, hydrogen could play a key role, because it can replace fossil fuels in some carbon intensive industrial processes, such as in the steel or chemical sectors, lowering GHG emissions. The EU Commission is currently implementing a hydrogen strategy but it takes time. See COM (2020) 301 final, *A hydrogen strategy for a climate-neutral Europe*, 8 July 2020.
21. International Transport Forum, *Electric mobility: Taking the pulse in times of coronavirus*, Covid-19 Transport Brief, 27 April 2020, accessed 12 June 2020 at www.itf-oecd.org.
22. The Dutch model can be considered one of the best practices in Europe where cycling has been developed by making cycling appealing and accessible to people of all income groups, see Dutch Cycling Embassy, *Dutch Cycling Vision*, October 2018.
23. The project is called '*Streetspace for London*', available on the web site Transport for London, accessed 5 August 2020 at https://tfl.gov.uk/travel-information/improvements-and-projects/streetspace-for-london.
24. The Cycle to Work Scheme is a tax exemption introduced with the Financial Act 1999 allowing employers to loan bikes and safety equipment to employees as a tax-free benefit.
25. In Belgium, there has been a voluntary cycling mileage allowance in force since 1997 and employers can provide employees with a company bike. A bike is not considered a taxable benefit for employees and 120% of the costs are deducted for employers.
26. Since 1 January 2020 employers may pay cyclists a (tax-free) mileage allowance of up to €0.19 per kilometre.

27. International Transport Forum, *Safe micromobility*, Corporate Partnership Board Report, February 2020, p. 14.
28. New personal mobility vehicles (PMVs) provide opportunities to their users but at the same time create some problems with street space sharing, road safety, and traffic offences that must be taken into account. See J. Zagorskas and M. Burinskiene, *Challenges caused by increased use of e-powered personal mobility vehicles in European cities*, Sustainability, 2020, no. 12, 273.
29. International Transport Forum, *COVID-19 transport brief: Re-spacing our cities for resilience*, accessed 12 June 2020 at https://www.itf-oecd.org/sites/default/files/respacing-cities-resilience-covid-19.pdf?fbclid=IwAR1mxucdmtT7hcy8zjeS_Ll3cihQelWVyFca5BlP1-rUa1-qecvsPx5Ct2M.
30. Lime and Bird are American companies dealing with shared transport services. They run e-scooters, bikes and e-bikes in various cities in the world.
31. New York Council approved a shared e-scooter pilot programme in the summer of 2020 and Bird arrived in Rome in June 2020. See Bird Cities Blog, 29 June 2020, accessed 24 May 2021 at https://www.bird.co/blog. See also *Rethink your ride with Lime*, Lime Blog, 15 July 2020, accessed 6 August 2020 at https://www.li.me/second-street/rethink-your-ride-with-lime.
32. International Transport Forum, *Transport connectivity: A gender perspective*, OECD Publishing, Paris, 2020; C. Duchène, *Gender and transport*, Discussion Paper no. 2011-11, April 2011.
33. The EU Commission announced in the European Green Deal that it would adopt a strategy for sustainable and smart mobility that will also address the challenge of multimodal transport. See COM (2019) 640 final 2.1.5.
34. International Transport Forum, *Transition to shared mobility*, May 2017; International Transport Forum, *A new paradigm for urban mobility*, November 2015; B. Dugua, G. Novarina and G. Trotta-Brambilla, *Strategie di multimodalità e articolazione tra urbanistica e trasporti: a Lione, Grenoble e Ginevra*, in Urbanistica, 2015, no. 156, 94–121.
35. Press release of the Municipality of Turin, 22 September 2020, accessed 5 October 2020 at http://www.comune.torino.it/ucstampa/2020/article_637.shtml.
36. Empirical findings indicate that congestion pricing increases daily bike-sharing use by around 5% to 5.8% in the short run, depending on the model specification. See OECD, *Evaluating the impact of urban road pricing on the use of green transport modes: The case of Milan*, Environment Working Paper no. 143, February 2019, p. 9.
37. The first Italian lockdown was announced in March 2020 and lasted until May 2020.
38. Decreto Legge 19 May 2020 no. 34 published in the *Gazzetta Ufficiale* 19 May 2020 no. 128.
39. The mechanism was introduced in 2018 with Law no. 145 of 30 December 2018, and entered into force 1 March 2019. During the XX Global Conference on Environmental Taxation a paper was presented dealing with the Italian ecobonus legislation. See A. Tomo, *'Ecobonus' and 'Ecotax': Two recent Italian fiscal measures to promote the decarbonisation in vehicles system*, in T. Zachariadis, J.E. Milne, M.S. Andersen and H. Ashiabor (eds), Economic Instruments for a Low-Carbon Future, Critical Issues in Environmental Taxation Series, vol. XXII, Edward Elgar Publishing, 2020, pp. 70–81.
40. M1 vehicles are vehicles for the transport of persons, having a maximum of eight seats in addition to the driver's seat.

41. Law no. 178/2020 extended this contribution for Euro 6 vehicles until June 2021 with the condition that a vehicle registered before 2011 is scrapped.
42. The English and the Belgian experience demonstrated the efficiency of tax mechanisms to promote the use of the bike to go to work, in this sense see European Cyclists' Federation, *Commuting: Who pays the bill?*, 2018, p. 7.
43. In favour of this idea see A. Gago, X. Labandeira and X. Lopez-Otero, *Taxing vehicle use to overcome the problems of conventional transport taxes*, in M. Villar, J.E. Milne, H. Ashiabor and M.S. Andersen (eds), Environmental Fiscal Challenges for Cities and Transport, Critical Issues in Environmental Taxation Series, vol. XXI, Edward Elgar Publishing, 2019, pp. 154–67.
44. N. Taleb, Antifragile: Prosperare nel disordine, Il Saggiatore, 2013.

PART V

Environmental support schemes in the midst of the pandemic

13. A taxonomy of environmentally sustainable activities to orient Covid-19 tax measures to environmental objectives

Sébastien Wolff[1]

1. INTRODUCTION

In 2018, the European Commission presented a plan for sustainable finance aiming at reorienting capital flows towards sustainable activities.[2] Among other measures, the Commission announced the development of a Taxonomy for sustainable economic activities. The Taxonomy and delegated acts will list such activities and provide minimum environmental standards for each of them.

In December 2019, the European Commission's chairwoman introduced a new strategic plan for the European Union ('The European Green Deal'),[3] aiming at reaching climate neutrality in 2050 by, that is, creating a European sustainable investment fund, revising the Energy Taxation Directive[4] ('ETD') and promoting a circular economy. In recent years and after two missed attempts for the Commission to revise the ETD, voices have been raised against the current provisions. To its credit, the ETD was drafted long before climate impact caused by the use of fossil energy was the main concern. The same point might be made for state aid regulation and value added tax (VAT), where completing the internal market and avoiding any hostile competition between member states were higher on the preoccupations list than environmental concerns at the time of their adoption.

Since the rapid outbreak of Covid-19 throughout the world, governments are facing requests from weakened sectors to benefit from public financial support.[5] The temptation is then high for governments to support economic activities with subsidies and tax incentives. However, not all activities are carbon-neutral or climate friendly: funding them might lead to supporting fossil energy and going against the international commitment under the Paris agreement and the main objective of the Green Deal. And Covid-19 has also shown that air pollution is directly linked to economic activity.[6]

The aim of this chapter is to investigate the opportunity and the pertinence to refer to a Taxonomy for selecting the beneficiaries of tax measures and subsidies. On the one hand, the selection of activities that contribute to one or several of the six objectives included in the Taxonomy will foster energy transition and environment protection; on the other, it will provide a unified definition of environmental activities for tax purposes and help to safeguard a fair competition across Europe when it comes to protecting the environment and tackling climate change.

In this chapter, we discuss the potential use of the Taxonomy for establishing a common standard for preferential regimes for both state aids in the field of energy or environment and energy taxation. The first section presents the Taxonomy destined originally to financial sector regulation and the economic activities listed within. The second section is then dedicated to the evaluation of the current regime and the numerous exemptions and preferential regimes included in the ETD and VAT directive. It also assesses the State Aid legal framework and Section 7 of the General Block Exemption Regulation (GBER) which is dedicated to environmental aids. Finally, the last section is an attempt to bring coherence with the Taxonomy into the energy taxation legal framework.

2. THE TAXONOMY OF SUSTAINABLE ACTIVITIES FOR FINANCIAL PRODUCTS

In 2018, the European Commission adopted a new plan for financing a sustainable growth,[7] where the reorientation of private and public funds to sustainable economic activities is identified as a key element for a transition to a greener economy. As part of this plan, three regulations were adopted by the Council and the Parliament: (1) the Benchmark regulation,[8] (2) Disclosure regulation[9] and finally (3) the Taxonomy.[10] The Benchmark regulation intends to include some sustainable dimensions in financial benchmarks, that is, making it mandatory for providers to offer a reference benchmark in line with the EU climate objective. The Disclosure regulation, interestingly, requires financial market participants and financial advisers to publish pre-contractual and periodical information about the sustainability of their activities and the products they proposed. Among other information, it imposes on the manufacturer of a financial product or to the investee company itself the publication of the percentage of sustainable activities falling within the Taxonomy criteria. Finally, the Taxonomy builds up a harmonised database of environmentally sustainable activities. For this purpose, the Commission will develop screening criteria demarcating sustainable activities from others.

According to the Taxonomy, an environmentally sustainable activity is:[11]

1. An activity contributing substantially to one or several of the six environmental objectives: (a) climate change mitigation; (b) climate change adaptation; (c) the sustainable use and protection of water and marine resources; (d) the transition to a circular economy; (e) pollution prevention and control; (f) the protection and the restoration of biodiversity and ecosystems;
2. An activity that does not harm any other objective;
3. An activity which is carried out in compliance with minimum safeguards identified in the regulation; and
4. An activity that meets the screening criteria specific to a certain area of business.

It is worth noting that the criteria should be assessed in a cumulative way, meaning that an activity will only be considered as sustainable if the four conditions are met.

The potential contribution of an activity to one of the six objectives is described in more detail in the Taxonomy provisions.[12] For instance, article 10 describes an economic activity that contributes substantially to the objective 'climate change mitigation' as follows:

> An activity contributes substantially to the stabilisation of greenhouse gas concentrations in the atmosphere at a level which prevents dangerous anthropogenic interference with the climate system consistent with the long-term temperature goal of the Paris Agreement through the avoidance or reduction of greenhouse gas emissions or the increase of greenhouse gas removals, including through process innovations or product innovations.[13]

Then the same article lists different activities regarded as serving the objective such (1) generating, transmitting, storing, distributing or using renewable energy in line with Directive (EU) 2018/2001, including through using innovative technology with a potential for significant future savings or through necessary reinforcement or extension of the grid; (2) improving energy efficiency, except for power generation activities; or (3) increasing clean or climate-neutral mobility.

For the development of screening criteria, expertise from European experts was gathered to develop a methodology to assess the impact of economic activities on climate change and on the environment. This scientific input makes the Taxonomy rather an environmental regulation than a financial one. Two different reports were published by the group of environment experts,[14] listing proposals of screening criteria for more than 140 economic activities, but only for two objectives linked with climate change. Ten major areas of the economy are covered: Forestry; Agriculture; Manufacturing; Electricity, gas, steam and air conditioning supply; Water, sewerage, waste and remediation; Transportation and storage; Information and communications; Construction and real estate activities; Financial and insurance activities; and Professional, scientific and technical activities.

For every activity, screening criteria provide a precise estimation of the figures to meet by market operators to fulfil the objective. Furthermore, specific conditions are included to enact the do-not-significantly-harm principle and the minimum safeguards. For car manufacturing – an example of a key activity sector for decarbonising the economy – screening criteria might be summarised as follows:

- To be considered as contributing substantially to mitigate climate change, the tailpipe emissions shall be limited to a maximum of 50g CO_2/km under the World harmonised Light-duty vehicles Test Procedure (WLTP) protocol until 2025. From 2026 onwards, emissions of CO_2 will be further limited to 0g CO_2/km;
- To comply with the do-not-significantly-harm principle, the following requirements shall be met:
  - Direct emissions to air from exhaust gases of internal combustion engines; for this specific criterion, it is interesting to note that the Taxonomy requirements go further than the current thresholds under Euro 6 norm,[15] imposing an additional effort of 10%;
  - Indirect emissions to air from the production of fuels and energy carriers;
  - Waste generation, with the application of the strengthened levels of recycling of the 'end-of-life of vehicles directive';[16]
  - Recycling of materials, in view of creating a circular economy;
  - Noise, as one of the parameters to evaluate tyres. With a special focus on tyres, the report proposed to go beyond tyre labelling regulation[17] requirements by adding an indicator on the abrasion.
  - Road safety, as all vehicles coming from the factory should be compliant with Regulation No 661/2009 which establishes standards for releasing a vehicle on the European roads.

From a legal perspective, it is interesting to note that the scope is not limited to vehicles intended to be driven within the European Union but is also applicable when European factories manufacture cars and light commercial trucks for foreign markets. In this respect, the effort to be considered as an environmentally sustainable activity for financial purposes has to be assessed at the level of the company. As we will discuss later in this chapter, it means that taxes levied at the production level rather than at the consumption level match particularly well with a potential application of the Taxonomy.

In general, the Taxonomy works as an aggregator of all environmental and climate concerns relating specially to a certain activity. In economic words, screening criteria are trying to encompass and mitigate all negative externalities caused by the economic activity in addition to its contribution to one or several environmental objectives.

3. THE CURRENT PORTFOLIO OF EXEMPTIONS AND PREFERENTIAL TAX REGIMES IN THE FIELD OF ENVIRONMENTAL AND ENERGY TAXATION

a. Exceptions and Preferential Regimes within the Energy Taxation Directive[18]

Before listing product exemptions and rate reductions of the ETD, it is important to recall that its first aim was not environmental. The ETD was adopted in the 1990s to avoid distortions of competition in the internal market and cover all excise levies. Per design, as every excise duty, it regulates production taxes. Due to this age, the current provisions of the ETD are dated and do not reflect the ambitious EU objectives in greenhouse gas (GHG) emissions reduction and protection of the environment.

The ETD does not create a specific tax but only imposes a certain level of taxation to a selection of energy products.[19] Therefore, excise rates might be different depending on the member states where it is levied. Certain member states, such France or Sweden, use several taxes to reach the minimum level of taxation imposed by the ETD.[20] For others, a specific levy was included in their tax system and is specifically designed for energy. For instance, the Irish tax on mineral oils is proportional to the carbon content to a certain extent since the revision of the Mineral Oil Tax bill.[21]

As long as the minimum levels of taxation included in the ETD are met, member states remain free to discriminate products based on their quality, the quantity produced, the usage or the business character of the consumption.[22] For instance, several member states decided to discriminate rates between low and high sulphur content gasoil used as propellant or as heating fuel.[23] Some others, such as Austria or Denmark, decided to grant a favourable rate for gasoil with a minimum content of biofuel. More originally, Hungary raises upwards its level of taxation when the price of crude oil is less than 50 USD per barrel.

By design, the ETD includes also several exemptions and preferential regimes, authorising member states to tax at different rates the same energy product. Some exceptions were purely transitional or are applicable only to very limited areas of member states' territories.[24] However, some other provisions which are not limited in time or to some territories are still in application. For instance, certain usages can justify a reduced rate, independently of their actual impact on the environment. It results in the fact that a similar product might be taxed differently according to its use, and that also for a similar use, the price paid is different depending on the member state or depending on the carbon nature of the product. Consequently, several scholars and the Commission itself pointed out that the current minimum levels of taxation imposed by the directive do not reflect their carbon content nor their pollutant potential.[25] This resulted in a specific paragraph in the new Green Deal strategy urging member states to consent to a reform of the ETD to meet the following aims:

- Aligning taxation of energy products and electricity with EU energy and climate policies, to contribute to the EU 2030 energy targets and climate neutrality by 2050;
- Preserving the EU single market by updating the scope and the structure of tax rates and rationalising the use of optional tax exemptions and reductions.[26]

Exemptions and reduced rates based on the use of fuel might be addressed with the help of a Taxonomy. Indeed, under the current drafting, business owners and companies might benefit from reduced rates under the ETD on the one hand and carry activities harmful for the environment on the other. It consequently jeopardises the new aim recognised to excise duties of sending a price signal on the climate impact of fossil fuels. The idea discussed in this chapter is not to revoke all preferential regimes but instead to use the Taxonomy to bring more selectivity. A targeted mapping of economic activities may help to refine the current regime to reorient tax expenditures to activities that are contributing to general objectives of the European Union and its member states.

In keeping with this spirit, exemptions and reduced rates relating to business use might be limited to companies carrying out an activity contributing substantially to one of the six objectives listed in the Taxonomy. Without being intended for tax purposes, the Taxonomy is well designed to match the objective of an excise system including environmental and climate concerns:

- Economic activities benefiting from ETD business preferential regimes are covered by the Taxonomy;
- Activity of producing energy is included in the Taxonomy, so are the screening criteria linked to the manufacturing of all energy products.

Indeed, the Taxonomy includes the production of energy in two objectives: substantial contribution to climate change mitigation and substantial contribution to climate change adaptation. However, only certain ways of generating energy are considered as environmentally sustainable. Among others, are listed the production of electricity from renewables, which does not fall into the scope of the ETD, but also the use of gas for electricity generation, for heating and for cooling. The screening criteria are relatively severe, as they use a declining threshold for GHG emissions reaching 0g/CO2 per unit by 2050. The addition of the Taxonomy criteria to benefit from the reduced business rates will consequently help to reinforce the environmental character of the ETD.

Moreover, the use of a Taxonomy will provide a better view on the amount of fossil energy used by member states to foster climate change mitigation and make it possible to align this objective with the Green Deal target.

b.   VAT

The EU tax on added value is one of the most advanced tax systems on consumption in the world and one of the most harmonised public levies at the European level.

As for the ETD, the main objective of VAT harmonisation was the completion of the internal market. However, as a consumption tax, the fourth recital of the last VAT directive[27] establishes another objective:

> A VAT system achieves the highest degree of simplicity and of neutrality when the tax is levied in as general a manner as possible and when its scope covers all stages of production and distribution, as well as the supply of services.[28]

The neutrality principle requires to limit operations falling outside of the scope and to avoid potential competition distortion due to preferential tax regimes. A limit of two reduced rates per member state was consequently imposed – with an absolute minimum rate of 5%. Annex 3 lists goods and services where a reduced rate can be applied but does not include any product or service harmful to the environment.

In our opinion, the most problematic provision consists in article 110 of the VAT directive.[29] This article states as follows:

> Member states which, at 1 January 1991, were granting exemptions with deductibility of the VAT paid at the preceding stage or applying reduced rates lower than the

minimum laid down in Article 99 may continue to grant those exemptions or apply those reduced rates.
The exemptions and reduced rates referred to in the first paragraph must be in accordance with Community law and must have been adopted for clearly defined social reasons and for the benefit of the final consumer.[30]

When adopted in 1991, the intention was to have a progressive phase-out. However, in 2020, 'parking rates' are still applied by several member states. One of the reasons might be that, when a member state decides to raise one of its 'parking rates', it will not be possible in the future to reintroduce a reduced rate on this product or service if not included in Annex 3.

From an environmental perspective, 'parking rates' are the biggest concern in the VAT system because of the wrong price signal they send. Indeed, in reason of their adoption in the 1980s, products and services benefiting from a reduced rate were not selected based on modern environmental concerns or climate change. It results that certain countries tax at preferential rates fossil fuels, despite their disastrous effect on the climate and the environment.[31]

Applied to consumption tax, the Taxonomy could limit reduced rates and exemptions to goods and services offered by economic operators compliant with the screening criteria. From a legal perspective, such an ambitious vision might be difficult in an international context. Indeed, in application of the General Agreement on Tariffs and Trade (GATT) provision on border adjustments[32] and to maintain a fair access to the European market for foreign producers, it is necessary to let producers located outside the European Union have the option to prove they comply with the screening criteria. Moreover, the adoption of a common standard for sustainable activities will impose harmonisation of the potential domains where a reduced rate could be applied and raise as a new objective for consumption tax the protection of the environment and of the climate.

c. **State Aids and Section 7 of the General Block Exemption Regulation**

The last area where environmental and energy concerns might echo is the control of state aids. As for other aids, tax expenditures or subsidies granted for environmental purpose through state resources, which distort or threaten to distort competition by favouring certain undertakings or the production of certain goods, are incompatible with the internal market in application of article 107 Treaty on the Functioning of the European Union (TFEU).[33] However, the treaty also includes the possibility to exempt certain categories of aids via a general scheme. This possibility was materialised in the adoption of the GBER[34] for certain areas of public intervention. It allows member states to support certain categories of activities without prior notification to the European Commission. Section 7 of the GBER is dedicated to aid belonging to the environmental protection field and contains all conditions for state aids to be declared compatible. However, the tax design is assessed more in details than the effective environmental impact. The too general environmental criteria engender a lack of precision, especially when compared to the criteria developed in application of the Taxonomy, both in the different dimensions they cover than in the severity of the requirements.[35]

By adding the Taxonomy requirements for an activity to be declared compatible with the treaty, public aids might be more accurately redirected to the right projects and companies and contribute therefore to Green Deal objectives. Moreover, it will help to bring coherence between objectives at the level of the Union and aids granted by member states.

4. A TAXONOMY TO BRING MORE COHERENCE IN THE FISCAL LANDSCAPE

The proposed introduction of a common database for environmentally sustainable activities for tax matters aims at fostering transparency for the taxpayer of tax expenditures directed to environmental and climate projects. With the help of the legislative bundle from the 'Action plan for sustainable finance',[36] it aims at increasing the amount of private capital and public expenses that are redirected to key activities for tackling climate change and fostering environmental protection, including in a Covid-19 context.

As illustrated in Figure 31.1, according to classical economic theory, capital comes from two different sources: from the state or from private investment. For the latter, the investment might come directly from private citizens, by buying shares or bonds issued by a company or from the banks acting as intermediaries. With the entry into force of the Taxonomy and Disclosure regulations, market participants – including banks – must disclose the share of sustainable activities of every financial product they market as sustainable. A similar obligation for tax expenditures granted by member states might help in monitoring progress in key areas of the energy transition.

To align fiscal provisions with climate and environment targets of the Green Deal, the following modifications could be envisaged in fiscal matters:

- In the *Energy Taxation Directive*, exemptions and reduced rates for business use could be limited to economic operators who are carrying out mainly activities contributing to one of the Taxonomy objectives. The requested share could be adjusted according to technological progress. Two main advantages might be found in these amendments: first, it maintains a fair playing field between economic participants by harmonising at

the European level areas where business exemptions and reduced rates can be granted by member states; second, it aligns ETD provisions with the objective of carbon neutrality in 2050.
- In the *VAT directive*, provisions could be revamped to repeal 'parking rates' and to introduce a requirement for the manufacturer of goods or services to comply with the screening criteria of the Taxonomy in order to benefit from a reduced rate. Again, the required share of compliant activities might be adjusted over time and the list of activities might evolve to match new technological developments.
- Finally, the *state aid legal framework* might be refined by integrating in the GBER the stronger screening criteria from the Taxonomy.

From a political perspective, according to article 113, enacting secondary law in fiscal matters requires unanimity at the level of the Council.[37] Reaching unanimity on potential reforms might not be a walk in the park, as shown by previous attempts from the Commission to redraft the ETD and the VAT directive. However, preferential tax regimes based on the evolution of the share of sustainable activities over time might be envisaged.

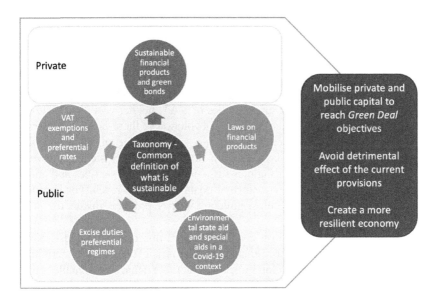

Figure 13.1   The use of the Taxonomy in the different fields of public policy

The proposal behind this chapter is obviously not to reform the entire tax system on the basis of tackling climate change and making environment protection the only top priority. It aims at unifying the definition of environmental sustainability in two interconnected areas of public intervention: taxation and banking regulation. With the rapid outbreak of Covid-19, the need for public funding is increasing, and billions of public money is reaching businesses. The conditions to benefit from such help are not predetermined and will certainly broadly vary between member states. In this specific context, one might find it interesting to dedicate the most generous financial support to businesses and companies that have already committed themselves to a product compliant with the most advanced climate and environmental standards, like the ones included in the Taxonomy. The current Covid-19 outbreak seems indeed to support the idea that a transition to more sustainable activities will make the economy more resilient to crisis and prevent additional threats due to climate change. Moreover, preserving the environment will limit the spread of diseases only present in pristine environments.

5. CONCLUSION

As presented in the first parts, the adoption of a Taxonomy for sustainable activities might constitute an important step to reach greater protection of the environment and to mitigate climate change. It makes the boundary between sustainable and not sustainable activities clearer and suggests a reflection about the real impact of investment decisions on environmental concerns.

As for financial regulation, climate change and environment protection were not the initial objectives of excise duties or VAT, neither was it for state aid control. However, due to the absence of evolution of these provisions during the last 15 years, the current tax regimes are becoming obsolete and lack adequacy with the current concerns and challenges. The existence of several preferential regimes supporting non-sustainable activities, services and goods are making climate and environmental goals difficult to reach. For instance, reduced VAT rates on the most pollutant energy products distort the price signal sent to the consumer.

Instead of trying to reform each legislation, this chapter suggests using for tax purpose the already existing Taxonomy of sustainable activities. Environmental experts develop screening criteria to delimit sustainable activities in all main areas of economic activity. We propose to use these screening criteria in order to insert a harmonised definition of sustainable activities to all main tax regulations. It could result in (1) limitation of a VAT reduced rate to goods and services with production processes in line with the Taxonomy criteria, (2) an excise preferential business regime granted only to companies and individuals carrying on sustainable activities responding to the Taxonomy standards – or in proportion of this compliance – and (3) a more ambitious and more precise legal framework for state aids.

In our opinion, the adoption of a common definition of sustainable economic activity will help to bring more transparency to the allocation of public funds in the field of climate or environment initiatives. Furthermore, it will create an equality between public and private financial resources dedicated to sustainable activities and maintain a level playing field among European businesses when it comes to advantageous tax regimes for environmental initiatives. Finally, it will be an important tool to reach the Green Deal objective for environment preservation and climate change mitigation. As the current Covid-19 epidemic emphasises the need for public support, a common standard for tax measures in favour of sustainable development will help to rebuild the economy in a greener way and make it more resilient to future crises.

NOTES

1. Sébastien Eric Wolff is a PhD candidate at the Catholic University of Louvain (Belgium) under the supervision of Pr. Dr E. Traversa, lecturer at the ICHEC Brussels Management School (Belgium) and guest lecturer at the Université de Lorraine (France).
2. Communication of 8 March 2018 from the Commission: 'Action Plan: Financing Sustainable Growth', COM/2018/097 final.
3. Communication of 11 December 2019 from the European Commission: 'The European Green Deal', COM/2019/640 final.
4. Council directive 2003/96/EC of 27 October 2003 restructuring the Community framework for the taxation of energy products and electricity, *OJ* L 283 of 31 October 2003, 51.
5. See for instance: OECD (2020). *Government support and the COVID-19 pandemic*. 14 April 2020, accessed 18 May 2021 at https://read.oecd-ilibrary.org/view/?ref=128_128572-w5qyf5699d&title=Government-support-and-the-COVID-19-pandemic; OECD (2020). *COVID-19 and fiscal relations across levels of government*. 31 July 2020, accessed 18 May 2021 at http://www.oecd.org/coronavirus/policy-responses/covid-19-and-fiscal-relations-across-levels-of-government-ab438b9f/.
6. See i.e.: Transport and Environment (2020). No going back: European public opinion on air pollution in the Covid-19 era, accessed 18 May 2021 at https://www.transportenvironment.org/sites/te/files/publications/Briefing%20-%20polling%20Covid-19%20%26%20mobility.pdf; He, G., Pan, Y. and Tanaka, T. (2020). The Short-Term Impacts of COVID-19 Lockdown on Urban Air Pollution in China. *Nature Sustainability*, 7 July 2020, 1005–10; European Energy Agency (2020). Air quality and COVID-19. 12 August 2012, accessed 18 May 2021 at https://www.eea.europa.eu/signals/themes/air/air-quality-and-covid19/air-quality-and-covid19.
7. 'Action Plan: Financing Sustainable Growth' (n 2).
8. Regulation (EU) 2019/2089 of the European Parliament and of the Council of 27 November 2019 amending Regulation (EU) 2016/1011 as regards EU Climate Transition Benchmarks, EU Paris-aligned Benchmarks and sustainability-related

disclosures for benchmarks. *OJ* L 317 of 9 December 2019, 17. Hereafter 'Benchmark regulation'.
9. Regulation (EU) 2019/2088 of the European Parliament and of the Council of 27 November 2019 on sustainability-related disclosures in the financial services sector. *OJ* L 317 of 9 December 2019, 1. Hereafter 'Disclosure regulation'.
10. Regulation (EU) 2020/852 of the European Parliament and of the Council of 18 June 2020 on the establishment of a framework to facilitate sustainable investment and amending Regulation (EU) 2019/2088. *OJ* L 198 of 22 June 2020, 13. Hereafter 'Taxonomy regulation'.
11. Taxonomy regulation, article 3.
12. Taxonomy regulation, articles 10 to 15.
13. Taxonomy regulation, article 10, par. 1.
14. Technical Expert Group on Sustainable Finance (2020). *Taxonomy report: technical annex*, March 2020, accessed 18 May 2021 at https://ec.europa.eu/info/sites/default/files/business_economy_euro/banking_and_finance/documents/200309-sustainable-finance-teg-final-report-taxonomy_en.pdf, 556.
15. Euro 6 norm is an emissions standard for light vehicles for type approval in the European Union established by Regulation (EU) 715/2017.
16. Directive 2000/53/EC 18 September 2000 on end-of life vehicles. *OJ* L 269 of 21 October 2000, 34.
17. Regulation (EC) No 661/2009 of the European Parliament and of the Council of 13 July 2009 concerning type-approval requirements for the general safety of motor vehicles, their trailers and systems, components and separate technical units intended. *OJ* L 200 of 31 July 2009, 1.
18. Council directive 2003/96/EC of 27 October 2003 restructuring the Community framework for the taxation of energy products and electricity. *OJ* L 283 of 31 October 2013, 53. Hereafter 'ETD'.
19. ETD, article 4.
20. In Sweden, the levy is composed of one energy tax and a CO2 levy.
21. Irish Tax and Duties (2020). 'Excise – Accounting for Mineral Oil Tax Manual', June 2020.
22. ETD, article 5.
23. It is the case in Austria, Belgium, Germany and Luxemburg.
24. As for instance the insular territories of Greece.
25. For an in-depth assessment of the current provisions of the ETD, see: European Commission (2019). 'Evaluation of the Council Directive 2003/96/EC of 27 October 2003 Restructuring the Community Framework for the Taxation of Energy Products and Electricity', SWD(2019) 329 final of 11 September 2019; Harding, M., Martini, C. and Thomas, C. (2016). Taxing Energy Use: Patterns and Incoherencies – Energy Taxation in Europe and the OECD. In Bardazzi, R., Pazienza, M.G. and Tonini, T. (eds), *European Energy and Climate Security*, Springer, 233–64; Deffaa, W. (2011). New Impetus for EU Taxation Policy. *Intereconomics* 2011 (46), 5, 287–96.
26. The EU Green Deal states as follows: 'Ensuring that taxation is aligned with climate objectives is also essential. The Commission will propose to revise the Energy Taxation Directive, focusing on environmental issues, and proposing to use the provisions in the Treaties that allow the European Parliament and the Council to adopt proposals in this area through the ordinary legislative procedure by qualified majority voting rather than by unanimity.'

27. Council directive 2006/112/EC of 28 November 2006 on the common system of value added tax, *OJ* L 347 of 11 December 2006, 1. Hereafter 'VAT directive'.
28. VAT directive, recital 5.
29. For a review of all concerns caused by the reduced rates and exemptions, see: de la Feria, R. (2014). *VAT Exemptions: Consequences and Design Alternatives.* WoltersKluwer; Jogels, H. (2014). A Lot to Do about Reduced VAT Rates. *EC Tax Review*, 2014 (23), 5, 244–6. For the system in general: Cnossen, S. (2011). Value-Added Tax and Excises: Commentary. In Mirrless, J. (ed.), *Dimensions of Tax Design: The Mirrless Review*, OUP, 370–86; Englisch, J. (2011). EU Perspective on VAT Exemptions. *Working Papers Oxford University Centre for Business Taxation*, 1111.
30. VAT directive, article 110.
31. For the full list of rates applied by member states: European Commission, *VAT rates applied in the member states of the European Union*, 1 January 2020, accessed 18 May 2021 at https://ec.europa.eu/taxation_customs/sites/taxation/files/resources/documents/taxation/vat/how_vat_works/rates/vat_rates_en.pdf.
32. More precisely GATT, article III.2. See also: Mehling M.A., Asselt, H. van, Das, K., Droege, S. and Verkuijl, C. (2019). Designing Border Carbon Adjustments for Enhanced Climate Action. *American Journal of International Law*, 113(3) 433–81; Holzer, K. (2014). *Carbon-Related Border Adjustment and WTO Law*. Edward Elgar Publishing; Weber, R.H. (2015). Border Tax Adjustment: Legal Perspective. *Climatic Change*, 133(3), 407–17; Pauwelyn, J. (2013). Carbon Leakage Measures and Border Tax Adjustments under WTO Law. In Van Calster, G. (ed.), *Research Handbook on Environment, Health and the WTO*, Edward Elgar Publishing, 448–506.
33. The European Commission published guidelines: EC (2014). Guidelines on State Aid for Environmental Protection and Energy 2014–2020. *OJ* C 200 of 28 June 2014, 1; see also Nicolaides, P. and Kleis, M. (2014). Critical Analysis of Environmental Tax Reductions and Generation Adequacy Provisions in the EEAG 2014–2020. *European State Aid Law Quarterly*, 13(4), 636–49; Villar-Ezcurra, M. (2017). The Concept of 'Environmental Tax' in a State Aid Context when a Fiscal Energy Measure is Concerned. *European State Aid Law Quarterly*, 16(1), 11–24.
34. Commission regulation (EU) No 651/2014 of 17 June 2014 declaring certain categories of aid compatible with the internal market in application of Articles 107 and 108 of the Treaty. *OJ* L 187 of 26 June 2014, 1.
35. Villar-Ezcurra, M. (2017). State Aids and Taxation in the Energy Sector: Looking for a New Approach. Englisch, J. (2017). Energy Tax Incentives and the GBER Regime. Respectively chapters 1 and 15 in: Maillo González-Orús, J. and Villar Ezcurra, M. (eds), *State Aids, Taxation and the Energy Sector*, Reuters; Boesherz, D. (2004). Community State Aid Policy and Energy Taxation. *EC Tax Review* 2004(4), 214–19; Merola, M. and Diaz, O. (2018). Energy and Environment. In: Nascimbene, B. and Di Pascale, A. (eds), *The Modernisation of State Aid for Economic and Social Development*, Studies in European Economic Law and Regulation, vol 14, Springer, 169–236; Maillo González-Orús, J. (2017). Balancing Environmental Protection, Competitiveness and Competition: A Critical Assessment of the GBER and EEAG. *European State Aid Law Quarterly*, 2017 16(1) 4–10.
36. 'Action Plan: Financing Sustainable Growth' (n 2).
37. Talus, K. (2016). *An Introduction to EU Energy Law*. OUP, 133; Terra, B.J.M. and Wattel, P.J. (2008). *European Tax Law*. 5th edn, Wolters Kluwer, 11 and ch. 7.

14. Assessing public aid for true green digital recovery: a matter of good tax governance in the European Union

Marta Villar Ezcurra and María Amparo Grau Ruiz[1]

1. INTRODUCTION

All around the world, the initial tax policy responses to face the COVID-19 crisis were focused on alleviating cash-flow problems through temporary measures.[2] After this understandably urgent reaction, it is now time to consider how an update of systemic aspects could play a key role in the European economic recovery in line with the UN Sustainable Development Agenda.[3]

When confronting the economic difficulties caused by the COVID-19 outbreak, the three main EU institutions claimed that Europe must emerge stronger from this crisis.[4] When devising new policies, the EU State aid law has become an important tool to contribute to the economic recovery. Although it has been relaxed to enable EU Member States to take swift and effective action to support citizens and undertakings,[5] the preservation of competition and productivity is crucial to overcome the economic crisis and benefit the ultimate consumer.[6] Simultaneously, an attempt has been made to support the twin green and digital transitions in accordance with EU objectives.[7] In addition, resource efficiency and the circular economy have been prioritized on the agenda.[8]

The targeted and proportionate application of the EU State aid control serves to ensure that any national support measure is effective in helping the affected undertakings during the COVID-19 pandemic, but also in allowing them to bounce back from the current situation. This broad and multifaceted perspective of the State aid regime for the recovery aims to be in line with the so-called 'Next Generation EU budget'.[9]

This chapter explores the current use of tax incentives and other financial measures under the scope of the EU law. It does not fully review the state of the art of the EU State aid regulation but lays down a basic framework of where to insert dynamic tax proposals to move towards the declared objectives. In parallel, it clearly shows the adaptability of the State aid regime, according to its nature and purpose.

The heart of the problem lies in designing better simultaneous control mechanisms of public aid to assure the well-functioning of the internal market in an open and competitive way. Lack of proper control entails serious risks, such as segmentation of the market. This could be to the detriment of social cohesion within the Union and consequently deserves careful attention. Some advantages could be derived from the use of cumulative control tools, or a comparative sector-by-sector analysis (e.g. the car industry) for a more transparent evaluation of the actual impact of public aid. In the process, coherence between ecologically driven strategies and the use of financial and tax measures within the traditional limits to harmful competition in the EU should be enhanced.

2. THE USE OF TAX INCENTIVES IN RESPONSE TO THE COVID-19 CRISIS

2.1 Global Reactions for (Green) Recovery Stimulus

In the UN Framework for the immediate socio-economic response to COVID-19[10] there are five streams of work 'connected by a strong environmental sustainability [...] to build back better'.[11] To that aim, it is

> imperative that the fiscal and monetary measures in response to the pandemic do not support economic activities that cause environmental degradation or do not offset negative externalities. The long-term behavioural impacts of monetary incentives to firms and households are also important. Fiscal policies can also shift the balance of incentives in favour of more sustainable choices and behaviour as the recovery takes hold.[12]

Thus, it seems essential to incorporate environmental conditions in any aid granted to contribute to the fulfilment of objectives of general interest, such as the construction of a carbon-neutral economy. Stimulus packages are often tied to decarbonization requirements. In particular, strict performance requirements should be imposed in exchange for government support. Occasionally, some projects not completed on time have risked losing tax incentives. Therefore, setting a clear and fair legal framework is key to incentivize the private sector towards targeted green behaviour.

In addition, private investment in green assets, renewable energy and energy efficiency can be encouraged through a strategic use of public finance. In fact, the investments considering environmental, social and governance criteria are performing better and proving more resilient to the volatility caused by COVID-19 than conventional funds.[13]

Both green jobs and resilient enterprises are to be created with well-targeted government support to green rather than brown activities, focusing public investment projects on boosting climate-smart infrastructure or technologies, avoiding carbon-intensive investments or by making support conditional on committing to emissions reductions targets. Integrating climate change measures into economic recovery packages and national economic planning will ensure collective and aligned action by governments, the United Nations system, development partners and the private sector.[14]

Of course, countries will follow varied pathways, both in economic recovery and in their energy transitions, according to their particularities and the choice of who pays for it.[15] The fiscal stimulus has been widely employed in many countries all over the world.[16] The diversity of views, priorities, abilities and needs, with the same aims of inclusiveness and a just transition, while connecting short-term to medium- and long-term decarbonization actions, is remarkable, as a recent International Renewable Energy Agency (IRENA) report shows.[17]

For example, for renewable and efficient transport, significant decarbonization can be achieved through electrification of the sector, if powered by renewables. Phasing out fossil fuel subsidies would also make investment in electric vehicles (EVs) more attractive. Either way, systemic shifts in the transport sector will require target-setting, as well as fiscal and financial incentives. So, recovery packages for the automobile industry can be tied to commitments to invest in EVs and higher-efficiency cars. Moreover, investment will be required in Research and Development and demonstration projects to benefit from the abundance of cost-competitive renewable power. The decarbonization of the transport sector will depend on policies as well as structural and behavioural changes. Finally, investment in renewables for end uses should be triggered with ambitious deployment plans, by announcing future targets in transport, together with financial and fiscal incentives to support the uptake of solutions.[18]

2.2 The Recent Approach in the EU: Greening State Aid

On the one hand, in the context of the Green Deal, the European Commission will make proposals to ensure that taxation supports the EU's objective of reaching climate neutrality by 2050. A recent tax package focuses on simplifying tax rules, removing tax obstacles for taxpayers in many sectors in the single market.[19]

On the other hand, focusing on the State aid regime, the Temporary Framework and its updates reveal an increasing use of the approved COVID-19 measures[20] and the different States' views on the path to recovery. This entails a risk of creating new imbalances if the proper justification is missing. Avoiding beggar-thy-neighbour policies and the North-South political divide intensifying is crucial. The introduction of some green requirements in the aid can help the achievement of environmental objectives:

> Providing economic opportunities to Mediterranean EU Member States with renewable resources (wind, solar-PV [photovoltaic] and CSP [concentrated solar power]) would allow the European countries that have suffered the most from the [...] crisis to benefit from their comparative advantages while contributing to the EU's energy security and its compliance with emission reduction and renewable targets.[21]

A central piece in the economic recovery is the EU Recovery Fund. It includes a reformed budgetary framework for the EU's own resources and an extraordinary temporary momentum financed with long-term debt. Keeping the internal market alive would push those who largely benefit from it to make concessions in conditionality. Any deal must strike a balance between funding and conditions; between reforms and solidarity. Different countries agree on the EU strategy and the need for a digital, inclusive and green recovery.[22]

Based on solidarity, cohesion, and convergence, on 21 July 2020, EU leaders agreed on a comprehensive package of EUR 1.824.3bn[23] which combines the multiannual financial framework and an extraordinary recovery effort, Next Generation EU. The European Council adopted on 11 February 2021 the regulation establishing the Recovery and Resilience Facility (RRF).[24] The package will help the EU to rebuild after the COVID-19 pandemic and will support investment in the green and digital transitions. After the provisional agreement between the Council and Parliament, the Recovery Fund centres on a EUR 390bn programme of grants and maintains: 1. the transfers from the Recovery and Resilience Mechanism; 2. solvency and strategic value chains support; 3. environmental transition social compensation; 4. health autonomy; and 5. cooperation. The major novelty is the issuance of EU debt which means a considerable step in the EU integration process.[25] Spain will receive EUR 140bn from this historic Recovery Fund.[26]

Although 'the flexibility created under the Stability and Growth Pact and the State aid regime as well as the determined action of the European Central Bank have created space for national action to prevent the collapse of the economy and to protect businesses, jobs and livelihoods',[27] large differences in the amount of State aid given by EU Member States have the potential to unlevel the playing field inside the EU.

The EU State aid rules enshrined in Articles 107 and 108 of the Treaty on the Functioning of the European Union (TFEU) only apply where financial support granted by EU Member States to undertakings distorts or threatens to distort competition in the internal market. However, as financial support either granted by non-EU authorities to undertakings in the EU, directly or through their parent companies outside the EU, is not covered by EU State aid rules, where foreign subsidies facilitate and distort the bidding in an EU public procurement procedure, there appears to be a regulatory gap. To resolve it, the European Commission has proposed a new instrument.[28] In this regard, the risk of foreign non-green aids should not be overlooked, as it could seriously harm the real implementation of the current EU strategy.

Some requirements of the temporary European Commission guidelines on State aids show the difficulties for North-South balances, as well as the tendency to deal with the problems of lack of transparency. Probably, this is why the Commission states that:

> in order to ensure that the financial support can flow to eligible undertakings, Member States should establish reasonable requirements to demonstrate the absence of links to a jurisdiction that features on the EU list of non-cooperative jurisdictions. At the same time, it is essential to guarantee that undertakings cannot circumvent the requirements for entitlement to financial support.[29]

The conditionality and the environmental standards in the EU State aid Temporary Framework and the aim of fairness in the field of taxation, both connected to the just transition to a green economy, will guide national plans for the recovery in a coordinated way and help the EU in the harmonization process.

3. THE USE OF TAX INCENTIVES IN THE TRANSPORT SECTOR

Due to its potential for green and digital recovery, the transport sector may serve us as a practical example to assess recent public aids in the EU.

3.1 Identifying Tendencies in a Broad Perspective

Global energy subsidies have remained large and are still consuming enormous fiscal resources in some countries. The global total number of direct energy sector subsidies – including those to fossil fuels, renewables and nuclear power – is estimated to have been at least USD 634bn in 2017, of which USD 447bn were for fossil fuels. Subsidies for petroleum products dominated the total, at USD 220bn, followed by electricity-related support to fossil fuels at USD 128bn. Subsidies for natural gas and coal in 2017 were estimated at USD 82bn and USD 17bn, respectively.[30]

The International Monetary Fund put the subsidies to fossil fuels at USD 5.2trn in 2017. It also calculated that if fuel prices had been set at fully efficient levels in 2015, estimated global CO2 emissions would be 28 percent lower, fossil fuel-related air pollution deaths 46 percent lower, tax revenues higher by 3.8 percent of global gross domestic product (GDP), and net economic benefits (environmental benefits less economic costs) at 1.7 percent of global GDP.

The current electrification targets mean challenges for policymakers worldwide, particularly in the transport sector. A recent study,[31] by applying the social cost of carbon and value of statistical life metrics to the emission change results, has concluded:

> if EVs replaced 25 percent of combustion-engine cars currently on the road, the United States would save approximately USD 17bn annually by avoiding damages from climate change and air pollution. In more aggressive scenarios – replacing 75 percent of cars with EVs and increasing renewable energy generation, savings could reach as much as 70bn dollar annually.

The makers of electric cars have benefited from federal tax credits for purchases of electric cars, as well as from fuel efficiency standards that favoured energy-efficient vehicles, further boosting the productivity of manufacturers through economies of scale.[32]

Transport accounts for a quarter of the Union's greenhouse gas emissions (GHE) and these continue to grow. The Green Deal seeks a 90 percent reduction in these emissions by 2050. Digital, automated mobility and smart traffic management systems will make transport more efficient and cleaner.[33] As in 2018 the European Commission highlighted, there is an ambitious agenda to promote more secure, clean and connected mobility, electrification being one of the priorities. In June 2019, the European Council held the strategy agenda for the next 5 years, with measures that aim to improve the environment in cities and the air quality.[34]

To progress towards these objectives within the framework of the Governance of the Energy Union and Action for the Climate EU Regulation[35] and other EU laws promoting energy transition,[36] Member States should present to the European Commission their integrated National Plans for Energy and Climate. The Member States have to include in their long-term strategies their energy efficiency measures in the transport sector, options to decarbonize included.[37]

During the COVID-19 crisis, the massive fiscal and financial repurposing made by governments, including the redirection of fossil fuel subsidies, are a glimpse of the future. They suggest that the status quo and business-as-usual are policy choices.[38]

The efforts to decarbonize the transport sector through electrification by incentivizing the adoption of EVs have gained significant momentum and, at some point, policy must focus also on their integration with existing power systems.[39] The EV owner might benefit from incentives provided in the balancing and ancillary service markets, at least temporarily. Smart meters, batteries and other storage technologies would require incentives such as subsidies and tax exemptions.[40]

3.2   Analysis within the EU

Nowadays, Member States can design ample aid measures to support specific companies or sectors suffering from the consequences of the coronavirus in line with the existing EU State aid framework. On 13 March 2020, the Commission adopted a Communication on a Coordinated economic response to the coronavirus outbreak setting out these possibilities. Thus, Member States can compensate specific companies or specific sectors for the damage directly caused by exceptional occurrences, such as the pandemic. This general regime is foreseen by Article 107(2)(b) TFEU, but State aid rules based on Article 107(3)(c) TFEU also enable Member States to help companies cope with liquidity shortages and those needing urgent rescue aid. A variety of additional measures, such as the *de minimis* Regulation and the General Block Exemption Regulation, can also be put in place by Member States immediately, without involvement of the Commission.

In the case of particularly severe economic situations, such as the one currently faced by all Member States, the EU State aid rules allow them to grant support to remedy a serious disturbance to their economy. This is foreseen by Article 107(3)(b) TFEU. On 19 March 2020, the Commission adopted a State aid Temporary Framework based on this specific legal ground to enable Member States to use the full flexibility of these rules. The Temporary Framework, as amended on 3 April and 8 May 2020 and extended on 13 October 2020, provides for different types of aid, which can be granted by Member States, among others, selective tax advantages and advance payments, support for coronavirus-related research and development; and targeted support in the form of deferral of tax payments and/or suspensions of social security contributions. The Temporary Framework will be in place until 30 June 2021 and until 30 September 2021 for recapitalization measures only.

Regarding the transport sector in general, most of the EU countries, such as France or Italy, are taking steps to EV production (following the experience of other countries like Norway). France is betting on electric cars in a plan of EUR 8bn to save their automobile industry.[41] In 2020, the German government had already allocated more than EUR 1 bn to the implementation and development of battery factories. The batteries constitute up to 40 percent of the value of EVs. In a similar vein, the agreement reached by the German government may indicate the direction in which the aid package to the automotive industry may go, focusing public investment on EVs and encouraging external and internal investment for the implementation of battery factories on national territory. In this respect, the European Union itself has a Strategic Action Plan for Batteries which states that between 20 and 30 gigafactories are necessary, which will have a potential value in the market of EUR 250,000 by 2025. It will probably create stable jobs with high qualifications and increase the national economic production.

These developments should be also considered in other countries, like Spain, where the car sector has already an important weight in terms of GDP. Therefore, COVID-19 can certainly play a catalytic role to transform the sector towards electrification. Greening at the moment the different tax incentives related to the transport sector will help the transformation of the car industry and will reorient citizens' behaviours, while hopefully creating new jobs.

4. POLICY DRIVERS FOR THE USE OF TAX INCENTIVES RELATED TO THE TRANSPORT IN SPAIN

When looking for the best measures to promote electromobility in Spain, policymakers must consider the essential finance principles of effectiveness and efficiency in the use of public support, as constitutionally required. Another useful criterion is the temporary nature of the incentives offered.

4.1 Identifying Asymmetries in the Pre- and Post-COVID Scenario

This crisis, like the one in 2010, has highlighted the problems of having an incomplete monetary union in Europe. The approach on the financing, and not on the necessary expenditure, could result in an insufficient final average expenditure, that would make Europe come out of the crisis later, with greater real divergences between countries.[42] Although the shock is symmetrical and hits all countries, its impact will be asymmetrical and will hit them unevenly, depending on country-specific factors (their productive structure, fiscal margin and the idiosyncrasies of the labour market). Spain faces this crisis with weak public finances, many spending needs and a high deficit and debt. Any reform should take this into account.

The need for a common fiscal policy is not only a question of solidarity, but mainly one of efficiency and sustainability of the single market and the euro. Support for businesses within Europe – with a justified exception from the rules on State aid – is already distorting the single market by depending on each individual State's financial capacity. If spending is conditioned to the financial capacity of each country, the most indebted will spend much less, the average spending will be much lower than necessary, the Eurozone will take much longer to get out of the crisis, and it will do so with a deepening of real divergences, something unsustainable in the long term.

The green transformation requires both technological innovation and environmental taxation. This comprises investing in infrastructure that accelerates the energy transition, internalizing through taxes the costs of climate change, deploying less emission-intensive technologies and innovating in more efficient production processes.

4.2 Challenges for the Vehicle Transport Sector and Current Tax Incentives Proposals

In Spain, the transport sector is critical for a green economic recovery. It is responsible for many of the diffuse emissions of the greenhouse effect and is also one of the major industrial sectors in the context of the national GDP. At the present time, it represents more than 40 percent of the emissions in Spain. For that reason, it is essential to support the automotive industry, to stimulate investment in innovation and its transformation, by encouraging the purchase of EVs and the installation of recharging points in public buildings or private housing. This is the prevailing line in large EU countries.

The 2021 Climate Change and Energy Transition Act[43] is based on the Climate Change strategy. It aims to favour the car sector and to promote investments in infrastructure as well as the public-private collaboration. A date for cars and light commercial vehicles to be vehicles with emissions of 0g CO2/km is explicitly set in 2040. Other measures will be put in place to facilitate the penetration of these vehicles, including measures to support Research, Development and innovation. However, during the parliamentary debate through the process of proposing amendments, some were unsuccessfully claiming that this date should be brought forward to 2035, that further reflection is needed on the way for a net reduction in road transport, especially for goods and private vehicle use, and that measures should also be taken to encourage a rapid transition of the heavy commercial goods and passenger transport sector to zero emission mobility as soon as possible by 2050.

In addition, it is worth noting that the Spanish digital agenda 2025 is aligned with the EU objectives, the 2030 Agenda and the Science, Technology and Innovation agenda. During 2020–22 structural reforms are aimed to mobilize EUR 70,000m of public and private investment around ten key axes, including digital connectivity, 5G technology promotion, digital competences, cybersecurity and digital transformation.[44] This will probably have an impact on the transport sector as well.

In fact, in line with the EU strategy, some new tax incentives for the automotive industry have already been put in place. The Corporate Income Tax Act 2014 (CIT) has been recently modified by Royal Decree Law 23/2020, of 23 June, approving measures in the field of energy and other areas for economic revival. For the tax periods initiating in 2020 and 2021, the freedom of amortization for investments made in the value chain of electric mobility, sustainable or connected is allowed. These are its main features: 1. investment in new elements of tangible fixed assets that involve the sensorization and monitoring of the production chain, as well as the implementation of manufacturing systems based on modular platforms or that reduce environmental impact made available to the taxpayer within the year 2020; 2. maintenance of employment. To this end, work will be done with the sector and the National Integrated Energy and Climate Plan will establish the intermediate objectives to be achieved by that date.

5. IN SEARCH OF A COHERENT FISCAL POLICY GOVERNANCE IN THE EU

5.1 The Relevance of an Implementation Frame

Apart from the EU strategies and national plans, several essential questions may arise when looking forward to the implementation of a coherent fiscal policy governance in the EU, aligned with both a green and a digital recovery.

Over time, in the short run pragmatic considerations have prevailed in many countries (e.g. effective fuel tax rates vary considerably from sector to sector and while it is not always immediately clear what kind of exemptions, liability caps or special arrangements that specific industries or target groups have obtained, these circumstances are, of course, crucial when a proper *ex post* evaluation of impacts and effectiveness is to be made). The impact of tax exemptions, non-payments and negotiated agreements for specific industrial sectors should be considered as accurately as possible. Auditors usually provide an independent review of company energy practices and could make recommendations for improvements. However, some recent proposals have been made in order to arrange contracts (e.g. contract for carbon differences) in a way that facilitates risks assumption. This strategy may help escaping the public controls through public accounting, so their eventual role in the European industrial decarbonization should be carefully analysed.

When searching for investment opportunities of public funding, special attention should be paid to environmental benefits, macroeconomic returns and speed of implementation. The G7 and many European countries have pledged to phase out inefficient fossil fuel subsidies by 2025. Government interventions in the post-COVID recovery could accelerate this process, in concert with measures for greater energy efficiency and structural changes in the economy to prevent demand for fossil fuels from returning to pre-pandemic levels.

As Skou Andersen pointed out, when using an *ex ante* model, strong assumptions are often involved, including perfect competition and fully rational actors, while the results will depend on the values of a range of intermediate variables.[45] Now, in the post-COVID-19 scenario, we should specially try to facilitate the future *ex post* control, where the analysis will be constrained by the collected historical data.

5.2 Balancing Recovery National Strategies with Control Mechanisms – the Lack of Transparency

Without a proper implementation frame, our EU Greening Recovery might lose its muscles and teeth: both its economic multiplier effect and its climate mitigation effectiveness; because the EU does not have a strong central government or an executive Weberian bureaucracy.[46] Thus, the financial implementation should try to minimize the risks and take advantage of the opportunities of both private and public financing. The public administration may lead the change: streamlining and innovating procedures, through public procurement, and building partnerships with civil society.

For example, the European Clean Trucking Alliance is demanding a clear pathway and political strategy to enable the rapid deployment of zero emission vehicles and infrastructure to the European Commission. Europe needs to accelerate the full decarbonization of the road freight sector based on a strategy taking into account total cost, scalability and sustainability of available carbon-neutral technologies coming from renewables. All transport-related sectors including the energy supply sector, gas stations and service providers need a strategic roadmap to introduce green and zero emission technologies. They agree that necessary COVID-19 recovery investments need to safeguard jobs and support long-term sustainable solutions, phasing out further support measures for fossil fuels at European and national level. Apart from several regulatory proposals (e.g. change the Alternative Fuels Infrastructure Directive into a Regulation to ensure a proper implementation or conclude the Eurovignette Directive revision mandating significant toll reductions for zero emission trucks), a dedicated EU funding scheme with grants is requested to support the road freight sector installing charging infrastructure in depots, purchasing zero emission vehicles and supporting other carbon-neutral technologies, coming from renewables.[47]

Some lessons can be learned on how to implement sound controls from the wide experience in dealing with State aid rules. Procedurally, the principle of proportionality[48] must be respected. In this field a notification to the Commission, together with its decision, creates legal certainty. Otherwise, disputes could arise in court from those who do not qualify for public support or those who finance the public support measure. However, the opening of a formal investigation obliges Member States to suspend implementation of their State aid measures, so caution is needed.

Additionally, on 23 July 2020, the Commission published its draft Regional Aid Guidelines. Although they are not applicable to transport or energy, some of their features may serve to design an effective control in general terms. For instance, aid should have an incentive effect, changing the behaviour of an undertaking in a way that it engages in additional activity contributing to the desired objective. The aid should not subsidize the costs of an activity that an undertaking would have incurred in any event. Enterprises should explain counterfactually what would happen if they did not receive the aid, and the Member States should carry out a credibility check of the counterfactual and confirm the incentive effect. General data in the sector and relevant particular data may serve to justify the behaviour, depending on the circumstances of each case.

When aid is awarded concurrently under several schemes, the total aid from all sources should not exceed the maximum permissible aid intensity per project. Cumulation checks should be carried out to prevent excessive aid, whenever aid is granted via automatic tax measures. *Ex post* evaluation should be required for schemes – considering their combined duration – with large aid budgets, or containing novel characteristics, or when significant market, technology or regulatory changes are foreseen. Aid maps and aid intensity ceilings could also facilitate implementation and control.

6. CONCLUSION

The EU State aid law has demonstrated since the very beginning of the current pandemic crisis its swift and flexible response. There is an increasing recognition of how multiple economic, social and institutional drivers exacerbate environmental risks. In order to assess how tax measures can be optimized to serve simultaneously as recovery instruments and greening tools, mastering the implementation options in the EU is critical. The fiscal and financial reactions to COVID-19 provide an opportunity for transformation and the creation of green jobs to 'build back better'. Fundamental to recovery will be early action on the transport sector. How and where tax measures are focused on energy transitions can bolster sustainable development, in the way to a desired fully decarbonized economy by the middle of this century.

NOTES

1. vilezc@ceu.es, Universidad San Pablo-CEU, CEU Universities, DIGICCTAX (C21/0720), RTI2018-098715-B-C22 DER project (MCIU/AEI/FEDER, UE);

grauruiz@ucm.es, University Complutense of Madrid, PI AudIT-S project (PID2019-105959RB-100).
2. CIAT/IOTA/OECD (2020), Tax Administration Responses to COVID-19: Measures Taken to Support Taxpayers, OECD, Paris, 21 April 2020. https://www.oecd.org/coronavirus/policy-responses/tax-administration-responses-to-covid-19-measures-taken-to-support-taxpayers-adc84188 (last accessed 15 May 2021).
3. Joint op-ed by President Sassoli, President Michel and President von der Leyen, 9 May 2020. https://ec.europa.eu/commission/presscorner/detail/en/ac_20_841 (last accessed 15 May 2021).
4. Id.
5. The European Commission has decided to extend the scope of the State aid Temporary Framework adopted on 19 March 2020. European Commission (2021), 28 January 2021, Commission prolongs and further expands Temporary Framework to support economy in context of coronavirus outbreak. https://ec.europa.eu/commission/presscorner/detail/en/ip_21_261 (last accessed 15 May 2021).
6. European Commission (2021), Informal consolidated version of the Temporary Framework for state aid measures to support the economy in the current COVID-19 outbreak. https://ec.europa.eu/competition-policy/system/files/2021-03/TF_informal_consolidated_version_as_amended_28_january_2021_en.pdf (last accessed 15 May 2021).
7. European Commission (2021), Competition: State aid, timeline table. https://ec.europa.eu/competition/state_aid/legislation/timeline_table_SA_final.pdf (last accessed 15 May 2021).
8. Bibas, R., J. Chateau and E. Lanzi (2021), Policy Scenarios for a Transition to a More Resource Efficient and Circular Economy, OECD Environment Working Papers, No. 169, OECD Publishing, Paris, https://doi.org/10.1787/c1f3c8d0-en.
9. In May 2020, the Commission proposed a modern long-term EU budget boosted by New Generation EU mobilizing a variety of instruments around three pillars. See Council Regulation (EU, Euratom) 2020/2093 of 17 December 2020 laying down the multiannual financial framework for the years 2021 to 2027 (OJ of the EU L 433/11, 22 December 2020 ELI: http://data.europa.eu/eli/reg/2020/2093/oj, last accessed 24 May 2021).
10. UN (2020), A UN Framework for the Immediate Socio-Economic Response to Covid-19, April 2020, pp. 1, 24. https://unsdg.un.org/sites/default/files/2020-04/UN-Framework-for-the-immediate-socio-economic-response-to-COVID-19.pdf (last accessed 15 May 2021).
11. 'The five streams of work that constitute this package include: 1. ensuring that essential health services are still available and protecting health systems; 2. helping people cope with adversity, through social protection and basic services; 3. protecting jobs, supporting small and medium-sized enterprises, and informal sector workers through economic response and recovery programmes; 4. guiding the necessary surge in fiscal and financial stimulus to make macroeconomic policies work for the most vulnerable and strengthening multilateral and regional responses; and 5. promoting social cohesion and investing in community-led resilience and response systems. These five streams are connected by a strong environmental sustainability and gender equality imperative to build back better.' See the UN Report, 2020, *supra* note 10, p. 1.

12. Id., p. 19. Frans Vanistendael (2019), Reflections on Sustainable Taxation, Revista Técnica Tributaria, vol. 4, issue 127. https://revistatecnicatributaria.com/index.php/rtt/article/view/522 (last accessed 15 May 2021).
13. While such funds were also hit by the financial turmoil, they have experienced only half of the decline observed by the S&P 500, delivering better returns during the crisis.
14. PAGE (2020), Reframing National Economies around Sustainability in a COVID-19 World, PAGE Thematic Briefs. https://www.un-page.org/files/public/page_ff_-_climate_change_jul_final.pdf (last accessed 15 May 2021).
15. Janet E. Milne and Marta Villar (2020), Renewable Electricity and Tax Expenditures: Lessons from Two Countries, Intertax vol, 48, issue 4, pp. 369–88 at 397.
16. PAGE (2021), Policy Responses: Fiscal Policy Measures. https://datastudio.google.com/reporting/fda0ecd7-f29c-4d0d-87a2-47cb6f91c852/page/YY5TB (last accessed 15 May 2021).
17. IRENA (2020), The Post-COVID Recovery: An Agenda for Resilience, Development and Equality, International Renewable Energy Agency, Abu Dhabi, p.5. https://www.irena.org/-/media/Files/IRENA/Agency/Publication/2020/Jun/IRENA_Post-COVID_Recovery_2020.pdf (last accessed 15 May 2021). Similarly, OECD (2021), Tax Policy Reforms 2021: Special Edition on Tax Policy during the COVID-19 Pandemic, OECD Publishing, Paris, https://doi.org/10.1787/427d2616-en (last accessed 15 May 2021).
18. FIA Foundation (2020), Renewable Energy Pathways in Road Transport, FIA Foundation Research Series, Paper 13, November 2020.
19. The Commission suggests a reform of the Code of Conduct related with the State aid regulation, improvements to the EU list of non-cooperative jurisdictions, and outlines the EU's approach to work together with developing countries in the area of taxation, in line with the 2030 Sustainable Development agenda. European Commission (2020), Fair and Simple Taxation: Commission Proposes New Package of Measures to Contribute to Europe's Recovery and Growth, 15 July 2020. https://ec.europa.eu/commission/presscorner/detail/en/ip_20_1334 (last accessed 15 May 2021).
20. An informal consolidated version is available and can be consulted. See *supra* note 6.
21. Gonzalo Escribano and Lara Lázaro (2020), Balancing Geopolitics Hit Green Deal Recovery: In Search of a Comprehensive Euro-Mediterranean Energy Script, ARI 95/2020, 15 July 2020.
22. María Amparo Grau Ruiz (2020), Condicionalidad, selectividad y afectación: ¿estrategias a considerar para la recuperación económica?, Revista Técnica Tributaria, vol. 2, issue 129. https://revistatecnicatributaria.com/index.php/rtt/article/view/13 (last accessed 15 May 2021). Monika Sie Dhian Ho and Charles Powell (2020), Spanish vs Dutch Views on the EU Recovery Fund, Eurobserver, 17 July 2020.
23. European Council (2020), A Roadmap for Recovery: Towards a more resilient, sustainable and fair Europe. https://www.consilium.europa.eu/media/43384/roadmap-for-recovery-final-21-04-2020.pdf (last accessed 15 May 2021).
24. European Council (2021), A Recovery Plan for Europe, https://www.consilium.europa.eu/en/policies/eu-recovery-plan (last accessed 15 May 2021).

25. Enrique Feás (2020), La UE acierta a corto y arriesga a largo plazo, Voz Populi. https://www.vozpopuli.com/opinion/ue-fondos-acuerdo_0_1375362912.html (last accessed 15 May 2021).
26. Bernardo de Miguel and Lluís Pellicer (2020), Spain could Get €140 Billion from EU's Covid-19 Recovery Plan, El País, 27 May 2020. A Roadmap for Recovery: Towards a More Resilient, Sustainable and Fair Europe. https://english.elpais.com/spanish_news/2020-05-27/spain-could-get-140-billion-from-eus-covid-19-recovery-plan.html (last accessed 15 May 2021). For updated data see https://www.lamoncloa.gob.es/temas/fondos-recuperacion/Paginas/index.aspx and http://www.realinstitutoelcano.org/wps/portal/rielcano_en/contenido?WCM_GLOBAL_CONTEXT=/elcano/elcano_in/zonas_in/ari35-2021-feas-steinberg-european-recovery-plan-figures-for-spain (both last accessed 15 May 2021).
27. Bernardo de Miguel and Lluís Pellicer, *supra* note 26, p. 3.
28. European Commission (2020), White Paper on levelling the playing field as regards foreign subsidies, Brussels, 17 June 2020, COM (2020) 253 final.
29. European Commission (2020), Commission Recommendation of 14 July 2020 on making State financial support to undertakings in the Union conditional on the absence of links to non-cooperative jurisdictions, Brussels, 14 July 2020, COM (2020) 4885 final, recital (7).
30. Id., pp. 99 and 175.
31. Amanda Morris, Widespread Electric Vehicle Adoption would Save Billions of Dollars, Thousands of Lives: Study Finds Improved Air Quality would Avoid Health and Climate Damages, NU, GeoHealth, 14 August 2020. https://news.northwestern.edu/stories/2020/08/widespread-electric-vehicle-adoption-would-save-billions-of-dollars-thousands-of-lives/?utm_source=nn_newsletter&utm_medium=email&utm_campaign=ev_0819 (last accessed 15 May 2021).
32. Id., p. 79.
33. European Commission, Sustainable Mobility: The European Green Deal, 11 December 2019. https://ec.europa.eu/commission/presscorner/detail/en/fs_19_6726 (last accessed 15 May 2021).
34. European Commission (2018), Europe on the move, Press Release 17 May 2018. https://ec.europa.eu/commission/presscorner/detail/en/IP_18_3708 (last accessed 15 May 2021). European Council (2019), A New Strategic Agenda 2019–2024. https://www.consilium.europa.eu/media/39914/a-new-strategic-agenda-2019-2024.pdf and Conclusions of 20 June 2019 (EUCO 9/19). https://www.consilium.europa.eu/media/39922/20-21-euco-final-conclusions-en.pdf (both last accessed 15 May 2021).
35. Regulation (EU) 2018/1999 of the European Parliament and the Council, of 11 December 2018, related to the Governance of the Energy Union and the Climate Action, OJEU L 328, 21 December 2018. https://eur-lex.europa.eu/legal-content/EN/TXT/?uri=uriserv:OJ.L_.2018.328.01.0001.01.ENG (last accessed 15 May 2021).
36. See European Commission, Fourth Report of Energy Union, 9 April 2019 (COM (2019) 175), pp. 14–27. https://ec.europa.eu/info/publications/4th-state-energy-union_en (last accessed 15 May 2021).
37. See paragraph 2.4.3, Annex IV of the Regulation.
38. UN Framework, *supra* note 10, p. 40.
39. The debate around options has tended to focus on Vehicle-to-Grid (V2G) based business models as the optimal approach. The limitations stem from existing electricity market price signals, battery degradation, low energy density of batteries

and the risk of voiding guarantees on batteries, etc. An alternative option is based on Vehicle Grid Integration (VGI). Although VGI does not include injection of the power back to the grid, it enables other features, such as balancing of the user's own consumption and self-generation, through, for example, rooftop photovoltaics (PV). VGI can emerge as the least-cost integration option for EVs until such time as the V2G option becomes economically viable. The Oxford Institute for Energy Studies (2020), A Viable Integration Option for Electric Vehicles. https://www.oxfordenergy.org/research/viable-integration-option-electric-vehicles (last accessed 15 May 2021).

40. See IRENA, *supra* note 17, p. 69.
41. RFI (2020), France Unveils 8 Bn-euro Plan to Revive Auto Sector through Electric Cars, 25 May 2020. https://www.rfi.fr/en/wires/20200526-france-unveils-8-bn-euro-plan-revive-auto-sector-through-electric-cars (last accessed 15 May 2021)
42. Federico Steinberg, Miguel Otero Iglesias and Enrique Feás (2020), ¿Recuperación o metamorfosis? Un plan de transformación económica para España, Informe Elcano, Informe 28, July 2020. http://www.realinstitutoelcano.org/wps/wcm/connect/410d3de1-9de8-44fe-9f5e-b5ddbe7ce965/Informe-Elcano-28-Recuperacion-o-metamorfosis-plan-transformacion-economica-para-Espana.pdf?MOD=AJPERES&CACHEID=410d3de1-9de8-44fe-9f5e-b5ddbe7ce965 (last accessed 15 May 2021).
43. Spain's first Climate Change and Energy Transition Act was approved in the Lower House of Parliament, after passing through the Upper House of Parliament, on 13 May 2021 promoting full decarbonization of the economy by 2050, with first upward revision of the current targets in 2023. See 121/000019 Draft Act of Climate Change and Energy Transition (OJ Cortes generales, Congreso de los Diputados 16 April 2021, Serie A, No. 19-1). https://www.congreso.es/public_oficiales/L14/CONG/BOCG/A/BOCG-14-A-19-5.PDF, for the text passed by the Senate https://www.senado.es/legis14/publicaciones/pdf/senado/bocg/BOCG_D_14_184_1815.PDF (both last accessed 15 May 2021) based on the Spanish Climate Change and Clean Energy Strategy. https://www.miteco.gob.es/es/cambio-climatico/legislacion/documentacion/cle_ene_pla_urg_mea_tcm30-178764.pdf (last accessed 15 May 2021).
44. Gobierno de España (2020), Plan España Digital 2025, https://www.lamoncloa.gob.es/presidente/actividades/Documents/2020/230720-Espa%C3%B1aDigital_2025.pdf (last accessed 15 May 2021).
45. Mikael Skou Andersen (2010), Europe's Experience with Carbon-Energy Taxation, 20 December 2010. http://sapiens.revues.org/index1072.html (last accessed 15 May 2021).
46. Jean-Michel Glachant (2020), Greening the Covid-19 Recovery in the European Union, Policy Brief, Florence School of Regulation, EUI, No. 31, July 2020, p. 2.
47. See https://clean-trucking.eu (last accessed 15 May 2021).
48. Phedon Nicolaides (2020), The Commission Must Act in Accordance with the Principle of Proportionality. State Aid Uncovered, 11 August 2020. https://www.lexxion.eu/stateaidpost/the-commission-must-act-in-accordance-with-the-principle-of-proportionality(last accessed 15 May 2021).

15. The purposefulness and serviceability of renewable energy support schemes in view of the COVID-19 crisis
Theodoros G. Iliopoulos[1]

I. INTRODUCTION

At the time of the celebrations for the new year in January 2020, very few, if not anyone, expected the unprecedented situation that the planet would experience a few weeks later. At that time, the coronavirus had only recently appeared in China[2] and the rest of the world largely received the news with sympathy, but indifference, and with the confidence or hope that it would all prove a regional and temporary epidemic. Unfortunately, the whole world would soon count casualties and one country after another would impose mobility restrictions and lockdowns. The COVID-19 pandemic has brought tragic consequences for human life and it has dramatically affected the whole range of human activity. Energy markets were not an exception.[3]

The deceleration in economic activity due to the confinement measures resulted in a general decrease of electricity consumption.[4] In Europe, from late March until mid-May 2020 it dropped by about 10% compared to the same period in 2019;[5] during the hard lockdown weeks, electricity generation dropped by 14%, with the biggest hit taken by production from lignite and hard coal, which dropped by more than 40%.[6] Similarly, the use of oil products in transport also plummeted during the lockdown, which dragged prices down.[7] On the contrary, renewable energy projects have managed to remain profitable and the generation of electricity from renewable energy sources (RES) in Europe in the first half of 2020 rose by 11%, thanks to the operation of new installations and to favourable climatic conditions.[8] Given the above, and without underestimating the fact that the recovery of the economic activity may reverse such generation and consumption patterns, there have been expectations that a side-effect of the COVID-19 crisis may be a solid boost for the energy transition. Before the outbreak of COVID-19, the EU legislature had emphasised the need for the use of financial instruments to facilitate and accelerate the deployment of RES and had reaffirmed that Member States may apply national support schemes for renewable energy sources (RESSS).[9] Article 2(5) of the recast Renewable Energy Directive 2018/2001 (RED II)[10] defines RESSS as

> any instrument, scheme or mechanism applied by a Member State, or a group of Member States, that promotes the use of energy from renewable sources by reducing the cost of that energy, increasing the price at which it can be sold, or increasing, by means of a renewable energy obligation or otherwise, the volume of such energy purchased.

Accordingly, the questions with which this contribution deals are (a) whether the enactment of RESSS in Member States retains its purposefulness in the landscape that emerged after the outbreak of the COVID-19 pandemic and, (b) if yes, how the supranational legal framework should change to ensure the serviceability of the RESSS. In terms of structure, after the chapter's introduction, the second part examines the normative foundation for the enactment of RESSS. Next, part III investigates the relationship between market failures and RESSS, especially after the COVID-19 outbreak. Part IV submits certain suggestions for the refinement of the supranational RES support legal framework. Part V concludes the chapter.

II. THE NORMATIVE FOUNDATION FOR THE ENACTMENT OF RESSS

The enactment of RESSS constitutes an intervention in the energy markets, for which Member States do not have carte blanche. Hence, it is important to delineate the systemic boundaries and the normative foundations that justify such interventions, as set by the supranational political economy structure.

The EU political economy is a combination of ordoliberalism and regulatory capitalism, as implied by primary law's connotations of the former and by the practice's links with the latter.

More specifically, Article 3(3) of the Treaty on European Union, which establishes the objectives of the EU, enshrines the model of a 'social market economy'.[11] This term is associated with the ordoliberal economic doctrine that, by way of showing a third way between pure laissez-faire liberalism and a Keynesian interventionist model, propounds a model of free competition that merges the economic and political sphere, so that economic activity be conducted in conformity with a specific political order, an *ordo*. This order may comprise economic and social goals, such as environmental and energy policy objectives. Thus, economic liberty is restrained by political choices made by the state and embodied by the law.[12] Within this framework, public intervention in principle aims to ensure that markets respect the *ordo*; if they do, non-economic policy objectives are expected to be realised too. However, intervening for actively pursuing social goals is also recognised as potentially necessary for an ethical outcome to be reached, as long as it does not distort the market and does not undermine the *ordo*.[13]

However, attaining social goals has not per se sufficed the EU legal order to accept public interventions in the market. Considerations of efficiency and market failures are taken into account, which alludes to the model of regulatory capitalism.[14] Regulatory capitalism's principal credo is that competitive markets lead to an efficient outcome, an optimal allocation of resources where no actor can be better off without another actor becoming worse off.[15] But in the event that markets prove unable to deliver an efficient outcome due to the existence of a market failure, that is, a 'failure of a more or less idealised system of price-market institutions to sustain "desirable" activities or to estop "undesirable" activities',[16] a corrective intervention is required.[17] Corrective interventions that address market failures, such as the activity of monopolies or the occurrence of imperfect information, can be paralleled to the ordoliberal mandate to sustain and restore the *ordo*. In fact, the coexistence of the two models denotes a paradigm that grants less 'regulation-free' space to markets and is more sensitive and reactive to market failures, also by addressing those that relate to social goals, like the energy transition.[18]

III. MARKET FAILURES AND RESSS

a) Market Failures and RESSS in General

Within the framework of the supranational political economy, the social goals of tackling climate change and developing RES[19] enable Member States to legitimately intervene in the market through RESSS, as long as there is a certain market failure impeding their attainment. However, secondary EU law contains neither RESSS-specific rules that would specify when such market failures occur nor bases or mechanisms that would ensure compliance with the abovementioned political economy structure. And although the RED II did introduce rules that impact on the design of national RESSS, it remained silent on the exact conditions justifying their enactment in the first place.

Nevertheless, one can find such conditions in the field of State aid law. In the absence of RESSS-specific secondary legislation before the RED II, State aid law has been the main instrument for a supranational intervention in national renewable energy support laws and policy. Indeed, the Commission has the competence to assess the compatibility with the internal market of the RESSS that constitute State aid.[20] In doing so, the Commission also makes considerations about the enactment and the design features of the RESSS under scrutiny on the basis of conditions declared in a soft law instrument, the Guidelines on State aid for environmental protection and energy (EEAG).[21]

The EEAG do link the need for State intervention with the presence of a market failure and they require that the specific problem that needs to be addressed is diagnosed and defined in advance.[22] Point 35 EEAG specifies what market failures may hamper a well-functioning secure, affordable and sustainable internal energy market. These are: negative externalities, positive externalities, asymmetric information and coordination failures.

From the above types of market failure, externalities are the most pertinent to RESSS. The term denotes the occurrence of unintentional external effects that an economic activity entails for actors not involved in it and for society; these effects are 'unaccounted for by market valuations'.[23] RES are directly linked with positive externalities, such as acceleration of clean energy transition, climate change mitigation or increase of energy security, which are not reflected by the price, demand and supply taking place in the market. Accordingly, RESSS aim to ensure that generators will be receiving a return for such social benefits that their activity provides.

But RES are also linked with the correction of negative externalities, particularly the negative external effects imposed by energy generation from fossil fuels, such as environmental damage, greenhouse gas emissions, resources depletion and air pollution. These social costs should be reflected in market transactions so that price signals about the harm caused lead to an increase in the price and a drop in the quantity of energy from conventional sources. A classic remedy to negative externalities is taxation,[24] but RESSS can also serve as an ancillary remedy because the development of RES replaces fossil fuels and, thus, it contributes to the reduction of supply of energy associated with negative externalities.[25]

The occurrence of negative externalities has, so far, been the only case of a market failure recognised by the EU legal order to be tackled by RESSS.[26] In fact, the Commission's State aid decisions about RESSS often make no explicit reference to a certain market failure; but when they do, they always identify a case of negative externalities.[27]

b)   Market Failures and RESSS after the COVID-19 Outbreak

The COVID-19 crisis caused a shock in the energy markets. It caused an overall reduction of oil and natural gas demand which 'led to an unprecedented reduction of their selling prices';[28] it accelerated the drop in electricity demand that was already happening due to the mild winter, which, in its turn, resulted in low prices across Europe.[29] Moreover, the overall reduced demand for energy is expected to 'trigger the largest ever annual fall in CO_2 emissions', with a fall by 5 to 8%.[30] Yet RES proved more resilient and, thanks inter alia to their flexibility and to the (near) zero production cost,[31] RES projects retained their profitability and the share of the generation of RES substantially increased.[32] As a result, in the first half of 2020 several EU Member States either closed coal plants or experienced long coal-free periods, and earned practical experience on how to run their grid with a high share of RES.[33] Seeing that the intermittency of renewables and the unstable production of energy have threatened security of supply and have thus impeded their development, the experience gained may prove crucial for the energy transition.

Given the above COVID-19-driven changes in the energy markets, one may argue that the externalities and the market failure analyses are now futile and may doubt that further intervention through RESSS is needed. However, this would be a rather short-sighted argument.[34] The recorded effects of the COVID-19 pandemic are ephemeral and do not suffice for one to celebrate the accomplishment of the energy transition. More specifically, the reduction in energy demand and the financial repercussions of the COVID-19 crisis are expected to cause a reduction in investments and in the growth of RES projects.[35] And yet the climate change and energy transition targets require that RES installations at least double in the decade of the 2020s, compared to the 2010s.[36] At the same time, while the share of RES has risen in the sector of electricity (also due to the overall drop of demand), RES have proven less resilient in the sectors of transport and heating and cooling, as their growth has decelerated.[37] Moreover, seeing that fossil fuel industries have proven over time to be qualified to sustain crises and preserve their key role in energy systems, they may sustain the pandemic crisis too (even though the price fluctuations pose risks, especially to the development of the liquefied natural gas trade).[38] And while meeting the Paris Agreement[39] target requires an annual 7.6% decrease of emissions globally,[40] emissions have already started to rebound with the lift of the strict confinement measures.[41] Besides, the short-lived, albeit notable, drop in emissions in 2020 has only negligibly contributed to the struggle against climate change.[42] And the drop in electricity demand is largely attributed to the 'dramatic reductions in services and industry',[43] which is well expected to be reversed when economic activity restarts.

Consequently, there are no grounds for complacency and one should not conclude that positive or negative externalities are not relevant to the field of RES any more. But the landscape that emerged after the COVID-19 outbreak also exacerbates other cases of market failure that had already been affecting RES, but have been so far rather disregarded. These are (a) barriers to entry and risk, and (b) insufficiency of merit goods.

First, RESSS may address barriers to entry and risk, which have been always present in the field of RES and have restrained or severely discouraged investors from entering the market.[44] Accordingly, RES investments are characterised by high upfront costs, especially for innovative technologies, while two important RES, wind and sun, are intermittent; generation flow is not constant, but unpredictable and dependent on weather conditions. The COVID-19 crisis could make the EU reconsider its current stance that 'risk or uncertainty do not in themselves lead to the presence of a market failure'.[45] With the world experiencing the deepest recession since World War II,[46] and with investments in RES expected to slow down in an environment of uncertainty, barriers to entry and risk should justify the enactment of RESSS that will back the efforts for the energy transition. Such RESSS may be investment-focused and facilitate the realisation of investments, such as tax exemptions or soft loans, but also generation-based and assist with the continuing generation of energy, such as market premiums and bidding procedures.

Second, RESSS may tackle the merit goods market failure. This market failure relates to goods which, by reason of their positive implications, are so meritorious that the actual supply and consumption are deemed insufficient. Merit goods generate positive externalities and they are thus closely related to them. Yet they are treated as a distinct category as they do not have a purely compensatory nature, but they also have a strong socio-political and ethical connotation, which broadens the economic analysis.[47] Since intervening in the market for ensuring the attainment of social goals is in accordance with the EU political economy, RESSS could be founded on a 'merit good' analysis. This would have an extra symbolic value as it would emphasise the EU's commitment to deliver the energy transition. Besides, as already noted, the development of RES is linked with positive effects, which become even more important after the COVID-19 outbreak: for instance, the promotion of RES entails less air pollution, which also means better health; in another example, investments in RES create jobs and they contribute to growth and, hence, to the financial recovery.[48]

In conclusion, in spite of certain positive side-effects of the COVID-19 crisis on the energy markets, market failures are still prevalent in the field of RES and RESSS retain their purposefulness. However, the COVID-19 crisis and its overall consequences escalate the need for serviceable RESSS.

IV. REFINING THE SUPRANATIONAL RENEWABLE ENERGY SUPPORT LAW

With recession in the EU being as deep as 8.3% in 2020[49] and with Member States needing to intervene through support policies in numerous fields to sustain the COVID-19 crisis,[50] the need for serviceable RESSS that will actually deliver the desired outcome and not waste resources is as great as ever. Member States retain the competence to design and enact RESSS;[51] but EU law, especially State aid law and the RED II, impacts on and delimits their discretion. In this regard, this part submits certain suggestions about refinements to EU law so that it better contributes to the serviceability of RESSS. Besides, the COVID-19 pandemic provides an opportunity for, or even necessitates, structural changes that will facilitate and enable the low-carbon energy transition. The legal suggestions put forward below constitute such structural changes, in the sense that they reform the normative framework that governs renewable energy policy and the promotion of RES.

To begin with, it is argued that the supranational legal order should accept that RESSS may be linked with more cases of market failure and that the current practice of the Commission, which only accepts RESSS for correcting negative externalities, should be abolished. The Commission's sceptical stance seems to derive from its older aspiration that RES would develop without the need for support,[52] which, however, has been unsubstantiated. In fact, the EU legislature has acknowledged that there is still need for RESSS for the policy targets to be reached, especially for the less developed technologies such as offshore wind or for self-consumption projects, and has recognised that the relevant decisions are left to the discretion of the Member States.[53] And the Commission itself has been tolerant and cursory when it scrutinises the RESSS that constitute State aid. Its assessments have never rejected a support scheme as incompatible with the internal market; they always affirm the necessity of the support granted, and not on the basis of a meticulous analysis, but on the basis of the presumption of point 115 EEAG that 'a residual market failure remains' in the field of RES. It is suggested that an accurate market failure analysis for the determination of the problem to be addressed and an illustration of the objectives of the intervention will assist, not in increasing the support granted, but in having better RESSS and in solidifying the necessity assessment. Properly identifying the problem offers clear criteria of assessment and allows a more accurate planning that leads to 'fit for purpose' RESSS that are diligently designed and are better equipped to harmoniously coexist with other instruments of environmental, climate change and energy policy. For instance, if the authorities aim to tackle the barriers or the excessive risk that smaller investors face they should opt for a support scheme with inherently lower risk, like a direct price instrument. In the event of barriers or risk for larger investors, or in the event of targeting a 'merit good' market failure by seeking the realisation of larger projects, tendering and bidding procedures for a certain amount of energy or for specific projects planned by the authorities may be the most suitable solution.[54]

Furthermore, while under the legal framework currently in force such appraisals can only occur at the supranational level as a part of a broader State aid compatibility assessment, it is argued that they should also (or rather, mainly) form part of the content of the RED II that lays down rules on RESSS. More specifically, Article 4(1) of the RED II affirms the importance of RESSS and Article 4(2) and (3) use a principle-based approach to set a framework that any RESSS for electricity shall conform with.[55]

These rules on the design of RESSS for electricity and on the effects that they should have on the market[56] deal with the performance of the RESSS. The RED II does not set down any rules in relation to the process before the enactment of RESSS that would for instance require national authorities to state reasons for their intervention or to have carried out an *ex ante* 'fit for purpose' scrutiny. However, thorough diligence can ensure, or at least increase the chances, that the national RESSS comply with the RED II requirements and can add coherence to the established RES support framework. The soft legal basis offered by the EEAG for examining the necessity of a support scheme may involve similar assessments, but it does not serve the same objective, as it has a different *ratio legis*: it is the State aid's compatibility with the internal market that is examined, and not the support scheme's suitability for delivering the envisaged outcome in accordance with the RED II provisions. Thus, the EU legislature can complement the RED II with the requirement that an 'energy market impact assessment' accompanies the enactment of RESSS. This suggestion draws inspiration from the environmental impact assessment, that is, the procedure set by Directive 2011/92[57] that ensures that the environmental implications of decisions are taken into account before the decisions are made. A similar, albeit not necessarily as elaborate, procedure in the field of the promotion of RES could ensure that a timely and careful consideration is given to the effects of a support scheme before its enactment.

But the serviceability of the RESSS is also dependent upon how they will operate in practice. As already noted, Article 4 of the RED II empowers Member States to enact RESSS that are market-based and market-responsive and do not unnecessarily distort electricity markets. This principle-based approach has the virtue of flexibility, as it allows *in concreto* assessments and does not entail an intensive intervention in the discretion of Member States. On the other hand, interpreting the indeterminate legal concepts of 'market-based', 'market-responsive' or 'unnecessary distortion' is a difficult exercise that might cause confusion and uncertainty and give rise to legal disputes. It is, hence, suggested that the Commission enacts a soft law instrument to guide Member States by proposing best practices and by elaborating on the principles enshrined by the RED II; for instance, how self-consumption schemes comply with the RED II;[58] or when remuneration under negative prices may still be compatible with these principles. The Commission could also update and link with the RED II the 'Guidance' on RESSS design that dates from 2013.[59] The interpretation given to design requirements included in the EEAG or in Regulation 651/2014[60] may serve as interpretive guidance.

In any case, the new instrument should also take the COVID-19 crisis into account and specifically guide Member States on how RESSS should be designed and how the relevant legal principles should be interpreted in view of the special circumstances of the pandemic. Indeed, one should reasonably expect that the foregoing indeterminate legal concepts may be construed differently during the COVID-19 crisis and the persistence of its implications. Of course, it is the Court of Justice of the EU that is exclusively competent to authentically interpret the RED II.[61]

Last, it is noted that the suggestions put forward in this contribution are in accordance with Article 194 TFEU and infringe neither the Member States' competences in the field of energy nor the Member States' rights in developing their energy policy.[62]

V. CONCLUSION

The pillars on which the efforts for an energy transition have been founded since the beginning of the last decade are now under pressure, not only because of the urgency of the climate change threat, but also because of the implications of the dramatic COVID-19 pandemic. Energy markets have suffered demand and price shocks, and the RES, as resilient as they have proven, are expected to experience a slowdown in their growth in the next couple of years due to the overall uncertainty and the deceleration in economic activity. But the COVID-19 crisis provides an opportunity for drastic and structural changes in the field of energy law before humanity gets locked into a 'business-as-usual' recovery. Accordingly, and without disregarding the need for demand response and energy storage strategies, this contribution focuses on the EU renewable energy support legislation and puts forward suggestions for its reform.

With market failures still existing in spite of certain ephemeral positive side-effects, such as a momentary rise of the RES share and a similar reduction in greenhouse gas emissions, the need for a corrective intervention through RESSS remains – if not increases. Until now, the Commission has adopted a rather narrow stance that only accepts the occurrence of negative externalities as a reason justifying the enactment of RESSS. At the same time, and rather at odds with the theoretically strict stance, the relevant assessments by the Commission in practice always identify such a market failure on the basis of a presumption in soft law, with no thorough analysis being conducted. It is, however, argued that the market failure analysis should change and become wider, but also more structured. The cases of positive externalities, barriers to entry and risk and merit goods need to be included in the market failure analysis for the enactment of RESSS. This is in line with the political economy of the EU, which may justify corrective interventions in the market for the sake of social goals.

Moreover, accepting that more types of market failure that are relevant to the field of RES should be accompanied by a more substantiated analysis will lead to an accurate identification of the problem that needs to be tackled. As a result, the enacted RESSS will be better equipped to lead to the attainment of the policy objectives. Such considerations should be integrated in a broader pre-enactment 'fit for purpose' assessment, delineated by the RED II. This will increase the coherence of the legal framework, as the RED II contains rules on the design of RESSS, but no rules on the procedure before a support scheme is enacted. The supranational legal framework currently in force only examines the necessity of a support scheme on the basis of the EEAG, under the State aid compatibility assessments of the Commission. In addition, it is argued that a soft law instrument should elaborate on the principles that determine the design of RESSS, by way of an interpretative guidance for Member States. This will contribute to the homogeneous interpretation and application of the RED II, but it will also allow the supranational legal order to suggest how the principle-based provisions of the RED II should be interpreted and applied, also in view of the special circumstances of the COVID-19 pandemic.

ENDNOTES

1. Theodoros G. Iliopoulos is a doctoral researcher in Energy and Environmental Law at Hasselt University. Contact: theodoros.iliopoulos@uhasselt.be. With the present paper, the author was awarded the 'GCET21 Young Researcher Award' in the virtual event GCET21 that was hosted by Vermont Law School in September 2020.
2. A. Wilder-Smith and D.O. Freedman, 'Isolation, Quarantine, Social Distancing and Community Containment: Pivotal Role for Old-Style Public Health Measures in the Novel Coronavirus (2019-Ncov) Outbreak' (2020) 27 *Journal of Travel Medicine* 1.
3. Cameron Hepburn, Brian O'Callaghan, Nicholas Stern, Joseph Stiglitz and Dimitri Zenghelis, 'Will COVID-19 Fiscal Recovery Packages Accelerate or Retard Progress on Climate Change?' [2020] *Oxford Review of Economic Policy* graa015.
4. Alireza Bahmanyar, Abouzar Estebsari and Damien Ernst, 'The Impact of Different COVID-19 Containment Measures on Electricity Consumption in Europe' (2020) 68 *Energy Research & Social Science* 101683.
5. 'Bruegel Electricity Tracker of COVID-19 Lockdown Effects' (*Bruegel.org*, 2020) <https://www.bruegel.org/publications/datasets/bruegel-electricity-tracker-of-covid-19-lockdown-effects> accessed 16 August 2020. See also 'EU's Electricity Consumption Lower in April 2020' (*Eurostat*, 2020) <https://ec.europa.eu/eurostat/web/products-eurostat-news/-/DDN-20200714-2?inheritRedirect=true&redirect=%2Feurostat%2Fweb%2Fcovid-19%2Fagriculture-energy-transport-tourism> accessed 16 August 2020.
6. 'Electricity Output Change in Europe by Fuel April 2020' (*Statista*, 2020) <https://www.statista.com/statistics/1114557/europe-electricity-generation-reductions-due-to-covid-19> accessed 16 August 2020.

7. Kelly Kingsly and Kouam Henri, 'COVID-19 and Oil Prices' [2020] SSRN Electronic Journal <https://papers.ssrn.com/sol3/papers.cfm?abstract_id=3555880> accessed 16 August 2020.
8. Dave Jones and Charles Moore, 'Renewables Beat Fossil Fuels' (*Ember*, July 2020).
9. Directive (EU) 2018/2001 of the European Parliament and of the Council of 11 December 2018 on the promotion of the use of energy from renewable sources [2018] OJ L328/82, recitals 11, 12, 16 and Article 4.
10. Ibid.
11. Consolidated version of the Treaty on European Union [2016] OJ C202/13 (hereafter TEU).
12. Paul James Cardwell and Holly Snaith, '"There's a Brand Talk, but It's Not Very Clear": Can the Contemporary EU Really be Characterized as Ordoliberal?' [2018] *Journal of Common Market Studies* 1053, pp 1058, 1063–4; Josef Hien and Christian Joerges, 'Dead Man Walking? Current European Interest in the Ordoliberal Tradition' [2018] *European Law Journal* 142, pp 145–7, 150; Werner Bonefeld, 'Freedom and the Strong State: On German Ordoliberalism' [2012] *New Political Economy* 633; David J. Gerber, 'Constitutionalizing the Economy: German Neo-Liberalism, Competition Law and the "New Europe"' [1994] *The American Journal of Comparative Law* 25.
13. Christian Joerges and Florian Rödl, '"Social Market Economy" as Europe's Social Model?' in Lars Magnusson and Bo Stråth (eds), *A European Social Citizenship?* (Peter Lang 2004), 125, pp 144–5; Christian L. Glossner, *The Making of the German Post-war Economy* (I.B. Tauris 2010), pp 47–8.
14. See for instance Communication from the Commission – Guidelines on State aid for environmental protection and energy 2014–2020 [2014] OJ C200/1; Commission, 'Guidance for the design of renewables support schemes' (Staff Working Document) SWD(2013) 439 final. See also Cardwell and Snaith (n 12), p 1058.
15. Evelyn Z. Brodkin and Denis Young, 'Making Sense of Privatization: What Can We Learn from Economic and Political Analysis?' in Sheila B. Kamerman and Alfred J. Kahn (eds), *Privatization and the Welfare State* (Princeton University Press 2014), 121; Klaus Mathis, *Efficiency Instead of Justice?* (tr Deborah Shannon, Springer 2009), ch 3; Thomas Miceli, *The Economic Approach to Law* (Stanford University Press 2004), ch 1.
16. Francis M. Bator, 'The Anatomy of Market Failure' [1958] *The Quarterly Journal of Economics* 351.
17. Joseph P. Tomain and Richard D. Cudahy, *Energy Law in a Nutshell* (West Academic Publishing 2017), pp 38–50; Niamh Dunne, *Competition Law and Economic Regulation* (Cambridge University Press 2015), ch 1; Robert Baldwin, Martin Cave and Martin Lodge, *Understanding Regulation* (Oxford University Press 2011), ch 2.
18. Ibid; Tony Prosser, 'Models of Economic and Social Regulation' in Dawn Oliver, Tony Prosser and Richard Rawlings (eds), *The Regulatory State: Constitutional Implications* (Oxford University Press 2010) 34; David Levi-Faur, 'Regulatory Capitalism: The Dynamics of Change beyond Telecoms and Electricity' [2006] *Governance: An International Journal of Policy, Administration and Institutions* 497; Giandomenico Majone, 'From the Positive to the Regulatory State: Causes and Consequences of Changes in the Mode of Governance' [1997] *Journal of Public Policy* 139.

19 See for instance Commission, 'The European Green Deal' (Communication) COM(2019) 640 final; Commission, 'United in delivering the Energy Union and Climate Action – Setting the foundations for a successful clean energy transition', COM(2019) 285 final; Commission, 'Accelerating Europe's transition to a low-carbon economy' (Communication) COM(2016) 500 final.
20 Consolidated version of the Treaty on the Functioning of the European Union [2016] OJ C202/47 (hereafter TFEU), Articles 107 and 108.
21 Communication (n 14); see also Antonios Bouchagiar, 'The Binding Effects of Guidelines on the Compatibility of State Aid: How Hard is the Commission's Soft Law?' [2017] *Journal of European Competition Law and Practice* 157.
22 Communication (n 14), point 34.
23 Bator (n 16), p 358. See also Emma Hutchinson, *Principles of Microeconomics* (University of Victoria 2017), ch 5; Peter Dorman, *Microeconomics* (Springer 2014); Steven C. Hackett, *Environmental and Natural Resources Economics* (M.E. Sharpe 2006), ch 14.
24 Shi-Ling Hsu, 'Prices versus Quantities' in Kenneth R. Richards and Josephine van Zeben (eds), *Policy Instruments in Environmental Law* (Edward Elgar Publishing 2020), 183, pp 183–98; Claudia Kettner, Daniela Kletzan-Slamanig, Stefan E. Weishaar and Irene J.J. Burgers, 'Designing Carbon Taxes: Economic and Legal Considerations' in Marta Villar Ezcurra, Janet E. Milne, Hope Ashiabor and Mikael Skou Andersen (eds), *Environmental Fiscal Challenges for Cities and Transport* (Edward Elgar Publishing 2019) 213.
25 Communication (n 14); Commission, 'Delivering the internal electricity market and making the most of public intervention' (Communication) C(2013) 7243 final, p 6.
26 See also Communication (n 14), point 115.
27 See for instance State Aid SA.50199 (2019/N), C(2019) 3122 final, para 45; State Aid SA.51306 (2018/N), C(2018) 6358 final, para 77; Aide d'État SA.46698 (2017/NN), C(2018) 1210 final, para 83; Aide d'État SA.49180 (2018/NN), C(2018) 6847 final, para 70; Aide d'État SA.48642 (2018/NN), C(2018) 7753 final, para 76; State Aid SA.49318 (2017/N), C(2018) 681 final, para 32; State Aid SA.44076, C(2017) 4988 final, para 85; State Aid SA.44666, C(2016) 7272 final, para 101; State aid SA.36196 (2014/N), C(2014) 5079 final, para 56.
28 Emilio Ghiani, Marco Galici, Mario Mureddu and Fabrizio Pilo, 'Impact on Electricity Consumption and Market Pricing of Energy and Ancillary Services during Pandemic of COVID-19 in Italy' (2020) 13 *Energies* 3357. See also Richard G. Smead, 'Oil and Gas in the Age of COVID-19: Where Do They Go from Here?' (2020) 36 *Natural Gas & Electricity* 22; Nelson Mojarro, 'COVID-19 Is a Game-Changer for Renewable Energy: Here's Why' (*World Economic Forum*, June 2020) <https://www.weforum.org/agenda/2020/06/covid-19-is-a-game-changer-for-renewable-energy> accessed 20 August 2020.
29 Massimo Schiavo, principal author, 'The Energy Transition and What It Means for European Power Prices and Producers: Midyear 2020 Update' (S&P Global Ratings, June 2020); Marcus Ferdinand, 'European Power and Carbon Markets Affected by COVID-19: An Early Impact Assessment' (*Independent Commodity Intelligence Services*, 2020) <https://www.icis.com/explore/resources/news/2020/03/27/10487371/european-power-and-carbon-markets-affected-by-covid-19-an-early-impact-assessment> accessed 24 August 2020.
30 Simon Evans, 'Analysis: Coronavirus Set to Cause Largest Ever Annual Fall in CO2 Emissions' (*Carbon Brief*, April 2020), <https://www.carbonbrief.org/analysis

-coronavirus-set-to-cause-largest-ever-annual-fall-in-co2-emissions> accessed 19 August 2020. See also Corinne Le Quéré, principal author, 'Temporary Reduction in Daily Global CO2 Emissions during the COVID-19 Forced Confinement' (2020) 10 *Nature Climate Change* 647.
31. Dave Jones, 'Analysis: Coronavirus has Cut CO_2 from Europe's Electricity System by 39%' (*CarbonBrief*, April 2020) <https://www.carbonbrief.org/analysis-coronavirus-has-cut-co2-from-europes-electricity-system-by-39-per-cent> accessed 19 August 2020; Juan M. Morales and Salvador Pineda, 'On the Inefficiency of the Merit Order in Forward Electricity Markets with Uncertain Supply' (2017) 261 *European Journal of Operational Research* 789.
32. IEA, 'Covid-19 Impact on Electricity-Analysis' (*IEA*, December 2020) <https://www.iea.org/reports/covid-19-impact-on-electricity> accessed 3 January 2021; Jones and Moore (n 8).
33. Jones and Moore (n 8); Mojarro (n 28).
34. Dieter Helm, 'The Environmental Impacts of the Coronavirus' (2020) 76 *Environmental and Resource Economics* 21, p 25.
35. Hepburn et al. (n 3); Jones and Moore (n 8); IRENA, 'The Post-COVID Recovery' (IRENA 2020); Brian Eckhouse and Chris Martin, 'Coronavirus Crushing Global Forecasts for Wind and Solar Power' [2020] *Bloomberg Green* <https://www.bloomberg.com/news/articles/2020-03-27/global-solar-wind-growth-will-be-erased-this-year-rystad-says> accessed 15 August 2020.
36. Ibid.
37. IEA, 'The Impact of the Covid-19 Crisis on Clean Energy Progress' (*IEA*, 2020) <https://www.iea.org/articles/the-impact-of-the-covid-19-crisis-on-clean-energy-progress> accessed 19 August 2020; IEA, '2020 and 2021 Forecast Overview' (*IEA* 2020) <https://www.iea.org/reports/renewable-energy-market-update/2020-and-2021-forecast-overview> accessed 19 August 2020.
38. Smead (n 28).
39. Paris Agreement to the United Nations Framework Convention on Climate Change, 12 Dec 2015, T.I.A.S. No. 16-1104.
40. UN, 'Emissions Gap Report 2019' (United Nations Environment Programme 2019).
41. Le Quéré et al. (n 30); Hepburn et al. (n 3).
42. Piers M. Forster, principal author, 'Current and Future Global Climate Impacts Resulting from COVID-19' [2020] *Nature Climate Change* 913.
43. IEA (n 32)
44. Brodkin and Young (n 15).
45. Communication (n 14), point 35(c).
46. Commission, 'Summer 2020 Economic Forecast: A Deeper Recession with Wider Divergences' (*EC Europa* 2020) <https://ec.europa.eu/info/business-economy-euro/economic-performance-and-forecasts/economic-forecasts/summer-2020-economic-forecast-deeper-recession-wider-divergences_en> accessed 21 August 2020; World Bank Group, 'Global Economic Prospects' (World Bank Group, June 2020).
47. Richard A. Musgrave, *The Theory of Public Finance* (MacGraw-Hill 1959). See also Leonardo Becchetti, Luigino Bruni and Stefano Zamagni, *The Microeconomics of Wellbeing and Sustainability* (Academic Press 2020), pp 250–51; Wilfried Ver Eecke, 'The Concept of a "Merit Good": The Ethical Dimension in Economic Theory and the History of Economic Thought or the Transformation of Economics into Socio-Economics' (1998) 27 *Journal of Socio-Economics* 133; Geoffrey

Brennan and Loren Lomasky, 'Institutional Aspects of "Merit Goods" Analysis' [1983] *Finanzarchiv* 183.
48 Jennifer Layke and Norma Hutchinson, '3 Reasons to Invest in Renewable Energy Now' (*World Resources Institute* 2020) <https://www.wri.org/blog/2020/05/coronavirus-renewable-energy-stimulus-packages> accessed 22 August 2020.
49 Commission (n 46).
50 Georgiana Pop and Ana Amador, 'To Aid and How to Aid: Policy Options to Preserve Markets' (2020) 19 *European State Aid Law Quarterly* 127.
51 Directive 2018/2001 (n 9), Article 4.
52 Guidance (n 14), pp 5–6; Communication (n 14) point 108. See also Theodoros Iliopoulos, 'Dilemmas on the Way to a New Renewable Energy Directive' [2018] *European Energy and Environmental Law Review* 210.
53 See Directive 2018/2001 (n 9), recitals 16–19, 22, 26 and Articles 4, 21, 22.
54 See Penelope Crossley, *Renewable Energy Law: An International Assessment* (Cambridge University Press 2019), ch 5; Cameron Hepburn, 'Carbon Taxes, Emissions Trading and Hybrid Systems' in Dieter Helm and Cameron Hepburn (eds), *The Economics and Politics of Climate Change* (Oxford University Press 2009) 365; Philippe Menanteau, Dominique Finon and Marie-Laure Lamy, 'Prices versus Quantities: Choosing Policies for Promoting the Development of Renewable Energy' (2003) 31 *Energy Policy* 799. See also Guidance (n 14), ch 3.1.7.
55 Theodoros Iliopoulos, 'Price Support Schemes in the Service of the EU's Low-Carbon Energy Transition' in Theodoros Zachariadis, Janet E. Milne, Mikael Skou Andersen and Hope Ashiabor (eds), *Economic Instruments for a Low-carbon Future* (Edward Elgar Publishing 2020) 2.
56 See also other provisions of the RED II, such as those in Articles 5, 6, 21 or 22.
57 Directive 2011/92/EU of the European Parliament and of the Council of 13 December 2011 on the Assessment of the Effects of Certain Public and Private Projects on the Environment, [2012] OJ L 26/1.
58 On self-consumption schemes see also Theodoros G. Iliopoulos, Matteo Fermeglia and Bernard Vanheusden, 'The EU's 2030 Climate and Energy Policy Framework: How Net Metering Slips through its Net' [2020] *Review of European, Comparative & International Environmental Law Special Issue* 245; Marta Villar Ezcurra and Carmen Cámara Barroso, 'Tax Incentives for Photovoltaic Power Self-consumption: An Analysis of the Spanish Experience' in Zachariadis et al. (n 55).
59 Guidance (n 14).
60 Commission Regulation (EU) No 651/2014 of 17 June 2014 declaring certain categories of aid compatible with the internal market in application of Articles 107 and 108 of the Treaty [2014] OJ L 187/1.
61 See TEU (n 11), Article 19.
62 On this discussion, see Kristin Haraldsdóttir, 'The Limits of EU Competence to Regulate Conditions for Exploitation of Energy Resources: Analysis of Article 194(2) TFEU' [2014] *European Energy and Environmental Law Review* 208; Angus Johnston and Eva van der Marel, '*Ad Lucem*? Interpreting the New EU Energy Provision, and in particular the Meaning of Article 194(2) TFEU' [2013] *European Energy and Environmental Law Review* 181.

PART VI

Lessons for allowance trading

16. Covid-19 and EU climate change linking

Stefan E. Weishaar

INTRODUCTION

In November 2019 the coronavirus (Covid-19) pandemic broke out, causing human suffering, fatalities and giving rise to an unprecedented wave of economic shutdowns that engulfed many countries around the globe.

There is the clear and present danger that this crisis leads to a new sense of urgency that diverts public attention away from other pressing problems such as the climate change crisis. Despite the positive effects of the economic downturn on global greenhouse gas (GHG) emissions, the climate crisis will not go away.

In recent years countries have already embarked upon a path of protectionism in the economic sphere. Given the economic setback in many countries, policymakers could approach the Covid-19 crisis by embracing protectionism even more and expanding it beyond the economic realm to other policy areas including climate change. This would be particularly grave as solutions to climate change require more concerted action, not less.

This chapter examines how Covid-19 affects climate change cooperation. It does this by examining how the Covid-19 crisis impacts the prospects for linking emissions trading systems (ETSs). It uses the European climate change policy as a case because the EU has the ambition to be the global climate change leader and it has experience in linking its ETS with other systems.

The chapter first reviews the current wider economic framework and the increasing emphasis of protectionism (part 1) before reviewing the positive but not structural effects Covid-19 has on climate change (part 2). Subsequently the chapter contributes to the linking literature by examining how susceptible linking is to protectionism (part 3). Part 4 builds upon insights gained and puts them into perspective by examining the effects of Covid-19 on cooperative approaches for climate change in the EU.

1. COVID-19 AND THE ECONOMY

Covid-19 has gravely impacted the economy. Early forecasts in March 2020 by the Organisation for Economic Co-operation and Development (OECD) suggested that global gross domestic product (GDP) growth in 2020 could be reduced by up to 1.5%.[1] Less than 2 months after the publication of the report the Secretary-General of the OECD has described even the most severe scenario contained therein as understating the true effects.[2] Estimates from June 2020 suggest that global GDP would decline by 6% in 2020 and trade would contract by 9.5% if no second wave came, and if there were a second wave global GDP would contract by 7.6% and world trade by 11.5%.[3] Covid-19 would then have given rise to the greatest global recession since the Great Depression. Not only the world as a whole but also Europe is being hit severely. Estimates from June 2020 suggest that the Eurozone's GDP would decline by 9.1% in 2020 if no second wave came, and if there were a second wave the Eurozone's GDP would decline by 11.5%.[4] The latest estimates for the Eurozone are more favourable as fiscal measures are taking root, predicting a somewhat milder decline for the Eurozone of 7.5% in 2020.[5]

The health crisis is thus swiftly turning both into an economic and financial crisis that was catching the world in an ill-prepared state. Due to increasing protectionism both the growth in the global GDP and in global trade have been on the decline since 2017,[6] underlining the mounting trade tensions between major economies.

Not only GDP and global trade are on the decline but also companies are not faring well. Global corporate debt levels are mounting and global corporate bond ratings have been low for the last decade and deteriorating, reflecting an unprecedented build-up of corporate bond debt since the 2008 financial crisis.[7]

Not only the corporate world is still under the impression of the 2008 financial crisis but also countries have not yet recovered from it. National debt figures measured in terms of GDP have increased markedly for 28 countries contained in the OECD data set from 56.8% on average in 2008 to 82.1% in 2019 and the number of countries with more than 100% debt have increased from four to eight during the same time period.[8] This is indicative that the fiscal measures that some countries have at their disposition at the beginning of the Covid-19 crisis are more restricted than during the 2008 crisis. Recent projections show that due to Covid-19 the OECD countries' debt in terms of percentage points of GDP will increase by 18.61% in a single wave scenario and by 26.63% in a second wave scenario.[9] It therefore does appear that fiscal expansion, as a solution to overcome the economic crisis, is approaching its limits.

Besides fiscal policy, nations can also rely on monetary policy to overcome a crisis situation. Examining the prospects of expansionary monetary policies to alleviate the economic crisis also gives little sign for optimism. Central bank interest rates have come down significantly from the 2008 financial crisis and some have even turned negative, indicating that a critical element of monetary policy seems to have reached its natural limits.

With the classical macroeconomic toolkit (fiscal and monetary policy) already heavily used and having reached the limits of its effectiveness in many countries, it is to be expected that the current crisis will be taking a long time to be resolved. There is the risk that the profound domestic economic and social problems overpower the urgency of the climate change crisis regularly emphasized by the IPCC (Intergovernmental Panel on Climate Change)[10] and give rise to more unilateral and protectionist measures.

Several governments have already reacted to Covid-19 with trade restrictions, particularly to prevent exports of medical supplies. The G20 countries had withdrawn 36% of these by mid-May, which is a positive development.[11] Nevertheless trade restrictions remain widespread, affecting an estimated 10.3% of G20 imports, and remain a concern.[12] Protectionist measures are prominently used at the moment and they have generated both contention and distrust between major trading partners that do seem to affect the willingness to cooperate in other areas. From a climate change perspective this is particularly grave because only cooperation can lead to success.

2. IMPLICATIONS OF COVID-19 ON CLIMATE CHANGE AND LINKING

The economic downturn resulting from the Covid-19 pandemic brought strong reductions in economic production, electricity demand and transportation. The daily global CO_2 emissions fell by 17% by early April 2020 vis-à-vis the mean 2019 levels; nearly half of this reduction was attributable to reductions in surface transport.[13] The aviation sector, which accounts for around 2% of global GHG emissions, is also in crisis. For 2020 the global passenger air traffic is projected to decline by 35% to 65%.[14] The overall emission reductions are of course dependent upon when pre-pandemic conditions return. Global emissions were projected to fall by 7% if some restrictions remain in place in 2020.[15] Reductions in GHG emissions of such an order of magnitude are welcome in light of the climate crisis. In order to contain global warming to 1.5°C above pre-industrial levels – the declared goal of the Paris Agreement – annual reductions of more than 6% are needed until 2030.[16] Covid-19 therefore offers some alleviation but of course is not sustainable itself as it does not bring the necessary structural changes that a transition to a low carbon society requires.

Against the backdrop of the economic downturn and increasing protectionism presented in the previous part a collaborative approach to climate policies is especially important as it reduces overall abatement costs hence enables countries to attain their emission reduction targets at lower costs. With cooperative approaches to climate change I am specifically referring to the linking of ETS.

The linking of ETS enables entities covered by an emissions trading scheme to freely use emission allowances issued by another trading scheme to meet its domestic compliance obligations.[17] Reflecting the increasing diversity and fragmentation in the various national and regional carbon mitigation strategies, linking research is also interested in the linking possibilities with other instruments such as taxation, performance standards, and so on.

Emissions trading is efficient and politically acceptable as it enables covered entities to identify themselves which entity has the lowest abatement costs and consequently which one should avoid emissions. Linking enables covered entities to take advantage of low abatement opportunities in other jurisdictions. The equalization of abatement costs across sectors and jurisdictions lowers the overall abatement costs and enables the attainment of a more ambitious environmental target at least cost.[18] It is estimated that if all OECD countries were linked, costs could be reduced by 25% to 55%.[19] There are also a number of other benefits and disadvantages associated with linking that have been discussed extensively in the linking literature and relate inter alia to synergy effects and policymaking.[20] These general weaknesses persist independent of the specific circumstances addressed in this chapter, namely the economic downturn due to the Covid-19 pandemic and the current political context of rising protectionism and EU policies. But in context of rising protectionism and economic contraction, linking climate change policies could help to keep a focus on climate change and to realize the necessary steps towards decarbonization at lower costs.

3. LINKING AND PROTECTIONISM

Linking of ETSs creates distributive effects between and within jurisdictions and thereby creates winners and losers from allowing trade between ETSs. Prospects of redistribution give rise to lobbying for the application of linking features that serve national interests or the private interests of particular stakeholders. This part therefore examines how susceptible linking is for protectionist sentiments.

A link between ETSs can be used and exploited by directing payment flows between linked systems. A link can also be used as a direct means to adversely affect the economy of the linking partner or used along traditional protectionist measures such as subsidies or border taxes.

Jurisdictions have several options to shape the redistribution pattern of allowances between linked ETSs. Strategically weakening one's environmental target is tantamount to a competitive currency devaluation in the sense that domestic entities are subject to a lower cost burden and could gain in competitiveness. Bringing additional sectors under the ETS can also alter redistribution patterns[21] if the newly added sectors are net buyers or sellers of allowances or if non-negligible administrative costs are placed upon the newly covered sectors. Even though such strategies can of course also be used independently of linking, in particular differences in environmental target setting are recognized as an important political barrier to linking.[22]

The linking literature has also established that economic shocks can spill over from one ETS to the other.[23] A point that has not yet received attention in the literature is that linking creates a direct connection of the real economy of the ETSs via the allowance market that can be exploited. Unlike the insights from trade theory that teach us that the linkages between economies are not immediate as prices are sticky and contracts are often concluded several months in advance,[24] the effects of changing allowance prices in linked ETSs may be felt more swiftly. Such developments may thereby hit the real economy of the linked jurisdiction much more rapidly than exchange rate fluctuations as allowances are required for production and have to be surrendered on a particular compliance date. By influencing the emission allowance market the real economy of the linked jurisdiction is therefore more vulnerable to price changes than mere changes in the exchange rates would indicate.

If an ETS is exporting allowances, the government could restrict the number of available allowances by, for example, increasing the auction reserve price, altering the auctioning schedules, reducing allowance sales or increasing domestic demand (for example, by adding sectors to the ETS or by asking public undertakings to buy additional allowances). Such measures could be described as 'beggar thy neighbour policies' if they benefit the jurisdiction that enacted them, while they harm other linked jurisdictions and trading partners.

Also more subtle ETS design features can be used to impact redistribution patterns in order to protect the economy. Examples include offsets, market management systems or carbon leakage measures.

Offsets can be used to direct transfers between linked systems. Offsets offer access to additional allowance sources and improve market liquidity but are often criticized regarding their environmental additionality. Differences in quality standards and quantitative restrictions spill over from one ETS to the other (back-door problem), undermine environmental integrity and give rise to transfers from one system to the other. Differences in offset rules are viewed to pose significant barriers to linking as they undermine political acceptability.[25]

Also ETS design choices are often co-determined by non-environmental considerations such as competitiveness concerns and supporting innovation and transition. Competition does not only take place between undertakings but also between economies and can take the form of regulatory competition as well. Market management systems (price floors, price ceilings, trigger prices, and so on) are therefore often included in ETS designs in order to manage overall allowance scarcity or market prices. Given their political sensitiveness, harmonization is described by the linking literature as being critical for linking.[26] Depending on their particular design, market management systems can protect domestic interests but also become vulnerable to policy changes in the linked system. Transfers between linked systems would, for example, arise if an allowance floor price would be supported by buying allowances from the market while linked ETSs would expand allowance liquidity.

Another critical issue for linking that can be used as a protectionist measure are differences in carbon leakage measures.[27] Linking levels the playing field between linked jurisdictions and thereby reduces the danger of carbon leakage, at least between the linked systems but not vis-à-vis third countries. But measures combating carbon leakage address environmental and competitiveness concerns and are oftentimes very political as they also give rise to redistributive effects. The underlying fear is that stringent carbon measures lead to a displacement rather than to an actual emissions reduction and that this undermines the environmental effectiveness and leads to deindustrialization. While the empirical evidence of carbon leakage is still debated, it is beyond doubt that the carbon costs of energy intensive trade exposed industries are mitigated via a variety of means. These can include ETS design measures but also protectionist measures that could include free allocation or financial transfers funded by carbon border tax adjustments. Clearly the granting of production subsidies or introducing border taxes can hardly be seen as trade liberalization.

The above treatment has shown that linking of ETSs exposes a jurisdiction to risks and makes it dependent upon developments abroad because a link can be exploited in various ways to further domestic interests via enticing transfers, harming the other ETS's economy and via traditional protectionist measures. It also can be used as a direct means to impact the real economy. The general approach suggested in the literature, when addressing the linking issues described above, is to reach *ex ante* legal agreements with linking partners. This would also be the logical approach to avoid the protectionist abuses identified above. Yet the dilemma of our times is that national interests also trump the rule of law. International agreements may be a weak safeguard when domestic interests are at play.

4. IMPLICATIONS FOR EUROPE

The forgoing parts have shown that protectionism is spreading and that things may get worse as a result of the Covid-19 crisis. It has also been shown that linking ETSs can be used to gain advantages over linked partners. This part therefore examines what implication this has for the further development of the European climate change policy and the linking of the EU ETS with other ETSs. In order to examine this, a brief introduction to the current European climate change policy is given.

For long the EU has aspired to become the global climate change leader and has some experience with linking. Linking ETSs[28] proved to be a cumbersome and not always a very successful way to expand EU influence in the area of climate change policies. The linking process with the Swiss ETS led to an alignment of the Swiss CO2 Act in 2011 to the rules of the EU ETS but a link was only established as of 1 January 2020. This linking process has therefore been taking very long. The link between the Australian Carbon Pricing System and the EU ETS never materialized because the Australian scheme was dismantled.

The EU ETS proliferation has not been very successful via linking, the EU is still a climate leader in the sense that it has set the most ambitious targets globally. For 2020 the EU aimed at reducing GHG emissions covered under the EU ETS by 20% below 1990 levels. For 2030 the EU ETS was strengthened to deliver a reduction of 43% below 1990 levels.[29] This European target was, however, not in line with the EU's 2050 target, nor with the objective of the Paris Agreement to contain global warming to 1.5°C if possible.[30]

Shortly before the 25th UN Climate Change Conference (COP25) the European Parliament approved a resolution declaring a climate and environmental emergency and calling upon the EU's President to include a 55% GHG emissions reduction target by 2030 in the European Green Deal.[31] The European Green Deal envisages climate neutrality by 2050.

The European Green Deal envisages an emission reduction target for 2030 of at least 50% and a plan for a 55% reduction. It also envisages the extension of the EU ETS to maritime transportation, construction and traffic and to reduce the free allowances to airlines over time.[32] Moreover it proposes to avoid carbon leakage by introducing carbon border taxes for specific sectors and to extend these over time.

The Commission recently presented its draft proposal for establishing the framework for achieving climate neutrality which obliges itself to review the Union's 2030 targets by September 2020 and to set a 2030 reduction target between 50%–55% below 1990 and to assess by June 2021 which legislation would need to be amended.[33] Given that the current EU level climate, energy and mobility targets are only projected to lead to GHG reductions of around 45% in 2030, compared to 1990 levels, much more needs to be done.[34]

The enhanced policy ambition of the EU must be concretized at a point in time when the climate change crisis rivals the Covid-19 crisis. As discussed above, Covid-19 has hit the European economy hard. The linking processes that the EU has embarked upon have not been easy and they took a lot of time. It also has been shown that linking makes countries dependent upon each other and that linking can be used in protectionist ways. Linking partners must be ready to trust each other, and trust that agreements would be observed, something that during an economic crisis, and against the current tensions between nations, is not easy.

This might explain why the appetite for linking is presently low. It bears mentioning that EU citizens are not only concerned about health and employment but remain also strongly concerned about climate change.[35]

There are, however, other important issues why linking the EU ETS to other trading systems is less likely to occur at the moment: the reason is that the challenges for the EU ETS are mounting with the increased climate ambition and clear ETS design solutions are not yet determined. This entails that a linked system would need to develop alongside the EU ETS rather than to be able to determine its own solutions.

The rising EU ambition to reduce GHG emissions means that installations covered by the EU ETS will need to reduce more – this will undermine European competitiveness. Thus far the EU ETS has not undermined the competitiveness of industry because almost all GHG emission reductions came from combustion (for example, energy generation). It is expected that this will change in the future when industry will need to start contributing to emission reductions in order to realize the strengthened targets.[36] An enhanced ambition will put both industry and politicians under pressure and tempt them to protect the EU economy. It is therefore not surprising that also the 2030 climate strategy provides for instruments to protect EU interests.

Less exposed EU ETS sectors will still receive some free allocation of emission allowances on the basis of benchmarks, but this will gradually be reduced and ultimately phased out by 2030.[37] Just like the energy sector, they will be subject to auctioning. The vast majority of sectors, covering 94% of industrial emissions, remain on the carbon leakage list and will continue to receive emissions for free.[38] Member States will also be entitled to continue to grant certain sectors support for increased electricity prices that have risen due to the passing on of carbon costs (indirect emission costs).[39] Moreover several European funds (regarding innovation and modernization) are available to help industry. Thus protectionist measures will continue to include different forms of subsidies (free allocation and financial aid measures) but these may become infeasible in light of the strong 2030 and 2050 emission reduction targets.

The New Green Deal therefore adds one important new element: a carbon border tax. Such a tax is envisaged to start with a number of selected sectors before being extended.[40] Of course taking World Trading Organization (WTO) compatible measures is subject to legal uncertainty relating to Articles III and XX of the General Agreement on Tariffs and Trade (GATT) and the specific requirements that a carbon tax measure is bound to persist for quite some time.[41] Especially now that the WTO Appellate Body is not operational. The interim solution to rely upon Article 25 Dispute Settlement Understanding (DSU) and to use former Appellate Body members to resolve appeals has only been reached by a few WTO members, the vast majority of members are not subject to this agreement.

It is therefore likely that even if an even-handed carbon tax measure were introduced by the EU, disputes could not be resolved under WTO rules and might lead other countries to impose protectionist measures. A negotiated approach by the EU would therefore appear expedient but the Commission seems to expect that a measure would raise funds swiftly so that they can be used for the Covid-19 rebuild of the EU economy.

Not only the introduction of the carbon border tax but also the extension of the EU ETS to maritime shipping is bound to give rise to disputes, as such a measure would necessarily involve a strong element of extraterritorial application of EU law. This was forcefully rejected several years ago when the EU ETS was extended to aviation. It may therefore be expected that such extensions will not be easily accepted by the international community.

CONCLUSION

It therefore can be concluded that the enhanced European climate ambitions bear a lot of conflict potential in them that can give rise to protectionist sentiments. Such developments may very well impede both the realization of stronger climate objectives and undermine cooperative approaches to climate policies. As presented in the parts on linking, protectionist sentiments could undermine the proliferation of larger linked ETSs. Linking offers attractive cost reductions and benefits that can be harnessed to support global climate change mitigation efforts but the European experience with linking with Switzerland and Australia has shown that linking can prove to be both cumbersome and fragile. Thus also independent of the pandemic linking was challenging.

Due to the deteriorated economic situation resulting from the pandemic and the environment of heightened protectionism in trade flows as well as the reduced trust among trading partners, one can expect that linking may be less attractive at the moment. Especially since it has been shown that linking could also be used as a protectionist measure.

Another reason why one might wonder if linking of ETSs is still a likely way forward is because of the expected conflicts relating to the strengthening of the EU ETS and the resulting impact on the covered industries. Examining the current developments of the EU ETS, linking is probably less likely to take place because of the regulatory framework, in particular when it comes to carbon leakage and carbon border taxes, which might need to be adjusted to the demands of trading partners.

Rather than new initiatives for linking, we might see more conservative forms of international cooperation, that is, the alignment of ETS design features and climate targets across jurisdictions. We might also see a heightened interest in carbon taxation as a form of raising tax income.[42]

Given the urgency of the climate situation, it is critical to avoid that Covid-19 also infects climate policy and that countries resent international cooperation. The climate crisis requires concerted action and one should not let a good crisis go by unused.

NOTES

1. OECD (2020), OECD Interim Economic Outlook: Coronavirus – the world economy at risk, 2 March 2020, p. 11.
2. OECD (2020), Coronavirus (Covid-19): Joint actions to win the war, available at https://www.oecd.org/about/secretary-general/Coronavirus-COVID-19-Joint-actions-to-win-the-war.pdf (accessed 26 May 2021), p. 1.
3. WTO Press release (2020),Trade falls steeply in first half of 2020, June 22nd, available at https://www.wto.org/english/news_e/pres20_e/pr858_e.htm, Table 1 (accessed 26 May 2021).
4. OECD (2020) OECD Economic Outlook, June 2020, The world economy on a tightrope, available at http://www.oecd.org/economic-outlook/june-2020 (accessed 26 May 2021).
5. OECD (2020), OECD Economic Outlook: Turning Hope into Reality, December 2020, available at https://www.oecd.org/economic-outlook (accessed on 5 January 2021).
6. OECD (2020), OECD Interim Economic Outlook: Coronavirus – the world economy at risk, 2 March 2020, p. 4.
7. Çelik, S., Demirtaş, G. and Iskasson, M. (2020), 'Corporate Bond Market Trends, Emerging Risks and Monetary Policy', OECD Capital Market Series, Paris, p. 14.
8. OECD (2020), General Government Debt (Indicator): Data excluding: Colombia, Iceland, Israel, Japan, Mexico, Switzerland, Turkey, available at https://doi.org/10.1787/cc9669ed-en (accessed on 5 January 2021).
9. OECD (2020), OECD Economic Outlook: All editions, OECD Economic Outlook: Statistics and Projections (database), available at http://www.oecd.org/coronavirus/en/data-insights/public-debt-projections-2019-21(accessed 26 May 2021).
10. IPCC (2018), Global Warming of 1.5°C: An IPCC special report on the impacts of global warming of 1.5°C above pre-industrial levels and related global greenhouse gas emission pathways, in the context of strengthening the global response to the

threat of climate change, sustainable development, and efforts to eradicate poverty, available at: https://www.ipcc.ch/sr15/download (accessed 26 May 2021).
11. OECD, WTO, UNCTAD, Reports on G20 Trade and Investment Measures,, 29 June 2020, Joint Summary, p. 2, available at https://www.oecd.org/daf/inv/investment-policy/23rd-Report-on-G20-Trade-and-Investment-Measures.pdf (assessed on 26 May 2021).
12. WTO (2020) WTO report on G20 shows moves to facilitate imports even as trade restrictions remain widespread, 29 June 2020, available at https://www.wto.org/english/news_e/news20_e/trdev_29jun20_e.htm (accessed 26 May 2021).
13. Le Quéré, C., principal author (2020), Temporary Reduction in Daily Global CO_2 Emissions during the Covid-19 Forced Confinement, *Nature Climate Change*. https://doi.org/10.1038/s41558-020-0797-x.
14. ICAO (2020), Effects of Novel Coronavirus (Covid-19) on Civil Aviation: Economic impact analysis, Air Transport Bureau, Montreal, Canada, 14 May, available at: https://www.icao.int/sustainability/Pages/Economic-Impacts-of-Covid-19.aspx (accessed 26 May 2021).
15. Le Quéré, C., principal author (2020), Temporary Reduction in Daily Global CO_2 Emissions during the Covid-19 Forced Confinement, *Nature Climate Change*, https://doi.org/10.1038/s41558-020-0797-x.
16. Doe H., (2020) Climate change, the coronavirus, and the economy, 25 May 2020, available at: https://www.rug.nl/news/2020/05/climate-change-the-coronavirus-and-the-economy (accessed 26 May 2021).
17. See Haites, E. (2003), Harmonization between National and International Tradeable Permit Schemes, CATEP Synthesis Paper, OECD, Paris, p. 5.
18. Türk, A., Mehling, M., Flachsland, C. and Sterk, W. (2009), Linking Carbon Markets: Concepts, case studies and pathways, *Climate Policy*, 9(4), 341–57, at p. 344.
19. Lazarowicz, M. (2009), U.K. Global Carbon Trading: A framework for reducing emissions, Office of Climate Change, London, U.K, p. 13.
20. See Weishaar, S.E. (2020), Linking of Climate Change Policies, in K.R. Richards and J. van Zeben (eds), *Policy Instruments in Environmental Law*, Elgar Encyclopaedia of Environmental Law, Edward Elgar Publishing, Cheltenham, UK and Northampton, MA, USA, pp. 389–405.
21. Metcalf, G. and Weisbach, D. (2012) Linking Policies when Tastes Differ: Global climate policy in a heterogeneous world. *Review of Environmental Economics and Policy* 6(1), 110–28.
22. Green, J.F., Sterner, T. and Wagner, G. (2014), A Balance of Bottom-up and Top-down Linking Climate Policies, *Nature Climate Change*, 4, 1046–1067.
23. Flachsland, C., Marschinski, R. and Edenhofer, O. (2009), To Link or Not to Link: Benefits and disbenefits of linking cap-and-trade systems, *Climate Policy*, 9(4), Special Issue Linking GHG Trading Systems, 358–72, at p. 361.
24. A fall in the real exchange rate often first leads to a deterioration of the current account reflecting the sluggish adaptation of the market to price changes in the short run. In the long run a fall in the real exchange rate leads to an improved current account. This is captured by the so-called J-curve. The J-curve effect lasts between 6 months and a year. See Paul Krugman and Maurice Obstfeld (1992), *International Economics*, 4th edn, Addison-Wesley, Longman, Reading, Massachusetts, p. 469.

25. Jakob-Gallmann, J. (2011), *Regulatory Issues in the Carbon Market: The Linkage of the Emissions Trading System of Switzerland with the Emissions Trading Scheme of the European Union*, Schulthess Verlag, Zurich, p. 140–42.
26. De Perthuis, C. and Trotignon, R. (2014), Governance of CO2 Markets: Lessons from the EU ETS, Energy Policy, 75 C, 100–106.
27. See Tiche, F.G. (2017), Linking Emissions Trading Systems, A law and economics analysis, PhD dissertation, University of Groningen, ch. 3.
28. See Article 25 Directive 2003/87/EC. Directive 2003/87/EC of the European Parliament and of the Council of 13 October 2003 establishing a scheme for greenhouse gas emission allowance trading within the Community and amending Council Directive 96/61/EC, OJ L 275, 25 October 2003, p. 32–46..
29. Directive (EU) 2018/410 of the European Parliament and of the Council of 14 March 2018 amending Directive 2003/87/EC to enhance cost-effective emission reductions and low-carbon investments, and Decision (EU) 2015/1814, OJ L 76, 19 March 2018, pp. 3–27.
30. I4CE and Enerdata (2018), Mind the Gap: Aligning the 2030 EU climate and energy policy framework to meet long-term climate goals, available at https://www.i4ce.org/download/mind-the-gap-aligning-the-2030-climate-and-energy-policy-framework-to-meet-long-term-climate-goals (accessed 26 May 2021).
31. European Parliament Press Release (2019), The European Parliament Declares Climate Emergency, Press Releases, 29 November 2019. The resolution also requests the Commission to ensure that all relevant legislative and budgetary proposals designed to limit global warming to under 1.5°C.
32. Von der Leyen, U. (2019), A Union that Strives for More: My agenda for Europe, Political Guidelines for the Next European Commission 2019–2024, p. 5, Available at: https://ec.europa.eu/info/sites/default/files/political-guidelines-next-commission_en_0.pdf (accessed 26 May 2021).
33. Proposal for a Regulation of the European Parliament and of the Council establishing the framework for achieving climate neutrality and amending Regulation (EU) 2018/1999 (European Climate Law), COM(2020)80 final, Brussels, 4 March 2020, Article 2(3) and 2(4).
34. Report from the Commission to the European Parliament and the Council, Preparing the ground for raising long-term ambition, EU Climate Action Progress Report, COM(2019) 559 final, 31 October 2019, p. 3.
35. Kantar (2020), Uncertainty: EU – hope – public opinion in times of Covid-19, A Public Opinion Survey Commissioned by the European Parliament, First results, 14 July 2020, p. 8, available at https://www.europarl.europa.eu/at-your-service/en/be-heard/eurobarometer/public-opinion-in-the-eu-in-time-of-coronavirus-crisis-2(accessed 26 May 2021).
36. Dechezleprêtre, A., Nachtigall, D. and Venmans, F., The Joint Impact of the European Union Emissions Trading System on Carbon Emissions and Economic Performance, OECD Economics Department Working Papers, , No. 1515, para 109.
37. Article 1(15.4) of Directive 2018/410 of 14 March 2018.
38. Articles 1(13a) and 1(15) of Directive 2018/410 of 14 March 2018.
39. Communication from the Commission Guidelines on certain State aid measures in the context of the system for greenhouse gas emission allowance trading post-2021 (2020/C 317/04), 25 September 2020.
40. Von der Leyen, U. (2019), A Union that Strives for More: My agenda for Europe, Political Guidelines for the Next European Commission 2019–2024, Available at:

https://ec.europa.eu/info/sites/default/files/political-guidelines-next-commission_en_0.pdf (accessed 26 May 2021).
41. McLure, C.E. Jr. (2011), A Primer on the Legality of Border Adjustments for Carbon Prices: Through a GATT darkly, CCLR, 2011/4, pp. 456–65; Holzer, K. (2014), Carbon Related Border Adjustment and WTO Law, Edward Elgar Publishing, Cheltenham, UK and Northampton, MA, USA, p. 98ff.
42. In the alternative the EU ETS could also be used to raise revenue, particularly if an auction reserve price would be introduced. Turning the currently quantity based instrument into a 'pricing' instrument is not something that has been favoured by the European Commission thus far and is therefore unlikely to be implemented.

17. Enforcing sustainable auction-based ETS in a post-COVID-19 world: evidence from and lessons for Northeast Asia

Joseph Dellatte and Sven Rudolph[1]

1. INTRODUCTION

Initial allocation and revenue use design features are often used as a leverage to ease policy implementation of greenhouse gas emissions emission trading schemes (GHG ETS). While GHG ETS have already been implemented in South Korea and China and are under consideration in Japan, full auctioning has so far not been deemed a worthwhile option, even though it would enhance the sustainability of the schemes.[2] Anxiety to lose competitiveness and fears of harsh political opposition from industrial and corporate sectors covered by the schemes have thus prevented GHG ETS from generating significant revenue in the region. However, the COVID-19 crisis raises the question on initial allocation and revenue use anew with two interdependent issues: (1) how to generate extra public revenues for financing the relaunch of affected economies, and (2) how to accelerate the energy transition.

Against this background, here we raise the question whether the COVID-19 global shock represents a new window of opportunity for overcoming national resistance to implementing revenue-raising GHG ETS in China, South Korea and Japan. We analyse how urgent post-COVID-19 policy concerns such as industrial relocation, Green Deal relaunch plans, and the need to find additional public revenue sources influence existing political barriers to the implementation of sustainable design features in GHG ETS, particularly full revenue-neutral auctioning and earmarking of revenues for environmental, economic, and social purposes in sustainable COVID-19-recovery programs.

We compare the three Northeast Asian countries' national response to the COVID-19 crisis and assess the impact these responses will probably have on current domestic barriers to the implementation of auction-and-earmarking-based GHG ETS. Methodologically we use document analysis with respect to national responses to the COVID-19 crisis and semi-structured expert interviews on the domestic barriers to implementing sustainable GHG ETS. Being part of a broader study, in this chapter we focus on the perception of the adoption of auction-based allocation among the three expert samples.

Based on the empirical evidence we identify a common rejection pattern toward auction implementation in GHG ETS in the sample. We show how this pattern is impacted by the COVID-19 crisis. And, we provide policy recommendation on how to exploit post-COVID-19 opportunities for enhancing Northeast Asian GHG ETS by lowering the barriers to revenue-raising design features.

2. PRE-COVID-19 CLIMATE POLICY IN NORTHEAST ASIA

Northeast Asia is the biggest absolute GHG emitting region in the world, China (10.9 $GtCO_2e^3$), Japan (1.3 $GtCO_2e$), and South Korea (0.673 $GtCO_2e$) are cumulatively responsible for 12.9 $GtCO_2e$ per year, which was more than one-third of global emissions in 2017.[4] With respect to climate policy, Northeast Asia at this very moment stands at a critical crossroads with respect to climate target development and carbon pricing policy implementation (Table 17.1).

The three Northeast Asian countries' policy responses to climate change differ in many aspects while they also share some similarities in their historical development. Japan is an Annex-I country with an absolute 26% GHG emissions reduction target compared to 2013 by 2030. Korea and China are both Annex-II countries. Korea intends to reduce its GHG emissions by 37% compared to a Business-as-Usual scenario by 2030. China plans to reduce CO_2 emissions per unit of gross domestic product (GDP) by 60–65% in 2030 from 2005 levels and intends to peak its GHG emissions around 2030.[5] The three countries recently pledged carbon neutrality, China for 2060 and the Republic of Korea and Japan for 2050.[6] In addition, the three countries are quite heterogeneous with respect to the constitutional and political situation. China is a one-party autocracy, while Japan and Korea are multi-party democracies.

In terms of GHG ETS, the region has seen a working national scheme in place in South Korea since 2015 and a linked sub-national ETS in Japan (Tokyo and Saitama ETS) since 2010/11.[7] China has been developing a national GHG ETS since 2017, which came into force in 2021.[8]

The Tokyo and Saitama ETS with just above 100 million tons of total GHG emissions in 2016 focus their linked ETS on the end-use of energy in large office buildings, while also including industrial emitters, thus covering around 1,800 facilities and a share of 21% of total CO_2 emissions. Emissions under the cap are supposed to be reduced by an average of 15% by 2020 and 35% by 2030 from average 2002–07 emissions. Initial allocation is fully free of charge, so no revenues are raised.

The Chinese national scheme was supposed to begin trading in 2020, but the COVID-19 outbreak has postponed the implementation of the first real trading phase. However, China has already implemented eight operating regional pilot GHG ETS in Shanghai, Beijing, Hubei, Tianjin, Fujian, Shenzhen, Guangdong and Chongqing since 2013. Still, the pre-COVID-19 political situation with respect to carbon pricing had already seen many barriers to sustainable GHG ETS design in the region. And even successful GHG ETS implementation resulted in programs that mostly excluded auctioning and government revenue raising in particular.

Table 17.1 Nationally determined contributions to the Paris Agreement and GHG ETS in Northeast Asia[9]

	China	Japan	Korea
NDC targets	Reduction of 60–65% of CO_2 emissions per unit of GDP	Absolute reduction of 26% of all GHG emissions by 2030 compared to 2013	Reduction of 37% of all GHG emissions by 2030 compared to Business as Usual
New objective announced	Peak before 2030 and carbon neutrality in 2060[10]	Carbon neutrality for 2050[11]	Carbon neutrality for 2050[12]
ETS	8 regional pilot ETSs (since 2013). National ETS scheduled for 2020 but delayed because of COVID-19 crisis	Tokyo and Saitama ETS (linked since 2011). Decision to implement a national ETS deferred after the Tohoku disaster in 2011. First carbon (fuel tax) in 2012	Korean ETS (since 2014)
Allocation method	National ETS: free allocation (benchmarking),[13] a portion is forecast to be auctioned later	Free allocation (grandfathering)[14]	2018–20: 97% freely allocated and 3% auctioned. From 2021: less than 90% freely allocated and more than 10% auctioned. EITE sectors received 100% free allocation

Globally, GHG ETS raised approximatively 21.61 billion US$ of public revenue, while carbon taxes yielded a slightly higher 23.67 billion US$ in 2019.[15] However, this represents only a very small portion of the approximatively 856 billion US$ revenues from environmental taxes or charges worldwide in 2018.[16]

In Northeast Asia, China, Japan and Korea collected 0.7%, 1.35% and 2.66% of GDP in environmental taxes in 2018, respectively.[17] Japan, the only country in the region with an explicit carbon tax in place, raised 2.43 billion US$ in carbon tax revenues in 2019.[18] Concerning GHG ETS, the Chinese and Japanese sub-national jurisdictions still allocate emissions allowances free of charge without generating extra costs to covered entities. The Korean ETS raised 179.27 million US$ in 2019,[19] but Korea intends to increase its still small share of allowances auctioned in the near future, which will increase costs for Korean firms (Table 17.1). Given the small absolute volume and public revenue share from carbon pricing in Northeast Asian countries, increasing GHG ETS revenues from the implemented or planned schemes represent a promising public income opportunity, particularly in times that require extra funds for sustainable economic recovery.

3. BARRIERS TO AUCTION-BASED GHG ETS IN NORTHEAST ASIA

With respect to research methodology, insights into barriers to auction-based GHG ETS in China, Japan and South Korea have been gained from a survey at COP25 in Madrid. The survey consisted of three expert samples from China, Japan and South Korea. All interviewees were country representatives in the negotiation teams of the Paris Agreement Article 6 Rulebook or advisors to the respective national delegations. The samples contained experts (n = 55) and negotiators from relevant government agencies and from the energy and corporate sectors. Semi-structured interviews were conducted before, during and after COP25 between October 2019 and January 2020.

Testing the possibility of implementing auction-based allocation involves analysing the effects of auctioning on stakeholders and their interests toward these effects. Auction increases the cost of carbon for covered firms but makes the initial allocation more efficient and fairer. Private costs increase because emission costs are fully charged to polluters thus following the strong polluter-pays principle (PPP). Cost-efficiency increases compared to free-of-charge allocation as there is no time lag between the allocation and the generation of the scarcity price, and because both transaction costs and administrative costs can be reduced. Also, the immediate scarcity price signal provides polluters with price certainty and sets immediate innovation incentives. Fairness increases as competitive distortions due to complex free-of-charge allocation are prevented. In turn, auctioning raises revenues for government bodies and considerably reduces the risk of over-allocation.[20]

Regarding the opinion of interviewees about the implementation of auction in their respective domestic GHG ETS, the interview results show that design features implying revenues such as auction-based initial allocation are often rejected both by polluters and economic government agencies. Especially in Korea and Japan, agents argued that these features are politically too difficult to settle with covered sectors. In the Korean case, auction-based allocation policy was even explicitly ruled out in the early-stage policy implementation process in order to obtain adherence from covered sectors (especially emission intensive trade exposed facilities, EITE) to the GHG ETS policy itself.

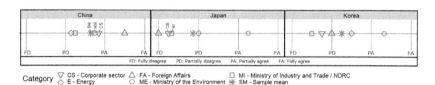

Figure 17.1   Do you agree to move to an auction-based allocation?[21]

As indicated in Figure 17.1, none of the three samples consequently agrees to auction-based allocation. More precisely, only Chinese representatives show an average opinion slightly in favor of auctioning. However, despite this slightly positive average opinion in China, a majority of policy-maker's agents interrogated – like NDRC[22] agents – reject auctions. Even agents from the Chinese Ministry of the Environment only display partial support for the idea. Meanwhile, on average, the two other samples from Japan and Korea, both democracies, disagree with the idea of a full auctioning. Here, a clear divide happens to exist in both samples between agents of the ministries of environment, slightly in favor of some sort of auction-allocation system, and the economic agents from industry, the corporate sector, the economic ministries and even from the foreign affairs agencies, which mostly reject auctions. It illustrates the strong constraints faced by authorities to increase the carbon burden on covered sectors and the influence of interest-groups on these issues. In country comparison, Japan seems to face the strongest opposition on average.

In spite of these observations, in the open questions part of the survey, a majority of government authorities' interviewees recognizes that the revenues generated by auctions would be a most welcome addition to the budget and could be used for financing innovation. However, given the data presented in Figure 17.1, this agency appetite for additional revenues and budget seems to have a lower incidence than the dominant fear of negative economic consequences and political pressure from covered entities due to the extra cost burden originating from full auctioning. In their comments, corporate sector interviewees justify their skeptical position based on expected competitive disadvantages, while economic ministries' representatives – METI[23] in Japan and Korea – describe this extra cost as politically explosive for generating strong political resistance from covered sectors to GHG ETS in its entirety. In addition, in Figure 17.1, the sections of representatives of the three countries that still believe auction could occur in the future happen to be less prevalent. In fact, explanations of their answers reveal interviewees' support to only some sort of partial auction that would explicitly not represent the majority of the initial allocation scheme.

Thus, similar response pattern to auctioning proposals can be identified among the three samples: If auctioning is implemented, government representatives expect strong opposition to this idea. Beyond EITE sectors' anxieties, opposition actually comes from a large part of the industrial sectors, concerned about the cost impact of the measure. Korean representatives specifically recognize that it would be challenging to change the current allocation rules in their GHG ETS and move from the current auctioning share toward full auction. They argue that it would affect the repartition of the effort between economic sectors and would hence reawaken opposition that had been hard to pacify during the initial implementation of the South Korean ETS.[24] Japanese governmental representatives confirm Korean experiences by stating that full auctioning would be very difficult to enforce in the current Japanese political context and thus could jeopardize any steps forward with respect to a national GHG ETS.

This argument also sheds light on a particular political strategy visible both in the Japanese and the Korean cases: According to the Korean interviewees, free allocation was used by government authorities to convince covered sectors to accept the scheme. This exploitation of auctioning as a political leverage to facilitate GHG ETS implementation embodies the compromise necessary to overcome resistance to carbon pricing by the covered sectors. In the Chinese case, resistance from covered sectors is less prevalent, but NDRC representatives still reject auction-based allocation, which might hint at a similar but less visible mechanism in place.

These results display a distinct barrier pattern, echoing the general political barriers to GHG ETS. During the GHG ETS policy process, policy-makers hold stakeholder consultations in order to negotiate special-interest wants and tailor the program design to the domestic needs. Government representatives' fears of harsh political oppositions from industry representatives meet and are reinforced by the factual anxiety of covered sectors' special-interest groups to face a genuine carbon cost that could endanger international competitiveness and reduce profits. This, in turn, encourages policy-makers to swap the design element of auctioning for political support for the policy itself, but by doing so jeopardizing a sustainable GHG ETS design including revenue-raising mechanisms features.

Table 17.2   COVID-19 measures and the environment in Northeast Asia[27]

	Total stimulus (in billion US$)	Percentage of GDP	Allocation for green transition (in US$)
China	594	4.1%	Not specified, but distinct 'New Infrastructure' investment plan of 1.4 trillion including green transportation
Japan	2,100	40%	102.8 million
Rep. of Korea	246.6	12.1%	25 billion

4.   NORTHEAST ASIA AND THE COVID-19 CRISIS

As has been the case across the world, the COVID-19 crisis has also severely affected people's lives in Northeast Asia. Despite relatively well-handled outbreaks, regional economies have been hit hard by lockdowns, travel restrictions and quarantines. In response, governments were forced to take unusual and costly actions to save their economies. These measures have been funded by national debt increases and money printing, are of the extensive type (fiscal measures, stimuli for small and medium-sized enterprises (SME), furlough, direct subsidies, and so on) and targeted citizens as well as all economic sectors.

However, obviously, the concrete direction of these relaunch plans has been politically motivated and varied across countries due to country-specific economic structures (Table 17.2). Unlike the EU 'Green-recovery' package that gives prominence to the ecological transition,[25] Northeast Asian relaunch policies do not carry a wide environmental dimension. China has adopted a relatively small relaunch plan compared to the size of its economy. The Chinese Premier Li Keqian even made no mention of climate change in his last speech in front of the National People's Congress in May. Although, he announced the continuity of a massive 'New Infrastructure' spending plan to target economic recovery and a green economic transition.[26] In Korea, the relaunch measures contain a so-called 'Green New Deal' of around 10% of the relaunch plan that directly targets the green transition of the economy. In Japan, though, the gigantic relaunch plan is at the moment dedicated to the preservation of the current economic structure with little resources directed to a green transition.

Nevertheless, green transition investments are not mentioned in the 594 billion US$ Chinese relaunch plan and it is not clear how the central government will fund this new spending. Still, China counts on its gigantic 1.4 trillion US$ 'New Infrastructure' investment plan to spark the economy if though it is not an explicit part of the Chinese post-COVID-19 relaunch plan. The New Infrastructure plan claims to target a green transition, mainly through new technologies, high-speed train development and electric vehicle subsidies. It also wants to give funding to local green initiatives at the provincial level.[28] In Japan, the 2.43 billion US$ revenues of the carbon tax do not compare in size to the 102.8 million US$ invested for green recovery in the Japanese post-COVID-19 relaunch plan. Only 74 million US$ of this are going to energy-efficient ventilation systems in public space and the construction of renewable energy facilities for companies, with the intention to bring back manufacturing to Japan; an additional 28 million US$ will be given to national parks.[29] In regional comparison, Korea is positioned as a pioneer with its genuine 'Korea Green New Deal' of 25 billion US$. The Deal heading through 2022 includes green remodeling of public facilities, building, housing and manufacturing facilities as well as direct stimulus to SME involved in the green economy.[30] Furthermore, the very small-yield auction in the South Korean (SK) ETS – approximatively 180 million US$ – gives Korean authorities plenty of room to generate more carbon pricing revenues to fund and expend their present green new deal.

Table 17.2 displays how the three countries have developed very different answers to the crisis and have adopted divergent political approaches to 'green relaunch'. Nevertheless, these three responses still follow the usual national pattern with respect to promoting the green transition. In addition to its relaunch plan targeting affected sectors, China also has a comprehensive plan of around 10% of its national GDP to foster the economy after COVID-19, which is supposed to at least partially target the green transition. In Korea, 1.2% of GDP equivalent is going to be spent on green stimulus. However, in Japan, only a very restricted amount of spending is going to be made on green features. It shows that the country with the greatest reluctance to auctioning (Japan) spends proportionally the most on the economic relaunch but dedicates the least to the green transition. These results illustrate that relaunch plans tend to confirm existing patterns in climate policy. It further demonstrates that making the decision to invest in green measures, in times of big spending, as in normal times, is a very political decision. That being said, not only could revenues from auctioning in domestic GHG ETS partially finance stimulus programs in the Northeast Asian countries, but it could also strengthen the political argument for using a bigger share for a green transition.

5. COVID-19 INFLUENCE ON PRE-EXISTING BARRIERS TO AUCTION-BASED GHG ETS

The COVID-19 crisis represents an unprecedented opportunity to change the predominant barrier-pattern toward auction-based GHG ETS and to build legitimacy for revenue-raising design elements. Indeed, as depicted in Figure 17.1, the traditional pattern generating blockage in the policy process is based on anxiety of government representatives to lose political support due to rather harsh resistance to auctioning from covered sectors. COVID-19, however, can change this opposition-equilibrium. It creates a situation in which major parts of COVID-19 recovery spending in Northeast Asia are safety measures to protect domestic companies affected by the pandemic. Thus, it constitutes the opportunity to apply a 'double dividend' type leverage by conditioning financial support on the acceptance of revenue raising by auction-based domestic GHG ETS. GHG ETS revenues could then finance the major part of the green measures of the relaunch plans. This option not only raises revenues for financing green relaunch plans, but also encourages green transition in the longer-term by structurally expanding government incomes and making domestic GHG ETS more sustainable. However, it does not mean a small group of emission-intensive actors should shoulder a disproportionate portion of the COVID-19 recovery but conveys to connect governmental relaunch funding recourse to the adherence to the PPP. It also creates a support coalition for building legitimacy for auction-based GHG ETS by linking the funding of green relaunch plans with the PPP.

The use of carbon revenues for funding green public policies is not new. Approximatively 70% of revenues generated from GHG ETS already tend to be allocated to 'green spending'.[31] Thus, revenues from GHG ETS auctions genuinely fit the post-COVID-19 finance needs of affected countries implementing relaunch plans, and they can also provide an additional incentive to include green measures. With respect to the political process, several studies have shown that clearly explaining to the public how carbon pricing revenues are used can increase the political support of carbon pricing policies.[32] Moreover, the more a jurisdiction exhibits weak support of carbon pricing, the more allocating revenues to environmental expenditures is beneficial to enhance social adherence to the measure. Hence, in the current situation, linking the funding of post-COVID-19 green relaunch plans to GHG ETS revenues could trigger a better understanding for carbon pricing in the region. More importantly, connecting GHG ETS auction-based allocation and revenue raising to COVID-19 relaunch plans would include carbon pricing in a wider policy context that is broadly perceived as necessary, which, in turn, is an important step for support-coalition building.[33]

More concretely, the adoption of an 'Auction and Invest Approach', where public spending for green transition is directly linked to carbon pricing revenue, appears promising.[34] For Northeast Asia, it means to adopt GHG ETS's auction-based allocation in the sectors targeted by COVID-19 stimulus. Table 17.2 directly gives a glimpse of where this auction and invest approach could be applied in the Northeast Asian case. In China, it signifies to pair auction-allocation experimentation to sectors concerned by the relaunch plan and providing funds for the 'New Infrastructure' package. In Japan, connecting auction-allocation rules to the stimulus received by industrial sectors would trigger significant revenues that could be used to source a genuine national green new deal. It also offers a new opportunity to negotiate the establishment of a national ETS that has recurrently been rejected by industrial sector representatives for many years.[35] In that aspect, it represents a powerful advocacy window that gives leverage to policy-makers to implement a more ambitious carbon pricing policy in the country. In the Republic of Korea, this auction and invest approach embodies an opportunity to structurally fund and increase the already existing 'Green New Deal' package.

This approach has the double advantages to find a sustainable source of finance for green stimulus in a transformative and disruptive period while at the same time reducing the political vulnerability of policy-makers with respect to opposition from covered sectors. In addition, the legitimacy of covered sectors' opposition to revenue-raising GHG ETS features can be weakened, if revenues are used for funding green stimulus packages.

6. CONCLUSION

In this chapter, we asked whether the COVID-19 crisis opens a new window of opportunity for overcoming domestic resistance (anxieties, political constraints and covered sector resistances) to auction-based GHG ETS in the three Northeast Asian countries of China, South Korea and Japan.

The empirical data analysed in this chapter shows that the strong rejection of auction-based allocations by covered sectors interest groups, particularly in Korea and Japan, and often supported by economic ministries prevents the implementation of revenue-raising features in GHG ETS.

The COVID-19 crisis, however, provides an unprecedented opportunity to resolve this barrier pattern, because additional government revenues are desperately needed to finance economic recovery programs, which will also benefit sectors usually in opposition to auction-and-revenue-earmarking design elements in GHG ETS.

Coupling post-COVID-19 crisis economic relaunch plans with the adoption of revenue-neutral auction-based allocation in Northeast Asian GHG ETS represents an auspicious solution. It means to condition financial support from relaunch plans to sectors covered by the respective GHG ETS on the support for auction-based allocation. Besides, this 'Auction and Invest Approach' to finance sustainable relaunch schemes by GHG ETS revenues fosters not only economic recovery but also effective and fair climate mitigation and adaptation.

In sum, the COVID-19 crisis offers a window of opportunity to overcome covered sectors' and linked government agencies' resistance to the strong PPP and to implement revenue-neutral full auctioning and sustainably earmarked revenue recycling in Northeast Asian GHG ETS. This unique chance should not be missed!

NOTES

1. Joseph Dellatte is a PhD candidate at the Graduate School of Economics and Dr Sven Rudolph is Associate Professor at the Hakubi Center / Graduate School for Global Environmental Studies at Kyoto University, Japan. Contact: jdellatte@icloud.com – ORCID: https://orcid.org/0000-0001-9829-4948.
2. Rudolph, S., Lenz, C., Volmert, B., and Lerch, A. (2012). Towards sustainable carbon markets: Requirements for effective, efficient, and fair emissions trading schemes. In Kreiser, Larry, Sterling Yabar, Ana, Herrera, Pedro, Milne, Janet E., and Ashiabor, Hope (eds). *Carbon Pricing, Growth and the Environment: Critical Issues in Environmental Taxation*, vol. XI (pp. 167–83). Cheltenham, UK and Northampton, MA, USA: Edward Elgar Publishing.
3. Gigaton of CO_2 equivalent.
4. European Commission. (2018). *Fossil CO2 Emissions of All World Countries*. Accessed 23 May 2021 at https://ec.europa.eu/jrc/en/publication/eur-scientific-and-technical-research-reports/fossil-co2-emissions-all-world-countries-2018-report; Rudolph, S., Lenz, C., Volmert, B., and Lerch, A. (2012). Towards sustainable carbon markets: Requirements for effective, efficient, and fair emissions trading schemes. In Kreiser, Larry, Sterling Yabar, Ana, Herrera, Pedro, Milne, Janet E., and Ashiabor, Hope (eds). *Carbon Pricing, Growth and the Environment: Critical Issues in Environmental Taxation*, vol. XI (pp. 167–83). Cheltenham, UK and Northampton, MA, USA: Edward Elgar Publishing.
5. UNFCCC. (2020). *Nationally Determined Commitments to the Paris Agreement*. Accessed 23 May 2021 at https://www4.unfccc.int/sites/NDCStaging/Pages/All.aspx.
6. Chemnick, J. and Storrow, B. (23 September 2020). China says it will stop releasing CO_2 within 40 years. *ClimateWire, EENews*. Accessed 23 May 2021 at https://www.eenews.net/climatewire/stories/1063714445/search?keyword=Xi+Jinping; Ha, T. (25 September 2020). South-Korea declares climate emergency, sets net zero target for 2050. *Eco-Business*. Accessed 23 May 2021 at https://www.eco-business.com/news/south-korea-declares-climate-emergency-sets-net-zero-target-for-2050; Farand, C. (21 October 2020). Japan set to announce 2050 net-zero emission target-report. *Climate Home News*. Accessed 23 May 2021 at https://www.climatechangenews.com/2020/10/21/japan-set-announce-2050-net-zero-emissions-target-report.
7. Rudolph, S., Aydos, E., Kawakatu, T., Lerch, A., and Dellatte, J. (2020). May link prevail! Or: a comparative analysis of lessons learnt from (not) linking carbon markets in Japan and Oceania. In Zachariaderis, T., Milne, J., Skou Andersen, M. (eds), *Economic Instruments for a Low-carbon Future*, Critical Issues in Environmental Taxation, vol XXII (pp. 98–113). Cheltenham, UK and Northampton, MA, USA: Edward Elgar Publishing.

Enforcing sustainable auction-based ETS in a post-COVID-19 world   253

8. Dellatte, J. and Rudolph, S. (2019). The way of the dragon: China's new emissions trading scheme and the prospects for linking. In Villar, M. (ed.) and Camara, C. (Cd.), *Environmental Tax Studies for the Ecological Transition: Comparative Analysis Addressing Urban Concentration and Increasing Transport Challenges* (pp. 97–105). Madrid: Thomson Reuters.
9. UNFCCC. (2020). *Nationally Determined Commitments to the Paris Agreement*. Accessed 23 May 2021 at https://www4.unfccc.int/sites/NDCStaging/Pages/All.aspx; Tokyo Metropolitan Government. (2015). *The Tokyo Metropolitan Environmental Security Ordinance 'Tokyo Cap-and-Trade Program' for Large Facilities*. Tokyo. Accessed 23 May 2021 at http://www.kankyo.metro.tokyo.jp/en/climate/cap_and_trade/index.files/TokyoCaT_detailed_documents.pdf; Ministry of Strategy and Finance of the Republic of Korea. (2012). *Act on the Allocation and Trading of Greenhouse Gas Emissions Allowances*. Accessed 23 May 2021 at http://www.lse.ac.uk/GranthamInstitute/wp-content/uploads/laws/1647.pdf; Ministry of the Environment of the Republic of Korea. (2018). *Second Allocation Plan*. Accessed 23 May 2021 at http://www.me.go.kr/home/web/board/read.do?pagerOffset=10&maxPageItems=10&maxIndexPages=10&searchKey=&searchValue=&menuId=286&orgCd=&boardId=883200&boardMasterId=1&boardCategoryId=&decorator= (in Korean); NDRC. (2017). *Chinese National ETS Regulations and Design Work Plan*. Accessed 23 May 2021 at https://www.ndrc.gov.cn/xxgk/zcfb/ghxwj/201712/W020190905495689305648.pdf (in Chinese).
15. World Bank. (2020). *Carbon Pricing Dashboard*. [Data set]. Accessed 23 May 2021 at https://carbonpricingdashboard.worldbank.org/map_data.
16. OECD. (2020). *OECD Pine Data Base*. [Data set]. Accessed 23 May 2021 at https://www.oecd.org/environment/tools-evaluation/environmentaltaxation.htm.
17. Ibid.
18. World Bank. (2020). *Carbon Pricing Dashboard*. [Data set]. Accessed 23 May 2021 at https://carbonpricingdashboard.worldbank.org/map_data.
19. Ibid.
20. Burtraw, D., Palmer, K., Munnings, C., Weber, P., and Woerman, M. (April 2013). Linking by degrees: Incremental alignment of cap-and-trade markets. (Resources for the Future department paper No. 1304). Washington, DC. Accessed 23 May 2021 at https://media.rff.org/documents/RFF-DP-13-04.pdf.
21. The results are organized in a Likert-type scale table depicting sub-categories of actors' opinions on auction-based allocation. The samples mean are given as an indication.
22. National Development and Reform Commission of China.
23. Ministry of Economy, Trade and Industry.
24. ICTSD. (January 2015). South-Korea launches national emissions trading system. *BIORES: International Centre for Trade and Sustainable Development*. Accessed 23 May 2021 at https://ictsd.iisd.org/bridges-news/biores/news/south-korea-launches-national-emissions-trading-system.
25. European Commission. (September 2020). *Recovery Plan for Europe*. Accessed 23 May 2021 at https://ec.europa.eu/info/strategy/recovery-plan-europe_en.
26. Fialka, J. (August 10 2020). Coal spree suggests China might loosen CO_2 goals. *ClimateWire*, *EENews*. Accessed 23 May 2021 at https://www.eenews.net/climatewire/2020/08/10/stories/1063707133?utm_campaign=Hot%20News&utm_medium=email&_hsmi=93012117&_hsenc=p2ANqtz-8xg3RD70z1LnUwIpBr2Ghkq9Dn_UbJgSjLlBaezjxpiBmDU79tqS4xQm7

miBJdZpEYV-73c6Gm6ptIdiMYKLSEXYwCTw&utm_content=93012117&utm_s.
27. UNESCAP. (2020). *COVID-19 Response Visualization in Asia*. Accessed 15 October 2020 at https://www.unescap.org/covid19#eo.
28. Liu, C., Li, L., Ting-Fang, C., and Kawase, K. (1 June 2020). China bets on $2tn high-tech infrastructure plan to spark economy. *NikkeiAsia Review*. Accessed 23 May 2021 at https://asia.nikkei.com/Business/China-tech/China-bets-on-2tn-high-tech-infrastructure-plan-to-spark-economy.
29. Regalado, F. (23 June 2020). Asia risk missing 'green' economic reset after coronavirus: Except in South-Korea, experts see absence of environmental resolve in the region. *NikkeiAsia Review*. Accessed 23 May 2021 at https://asia.nikkei.com/Spotlight/Asia-Insight/Asia-risks-missing-green-economic-reset-after-coronavirus.
30. UNESCAP. (2020). *COVID-19 Response Visualization in Asia*. Accessed 15 October 2020 at https://www.unescap.org/covid19#eo.
31. Carl, J. and Fedor, D. (2016). Tracking global carbon revenues: A survey of carbon taxes versus cap-and-trade in the real world. *Energy Policy*, 96(9), 50–77.
32. Carattini, S., Carvalho, M. and Fankhauser, S. (2018). Overcoming public resistance to carbon taxes. *Wiley Interdisciplinary Revue Climate Change*, 9(5), E531.
33. Leigh, R. (2019). Policy perspective: Building political support for carbon pricing – Lessons from cap-and-trade policies. *Energy Policy*, 134(11), Accessed 15 October 2020 at https://www.sciencedirect.com/science/article/abs/pii/S0301421519305737.
34. Ibid.
35. Keidanren. (19 March 2019). *Proposal on Japan's Long-term Growth Strategy under the Paris Agreement: Business-led Innovation to Address Challenges towards Decarbonization*. Keidaren: Japan Business Federation. Accessed 15 October 2020 at https://www.keidanren.or.jp/en/policy/2019/022.html.

Index

Africa 55
ageing population 56
aggressive tax optimization 91
Agreement on Subsidies and Countervailing Measures (SCM Agreement) 144, 145
Agreement on Trade-Related Investment Measures (TRIMs Agreement) 143
agriculture 50
airlines 70, 231, 237
alignment of ETS design features 238
allowance market 233
Amazon region
    Brazil 133
    Perú 103, 105–6
Amazonian forest 98, 149
Aneel 148
antifragility 178
Argentina
    carbon tax 111–25
        effectiveness to finance environmental expenditures 116–18
        effectiveness to reduce fuel consumption 115–16
        legal context 112–13
        settlement process 114–15
        taxable event 113–14
    Decreto 488/2020 111, 118–20, 121
    Liquid Fuels and Natural Gas Tax 112, 113
    Liquid Fuels Tax 113
Asia, Northeast *see* Northeast Asia
asset purchase programme (APP) 30
auction and invest approach 251–2
auctioning 233, 236
    enforcing sustainable auction-based ETS 242–54
Australia 235

aviation sector 70, 231, 237

barriers to entry 218–19, 220, 222
batteries for electric vehicles 204–5
Baumol, W.J. 53
'beggar thy neighbour' policies 233
bicycle lanes 173, 175
bicycles 71, 170, 173, 175, 176
    e-bikes 173
Biden, J. 35
bioelectrification 148
biofuels 140–53
Biofuture Platform 147–8
Bird 174, 181
Birol, F. 67
border carbon adjustment (BCA) 26–8, 31, 60, 91, 165, 235, 237
Boston Consulting Group (BCG) 170
Brazil 126–53
    'Convergência pelo Brasil' 132
    Emergency Benefit for Supporting Employment and Income 128
    emissions from transport 141–2
    environmentally-oriented tax policies and economic recovery 130–3
    Extraordinary Tax, Financial and Procurement Regime ('war budget') 127–8
    Federative Emergency Financial Aid 128
    fiscal measures and Covid-19 127–30
    Inovar-Auto Programme 140, 143–4, 145, 150
    intended Nationally Determined Contribution (iNDC) 141–2
    New Automotive Regime 143
    possible prognosis of post-pandemic fiscal measures 133–6

255

Proalcool programme (National Alcohol Program) 146
proposals for sustainable tax reform 134–5
tax incentives for electric vehicles and biofuels 140–53
orientation towards biofuels 148–9
RenovaBio Programme 140, 142, 146–8, 149, 150
Rota 2030 Programme 140, 142, 143–6, 148, 149–50
Brussels 173

Cambridge Econometrics 28
carbon border adjustment 26–8, 31, 60, 91, 165, 235, 237
carbon dioxide concentrations 169
carbon dividend 25–6
carbon emission intensity (CEI) of production chains 82, 85–91
Carbon Emission Intensity Ratio (CEIR) 87
carbon labelling 86–91
carbon leakage measures 234, 236
carbon neutrality 20–33
carbon pricing 3–6
    to achieve carbon neutrality in the EU 20–33
        level of the carbon price 24–5
    mitigation effectiveness 12
    Perú 96–110
    role of 21–2
    see also emissions trading systems (ETSs); carbon taxation
carbon taxation 238
    Argentina see Argentina
    as a climate mitigation tool 4–6
    Green New Dividend 34–47
    post-crisis assessment 3–19
    reasons for 21
    revenue neutral in the US 34–5, 38–44
Carney, M. 51
cars 170
    discouraging car travel 174–5
    electric see electric vehicles
    Italy 175–6
    screening criteria for manufacturing 187–8

Cassim, Z. 74, 75
CBIOs (decarbonization credits) 147, 150
CBS (social contribution on transactions with assets and services) 131
China 214, 242–54
    barriers to auction-based ETSs 245–8
    Covid-19 influence on 250–2
    climate policy 243–5
    and the Covid-19 crisis 248–9
    'New Infrastructure' investment plan 248–9, 251
CIDE-fuel 131, 135
Citizens Climate Lobby (CCL) 38
Clement, M. 148
climate change cooperation 229–41
    Covid-19 and the economy 229, 230–1
    implications of Covid-19 on climate change and linking 231–2
    linking and protectionism 232–4
        implications for the EU 235–7, 238
climate change mitigation sustainable economic activities 186, 187
climate justice 106
Climate Leadership Council (CLC) 38
coal prices 10–11
coal taxes 12
Coalition of Finance Ministers countries 3–19
Coalition of Green Capital 40
COFINS 129, 131, 133
coherence 192–4, 199, 207–9
Collaborative Advocacy Network (RAC) 134
command-and-control measures 20
Commission v France 82–3
Commission v United Kingdom 83
competitiveness 236
comprehensive energy price reform 12–15, 16
containment and mitigation 171
control mechanisms 208–9
Convention on Climate Change 22, 97
corporate debt 230
corrective interventions 216
covered sector interest groups 245–8, 251, 252

Covid-19 pandemic 55, 169, 214, 229
  Brazil
    effects 126
    fiscal measures 127–30
  economic recovery *see* economic recovery
  effects in Perú 99–101
  impact on the economy 229, 230–1
  impact on transport emissions 141
  impact on urban transport 169–71
  implications on climate change and linking 231–2
  market failures and RESSS 217–19
  Northeast Asia and 248–9
    Covid-19 influence on barriers to auction-based ETSs 250–1
  tax provisions in Italy 155–6
  use of tax incentives in response to 199–202
customs duties 163–5

Da Silva, D. 116
Davos 133
debt financing 29–30
debt recovery programmes 16–17
decarbonization 12, 68
decarbonization credits (CBIOs) 147, 150
deforestation 100–1, 149
delegated acts 52
Democrats 36, 37–8
destination principle 27
Diaz, D. 25
diesel 115–16, 118–19
digital levy 31
digital transition 206
directional stability 70
displaced jobs 43
distribution 73, 89
  carbon tax revenue in Argentina 116–18
  impact of modifying the ISC in Perú 105
  linking of ETSs 232–4
do-not-significantly-harm principle 68, 69, 186, 187
double dividend 53, 56–7, 85, 250
dynamic efficiency 20

e-bikes 173
e-scooters 173, 177
EAERE Statement 22
ecobonus 175–6
economic recovery 66–80
  approaches 68–74
  Brazil's environmentally-oriented tax policies and 130–3
  crisis as opportunity 66–8
  EU action plan for 29–31, 85, 90, 162–3, 166, 204
  recovery measures so far 74–5
'Economists' Statement on Carbon Dividends' 22
'Economists' Statement on Carbon Pricing' (EAERE Statement) 22
ecosystem services 98
EEAG (Guidelines on State aid for environmental protection and energy) 217, 220, 221
efficiency 178
elasticity of demand 25
electric vehicles 41, 172, 175–6
  incentives for charging infrastructure 159–60
  state aid 200, 203–4, 204–5
  tax incentives in Brazil 140–53
  tax incentives in Spain 206–7
electricity
  fall in demand 214, 217, 218
  generation 190, 214
    from renewables 218
  prices 10–12
emergency aid 68, 69, 70–2, 74, 75, 128, 194
emissions 3, 21, 169
  growth projections 7, 8
  Northeast Asia 243
  profile in Perú 97
  reductions
    Coalition of Finance Ministers member countries 4, 7–9, 10, 12, 13
    due to Covid-19 218, 231
    EU strategy for 22–4
    EU targets 23–4, 235–6
    how carbon taxation achieves reductions 21
    Northeast Asia 243–4
    Paris Agreement 3

from transport
　　Brazil 141–2
　　EU 203
　　US sectors 40
emissions trading systems (ETSs) 4–5, 12
　　enforcing sustainable auction-based ETSs 242–54
　　EU ETS *see* European Union (EU)
　　linking 229, 231–8
　　and protectionism 232–4, 235–7, 238
energy demand 217
energy efficiency
　　buildings 72
　　incentives in Italy 159–60
energy intensity of GDP 7
energy market impact assessment 221
Energy Policy Tracker 74, 75
energy prices 10–12, 16
　　reform 12–15, 16
energy saving 25
energy-saving materials 83
energy taxation, reasons for 20–1
environmentally sustainable activities Taxonomy *see* Taxonomy for environmentally sustainable activities
EPE (Brazilian Energy Research Company) 141, 146, 148
equity 42–3, 73
ESG (environmental, social and governance) criteria 132–3, 199–200
ethanol 146, 149
European Central Bank (ECB) 30
European Charter of Fundamental Rights 82
European Citizens' Initiative 25
European Clean Trucking Alliance 208
European Environment Agency (EEA) 54, 59
European Green Deal (EGD) 31–2, 52, 60, 161–2, 165, 184, 189, 195, 203, 235, 237
　　VAT 81, 84–5
European Investment Bank (EIB)
　　Guarantee Fund for Workers and Businesses 30

European Stability Mechanism (ESM)
　　Pandemic Crisis Support 30
European Union (EU)
　　action plan for sustainable finance 2018 184, 185, 192
　　Benchmark regulation 185
　　border carbon adjustment 26–8, 31, 60, 91, 165, 235, 237
　　Carbon Border Adjustment Mechanism 31, 60, 91
　　carbon pricing to achieve carbon neutrality 20–33
　　carbon dividend and fiscal reform 25–6
　　level of the carbon price 24–5
　　institutional developments 31–2
　　Communication on a Coordinated economic response to the coronavirus outbreak 204
　　Covid-19 Recovery Plan 29–31, 85, 90, 162–3, 166, 204
　　customs duties as environmental taxes 163–5
　　delegated acts 52
　　Directive 2019/904 158
　　Disclosure regulation 185
　　Draft Directive on carbon-energy tax 22–3
　　Emissions Trading System (ETS) 23, 26–7, 31, 60–1, 90
　　extension within the EU 28–9
　　linking and protectionism 235–7, 238
　　Energy Taxation Directive (ETD) 60, 184, 188–90, 192–3
　　General Block Exemption Regulation (GBER) 185, 191–2, 193
　　global leadership role 164, 166
　　Guidelines on state aid for environmental protection and energy (EEAG) 217, 220, 221
　　impact of Covid-19 on the Eurozone GDP 230
　　need for environmentally related tax reforms 53–61
　　Next Generation EU (NGEU) 29–30, 85, 198, 201

Non-Financial Reporting Directive
    (NFRD) 52
reconciling tax and environmental
    policies 81–94
Recovery Fund 201
Recovery and Resilience Facility
    (RFF) 201
Regional Aid Guidelines 209
Renewable Energy Directive
    2018/2001 (RED II) 215,
    219, 220–2, 223
renewable energy support schemes
    see renewable energy sources
    support schemes (RESSS)
revision of Council Directive
    2003/96/EC 161, 162
state aid *see* state aid
Strategic Action Plan for Batteries
    205
strategy for curbing emissions 22–4
Taxonomy *see* Taxonomy for
    environmentally sustainable
    activities
VAT *see* value added tax (VAT)
VAT Committee 90
VAT Directive 83, 84, 88–9, 190–1,
    193
excise tax (ISC) 101–2
    problems of 102
    transformation to a carbon price
        103, 104–5
exemptions 188–92
externalities 49–65, 135, 217
    internalization of external costs 49,
        50–1, 53

fee and dividend policy 38–40
    Green New Dividend 40–4
feebates 5, 12
Fernández, A. 112
financial crisis of 2008 67–8, 75
financial transaction tax 31
financing environmental expenditures
    111–12, 116–18, 121
financing of recovery policies 73–4
fiscal policy 230–1
    coherence in 192–4, 199, 207–9
    role concerning the transport sector
        171–2

fiscal stimuli 171
    Brazil 127–30
    green recovery 199–200
'fit for purpose' assessment 220–1, 223
flexible fuel vehicles 146, 148–9, 150
fossil fuels
    prices 10–12, 16
        reform 12–15
    subsidies 14–15, 74, 202–3, 207
        Perú 103, 104–5
France 170, 204
    VAT on diesel 82
fuel consumption 111–12, 115–16, 121
fuel switching 25
further education 72

G20 74, 75, 231
gasoline
    consumption in Argentina 115–16,
        118–19, 120
    prices 10–11, 25
        super gasoline price 115,
            118–19, 120
GDP 7, 59, 230
General Agreement on Tariffs and Trade
    (GATT) 27–8, 143, 191, 237
general distribution system 116–18
Germany 29, 69, 70, 71, 73, 204–5
    2008 crisis response 67–8
GHG emissions *see* emissions
global recession 230
Global Risks Perception Survey 54
governance 90
government agencies' representatives
    245–8, 251, 252
Grassi, M.C.B. 147
green banks 41, 42
green bonds 41–2, 43
green economic recovery 66–80
Green New Dividend 34–47
green products, costlier 50
'green skills' opportunities 72
green transition 248–9, 250–1
greening state aid 200–2
Guidelines on state aid for environmental
    protection and energy (EEAG)
    217, 220, 221
Guimarães, L.H. 148
Gutman, V. 98

habits in urban transport 170–1, 172
Hardin, G. 21, 51
hardship, focus on 69
harmfulness index (INC) 101–2, 104–5, 107
heavy-polluting industries 135
Henrique Guimarães, L. 148
High-Level Commission on Carbon Pricing 24
Hippocratic Oath 68
hybrid flexible fuel technology 146, 148–9, 150
hybrid vehicles 145–6, 148–9
hybridization process 146

IBS (tax on goods and services) 131, 134, 135
ICMS (consumption tax) 131, 133–4, 138
impact investors 51
implementation frame 207–8
import substitution policy 143, 151
imported parts and components 144, 145
Imposto sobre a Propriedade de Veículos Automotores (IPVA) 149
INC (harmfulness index) 101–2, 104–5, 107
incentives
    electric vehicles and biofuels in Brazil 140–53
    Italy 159–60
    urban mobility 173–8
    use in response to the Covid-19 crisis 199–202
    use in the transport sector 202–7
    Spain 205–7
income inequalities 57
indigenous peoples 98, 105–6
indirect land use change (ILUC) 149
inequality 57, 73
Inglis, B. 36
innovation 142
Inovar-Auto Programme 140, 143–4, 145, 150
Intergovernmental Panel on Climate Change (IPCC) 3, 39, 97, 231
internalization of external costs 49, 50–1
    theory 53
international agreements 164

International Council on Clean Transportation (ICCT) 146, 149
International Energy Agency (IEA) 141, 142
International Monetary Fund (IMF) 203
International Renewable Energy Agency (IRENA) 200
International Transport Forum (ITF) 172, 174
IOF (tax on financial operations) 129
IPI (tax on manufactured products) 129, 133, 143–4, 145
IPTU (urban estates tax) 131
IPVA 149
Ireland 188
IRPEF (personal income tax in Italy) 155, 159, 160
ISC see excise tax (ISC)
Italy 26, 155–68
    customs duties as environmental taxes 163–5
    deduction for IRPEF 159, 160
    incentives for specific interventions 159
    OECD, EU and energy taxation 160–3
    plastics tax and tax on the consumption of sweetened beverages 157–9
    tax legislation at the time of the Covid-19 pandemic 155–6
    transferability of tax credit 159–60
    urban transport 175–7
ITR (Rural Territorial Property Tax) 135

Jacobson, M. 39
Japan 242–54
    barriers to auction-based ETSs 245–8
        Covid-19 influence on 250–2
    climate policy 243–5
    and the Covid-19 crisis 248–9
    relaunch plan 248, 249
jobs, preservation of 73

Keeter, S. 36
Korea, South 242–54
    barriers to auction-based ETSs 245–8

Covid-19 influence on 250–2
climate policy 243–5
and the Covid-19 crisis 248–9
Green New Deal 248, 249, 251
Kyoto Protocol 22

L-category vehicles 173–4
labour taxes 56
Land-Use, Land-Use Change and Forestry (LULUCF) sector 97, 100–1
Latin America 97
see also Argentina; Brazil; Perú
legitimacy 90–1
Li Keqian 248
life cycle assessment (LCA) 86–91
Lilliestam, J. 67
Lime 174, 181
linking of ETSs 229, 231–8
implications of Covid-19 231–2
and protectionism 232–4
implications for the EU 235–7, 238
London 173
low CEI ratio products 88–9

Macri, M. 111
mandatory CEI assessment 89
Mandela, N. 59
maritime shipping 237
market-based RESSS 221
market failures 49, 216
and climate change in Perú 98
and RESSS 216–19, 220, 222
after the Covid-19 outbreak 217–19
in general 216–17
market management systems 233–4
market-responsive RESSS 221
Markey, E. 37
Mediterranean EU member states 201
Meinrenken, C.J. 87–8
merit goods market failure 218, 219, 220
micro-mobility 173–4, 176–7
Milan 173, 175
Milne, J. 115
mining 55
mobility bonus 176–7
monetary policy 231

Montreal 173
Moore, F. 25
motorcycles 175–6
Multiannual Financial Framework (MFF) 30, 31
multimodal transport 174
Mundaca, L. 171

National Carbon Emissions Intensity (NCEI) 87
national debt 156, 230
National Plans for Energy and Climate 203
National Recovery Plans 60
Nationally Determined Contributions (NDCs) 3
Perú 100–1
natural gas prices 10–11
negative externalities 49, 217, 222
Netherlands Enterprise Agency 147
neutrality principle 190
Next Generation EU (NGEU) 29–30, 85, 198, 201
non-financial reporting 52
non-recycled plastic 31
Northeast Asia 242–54
barriers to auction-based ETSs 245–8
influence of Covid-19 on 250–2
and the Covid-19 crisis 248–9
pre-Covid-19 climate policy 243–5

Ocasio-Cortez, A. 37
offsets 233
oil subsidies 74
ordoliberal economic doctrine 215–16
Organisation for Economic Co-operation and Development (OECD) 54–5, 111, 112, 142, 230
phases of the pandemic 171–2
Tax and Fiscal Policy in Response to the Coronavirus Crisis 130, 132
Taxing Energy Use 160–1
Ortiz, E. 98, 99, 102
own resources 30, 31

pandemic-emergency purchase programme (PEPP) 30

Paris 173
Paris Agreement 22, 43, 96, 161, 164, 167, 218
    commitments 3
    NDCs in Northeast Asia 244
'parking rates' 191, 193
Pearce, D. 53
penalizing mechanism (VAT) 88
Pereira, G.A.G. 147
Perú 96–110
    complementary measures 105–6
    effects of Covid-19 99–101
    emissions profile and climate conditions 97
    excise tax (ISC) 101–2
        transforming 103, 104–5
    market failures and climate change 98
    National Program for the Conservation of Forests for the mitigation of climate change (PNCB) 99
    Remuneration Mechanisms for Ecosystem Services (MRSE) 99
    socio-economic context of climate profile 97–8
    socio-economic instruments for climate change 99
    subsidies 102–3
        substitution or elimination of 103, 104–5
petrol *see* gasoline
photovoltaic (PV) energy 71
    incentives in Italy 159–60
Pigou, A.C. 49, 53, 58
Pigovian tax 53
PIS 129, 131, 133
Pizarro, R. 104
plastic containers for drinking water 158–9
plastics tax 157–9
political barriers to ETS auctioning 245–8, 251–2
polluter-pays principle 50–1, 61–2
population ageing 56
Porter Hypothesis 50
positive externalities 49, 217, 222
poverty
    Argentina 119

Perú 97–8
power storage 71
preferential tax regimes 188–92, 193, 194–5
private capital 192–4, 195
production chains 82, 85–91
proportionality principle 208
protectionism 229, 231, 237
    linking of ETSs and 232–4
        implications for the EU 235–7, 238
public aid *see* state aid
public capital 192–4, 195
public debt 156, 230
public goods 98
public health 68, 70–2
public opinion on climate change 35–6, 37–8
public transport 71, 175

qualified majority voting 162
Quinet Commission Report 25

race 42
Reagan, R. 37
recovery and resilience plans 30
redistribution 232–4
    see also distribution
regulations 12
regulatory capitalism 216
relaunch plans 248–9, 250–1, 251–2
renewable energies
    electricity generation from 218
    investment in 71
    solar 39, 41, 71, 159–60
    wind 39, 41
renewable energy sources support schemes (RESSS) 214–27
    market failures and 216–19, 220, 222
        after the Covid-19 outbreak 217–19
        in general 216–17
    normative foundation 215–16
    refining the supranational renewable energy support law 219–22
RenovaBio Programme 140, 142, 146–8, 149, 150
renters 42–3

Republicans 36, 37–8
resilience 178, 194
restoration of public finances 171–2
revenue neutral carbon tax/pricing 34–5, 38–44
revenue neutral tax reforms 60
revenues
    from carbon pricing 25–6
    from carbon taxes 5, 9–10, 11, 14–15, 244–5
    from environmental taxes in the EU 54, 56
    from ETSs 244–5, 250–1
    recycling 74
    from vehicle taxes 177
Richter, J.L. 171
risk 218–19, 220, 222
road freight sector 208
road fuel taxes 12
Rota 2030 Programme 140, 142, 143–6, 148, 149–50
Rubini, L. 145

Saint-Amans, P. 56
Salassa Boix, R. 115, 116
San Martín region, Perú 106
Sanders, B. 37
SARS outbreak 169
Schapiro, M. 145
SCM Agreement 144, 145
scooters 170, 176
    e-scooters 173, 177
scrapping premium 67–8
screening criteria 186–8, 190, 191, 193, 194–5
Seattle 173
seismic risk reduction incentives 159–60
selective tax 133, 134, 135
selling and importing vehicles 144
shared mobility services 174
Sierra Club 39
single-use plastics tax 157–9
Skou Andersen, M. 208
social contribution on transactions with assets and services (CBS) 131
social distancing 170
social marginal cost charging 51
social market economy 215–16
socio-environmental principles 134

soft drinks tax 157–9
soft law 217, 219–22, 223
soft mobility 173, 175–7
solar energy 39, 41
    photovoltaic (PV) 71, 159–60
solution aversion 36
Solutions Project, The 39
South Korea *see* Korea, South
Spain
    Climate Change and Energy Transition Act 206
    Corporate Income Tax Act (CIT) 206–7
    tax incentives related to transport 205–7
special distribution system 116–17, 118
state aid 198–213
    coherent fiscal policy governance in the EU 199, 207–9
    EEAG guidelines 217, 220, 221
    greening 200–2
    and renewable energy support 216–17
    RESSS 219, 220
    tax incentives related to transport 202–5
        Spain 205–7
    Taxonomy and 184, 191–2, 193, 194, 195
    Temporary Framework 204
    use of tax incentives in response to the Covid-19 crisis 199–202
static efficiency 20
Stern, N. 24, 49
Stiglitz, J. 24
structural change 68, 70–2
subsidies 53, 202, 236
    elimination in Brazil 135
    fossil fuels 14–15, 74, 103, 104–5, 202–3, 207
    Perú 102–3, 104–5
        elimination and substitution 103, 105–6
sugar cane 146, 149
super gasoline price 115, 118–19, 120
SURE (Support to mitigate Unemployment Risks) 30
sustainability bonds 43
sustainable development 67

sustainable financing Taxonomy *see*
    Taxonomy for environmentally
    sustainable activities
sustainable regional development 134–5
Swapfiets 175
Sweden 26
sweetened beverages, tax on
    consumption of 157–9
Switzerland 235
systems approach to fiscal reform 59–61

Taleb, N. 178
tax credits 158–9
    transfer 159–60
tax on financial operations (IOF) 129
tax incentives *see* incentives
tax on manufactured products (IPI) 129,
    133, 143–4, 145
tax reform
    EU
        action plan in the pandemic
            crisis 162–3
        carbon dividend and 25–6
        need for environmentally
            related reform 53–61
        green tax reform in Brazil 134–6
    Italy 155–60, 166
Taxonomy for environmentally
    sustainable activities 51–2,
    184–97
    coherence in the fiscal landscape
        192–4
    current portfolio of exemptions
        and preferential tax regimes
        188–92
        Energy Taxation Directive
            188–90
        state aids 191–2
        VAT 190–1
teleconferencing 170
teleworking 170
Thöne, M. 69
Toyota 148
trade restrictions *see* protectionism
Tragedy of the Commons 21, 51
training 72
transport 40, 200, 208
    emissions in Brazil 141–2
    urban mobility *see* urban mobility
    use of tax incentives 202–7

Spain 205–7
Treaty on the European Union (TEU)
    215
Treaty on the Functioning of the
    European Union (TFEU) 31, 82,
    191, 222
    state aid rules 201–2, 204
TRIMs Agreement 143
Trinidad, C. 98, 99, 102
Turin 174

unemployment 100
United Nations
    Agenda 2030 for Sustainable
        Development 158, 164, 165,
        167, 198
    Framework Convention on Climate
        Change 22, 97
    Framework for the immediate
        socio-economic response to
        Covid-19 199
United States (US) 69–70
    American Clean Energy and
        Securities Act 36
    American Recovery and
        Reinvestment Act 2009 68,
        171
    Energy Innovation and Carbon
        Dividend Act (EICDA)
        38–40
    Green New Deal 34, 37–8, 42
    Green New Dividend 34–47
    impediments to climate action 35–7
    National Climate Bank 40
    New Deal 34, 37
    revenue neutral carbon pricing 34–5,
        38–44
    Superfund Amendments and
        Reauthorization Act 27–8
universalization 90
unnecessary distortion 221
urban mobility 71, 169–82
    future perspectives for tax policies
        and 172–5
    how the Covid-19 pandemic is
        changing habits 170–1, 172
    Italy 175–7
    new challenges 169–70
    role of fiscal policy in the pandemic
        171–2

user-pays principle 50, 62

value added tax (VAT) 81–94, 184, 193, 194
    application of LCA-based carbon intensity models to 88–91
    environmental-tax paradox 82–5
    exemptions and preferential regimes 190–1
    greening 85–8
    reduced rates for targeted products 88–9
vehicle tax system revenues 177
von der Leyen, U. 23–4, 25, 61, 165
Von der Leyen Commission 84

Waxman–Markey climate bill 36
wildfires 35, 133
wind energy 39, 41
women 174
work 72
World Economic Forum 133
World Health Organization 169
World Trade Organization (WTO)
    dispute over the Inovar-Auto Programme 140, 143–4
    rules 27, 145, 237
Wuhan 170

Zhao, R. 86–7
zombie banks 68